WHEN EAST ASIA MEETS SOUTHEAST ASIA

Presence and Connectedness in Transformation Revisited

WHEN EAST ASIA MEETS SOUTHEAST ASIA

Presence and Connectedness in Transformation Revisited

Edited by

Yumi Kitamura
Kyoto University, Japan

Alan H Yang
National Chengchi University, Taiwan

Ju Lan Thung
Indonesian Institute of Science, Indonesia

World Scientific

NEW JERSEY • LONDON • SINGAPORE • BEIJING • SHANGHAI • HONG KONG • TAIPEI • CHENNAI • TOKYO

Published by

World Scientific Publishing Co. Pte. Ltd.
5 Toh Tuck Link, Singapore 596224
USA office: 27 Warren Street, Suite 401-402, Hackensack, NJ 07601
UK office: 57 Shelton Street, Covent Garden, London WC2H 9HE

Library of Congress Cataloging-in-Publication Data
Names: Kitamura, Yumi, editor. | Yang, Alan Hao, editor. | Thung, Ju-Lan, editor.
Title: When East Asia meets Southeast Asia : presence and connectedness in transformation revisited / edited by Yumi Kitamura, Kyoto University, Japan, Alan H Yang, National Chengchi University, Taiwan, Ju Lan Thung, Indonesian Institute of Science, Indonesia.
Description: New Jersey : World Scientific, [2023] | Includes bibliographical references and index.
Identifiers: LCCN 2022007581 | ISBN 9789811250651 (hardcover) | ISBN 9789811250668 (ebook) | ISBN 9789811250675 (ebook other)
Subjects: LCSH: East Asia--Economic conditions. | Southeast Asia--Economic conditions. | East Asia--Foreign economic relations--Southeast Asia. | Southeast Asia--Foreign economic relations--East Asia.
Classification: LCC HC412 .W436 2023 | DDC 337.1/5--dc23/eng/20220218
LC record available at https://lccn.loc.gov/2022007581

British Library Cataloguing-in-Publication Data
A catalogue record for this book is available from the British Library.

For any available supplementary material, please visit
https://www.worldscientific.com/worldscibooks/10.1142/12679#t=suppl

Desk Editors: Aanand Jayaraman/Lixi Dong

Typeset by Stallion Press
Email: enquiries@stallionpress.com

https://doi.org/10.1142/9789811250668_fmatter

About the Editors

Yumi KITAMURA is an associate professor at the Kyoto University Library, Japan. Her main field of study is Southeast Asian Studies and Library and Information Science. She has been actively involved in research and education in both Japan and Indonesia. Her recent publications include the following "Long way home: The life history of Chinese-Indonesian migrants in the Netherlands" in *Wacana, Journal of the Humanities of Indonesia*, "The Re-recognition of Confucianism in Indonesia: An Example of China's Soft Footprint in Southeast Asia," in Diokno M. S. I., Hsiao, H.-H. and Yang, A. H., (Eds.), *China's Footprints in Southeast Asia*. NUS Press, and "Parallel Development: Southeast Asian Studies and Library Collections", in Khoo B. T., and Suryomenggolo, J., (Eds.), *States and Societies in Motion: Essays in Honor of Takashi Shiraishi*. NIAS, 2020.

Alan Hao YANG is a distinguished professor of Southeast Asian Studies at the Graduate Institute of East Asian Studies (GIEAS) and Deputy Director of the Institute of International Relations (IIR) at the National Chengchi University (NCCU), Taiwan. He has been engaging in Think Tank Diplomacy. Yang's research interests cover International Relations Theories, International Relations and Regionalism in Southeast Asia, Environmental Governance and Disaster Resilience, Border Politics and Politics of Resistance in Southeast Asia, Foreign Policy and Soft Power Analysis with specific focus on China's Confucius Institute, and Taiwan's New Southbound Policy (NSP). He has published more than 90 journal articles in leading international journals as well as Taiwanese ones such as *Pacific Review*, *Pacific Affairs*, *Politics and Governance*, *Journal of*

Asian Public Policy, *Issues and Studies*, etc. Dr. Yang's latest publications include *The Volatility and Future of Democracies in Asia*, co-edited with Dr. Hsin-Huang Michael Hsiao (published by Routledge in 2021).

Dr. Yang is a frequent contributor to the platforms for international and strategic analyses such as *Global Taiwan Brief*; *The National Interests*; *The Diplomat*; *PacNet Commentary*; *Taiwan Insight*; *Rappler*; and *East Asia Forum*.

Ju Lan THUNG is a senior researcher at the Research Center for Society and Culture — The Indonesian National Research and Innovation Agency (BRIN Indonesia). She graduated from the Ph.D. Program in Sociology at La Trobe University, Melbourne, Australia in 1998. She has written several articles on Chinese and Indonesian ethnicity and various social issues, such as, "Agama dan Identitas Orang Tionghoa di Indonesia" (Religion and Identity of Chinese in Indonesia), in *Revolusi Tak Kunjung Selesai: Potret Indonesia Masa Kini* (Unfinished Revolution: Indonesia's Contemporary Portrait), KPG & IRASEC, 2017; "Memahami Etnisitas di Perkotaan: Politik Inter-Ruang di Kota Multikultural" (Understanding Ethnicity in Urban area: Politics of Interspace in Multicultural City), *Journal Masyarakat & Budaya*; "Confucius Institute at University Al Azhar, Jakarta: The unseen power of China," *Wacana, Journal of the Humanities of Indonesia*; *Iptek dan Masyarakat: Problematik Agrikultura di Indonesia* (Science, Technology and Society: Agricultural Problematics in Indonesia), LIPI Press, 2019; and "Politics of Difference: Ethnicity and Social Class Within the Indonesian Middle Class in Digital Era," *Journal Antropologi Indonesia*, published online: http://journal.ui.ac.id/jai; Papua dan Solusi Budaya (Papua and Cultural Solution), in Emansipasi Papua (Papuan Emansipation) Impartial, 2021.

https://doi.org/10.1142/9789811250668_fmatter

Contents

https://doi.org/10.1142/9789811250668_fmatter

Introduction

Crafting the People-Centered Connectedness in Southeast Asian Regionalism

Yumi Kitamura, Alan Hao Yang and Ju Lan Thung

Under the influence of globalization and regionalization, in which the compression of time and space is being accompanied by transnational mobility as the everyday life practices, the traditionally defined regions and regional communities have been reshaped with completely different connotations. The traditional geographical boundary as the territorial demarcation between regions and countries has gradually faded. The academic undertaking with state orthodoxical unit-of-analysis has been loosened due to the emergence of bottom-up and border-crossing challenges. Hence, much attention has been attracted to the rise of the people-centered connectedness in shaping the international and regional order.

This book argues that the emergence of the widely recognized people-centered connectedness reveals at least three features (the 3Es features): encountering, engaging and empowering. Encountering refers to the fusion of the internal encounters and external stimuli of forces in terms of goods, capitals, interests, and even ideas among stakeholders; not necessarily limited to state actors per se. Engaging refers to the specific interactions among stakeholders (which includes cooperation, confrontation and the collaboration aimed at resolving conflicts). Empowering refers to the process by which stakeholders obtain (or are empowered with) the capacity to alter the *status quo* in the process of encountering and engaging. We argue that in particular to Southeast Asia, a region in the Indo-Pacific that has clearly demonstrated an overarching architecture of regional integration and collective efforts. Nourishing the awareness toward establishing a regional community, can be regarded as a particularly vivid case of the interaction of neighboring countries practicing various forms of people-centered connectedness, which corresponds to the thematic focus of this book, *When East Asia Meets Southeast Asia*.

The political landscape of East and Southeast Asia has been changing drastically since the turn of the century. It is no doubt that much of the changes are the results of the People's Republic of China's economic growth and its diplomacy projected by hard, soft, and sharp power. Disputes in the South China Sea among China, Taiwan, and several Southeast Asian countries after 2010 are one of the consequences of China's assertive use of hard power. Another significant example is the advancement of the Belt and Road Initiative (BRI) since late 2013, which has lead to various projects of infrastructure projects in over 70 countries including some in Southeast Asia. The penetration of China's power and influence within Southeast Asia has been escalated with the promotion on vaccine diplomacy against COVID-19 and Beijing's export of one-party-rule authoritarianism through sharp power and purposeful socio-economic statecraft, particularly for its panopticism for the ongoing pandemic governance. Various international factors such as the repositioning of the United States in Asia under the Biden administration and the sudden coup in Myanmar in February 2021 complicate the picture even further.

Following these changes, several works have been published to examine the international relations (IR) between China and Southeast Asia from various perspectives in recent years. For example, Shambaugh (2021) provides an overview of the competition between the United States and China through their diplomacies in Southeast Asia, while Emmerson's (2020) edited volume analyzes the up-to-date economic dependence of Southeast Asian countries on China and unpacks Southeast Asian attitudes toward and perception of China. Moreover, Gagliano (2019) examines the rivalry of the two giants in the South China Sea by looking into the decision-making of five countries such as Malaysia, the Philippines, Vietnam, Brunei and Indonesia. In terms of Beijing's soft power or socio-economic influence of Beijing, Lampton *et al.* (2020) co-authored *Rivers of Iron* to examine Chinese president Xi Jinping's effort to create an inter-country railway system connecting China and its seven Southeast Asian neighbors and the political, social, and economic implications. A similar undertaking is Chen's (2020) study of the Asian Infrastructure Investment

Bank (AIIB). He utilizes the IR theories to examine AIIB and argues that the bank is still evolving. He also examines the interaction of power, interests and status to determine whether the bank will go wild. Theoretically, AIIB's shape of the AIIB will influence global strategic conditions and global perceptions of the bank itself, consequently affecting China's metanational influence.

In addition to the leadership in global infrastructure projects, from the perspective of soft power, Peng ed. (2021) presents how the COVID-19 pandemic reshaped the relationship between China and Southeast Asian countries with detail. Diokno *et al.* (2019), on the other hand, details China's relationship with each state in Southeast Asia outside of security issues from various perspectives. These recent studies mainly focus on the influence of China-Southeast Asian relations.

Evidently, Southeast Asia is also known for its large number of Chinese overseas residents. The positioning of Chinese overseas communities in each country were first shaped by the colonial government and then by the IR between the newly independent countries in Southeast Asia and the newly established People's Republic of China. In addition, the popular images of China affected the acceptance and non-acceptance of Chinese overseas within the country. In other words, Chinese overseas communities were never free from the IR of that time. To some extent, this complex position of Chinese overseas residents is reflected in how China studies were developed in Southeast Asian countries. Ngeow's (2019) edited volume presents an interesting view by examining into how China has been studied in countries in Southeast Asia. Shih *et al.* (2019) also explore the academic discourses on China in South and Southeast Asia with a greater focus on the perspectives of Chinese overseas residents.

While these works bring us new perspectives on China and Southeast Asia, the position of the Republic of China (ROC) or Taiwan in Southeast Asia remains underexplored. To fill this gap, this book intends to examine the relationship between East Asia and Southeast Asia through three themes — namely, historical perspectives, economic flows of capital and people, and socio-cultural connections, with a strong focus on Taiwan. While a substantial number of chapters in this book is on the Chinese overseas in Indonesia and their connections with China and Taiwan both historically and contemporarily, this book also provides comprehensive knowledge on the different levels of international relations levels between East Asia and Southeast Asia.

Part 1, "Contending Regional Approaches," consists of four chapters to guide the readers in gasping the involvement of East Asia in the historical context. Lim's chapter takes a broad overview of the relationship between Taiwan and Southeast Asian countries during the Cold War. It focuses on how the Taiwan government cultivated new allies through cultural diplomacy, economic diplomacy and military assistance as part of its anti-communist agenda in East and Southeast Asia. Following Lim's chapter, Yang highlights the Taiwan's diplomatic strategy, moving from Go South Policy to the New Southbound Policy, toward Southeast Asia after the Cold War and explains how the Taiwanese mentality has shifted from "Taiwanese Asia" to an "Asian Taiwan" through the examination of the transformation and progress of the Go South Policy over the past 30 years. His chapter addresses the practice of encountering and engaging of Taiwan's regionalizing efforts. Chapters by Chang and Kano are overviews on China-Southeast Asia and Japan-Southeast Asia relations. Hence, Chang's chapter focuses on the recent development in China's aid diplomacy, including BRI and AIIB and the dilemmas relating to them. In additions, Kano provides a century-long economic history between Japan and Southeast Asia with very rich statistical data on the international trade and direct investment.

Part 2, "Economic Flows of Capital and People," consists of seven chapters mainly examining the flows of capital and people between Indonesia and Taiwan from the colonial period to the present and how this flow changed both societies. The authors in this part are a balance of academics and practitioners. Chen's chapter brings us back to Batavia at the beginning of the 20th century and examines the international business network of prominent Hakka families between Indonesia and various places in East Asia, such as Taiwan, Hong Kong and Kobe. Yoshida examines the connection among the Dutch East Indies, Taiwan, and Japan of the same period from different perspectives. In Yoshida's chapter, he explores the nationality problem of Taiwanese-Japanese or "Taiwan sekimin", who migrated from Taiwan to the Dutch East Indies at the beginning of the 20th century. He also provides insight into the history of the modern passport system.

While Chen's and Yoshida's chapters explore the historical connections between Southeast Asia, Taiwan, and Japan, the next five chapters highlight the contemporary issues in terms of the flows of capital and people. Hew's chapter focuses on the recent Hui migrants in Malaysia. The Hui are Mandarin-speaking Chinese Muslims. His research shows how the piety motivated their migration. Hsu provides both a historical overview and an update on their (Taiwanese entrepreneurs) and their companies in Southeast Asia, emphasizing their importance during the COVID-19 pandemic. Yokota's chapter explains the marriage migration of Chinese Indonesians from Singkawang in West Kalimantan, Indonesia, to Taiwan. Setyaningsih examines the impact of the New Southbound Policy on the Taiwan-Indonesia relationship. While the New Southbound Policy stresses people-to-people relations, the real life experiences of migrant workers and Taiwan as host society are facing several challenges. Finally, Kevin Chen, from the practitioner's perspective, shares his experience as the founder of One-Forty, a non-profit organization that tries to empower migrant workers from Southeast Asia based in Taiwan and provides insights into a more diverse and inclusive Taiwan.

Part 3, "Socio-Cultural Connections," consists of three chapters. This part is a unique contribution to the scholarship that focuses on the transformation of both traditional and popular culture in Southeast Asia, China and Taiwan by focusing on different agents. Wirawan uncovers Chinese Indonesia perception of East Asian countries by examining social and cultural articles on Taiwan and China published in the Chinese Indonesian popular magazines during the first decade of Indonesian independence (1945–1955). Fushiki explores one of the performing arts in Indonesia, *Wayang potehi*, a glove puppet show mostly performed in Klenteng (Chinese temples) and compares it with Potehi (Budaixi) in Taiwan. Barker explores the connection and encounters between Malaysia, Taiwan, Hong Kong, and China by looking into the Chinese-language film industry in Malaysia.

Undoubtedly, it is difficult to predict the political landscape in East and Southeast Asia in the next decades, but the dynamics of flows between the two transcend politics. We hope this book displays the richness of those flows from both historical and contemporary perspectives and sheds light on the further understanding of the configuration of regionalism in East and Southeast Asia. We firmly believe that the ties between East Asia and Southeast Asia will become stronger and even closer, facilitated by the mutual reinforcement of encountering, engagement and empowering among stakeholders.

The drafts of several chapters in this book were presented in two international seminars supported by JSPS KAKENHI [15KK0118], Fund for the Promotion of Joint International Research. Namely, International Workshop on Making Global Trajectories of Chinese Diaspora Studies in Asia, in November 2017 at The Indonesian Institute of Sciences (reorganized as the National Research and Innovation Agency: BRIN in 2021) in

Jakarta, Indonesia and (two-day workshop 5-6 November 2017) and Contextualizing Taiwanese & Chinese Presented in Southeast Asia and Southeast Asians in Taiwan–in Both Historical and Contemporary Perspectives, in March 2019 at the Institute of International Relations, National Chengchi University, in Taipei, Taiwan, with the support of IIR flasgship project granted by the Ministry of Education of Taiwan. Therefore, Special thanks of the editors go to JSPS, LIPI/BRIN, IIR, and Kyoto University for their kind endorsement and institutional assistance to make the publication possible.

References

Chen, I., ed. (2020). *Configuring the Asian Infrastructure Investment Bank: Power, Interests and Status*. London and New York, Routledge.

Diokno, M. S. I., Hsiao, H.-H. M. and Yang, A. H., eds. (2019). *China's Footprints in Southeast Asia*. Singapore, NUS Press.

Emmerson, K. D. (2020). *The Deer and the Dragon: Southeast Asia and China in the 21st Century*. Stanford, Shorenstein Asia-Pacific Research Center.

Gagliano, J. A. (2019). *Alliance Decision-Making in the South China Sea: Between Allied and Alone*. Abingdon, Routledge.

Lampton, D. M., Ho, S. and Kuik, C.-C. (2020). *Rivers of Iron: Railroads and Chinese Power in Southeast Asia Oakland*, University of California Press.

Ngeow, C. B. (2019). *Researching China in Southeast Asia*. London and New York, Routledge.

Peng, N., ed. (2021). *The Reshaping of China-Southeast Asia Relations in Light of the COVID-19 Pandemic*. Singapore, Springer.

Shambaugh, D. (2021). *Where Great Powers Meet: America & China in Southeast Asia*. New York, Oxford University Press.

Shih, C.-y., Manomaivibool, P. and Marwah, R. (2019). *China Studies in South and Southeast Asia: Between Pro-China and Objectivism*. Singapore, World Scientific.

Part 1

Contending Regional Approaches

https://doi.org/10.1142/9789811250668_0001

Chapter 1

The Diplomatic Efforts of the Republic of China Toward Southeast Asia, 1950–1978

Jason Lim

Senior Lecturer in Asian History,
University of Wollongong, Australia

Introduction

With the proclamation of the founding of the People's Republic of China (PRC) in 1949, the government of the Republic of China (ROC) retreated to Taiwan. Chiang Kai-shek, who had resigned in early 1949 to take responsibility for the military blunders by the Kuomintang (KMT) on the mainland against the Chinese Communist Party (CCP), resumed as President in 1950. The defeat of the KMT on the mainland came just as Southeast Asia was going through a period of decolonization. From the proclamation of independence of the Democratic Republic of Vietnam (or North Vietnam) in 1945 to the secession of Singapore from Malaysia in 1965, local nationalist leaders began taking charge of running their own countries from departing European colonial powers. Independence was followed by a nation-building process in a Cold War environment. North Vietnam was a communist state, but non-communist regimes in Southeast Asia faced military and political opposition from internal communist parties. The year 1975 saw the fall of South Vietnam and the overthrow of non-communist regimes in Laos and Cambodia.

The importance of Southeast Asia as an ideological battleground was not lost to the ROC but we know little of its concerns about Southeast Asia. Scholarship on the Cold War in East and Southeast Asia focusses exclusively on American interests against Chinese activities and influence. Therefore, in this struggle for influence in Southeast Asia, it is assumed that the ROC, as a small country of 13,890 square miles (35,975 square kilometers) and a population of 6.5 million in 1950 (*Daily Telegraph*, 1950), is not able to exert any influence in the region. The ROC had established diplomatic relations with two Southeast Asian countries — Thailand in 1945 and the Philippines in 1948 — but that was achieved before the retreat to Taiwan. North Vietnam, Burma and Indonesia all recognized the PRC in 1950. After moving its capital to Taipei, the ROC established diplomatic relations with the Republic of Vietnam (or South Vietnam) in 1956, Cambodia in 1958 (for about three months) and Laos in 1962 (for a short 114 days). The ROC continued to monitor the decolonization process in Southeast Asia. After Malaysia gained independence in 1957, followed by Singapore's proclamation of independence in 1965, the ROC swiftly moved to cultivate diplomatic relations. Despite their efforts, Leifer argued that "Taiwan's diplomatic links within South-East Asia had been limited". These links had been limited to the Philippines, Thailand and South Vietnam because the "correspondence of special relations with the United States was a critical factor" (Leifer, 2001: 175). However, by limiting himself to the three Southeast Asian countries that the ROC has diplomatic relations, Leifer excluded the ROC's involvement with Southeast Asia outside official ties.

The inclusion of the ROC serves as a counterbalance to prevailing scholarship that focuses on Chinese and American involvement in Southeast Asia. This chapter will assess the relationship the ROC has with Southeast Asian countries from 1950 to 1978 through the use of selected records held in Taiwan — mainly at the Academia Historica (國史館), the National Archives Administration (檔案管理局), the Archives of the Institute of Modern History Academia Sinica (中央研究院近代史研究所檔案館) and the Kuomintang (KMT) Party Archives (中國國民黨中央文化傳播委員會黨史館) — and supplemented by archival records located in the Hong Kong Government Records Service, the National Archives of Australia and the National Archives of Singapore. These materials suggest that the ROC was a major player in Southeast Asia, largely through cultural and economic diplomacy.

ROC Interests in Southeast Asia

The ROC remains in the periphery of research scholarship on the Cold War in East and Southeast Asia because it had been placed within the strategic and military network of the United States' containment policy against the spread of communism from the PRC. Studies on the ROC during the Cold War focus largely on the two Taiwan Strait Crises of 1955 and 1958 when the PRC threatened to invade Taiwan, and the ROC's relationship with the United States (Roy, 2003: 105–151; Lin, 2016; Pang, 2019). However, according to a recent study by Lin Hsiao-ting, the ROC was active in Southeast Asia with its involvement in anti-communist activities during the Laotian Civil War, the Vietnam War and assistance to rebels in Indonesia in the 1950s (Lin, 2015: 267–306). I have also written about the co-operative efforts of the ROC and South Vietnam between 1955 and 1963 to work toward an East Asian cultural solidarity through Confucianism and East Asian culture in order to counter the spread of communism from the PRC and North Vietnam (Lim, 2014: 119–156).

As a state on a constant vigilance against an invasion from the PRC, anti-communism became the lynchpin of ROC foreign policy. In 1952, a report was prepared for Vice-President Chen Cheng on American, British and French defenses against any attempt by the CCP to invade Southeast Asia. The report was clearly unimpressed with the three Western powers for not working together against the threat (Chen, 1952). The presence of the British and American military was pivotal to ROC interests in Southeast Asia. The Americans became involved with South Vietnamese affairs after the Geneva Conference of 1954. Singapore had a huge naval base until the British military withdrawal in 1971. The governments of Malaysia and South Vietnam were fighting communist insurgencies. President Chiang even warned about the dangers of communism taking over Malaya to a visiting trade mission from Malaya and Singapore 25 days before Malaya became independent on August 31, 1957 (Zhonghua Minguo Shishi Jiyao Bianji Weiyuanhui, 1992: 332–334). There was a civil war in Laos from 1959 to 1975. Prince Norodom Sihanouk wanted Cambodia to be non-aligned so he had included the leftist Pracheachon party in his government.

Three factors worked to the advantage of the ROC in its outreach to Southeast Asia. First, despite being a recipient of American economic aid from 1950 to 1965, the ROC economy grew at a phenomenal rate. Industrialization that had started with the First Four-Year Plan (1953–1956) had boosted the Taiwanese economy. By 1959, Taiwan had "the highest standard of living in Southeast Asia (*sic*)" (Walker, 1959: 122). Trade soared. In 1963, total trade for the ROC was US$693.9 million; 10 years later it hit US$8,275.9 million. The main export markets of the ROC were the United States and Japan but by 1973, major export destinations included Singapore and Indonesia (Han, 1974). The ROC economy became a success story that other countries could learn. The *Canberra Times* reported in 1967 that "some economists are now describing Taiwan (Formosa) as coming into the category of developed nations rather than developing ones" (Chou, 1967: 22). *The Straits Times*, the main English-language daily in Singapore, reported in 1968:

> The best place to see how the Chinese communists failed to bring the Chinese people the "good things in life" is not in China. It is on the island of Taiwan ... Taiwan, only 90 miles from the mainland, is wide open to Americans to view the hottest economic spectacle in Asia. (Brown, 1968: 11)

The economic take-off of the ROC gave the country credibility in Southeast Asia. In a bid to discourage newly emerging nations in Southeast Asia from establishing diplomatic ties with the PRC, the ROC promoted itself as a place to train technicians in agriculture and industry. With Burma, Indonesia and North Vietnam recognizing the PRC, the ROC worked to promote closer economic ties with the remaining Southeast Asian countries, even if there was no exchange of ambassadors. As Wang noted, "many third world nations began to see Taiwan's success as a model for their own development" (Wang, 1990: 5).

The second factor is the projection of the image that the ROC was the true repository of Chinese culture, a point that was underlined to appeal to the overseas Chinese living in Southeast Asia. In 1968, it was estimated that about 75% of ethnic Chinese outside China reside in Southeast Asia (Chang, 1968: 99). The KMT and President Chiang continued to claim themselves as the rightful government of all of China and that the CCP regime in Beijing intended to destroy Chinese culture and traditions. The latter view was reinforced with the smashing of the "Four Olds" during the Cultural Revolution in the PRC from 1966. The ROC also used cultural traditions and history as bulwarks against communism. The KMT continued to court the loyalty of the overseas Chinese at a time when the decolonization movement in Southeast Asia was in full swing. Unfortunately for the KMT, the

Chinese in Southeast Asia were descendants of migrants from Fujian and Guangdong provinces and so they had no historical, cultural, social or family links with Taiwan. The only link that an overseas Chinese could have with Taiwan was a political one through support for the KMT.

The third factor was the image of an ROC that could not be divorced from its domestic politics and its military rivalry with the PRC during the Cold War. The ROC military consisted of about 600,000 men that was described in the mid-1960s as "the best-trained and organized in non-communist Asia today" (Jackson, 1966: 18). This was a sizable force in the region for a small country. The formidable strength of the ROC armed forces appealed to President Ngo Dinh Diem of South Vietnam, who told reporters in 1959 that the ROC military could be involved alongside South Vietnamese forces in a conflict with North Vietnam (National Archives Administration, 1959). A strong ROC military working in co-operation with South Vietnam would be a psychological boost in the event of any victory for one party.

The imposition of martial law in Taiwan since 1949 was of little concern to Southeast Asia. In the decolonization process tied closely with the Cold War environment, newly emerging nationalist leaders in Southeast Asia paid scant attention to democracy and human rights. The survival of these new nations against military and psychological threats from communist forces (whether domestic or foreign) remained paramount in the minds of Southeast Asian leaders. There were armed communist groups in Malaya, Thailand, the Philippines, Cambodia, Laos and South Vietnam. A pro-communist political party, the Barisan Sosialis, was also active in Singapore. Any communist movement was a hindrance to nation-building goals in Southeast Asia. The communist threat, however, was uneven across the region. It was strong in South Vietnam as the National Liberation Front (known as "Viet Cong" by American forces) remained allied with North Vietnam, but it was weak in Thailand. In the Philippines, the rebellion by the Partido Komunista ng Pilipinas (PKP) was over by 1954, as was the emergency against the Malayan Communist Party (MCP) by 1960. The Partai Komunis Indonesia (PKI) was alleged to be the mastermind behind a failed coup in Indonesia in 1965 and banned the following year. In Singapore, two mass arrest operations in 1963 effectively crippled the Barisan Sosialis. In this Cold War environment, Wang noted that "the majority of its East Asian neighbours were anticommunist in their foreign policies and demonstrated their sympathy toward Taipei by supporting ROC's international position". That "international position" was its standing on world anti-communism (Wang, 1990: 4–5).

The almost invisible role of Taipei during the Cold War arises from how the world, including the United States, view the ROC. The ROC was regarded as nothing more than "a pariah state" because it was "a one-party, US-client, garrison state". Its claims to represent all of China was not taken seriously internationally (Copper, 1997: 10). Indonesian Foreign Minister Adam Malik suggested in August 1967 that his country would recognize the Chiang government only if the ROC changed its name to the "Republic of Taiwan" since "Taiwan could not claim itself as the 'owner' of mainland China" (*The Straits Times*, 1967: 17).[1] The ROC also claimed to represent all overseas Chinese through the Overseas Chinese Affairs Commission in Taipei. However, only hardcore KMT supporters outside Taiwan would recognize that representation as a fact. These negative views of the ROC present a contradiction in the country's foreign affairs. On the one hand, if the ROC was a pariah state, it would have few friends. A pariah state has no interest in its neighbors and its neighbors care little about its existence. However, the large extent of files housed in the archives in Taiwan reveal the role of the ROC in nation-building projects in Southeast Asia during the Cold War. Its claim as a representative of all overseas Chinese was not heeded in Southeast Asia because newly emerging nations focused on assimilating their Chinese populations.

The relationship between the ROC and Southeast Asian countries (except North Vietnam, Burma and Indonesia) can be summarized as having three approaches:

- Cultural diplomacy — the promotion of Taiwan as a Chinese repository, a suitable place for Chinese tertiary education and concern for the plight of the overseas Chinese;
- Economic diplomacy — the promotion of agricultural and scientific knowledge, technical assistance, involvement in industrialization, and promotion of trade; and
- Military assistance — building up of armed forces, sales of weapons, and involvement in military conflicts and propaganda warfare against the spread of communism.

While these three approaches were used, some Southeast Asian countries mattered more to the ROC than others. Priority was placed on

[1] I thank Professor Leo Suryadinata at ISEAS-Yusof Ishak Institute for bringing this event to my attention.

winning new allies in Southeast Asia and so the ROC used all three approaches toward the newly decolonized states of South Vietnam, Malaya (later Malaysia) and Singapore, which gained independence between 1955 and 1965. While Malaysia and Singapore held back diplomatic relations with the ROC, they organized economic assistance schemes and cultural exchange programs with the ROC. Singapore declined official relations with the ROC because, in the recollections of S. Rajaratnam, the foreign minister in 1965, "we decided to have good relations discreetly with the Taiwanese and with the People's Republic of China, without antagonising either" (Chan and ul-Haq, 2007: 478). Singapore also had a policy of recognizing only "one China" and that the dispute between the ROC and the PRC was an internal affair (Lee, 2006: 620). The ROC opened a trade office in Singapore in 1969 but Singapore avoided opening its own trade office in Taipei until 10 years later. Lee Kuan Yew also took great lengths to not publicize "a mystery visit" to Taiwan, avoiding reporters at a stopover in Hong Kong on his return to Singapore. The Singapore Commission in Hong Kong also refused to confirm whether Lee actually visited Taipei (Press Library Files, 1973–1974). Malaysia withheld official recognition of the ROC as some members of the ruling coalition pointed out that the country should be "instilling amongst the local Chinese a sense of belonging and common loyalty towards Malaysia" (Department of Foreign Affairs, 1958–1988). The Malaysian Prime Minister, Tunku Abdul Rahman, was also "anxious not to do anything which might embarrass him in his efforts to attend the Afro-Asian Conference" (Department of Foreign Affairs, 1958–1988).[2]

Less time and effort were spent on strengthening ties with Thailand and the Philippines as the ROC worked on an assumption that state-to-state relations were strong since relations were established between 1945 and 1949. Thailand and the Philippines had anti-communist regimes and both states were members of the South East Asia Treaty Organisation (SEATO). Burma, Indonesia and North Vietnam were regarded as lost causes since all three states recognized the PRC and consequently wanted to have very little contact with the ROC. Laos and Cambodia had diplomatic relations with the ROC for very short periods of time, which showed how challenging it was for both states to remain neutral during the Cold War in neighboring Vietnam.

[2]Notes on the visit of the ROC Foreign Minister to Malaysia, July 13, 1965.

Cultural Diplomacy

Cultural diplomacy is the international promotion of a country's political, social and cultural values. It was an important aspect of foreign relations for the ROC as it introduced Southeast Asian peoples (especially the overseas Chinese) to what the ROC considered "real" Chinese culture in Taiwan. The ROC promoted culture, history and traditions as incompatible with communism. Cultural artefacts representing Chinese heritage were promoted by the ROC. Carey wrote that "cultural artefacts ... can reflect any aspect of the state's culture, and can involve food, visual art, literature, cultural exchange programs, academic exchange and overseas student programs, and language classes to name a few" (Carey, 2018: 3). Cultural diplomacy gained greater impetus once the Cultural Revolution was launched in the PRC in May 1966, with President Chiang launching the Chinese Cultural Renaissance Movement in response in November that year.

In promoting itself as the center of Chinese culture, the ROC encouraged the learning of everything associated with China including Confucianism, language (Mandarin), philosophy, art, history and literature. The ROC made arrangements for overseas Chinese students from Southeast Asia to complete post-secondary and tertiary education in Taiwan. Non-Chinese students were also invited to Taiwan for cultural visits or exchange programs. They would be exposed to what the KMT government hoped would be positive aspects of Chinese society — law and order, culture, land reform, industrialization and the arts. The ROC signed cultural agreements with Southeast Asian nations before conducting cultural exchange programs. Cultural groups or missions could be sent to Southeast Asia to let the latter understand Chinese culture on Taiwan. The cultural exchange programs, however, actually showcased Taiwan to Southeast Asian students because they could understand Taiwanese society, culture and economy. The programs highlighted "Taiwan" rather than "China". As the PRC descended into economic and social chaos from the late 1950s, the positive images of Taiwan and the military posturing of the PRC were used to gain sympathy from overseas Chinese students.

Understanding Chinese culture was also promoted in Southeast Asia. In June 1956, the ROC invited 28 educationists, historians and reporters from the Philippines for a visit to Taiwan. Upon their return to Manila, they formed the Philippine–China Cultural Association to push for the deepening of cultural ties between the two countries. In January 1957, the ROC donated 500 books on Confucianism to the Philippine Ministry of Education and later donated another 800 books on history (Chen, 2004: 54). When both countries signed a Cultural Convention on June 18, 1970, they agreed on the learning of each countries' language, history, literature, philosophy and culture. There was also an exchange of university professors, setting up scholarships and research grants, organization of cultural performances, and the exchange of films, television programs and radio programs (*ibid.*: 55).

Cultural diplomacy went together with anti-communism. As cultural links were forged with South Vietnam, the KMT government used culture and history as the backbone of the relationship. President Chiang and the KMT promoted the view that culture and heritage were incompatible with communism. Confucianism, not communism, connected the peoples of the ROC and South Vietnam. There was a view that societies in China, Japan, Korea and Vietnam had their origins in Confucianism (Zhu, 1958: 4). The winning of hearts and minds was a part of psychological warfare during the Cold War as President Chiang and the KMT made communism unappealing in East Asia. Through the promotion of Confucianism as the bedrock of East Asian culture, the ROC strengthened educational, academic and cultural ties with South Vietnam. Cultural and educational exchanges emphasized the Confucian legacy. The learning of Mandarin was used to promote East Asian solidarity as the use of the Chinese script was well-documented in the region. Yet the ROC promoted a superficial appreciation of Confucianism, with the focus merely on understanding how Confucianism shaped China and Vietnam in ancient times, but what was taught in schools and promoted publicly remained disconnected to the real world of the 1950s.

Since the ROC was focused on all things Chinese, Singapore was of great interest because about 75% of the 1,634,000 people were ethnic Chinese in 1960 (Purcell, 1965: 3). In the absence of diplomatic relations with Singapore, the ROC promoted itself as a Chinese society untainted by communism, where tradition was kept alive alongside thriving culture and the arts. The message of a Chinese non-communist society was deemed acceptable by Lee Kuan Yew government in Singapore. It resonated with the message the Lee government promoted that the outward forms of Chinese traditions and culture such as music, drama, performance and art were acceptable expressions of Chinese-ness, and that questions of Chinese-ness should not be used as political tools in a chauvinistic or communalistic agenda in Singapore. The ROC trained academics from Nanyang University on Chinese culture and sent Chinese teachers to Singapore (Qiaowu Weiyuanhui Qiaowu Yanjiushi, 1969: 42–43).

The island's main universities — in particular National Taiwan University, National Taiwan Normal University, National Chengchi University and National Cheng Kung University — were utilized to draw in overseas Chinese students. Studying in Taiwan was exported as an attractive package to the overseas Chinese and designed to prevent them from taking up tertiary education in China. Purcell believed that the Great Leap Forward in the PRC from 1958 had made the situation in China "even less propitious" for Chinese students in Malaya and Singapore (Purcell, 1965: 352). In an interview with the National Archives of Singapore, Lee Sing Tiong, a beneficiary of the scheme, recalled that every overseas Chinese student would get a return air ticket. In addition, these students paid a third of the tuition fees and had subsidized hostel rents (Lee, 1998). Fong Chan Yoon, who attended National Taiwan University, recalled visiting farms in Taiwan which helped him understand how land reforms in Taiwan had worked. He was also impressed with the efficiency of the police in Taiwan *during martial law* as they solved robbery cases within "two or three hours", citing the example of a friend who had her purse stolen. He concluded that there "not many bad people because of martial law" (Fong, 2001).

Taiwanese assistance was also given to the public service in Singapore. In May 1968, Professor Yu Yuen-Chen, an architect based in Taipei, was invited to submit plans for a Chinese-themed garden as a *free service* to the Jurong Town Corporation (JTC) (Ministry of Foreign Affairs, 1965–1970).[3] Professor Yu saw the project as "an effective way of constructing mutual friendship between these two Nations, especially because there are so many Overseas Chinese in your country" (Ministry of Foreign Affairs, 1965–1970).[4] The Chinese Garden (裕華園) was eventually opened on April 18, 1975. In building a garden that appealed to a form of "Chinese-ness", the Singapore government had approached the ROC, who was more than willing to help.

[3]Letter from Chairman-Designate of JTC to ROC Consul at Kuala Lumpur, May 29, 1968.

[4]Letter from Yu Yuen-Chen to Chairman of the JTC, July 8, 1968.

Economic Diplomacy

While the foreign policy of Taiwan was centered on an anti-communist agenda, the KMT government worked on the basis that the best anti-communist platform was the provision of technical and economic assistance to non-communist or anti-communist allies. Economic development and the raising of living standards in Southeast Asia would make communism — and the chaos and violence that came with it in North Vietnam and the PRC — unappealing. By the late 1950s, when it became clear to the KMT that they could not retake the mainland from the CCP, the government got down to developing Taiwan with the construction of roads, bridges, dams, schools and universities. Between 1952 and 1962, real national income of Taiwan doubled (Buss, 1964: 679). The ROC launched its International Technical Cooperation program in 1959 with a focus on agricultural development. Its claim to be an expert on agriculture stemmed from its successful land reform program under Vice-President Chen Cheng in the 1950s. The program was extended to Southeast Asia in 1963 with the following aim:

> This Program will afford the participants, selected by their respective governments, the opportunity of observing at first hand and studying and discussing in person with the competent Chinese authorities and agricultural experts how the problems relating to their respective fields have been met in this island (Ministry of Foreign Affairs, 1963–1966).

The ROC invited Thailand, the Philippines, Malaysia and South Vietnam to be involved with the program. The Philippines signed an agreement with the ROC on training Filipinos in agricultural technology on August 23, 1964. A month later, the ROC sent three specialists to the Philippines for five months to teach farmers the latest methods in sowing and harvesting such as irrigation, pest control, transplanting and fertilization (Chen, 2004: 74). The ROC helped the Philippines with its first rice station in Luzon in 1966. Sitting on 3,400 hectares of land, it employed 1,500 farmers (Chen, 2004: 74–75).

Malaysia was dependent on agriculture, especially rubber. The ROC actively promoted exchange visits by Malaysian politicians and public servants to Taiwan, with tours of agricultural facilities, farms and schools. The knowledge gained from such visits would be brought back to Malaysia where, it was hoped, the Malaysian government would utilize that knowledge to improve agriculture and animal husbandry. Malaysian Prime Minister Tunku Abdul Rahman told journalists in 1964 that "they [the ROC] are experts and they can help us a lot here" (Department of Foreign Affairs, 1958–1988).[5] Under the auspices of the International Technical Cooperation, Malaysia sent several groups of parliamentarians and public servants to Taiwan to observe factories, plants, schools and farms in Taiwan between 1965 and 1966. Some high-profile Malaysians went on these tours, including Thong Yaw Hong, Deputy Director-General of the Malaysian Economic Planning Unit, in February 1965, and Haji Mohamed Ghazali bin Jawi, Minister of Agriculture and Co-operatives, in July 1965. There was also a Malaysian Trade Mission of 12 merchants, traders and industrialists led by Senator Dato T. H. Tan that visited Taiwan in November 1965 (Ministry of Foreign Affairs, 1965a, 1965b). In August 1970, Malaysia and the ROC signed an agreement on economic co-operation. Malaysia sent a representative to study the port facilities at Kaohsiung and the ROC sent a technical mission to Malaysia to help set up an export processing zone (Chen, 2004: 31). Despite not having diplomatic relations, and resisting ROC appeals for official recognition, Malaysia was a beneficiary of the International Technical Cooperation program.

The ROC was also involved with scientific and engineering projects in South Vietnam before the start of the International Technical Cooperation program. In July 1958, Li Kwoh-ting led an Economic Goodwill Mission of agricultural and industrial experts to South Vietnam for 36 days to study the agricultural and industrial development of South Vietnam. After touring mainly Mekong River Delta, the highlands and the eastern coastal provinces, the mission produced a report that gave proposals on improving South Vietnamese agriculture and industry (Economic Good Will Mission of the Republic of China to Vietnam, 1958). The Republic of China Power Mission arrived in Saigon in November 1964 and worked to help South Vietnam generate electricity in the country. By August 1965, South Vietnam asked for 20 more engineers and technicians from Taiwan Power Company, a state-owned company, to work on commercial operations, management and accounting (Ministry of Foreign Affairs, 1965c). The ROC and South Vietnam also organized eight Economic Cooperation Conferences that alternated between Taipei and Saigon from 1960 to 1973. These conferences saw the ROC provide US$2 million in technical

---

[5] Foreign Minister Visits Asian Neighbours. *China News*, October 9, 1964.

assistance and machinery to South Vietnam, including US$400,000 in grain processing equipment (Chen, 2004: 291).

Military Assistance

The ROC closely monitored the work of the SEATO, the political and military situation in both North and South Vietnam, and communist movements in Southeast Asia. However, it did not join SEATO when it was organized in 1954 as it criticized the organization for not using anti-communism as its foundation (Free China Review, 1954). Wang Sheng led a military mission to South Vietnam in May 1960 and he suggested to President Diem that a political warfare center be established in the South Vietnamese military. The ROC set up the Psychological Warfare Training Centre in South Vietnam on February 7, 1961. From May 1961 to January 1962, the ROC trained 240 officers on political warfare. A Political Warfare Department was eventually set up in South Vietnam in December 1964. The ROC sent military advisers to South Vietnam from July 1966 and the ROC Military Advisory Group in Vietnam was organized in February 1967. The Group officially ended its work in March 1973 following the Paris Peace Accords (Chen, 2004: 296–299). A few officers, however, remained in Saigon until they were ordered by the ROC government to return to Taipei in April 1975.

Malaysia expressed an interest in purchasing weapons from the ROC. In July 1965, the Malaysian government accepted an offer of about 5,000 carbines from the ROC for the local Defence Corps of the Territorial Army, while declining an offer for the building of a munitions plant by the ROC (Department of Foreign Affairs, 1958–1988).[6] The ROC also offered army training facilities to the Malaysian Army and two military missions from Malaysia visited Taiwan. The ROC Army also specialized in "anti-communist training" which is offered to Malaysia (*ibid.*).[7] Malaysia also sent a "large delegation" to the Asian People's Anti-Communist League in 1964 (*ibid.*),[8] an organization spearheaded by President Park Chung-Hee

[6]Letter from W. A. Vawdrey, First Secretary in the Australian High Commission in Kuala Lumpur, to the Department of External Affairs, Canberra, July 16, 1965.

[7]Notes on the visit by the ROC Foreign Minister, July 13, 1965.

[8]Letter from W. A. Vawdrey, First Secretary in the Australian High Commission in Kuala Lumpur, to the Department of External Affairs, Canberra, April 2, 1965.

of South Korea and President Chiang. Similarly, as a small city-state, Singapore lacked land and facilities to train its armed forces. Lee Kuan Yew brought up this issue to Premier Chiang Ching-kuo during the former's visit to Taiwan in 1974. In April 1975, Singapore and the ROC agreed on the training of Singapore Armed Forces personnel in Taiwan under the code name "Exercise Starlight" (Lee, 2006: 622). The ROC also offered to help Singapore set up its own Air Force in 1967, and provided pilot training and technicians in 1971 (Chen, 2004: 10–11).

Relations with Indonesia

Both the PRC and the ROC saw relations with Indonesia as key to gaining a foothold on Southeast Asia. Indonesia was a dominant country in the region due to its size, population and, very importantly for the PRC and ROC, overseas Chinese presence in the country. At a conference in Colombo in April 1954, Indonesia proposed an Afro-Asian conference of newly independent countries. In December 1954, the "Colombo Five" of Burma, India, Ceylon, Indonesia and Pakistan agreed there should be such a conference in Indonesia. U Nu, Prime Minister of Burma, was adamant that the PRC should be invited to what eventually became the Bandung Conference but he threatened that Burma would to withdraw if the ROC was invited too. The organization of the conference revealed President Sukarno's struggle toward making the conference truly "non-aligned". Both Koreas were not invited but invitations were extended to the two Vietnams (Mackie, 2005: 63–65). The Bandung Conference could not be politically neutral since only one of the two claimants of all of China was invited.

Although Indonesia had recognized the PRC, the ROC still paid close attention to political developments within the country. In particular, the ROC focused on the influence of the PKI on Indonesian government and politics. The ROC was suspicious of President Sukarno since he had included members of the PKI in his government. In February 1958, disgruntled army units mainly in the islands of Sumatra and Sulawesi rebelled against the Indonesian government. They had issued an ultimatum to Jakarta to remove unnamed "communist sympathizers" from the Cabinet and a new government installed that would not have any communist ministers. The supposed anti-communist agenda of the rebels — now known as the Revolutionary Government of the Republic of Indonesia (PRRI) — attracted the attention of the ROC government.

The PRRI received arms and munitions and there were reports of foreign aid from Western governments. The ROC was complicit in its support for the rebels — rebel aircraft allegedly flew out of Taiwan on bombing missions or dropping aid (Doeppers, 1972: 190–191). In response, Sukarno closed down 18 Chinese newspapers in Indonesia on April 18 regardless of their political sympathies (Chen, 2004: 446). Mass arrests of pro-ROC Chinese in Indonesia were conducted on May 5. PRRI representatives also arrived in Taiwan for discussions on June 26. The "unexpectedly resolute" (Doeppers, 1972: 183) military response by the Indonesian government, however, resulted in the collapse of the PRRI by 1961. While the PRRI had an anti-communist agenda, influential Indonesians in government and the military saw the rebellion as an active attempt to break up the Indonesian state (Doeppers, 1972: 195). Indonesian politicians became suspicious of foreign attempts by the United States (through the Central Intelligence Agency), Australia, the United Kingdom and the ROC of causing civil war in Indonesia. Former Indonesian Foreign Affairs Minister Ide Anak Agung Gde Agung wrote in 1973:

> Arms dropped by unidentified airplanes ... bore the identification of the US army. This does not prove, of course, that the US government had intervened directly. Those US arms very probably came through the Kuomintang government in Taiwan. But if the US were really to be given logistic support, the perfect medium for the funnelling of supplies would have been the Taiwan government (Agung, 1973: 261).

The alleged coup and violence in Indonesia in 1965 gave the KMT government the opportunity to improve ties with Indonesia. Indonesia accused Beijing of actively supporting the PKI and relations between the two countries were finally broken in 1967. The KMT keenly observed events unfolding in Indonesia. There was a question on the possibility of diplomatic relations between the ROC and Indonesia (Deng, 1968). In September 1967, the ROC sent a delegation to Jakarta to negotiate a loan to Indonesia of US$20 million (Qian, 1967). Taipei had been opportunistic enough to see where Beijing had apparently failed in its diplomatic relations to jump in and occupy the space that Beijing had left behind. Unfortunately, Indonesia restricted relations with the ROC to trade ties. Despite the break in diplomatic relations between the PRC and Indonesia, the latter continued to adhere to the One-China Policy (*The Straits Times*, 1967: 17). Malik's suggestion referred to earlier that the Chiang government change the country's name to the "Republic of Taiwan" was not taken seriously by Chiang Kai-shek, who was bent on recovering mainland China from the CCP.

Conclusion

An overview of the diplomatic overtures by the ROC toward countries that did not recognize the PRC shows that the country had been successful in winning allies, even if those allies stopped short of full recognition. Through cultural and economic diplomacy, and provision of military assistance and training, the ROC had shown itself committed to an anti-communist agenda that most Southeast Asian countries found acceptable. As new states appeared in Southeast Asia, the ROC provided timely and needed assistance in technical expertise in agriculture and industry. The record of the ROC in introducing economic change such as land reforms in Taiwan had given it the experience that it could share with Southeast Asian countries. Despite reservations from countries such as South Vietnam and Malaysia that the ROC was focused on the local ethnic Chinese population, government leaders welcomed any assistance from the ROC. The role of the ROC in promoting goodwill with Southeast Asian countries was a positive one. In September 1963, Dato Haji Mohamed Noah bin Omar, Speaker of the Malaysian House of Representatives, said that diplomatic relations with the ROC were "inevitable" (*The Straits Times*, 1963).

The United Nations General Assembly Resolution 2758 on October 25, 1971 was a turning point for the ROC. The resolution called for the expulsion of "the representatives of Chiang Kai-shek" and the taking over of the "China" seat in the United Nations (UN) by the PRC. The UN General Assembly voted 76 to 35 with 17 abstentions. Southeast Asian countries were divided on the issue. Malaysia and Singapore joined Burma and Laos, and voted for the PRC to take the "China" seat. The Philippines and the Khmer Republic (Cambodia) voted against the resolution, while Indonesia and Thailand abstained (UN General Assembly, 1971). The resolution meant that the PRC could step into the shoes once filled by the ROC.

Under the PRC's "One-China Policy", any country establishing diplomatic ties with Beijing must sever all official relationships with Taipei. Malaysia became the first country in Southeast Asia to recognize Beijing on May 31, 1974, followed by the Philippines on June 9, 1975, and

Thailand on July 1, 1975.[9] In March 1975, when it became clear that the fall of Saigon was imminent, the ROC issued passports to Vietnamese of Chinese descent and sent vessels to pick up more than 1,000 people who had chosen to leave South Vietnam (Chen, 2004: 293–294). President Chiang died in Taiwan on April 5, 1975 and was succeeded by Yen Chia-kan. South Vietnamese President Nguyen Van Thieu resigned on April 21, 1975 and fled to Taipei when he met Madame Chiang Kai-shek and Premier Chiang Ching-kuo. Saigon fell to the North Vietnamese on April 30, 1975, marking the end of the Vietnam War.

The diplomatic overtures by the ROC in earlier decades meant that Malaysia, the Philippines and Thailand were willing to downgrade relations to an unofficial level rather than break ties with Taipei completely. In response to Malaysia's recognition of the PRC, the ROC Ministry of Foreign Affairs noted that despite the absence of diplomatic relations, the peoples of Malaysia and the ROC continued to have close cultural and economic ties (*ibid.*: 35). Malaysia also sought a way out when it issued a statement that while it no longer had any official relations with "Taiwan" (not the ROC), "all trade relations, investment and tourism between Malaysia and Taiwan will be continued by private individual *(sic)* based on people-to-people relations and on a local basis."[10] A "Far East Travel and Trade Centre" representing Taiwan was opened in Kuala Lumpur in August 1974. In 1977, the Taipei office of Malaysian Airlines began issuing visas to Taiwanese visiting Malaysia. Similar arrangements were made between the ROC, Thailand and the Philippines. Singapore continued to maintain trade offices as unofficial relations with the ROC.

However, it was ironically in Indonesia — the country the ROC worked so hard to secure recognition — that good relations paid off for Taiwan. The collapse of the Sukarno regime had given way to the pro-Western government of Suharto, who mended ties with the ROC, albeit unofficially. In 1970, the Indonesian Chamber of Commerce (KADIN) was set up to deal with trade and immigration issues with the ROC in the absence of an embassy. The ROC reciprocated in 1971 with the founding of the Chinese Chamber of Commerce to Jakarta. The opening of both offices was followed by visits from Indonesian politicians, military officers and public servants to Taiwan. In 1976, Taiwan and Indonesia signed

[9] Singapore recognized the PRC on October 3, 1990.

[10] Statement by the Malaysian Government on the Termination of Consular Relations with Taiwan, May 31, 1974.

a technical co-operation agreement in agriculture and since then, Taiwan has sent technical missions to Java.

ROC diplomacy had been successful in preserving ties with Southeast Asia since the departure of the ROC from the UN and the subsequent switching of diplomatic recognition from Taipei to Beijing did not mean the end of all diplomatic ties. As the 1970s grew to a close, the ROC had shifted the center of its foreign policy from one that sought to contain the spread of communism out of mainland China, to one of engagement with Southeast Asia through increasingly unofficial channels. There is a perception that Taiwan's future rests with Southeast Asia. The region had become increasingly important and Taipei looked to prioritizing its relations with Southeast Asian nations. It set the scene for the introduction of a New Southbound Policy in Taiwan in 2015 to enhance co-operation and exchange with Southeast Asian countries.

References

Agung, I. A. A. G. (1973). *Twenty Years Indonesian Foreign Policy 1945–1965*. The Hague, Mouton.

Brown, C. (1968). The Chinese Economic Success That Is Taiwan. *The Straits Times*, September 14, https://eresources.nlb.gov.sg/newspapers/Digitised/Article/straitstimes19680914-1.2.80?ST=1&AT=search&k=%22the%20chinese%20economic%20success%20that%20is%20taiwan%22&QT=%22thechineseeconomicsuccessthatistaiwan%22&oref=article.

Buss, C. A. (1964). *Asia in the Modern World: A History of China, Japan, South and Southeast Asia*. New York, Macmillan.

Carey, J. M. (2018). Cultural Diplomacy: Australia's Chance in the Pacific. *Quarterly Access*, 11(2): 1–5, https://www.internationalaffairs.org.au/wp-content/uploads/2018/07/QuarterlyAccessMagazineVol.11_Iss.2.pdf.

Chan, H. C. and ul-Haq, O., eds. (2007). *S Rajaratnam: The Prophetic and the Political*, 2nd edn. Singapore, Institute of Southeast Asian Studies and Graham Brash.

Chang, S.-D. (1968). The Distribution and Occupations of Overseas Chinese. *Geographical Review*, 58(1): 89–107.

Chen, C. (1952). *Guoji Waijiao Ziliao Huibian Disance: Meiying dui Dongnanya zhi Zhengce* 國際外交資料彙編第三冊：美英對東南亞之政策 (Compilation of International Foreign Affairs Materials: The Policy of the US and UK on Southeast Asia) (accession number 008-010602-00017-022). Chen Cheng Vice-Presidential Archives, Academia Historica (國史館), Taipei, Taiwan.

Chen, H. 陳鴻瑜 (2004). *Zhonghua Minguo yu Dongnanya Geguo Waijiao Guanxi Shi* (1912–2000) 中華民國與東南亞各國外交關係史 (1912–2000) (Diplomatic relationships between the Republic of China and Southeast Asian nations 1912–2000). Taipei, Dingwen Shuju.

Chou, E. (1967). Taiwan Now a "Developed" Country. *Canberra Times*, December 20, https://trove.nla.gov.au/newspaper/article/107038060?searchTerm=taiwan%20developed%20country.

Copper, J. F. (1997). *The Taiwan Political Miracle: Essays on Political Development, Elections and Foreign Relations*. Lanham, East Asia Research Institute and University Press of America.

Deng, T. Y. 鄧鐵英 (1968, December 7). Yinni Zhonggong de Yichang Emeng 印尼中共的一場噩夢 (Indonesia, a Nightmare for the Chinese Communist Party), *Xinwen Tiandi* 新聞天地, 1086. General Archives (accession number 一般588/488), Kuomintang Party Archives, Taipei, Taiwan.

Department of Foreign Affairs (1958–1988). *Correspondence*. Taiwan — Relations with Malaysia and Singapore (Accession number A1838, 519/3/22 Part 1), National Archives of Australia, Canberra, Australia.

Doeppers, D. F. (1972). An Incident in the PRRI/Permesta Rebellion of 1958. *Indonesia*, 14: 183–195.

Economic Good Will Mission of the Republic of China to Vietnam (1958). *Report on Vietnam's Agriculture and Industry*. Taipei, Economic Good Will Mission of the Republic of China to Vietnam.

Fong, C. Y. (2001, October 18). *Interview by Jason Lim* [Tape recording]. Accession number A002332/20/07. Oral History Centre, National Archives of Singapore, Singapore.

Free China Review (1954). *SEATO and NEATO*, September 1, https://taiwantoday.tw/print.php?unit=4&post=6549.

Han, L. (1974). *Taiwan Today*. Taipei, Institute of International Relations.

Jackson, D. G. M. (1966). *Formosa and the Chinese Nationalists*. Melbourne, The Hawthorn Press.

Lee, K. Y. (2006). *From Third World to First — The Singapore Story: 1965–2000*. Singapore, Marshall Cavendish Editions and the Straits Times Press.

Lee, S. T. (1998, November 20). *Interview by Yap Wee Cheng* [Tape recording]. Accession Number A002066/22/14. Oral History Centre, National Archives of Singapore, Singapore.

Leifer, M. (2001). Taiwan and South-East Asia: The Limits of Pragmatic Diplomacy. In R. L. Edmonds and S. M. Goldstein (eds.), *Taiwan in the Twentieth Century: A Retrospective View* (pp. 173–185). Cambridge, Cambridge University Press.

Lim, J. (2014). Confucianism As a Symbol of Solidarity: Cultural Relations between the Republic of China and the Republic of Vietnam, 1955–1963. *Issues & Studies*, 50(4): 119–156.

Lin, H. 林孝庭 (2015). *Taihai, Lengzhan, Jiang Jieshi: Jiemi Dang'an Zhong Xiaoshi de Taiwan Shi 1949–1988* 台海．冷戰．蔣介石：解密檔案中消失的台灣史 (The Taiwan Strait, the Cold War and Chiang Kai-shek: Missing Portions of Taiwanese History in the Declassified Archives, 1949–1988), Taipei, Lianjing Chuban.

Lin, H. (2016). *Accidental State: Chiang Kai-shek, the United States, and the Making of Taiwan*. Cambridge, Harvard University Press.

Mackie, J. (2005). *Bandung 1955: Non-Alignment and Afro-Asian Solidarity*. Singapore, Editions Didier Millet.

Ministry of Foreign Affairs (1963–1966). *Correspondence*. Dongnanya Jishu Hezuo Nongye Jishu Yantaohui — Jianbao Ziliao 東南亞技術合作農業技術研討會~簡報資料 (Technical Cooperation in Southeast Asia — Agricultural Technology Conference — Newspaper Articles) (Accession number 020-010604-0025), Academia Historica (國史館), Taipei, Taiwan.

Ministry of Foreign Affairs (1965a). *Correspondence*. Malaiya (Malaixiya) Renshi Fanghua (san) 馬來亞(馬來西亞)人士訪華(三) (Malayans (Malaysians) visiting the ROC, Volume 3) (Accession number 020-100900-0098), Academia Historica (國史館), Taipei, Taiwan.

Ministry of Foreign Affairs (1965b). *Correspondence*. Malaiya (Malaixiya) Renshi Fanghua (si) 馬來亞(馬來西亞)人士訪華(四) (Malayans (Malaysians) Visiting the ROC, Volume 4) (Accession number 020-100900-0099), Academia Historica (國史館), Taipei, Taiwan.

Ministry of Foreign Affairs (1965c). *Correspondence*. Yuenan Ruan Gaoqi Zongli Fanghua 越南阮高奇總理訪華 (Visit to China by *Vietnamese* Prime Minister Nguyen Cao Ky) (Accession number A303000000B/0054-12.22/9), National Archives Administration (檔案管理局), Taoyuan County, Taiwan.

Ministry of Foreign Affairs (1965–1970). *Correspondence*. Zhongxin Guanxi 中新關係 (Sino-Singaporean relations) (Accession number 11-01-07-07-01-001), Archives of the Institute of Modern History Academia Sinica (中央研究院近代歷史研究所檔案館), Taipei, Taiwan.

National Archives Administration, Accession number 0046/12-1, *Zhongyue Guanxi* 中越關係 (Sino-Vietnamese relations), letter from Ministry of Foreign Affairs to President Chiang and Premier Chen Cheng, January 13, 1960, Appendix Included Typed Text of "Viet-nam Glad to Have Aid of Chiang Forces", *Chicago Tribune*, December 30, 1959.

Pang, Y. H. (2019). *Strait Rituals: China, Taiwan, and the United States in the Taiwan Strait Crises, 1954–1958*. Hong Kong: Hong Kong University Press.

Press Library Files (1973–1974). *Newspaper Clippings.* Prime Ministers — Lee Kuan Yeu *(sic)*, Singapore Prime Minister (accession number HKRS70-7-718-1), Hong Kong Government Records Service, Hong Kong Special Administrative Region, People's Republic of China.

Purcell, V. (1965). *The Chinese in Southeast Asia.* London, Oxford University Press.

Qian, H. Y. 錢浩異 (1967, October 14). Yinni Xishou Wo Fangong Jingyan 印尼吸收我反共經驗 (Indonesia Learns from Our Anti-Communist Experiences), *Xinwen Tiandi* 新聞天地, 1026. General Archives (accession number 一般 586/442), Kuomintang Party Archives, Taipei, Taiwan.

Qiaowu Weiyuanhui Qiaowu Yanjiushi 僑務委員會僑務研究室 (1969). *Zhonghua Wenhua Fuxing Yundong Zai Haiwai* 中華文化復興運動在海外 (The Chinese Cultural Renaissance Movement overseas). Taipei, Qiaowu Weiyuanhui Qiaowu Yanjiushi.

Roy, D. (2003). *Taiwan: A Political History.* Ithaca and London, Cornell University Press.

The Daily Telegraph (1950). An Island to Keep from the Reds: Formosa — Chiang's Last Refuge, January 2, https://trove.nla.gov.au/newspaper/article/248995021?searchTerm=an%20island%20to%20keep%20from%20the%20reds.

The Straits Times (1963). Diplomatic Ties with Taipeh Inevitable, Says Dato Noah, September 3, https://eresources.nlb.gov.sg/newspapers/Digitised/Article/straitstimes19630903-1.2.49?ST=1&AT=search&k=%22diplomatic%20ties%20with%20taipeh%20inevitable%22&QT=%22diplomatictieswithtaipehinevitable%22&oref=article.

The Straits Times (1967). Chiang Must First Change Govt Name, August 31. Retrieved from microfilm NL12196, Lee Kong Chian Reference Library, National Library Board, Singapore.

UN General Assembly (1971). 1976th Plenary Meeting of the 26th Session of the United Nations General Assembly. A/PV-1976, United Nations Digital Library, New York, United States, https://digitallibrary.un.org/record/735611?ln=en.

Walker, R. L. (1959). Taiwan's Development as Free China. *Annals of the American Academy of Political and Social Science*, 321: 122–135.

Wang, Y. S. (1990). Foundation of the Republic of China's Foreign Policy. In Y. S. Wang (ed.), *Foreign Policy of the Republic of China on Taiwan: An Unorthodox Approach* (pp. 1–12). New York, Praeger.

Zhonghua Minguo Shishi Jiyao Bianji Weiyuanhui 中華民國史事紀要編輯委員會 (1992). *Zhonghua Minguo Shishi Jiyao (Zhonghua Minguo 46 nian 7 zhi 9 yuefen)* 中華民國史事紀要（中華民國46年7至9月份） (Records of Historical Events in the Republic of China). Xindian, Zhonghua Minguo shiliao yanjiu zhongxin.

Zhu, K. 朱凱風 (1958). Zhongyue Wenhua Tongchu Yiyuan 中越文化同出一源 (Chinese and Vietnamese Culture Come from a Common Source). *Zhongguo yizhou* 中國一周 *China Weekly*, 422: 4.

Appendix: Independence of Southeast Asian Countries from 1945 to 1978

Country	Independence from	Proclamation of independence	Remarks
Cambodia	France	November 9, 1953	
Indonesia	The Netherlands	August 17, 1945	The Dutch recognized Indonesian independence in 1949.
Laos	France	October 22, 1953	
Malaysia	United Kingdom	August 31, 1957	Malaya proclaimed independence in 1957 and joined Sabah, Sarawak and Singapore to form Malaysia in 1963.
Philippines	United States	July 4, 1946	
Myanmar (Burma)	United Kingdom	January 4, 1948	
Singapore	Malaysia	August 9, 1965	Singapore achieved full internal self-government in 1959, joined Malaysia in 1963, and seceded from it in 1965.
Thailand	—	—	Thailand was never colonized.
Vietnam, North	France	September 2, 1945	

(*Continued*)

(*Continued*)

Country	Independence from	Proclamation of independence	Remarks
Vietnam, South	France	October 26, 1955	Geneva Conference of 1954 divided Vietnam into two states. The Republic of Vietnam was proclaimed in 1955. It collapsed in 1975 and merged with North Vietnam in 1976.

https://doi.org/10.1142/9789811250668_0002

Chapter 2

Unpacking Taiwan's Presence in Southeast Asia: The International Socialization of the New Southbound Policy

Alan Hao Yang

Distinguished Professor, Graduate Institute of East Asian Studies and Deputy Director of Institute of International Relations, National Chengchi University, Taiwan

Introduction

Regionalism and regionalization are the two main axes of theoretical perspectives on contemporary regional integration as well as regional community building in Asia-Pacific and beyond (Beeson, 2014; Söderbaum, 2016; Dent, 2016). The former focuses on the outcomes of intergovernmental collaboration, whereas the latter explores how social driving forces hidden behind the state-centrism foster transnational linkages (Beeson, 2014: 5). Regionalism carries a tinge of state-centrist approach. Its goals are to safeguard peace and stability in the region, reduce confrontation and prevent the sudden outbreak of unforeseen hostilities (Mansfield and Milner, 1997: 3; Severino, 2009: 5–6, 16–18; Calder and Ye, 2010: 225–250). A recent focus of regionalism is aimed at fostering exchanges and integration among regional economies for the purpose of creating common interests for regional stakeholders through institutional frameworks or informal networks (Combes *et al.*, 2008; Fithra, 2016; Eko, 2017). Regionalization, on the other hand, takes society as its focus and employs civic forces to create intricate linkages among societies and build transnational communities, to some extent, in pursue of "soft regionalism" (Hurrell, 1995: 39–40).[1] The process of regionalization usually adopts a bottom-up approach to foster regional networks and further advance the regional community (Hatch, 2010; Klecha-Tylec, 2017).

The IR literatures habitually look at regional integration through the lens of regionalist approach with a focus on the policy and behavior of the state (Hobson, 2000; Blackwill and Harris, 2016). Nevertheless, the making of transnational communities in various regions today tells us that a more accurate understanding of such integration efforts is in great demand. It is imperative to "bring society back in" by highlighting the role and capacity of transnational actors and the micro-process of networks in the making of regional society.

Taiwan is a vivid case of re-examining regionalization in Asia. It is located where Northeast Asia and Southeast Asia meet and has always been searching for its identity as well as "holding a more advantageous position" within Asia (Office of the President, 2017a). On the one hand, it was a matter of wishing to break free from the constraints of cross-strait relations with China, while on the other hand, Taiwan hoped to become part of Asian integration. Since the 1990s, Taiwan's government actively explored relations with Southeast Asian countries, including a much earlier plan for Taiwan business (*Taishang*) to expand into the regional production bases and, shortly later, the bilateral investment project and special economic zone development plan led by the then Kuomintang (KMT) government and followed by both leaders of KMT and Democratic Progressive Party (DPP) (Chen, 2002; Cooper, 2015: 140–141). Twenty years later, the legacy of previous endeavors became the foundation the DPP government to activate its New Southbound Policy (NSP) since the early 2016 (Yang and Hsiao, 2015: 226–227; Glaser *et al.*, 2018: 6–9). The core orientation of the NSP is the repositioning of Taiwan's development and growth strategy, from being state-managed to becoming social interchange-based, from being pure profit-based to becoming people-centered (Yang, 2016; 2017a).

---

[1]A narrow definition of regionalization is the process driven by market forces see Hatch (2010: 6–7).

The development of the NSP has at least two connotations. On the domestic front, Taiwanese society had become increasingly knowledgeable about and familiar with its neighbors in Southeast Asia over the years so that with the promotion of the NSP things just fell into place. On the international level, the planned content of the NSP highlights that this country's "regional strategy for Asia" is reinventing itself by incorporating more local and regional development needs as the main issue the NSP ought to address (Office of the President, 2017b). Although there is room for policy improvement, the NSP has for sure unveiled Taiwan's path of international socialization as it participates in the ASEAN-led community building process.

Yet, who is socializing whom in Taiwan's relationship with its neighbors after all? Is international socialization the result of one-directional social impact? Or is it owed to bi-directional social exchange? How can such an everlasting socializing process stimulate or strengthen social linkages? This is where the problematique lies with the strategic interaction between Taiwan and Southeast Asia and what this chapter aims to explore and delineate. In this regard, this chapter consists of four parts: the first part recaps the theoretical basis and main focus of international socialization and social linkages. The second part discusses the positioning of Taiwan's Go South Policies in the past and describes, starting with the shift from the mentality of "*Taiwanese Asia*" (*taiwan de yazhou*, 臺灣的亞洲) to an "Asian Taiwan" (*yazhou de taiwan*, 亞洲的臺灣), in detail how Taiwan's long-term southwards engagement initiatives blends into the international socialization processes in the region. Part three highlights the relations the key actors and stakeholders involved in the NSP, such as transnational actors, are planning with the community and new social linkages that are currently being promoted. These include the roles and capacities of Taiwanese presence in Southeast Asia and Southeast Asian immigrants in Taiwan. Lastly, this chapter concludes by wrapping up Taiwan's international socialization in Asia.

International Socialization: Learning to be Regionalized

IR literatures studying on international socialization focuses on the causal effect between the international and domestic levels. Most studies explore how international norms and institutions affect the development and change of domestic law, policy and social practices. This interstate conceptualization of socialization is prevalent in works among leading IR scholars (Schimmelfennig, 2000; Alderson, 2001; Checkel, 2003; Flockhart, 2006).

There are two contending arguments of interstate conceptualization. The first of which emphasizes the institutional process of socialization. For example, Checkel (2003) delineates how Council of Europe shapes the changes of agent preferences of European countries whereas Greenhill (2010: 131–133) investigates the way how international governmental organization (IGO) mediated socialization facilitates its member states to comply with human rights norms. A recent discussion on state and individual socialization of adaptation of intellectual property norms by Morin and Gold (2016) using the triangulated data to examine the contradiction and intractability of the two-level socialization. In terms of institutional perspectives, socialization refers to the effectiveness of governance or setting up the "habits of cooperation" in making member countries comply with relevant norms (Johnston, 2003: 108).

A second perspective, with specific focus on individual state actor, highlights either the enabling capacity of great powers to influence the process of international socialization by manipulating material incentives and altering the substantive beliefs (Ikenberry and Kupchan, 1990: 285) or the negotiating capability of rising powers being socialized into the international order while reshaping it when they enter (Terhalle, 2011). For example, Makarychev (2017) looks at Russia's growing engagement with the Asia-Pacific as its strategic efforts of international socialization. Sueo Sudo contends Japan's ASEAN policy is to pursue multilateralism by promoting its changing patterns of foreign policy streams, a shift from dependence on the United States to an autonomous policy stance, and practicing its multilateral diplomacy in the region (Sudo, 2015: 239). Furthermore, Abe government of Japan advances the sharing of norms and principles of "rule of law" in the region as the effort to socialize its regional counterparts in Southeast Asia and beyond (The National Institute for Defense Studies, 2017: 252). Shambough (2013: 131) argues that China "seems stuck somewhere" between the two phases of international socialization, that is, the feigned compliance through a conscious and instrumental calculation and the internalization with deeply transformed identity. Since late 2013, the Belt and Road Initiatives (BRI), regarded as a new Long March, casts soft propaganda (*The Chinese dream*) and hard performance (*Economic strength seamlessly backed up by investment, production and political support*) for the purpose of socializing the neighboring countries to corroborate with the global rise of China (Yang, 2017b).

Comparing with the macro (*structural* and *power politics-oriented*) and meso (*institutional*) account for international socialization in contemporary IR literatures, this chapter explores the micro-process of socialization by highlighting the importance of *learning*. It holds that in the regional context socialization manifests itself in some sort of learning process. At the regional level, this chapter non-exhaustively identifies three types of learning as *interest-based, institution-based* and *interaction-based*. First, interest-based learning emphasizes an exchange of tangible or non-tangible interests. When a great power with abundant power resources tries to socialize a small country, material incentives will be provided with the small country to demand its compliance with norms set by great power, and further internalize its policy references with great power's interests.[2] The socialization of small country through interest-based learning easily degrades into one-directional manipulation of power politics in which the bullying government plays the key role.

Second, institution-based learning refers to the familiarization and socialization of member states with relevant norms, rules and procedures in the process of being a member of some international institutions. In doing so, member states take a unanimous stance within the institutional framework to encourage and implement collective actions. Such institution-based learning emphasizes that international organizations and institutions foster corresponding behaviors and common beliefs through the diffusion of values, identities, norms and best practices, bearing in mind the game rules agreed by all. In Southeast Asia, to follow the ASEAN Way defined by its members is the process of institution-based learning of soft regionalism and flexible consensus in pursuing regional integration (Acharya, 1997).

In contrast to the above-mentioned framework of the state-centric socialization, interaction-based learning is clearly more dynamic. At the regional level, it describes how the actors utilize learning to internalize the interacted knowledge, norms and interests for the purpose of making them

[2]The case of "One China Policy" firmly advocated by the People's Republic of China (PRC) is a vivid example of how Beijing socializes its Southeast Asian counterparts with a formatted norm in dealing with bilateral and multilateral relationship with Taiwan.

a part of regional development scheme. It is a learning process of being regionalized. Hence, interaction is conducive to emulation and learning and makes the actor as a node in the institutional network as well as a member of the community. Similar to the idea of "reciprocal socialization" (Terhalle, 2011), as the institution solidifies the learning process, the collective action resulting from learning among members of "we group" is also likely to reshape the institution and the learning criteria.

Apart from the state-centric conceptualization, the interaction-based learning process involves various stakeholders aside from government and therefore foster diverse social linkages. In particular, this chapter focuses on two kinds: *The epistemic communities* and *the transnational actors*. With regard to epistemic communities, termed as "a network of professionals with recognized expertise and competence in a particular domain and an authoritative claim to policy-relevant knowledge within that domain or issue-are" (Haas, 1992: 3), socialization occurs during the policy learning process as the norms and rules of the external environment are internalized as part of policymaking. Thanks to the learning process during socialization, epistemic communities are able to design more well-rounded policies that match the current dynamics so as to establish frameworks and projects to promote social linkages.

The socialization of transnational actors entails learning how to interact with other stakeholders for the purpose of becoming part of the transnational civil society and realizing the ideal of regional community. Having learned through socialization process, transnational actors will take advantage of their in-depth understanding of different political, social, economic and cultural systems to shape new shared interests and identities. Meanwhile, they will utilize the interaction to cultivate diverse social linkages.

This chapter argues the *epistemic communities* play a crucial role in imagining policy agenda and frameworks, considered as initiators of international socialization and social networks at a regional level, whereas the *transnational actors* are therefore agents/executors of regional socialization and at the same time practitioners of social networks at a regional level.

The following sections will employ Taiwan's policies toward Southeast Asia as a case study to portray its practice of international socialization. It will first explore the learning pathway of epistemic communities in "becoming part of Asia" (Miller and Wich, 2011) and then look into the updated socialization dynamics and micro-process driven by various transnational actors.

Taiwan's Going South Efforts

Amid a volatile international environment Taiwan continued to promote its going south efforts. The earliest goal of Taiwan's "Go South Policy" (*nanxiangzhengce*, 南向政策) was to break out of the political framing of cross-strait rivalry and to reduce its economic reliance on China (Glaser *et al*., 2018: 6). Taiwan government launched the Go South Policy to steer Taiwan's trade and investment toward Southeast Asia. However, since the policy initiatives in its early stage still lacked solid understanding of the neighboring countries and regional societies, Taiwan, as an outlying island in Asia, developed a sense of alienation from its periphery and came to regard Southeast Asia merely as a production base and investment target for *Taishang*. Even though every Taiwanese Presidents after Lee Teng-hui faced severe political pressure to seek the island country's international space, they all considered Southeast Asia as a promising region to explore strategic possibilities and functional ties with neighboring countries. Nevertheless, political leaders of Taiwan still harbored an instrumentalist attitude, imagining Asia or even influencing Asia from a Taiwanese perspective that caused estrangement between Taiwan and the regional community.

To get rid of this interest-based dilemma, Taiwan government and society reinvented themselves in recent years trying to respond to the *people-centered* development agenda promoted and practiced by the Association of Southeast Asian Nations (ASEAN) and its member states. This constitutes a community-deepening project that transitions from the mentality of "*Cross-strait Taiwan*" (*liangan de taiwan*, 兩岸的臺灣) via a muddling through process of "*Taiwanese Asia*" and develops toward an "*Asian Taiwan*". The transformation of these three structures represents a paradigm shift among Taiwan's epistemic communities regarding the Go South concept that deserves closer investigation.

A cross-strait Taiwan

The cross-strait factor constitutes Taiwan's curse in foreign relations. From the hot competition during the Cold War period to the cold peace after the Cold War, Taiwan has never been able to break through the structural constraint of cross-strait relations (*Reuters*, 2013; Rowe, 2017). On the political front, the KMT government on the one hand maintained the Greater China party-state ideology after it relocated to the island. As a result, Taiwan's epistemic communities during KMT administrations gave priority consideration to the cross-strait or China factor when floating any ideas regarding political development and external relations, which in return constricted Taiwan's regional participation in terms of capacity and strategy (for example, the 1992 Consensus, see Huang and Li, 2010: 153–162). On the other hand, Beijing has never renounced its threat to use military force to unify with Taiwan, and the continued undermining of Taiwan's international capacity through verbal intimidation and international pressure remains Taiwan's most severe challenge (de Lisle, 2016; Easton, 2017).

On the economic front, China's magnetic effect on Taiwan is the key. In the wake of its opening and reform policy in the late 1970s, China became the world's factory, attracting attention among Taiwanese enterprises also thanks to a culturally and linguistically close environment. In 1988, China announced the *Provisions of the State Council Concerning the Encouragement of Investments by Compatriots from Taiwan* (*guanyu guli taiwan tongbao touzi de guiding*, 關於鼓勵台灣同胞投資的規定) to entice Taiwanese entrepreneurs into expanding across China (Investment Promotion Agency of MOFCOM, 1988). After Taiwan announced the *Regulations on Managing Indirect Investment or Technological Cooperation in the Mainland Area* (*dui daludiqu jianjietouzi huo jishuhezuo guanlibanfa*, 對大陸地區間接投資或技術合作管理辦法) in 1990 (MOEAIC, 1990), *Taishang* quickly increased their presence in China, expanding from the Pearl River Delta (*zhujiang sanjiaozhou*, 珠江三角洲) to the Yangzi River Delta (*zhangjiang sanjiaozhou*, 長江三角洲), and continued moving further inland westward.

This challenge of having to face Chinese pressure and the difficult cross-strait situation in the political and economic spheres amounted to structural constraints that "repressed Taiwan with cross-strait relations". As China continues to grow more powerful, any Taiwanese leader must ponder ways to actively break the encirclement by China. Against this backdrop, nearby Southeast Asia, rather than Taiwan's diplomatic allies in far-flung Latin America and Africa, became the strategic choice of Taiwan government.

A Taiwanese Asia

In the 1990s, Taiwan started to democratize and bid farewell to its authoritarian of the past. Bearing political pressure from China, a democratized Taiwan must be more active and flexible in developing its foreign policy. Then President Lee Teng-hui began to conceive and promote the first wave of Go South Policy. In combination with his "go slow, be patient" (*jieji yongren*, 戒急用忍) approach toward China, the Go South Policy was interpreted as an option that allowed to counterbalance the westwards trend and slow China-bound investment from Taiwan. This government-proposed new policy orientation depended on the forces of the public sector, state-owned enterprises and KMT-affiliated business to break through the structural constraints of the "Cross-strait Taiwan" (Yang and Hsiao, 2015: 216–218). Meanwhile, the Policy also meant to establish intergovernmental linkages in flexible forms with Southeast Asian countries. Taiwan government, the public sector, state-owned enterprises and government-related institutions became the subjects that shaped the Policy with a strong "Taiwanese Asia" consciousness.[3]

Taiwan's epistemic communities also began to investigate the relations between Taiwan and the major countries in Southeast Asia, studying how Southeast Asia could be inserted into the strategic environment that Taiwan developed for its foreign relations. The founding of think tanks,[4] research centers[5] and research program[6] amplified the capacities and networks of the epistemic communities and fostered initial understanding of Southeast Asia in Taiwanese society.

The first wave of going south efforts established a modern bilateral framework and functional co-operation between Taiwan and Southeast Asian countries such as the visits between political leaders,[7] upgrading and renaming Taiwanese representative offices in the region, the signing of bilateral agreements, and setting up ministerial level dialogue mechanism in the 1990s (see Table 1). In 1994, Taiwan further adopted the

---

[3]The policy served as Taiwan's regional approach to act as the logistic hub in Asia.

[4]For example, the secretariat of Taiwanese participatory group for the Council for Security Cooperation in the Asia-Pacific (CSCAP) was set up at the Institute of International Relations (IIR) as the platform to practice track II diplomacy with leading think tanks in ASEAN and Asia-Pacific countries.

[5]The Centers for Southeast Asian Studies were set up in Tamkang University, National Chi Nan University, National Cheng Kung University and National Sun Yet-sen University to promote area studies of Southeast Asia.

[6]The leading research institution in Taiwan, Academia Sinica, initiated its Program for Southeast Asian Studies (PROSEA), in 1994 with specific focus on nourishing Southeast Asian studies and then upgraded into the Center for Asia-Pacific Area Studies (CAPAS) in 2003.

[7]Political leaders such as Fidel Ramos from the Philippines, Mohamad Mahathir from Malaysia, and Lee Kuan Yew and Goh Chok Tong had paid visits to Taiwan whereas Lee Teng-Hui visited Singapore, the Philippines, Indonesia and Thailand.

Table 1: Bilateral agreements between Taiwan and Southeast Asia countries (selective items on trade and investment issues in the 1990s)

Country	Date	Titles
Vietnam	1993/4/21	Agreement between the Taipei Economic and Cultural Office in Hanoi and the Vietnam Economic and Cultural Office in Taipei on the Promotion and Protection of Investments
	1993/7/29	Memorandum of Understanding on the Promotion of Investment (between the Industrial Development & Investment Center in Taipei and Investment Transaction Center in Hanoi)
	1998/4/6	Agreement between the Taipei Economic and Cultural Office in Hanoi and the Vietnam Economic and Cultural Office in Taipei for the Avoidance of Double Taxation and the Prevention of Fiscal Evasion with respect to Taxes on Income
Philippines	1992/1/27	Agreement between the Taipei Economic and Cultural Office and the Manila Economic and Cultural Office for the Promotion and Protection of Investments
	1994/7/2	Memorandum of Understanding between the Manila Economic and Cultural Office (Party A) and the Taipei Economic and Cultural Office (Party B) on the Promotion of Investments and Exports in the Textile and Apparel Industry
Singapore	1990/4/9	Agreement between the Industrial Development & Investment Center in Taipei and the Economic Development Board in Singapore on the Promotion & Protection of Investments
Malaysia	1993/2/18	Agreement between the Malaysian Friendship and Trade Centre, Taipei and the Taipei Economic and Cultural Office in Malaysia for the Promotion and Protection of Investments
	1996/7/23	Agreement between the Taipei Economic and Cultural Office in Malaysia and the Malaysian Friendship and Trade Center in Taipei for the Avoidance of Double Taxation and the Prevention of Fiscal Evasion with respect to Taxes on Income

(*Continued*)

Table 1: (*Continued*)

Country	Date	Titles
Thailand	1996/4/30	Agreement between the Taipei Economic and Trade Office in Thailand and the Thailand Trade and Economic Office in Taipei for the Promotion and Protection of Investments
	1999/7/9	The Taipei Economic and Trade Office in Thailand and the Thailand Trade and Economic Office in Taipei for the Avoidance of Double Taxation and the Prevention of Fiscal Evasion with respect to Taxes on Income
Indonesia	1990/2/9	Memorandum of Understanding between the Taipei Economic and Trade Office and the Indonesian Chamber of Commerce in Taipei Concerning Co-operation for the Promotion of Investment
	1990/12/19	Agreement between the Taipei Economic and Trade Office and the Indonesian Chamber of Commerce to Taipei for the Promotion and Protection of Investments
	1995/3/1	Agreement between the Taipei Economic and Trade Office and the indonesian Economic and Trade Office to Taipei for the Avoidance of Double Taxation and the Prevention of Fiscal Evasion with respect to Taxes on Income

Source: Treaty Database of the Ministry of Foreign Affairs (R.O.C.), retrieved on February 13, 2022 from <http://no06.mofa.gov.tw/mofatreatys/Index.aspx>.

Guideline on Enhancing Economic and Trade Relations with Southeast Asia (*jiaqiang dui dongnanya diqu jingmaohezuo gangling*, 加強對東南亞地區經貿合作綱領) formally setting up the tone of regional engagement.

Following policy direction endorsed by Taiwan government, then state-owned enterprises went to Southeast Asia as emerging transnational actors, triggering an investment rush and the mounting numbers of trade volume. In 1994, Taiwanese investment in Southeast Asia grew from US$1.17 billion in 1993 to US$4.98 billion in 1994, whereas its investment to China fell from US$3.17 to US$962 million (Glaser *et al.*, 2018: 6). The two-way trade soared 22.5%, increasing from US$16.4 billion in 1993 to US$20.2 billion in 1994 (see Table 2). Of course, investment by state-owned enterprises had also the effect of driving the expansion of small- and medium-sized enterprises into Southeast Asia. In the 1990s, for example, there were more than 2,000 Taiwanese electronics companies

Table 2: Taiwan's trade with Southeast Asia (Selective Years/ USD million)

	GSP					NSP	
Country/Year	**1993**	**1994**	**1995**	**1996**	**1997**	**2016**	**2017**
Southeast Asia	16,438.90	20,212.86	25,544.65	26,693.20	29,708.24	78,444.67	89,599.85
Brunei	76.20	77.15	72.35	99.23	91.19	134.08	235.21
Indonesia	2,908.52	3,547.31	4,019.20	3,839.73	4,318.46	7,046.76	8,092.18
Cambodia	9.56	11.89	33.96	68.15	93.42	728.49	727.36
Laos	8/04	16.53	23.27	12.57	16.58	21.06	22.31
Myanmar	26.73	44.28	63.45	67.92	85.77	281.86	295.46
Malaysia	3,610.63	4,550.89	5,852.18	6,518.83	7,236.60	14,095.94	17,551.13
Philippines	2,395.85	2,683.09	2,276.69	2,771.41	3,616.97	10,863.29	11,871.60
Singapore	4,756.11	5,771.34	7,362.76	7362.12	8.044.76	23,669.61	26,340.89
Thailand	2,991.85	3,548.87	4,556.87	4,461.18	4,488.89	9,308.85	10,740.46
Vietnam	655.41	961.51	1283.91	1492.05	1688.60	12,294.72	13,623.23

Source: Burea of Trade, R.O.C., (data base of trade statistic), retrieved from <http://cus93.trade.gov.tw/FSCE000F/FSCE000F>.

invested in Malaysia and facilitated the regional expansion of value chains in Southeast Asia (Hsu, 2017: 65).

To some extent, the encouraging outcomes of the Go South Policy at the time in promoting trade and investment shows that Taiwan government fulfilled the needs of the national economic transformation such as the relocation of "sunset industries" and the search for skilled labors, and, moreover, tried to counterbalance westwards movement of *Taishang*. Still, it drew criticism for apparently respecting Southeast Asia while Taiwan actually regarded the region as an appendage to advance the "Taiwan model" (Ngeow, 2017: 103). Some argued Taiwan was imitating the United States and Japan as it fanned out across the region with the "culture of a secondary imperial power" (Chen, 2010; Weber, 2016: 188) and treated Southeast Asia as the southward extension of its economy, culture and politics.

Economic networks and expansion activities conceived on the basis of such a "Taiwanese Asia" implied a strong belief that Taiwan's development experience could serve as catalyst or guide for Asia developing countries. This happened both during the presidencies of Chen Shui-bian as well as Ma Ying-jeou. Confronted with a stronger China, they both saw this as a remedy to overcome Taiwan's predicament in foreign relations. Both presidents also continued the existing guideline on economic and trade relations and even expanded the scope of countries and work items covered by it.[8]

Amid these moves, the epistemic communities, taking an interest in the development of the economy and free trade, played an important leading role.[9] The only difference was that President Chen, paying much attention to the political indigenization of Taiwan, did not prioritize "cross-strait Taiwan" turning instead to making good use of the networks that the DPP had cultivated as opposition and democratic political party in the past.

[8]During Ma administration, universities and colleges were encouraged to recruit more students from Southeast Asia to study in Taiwan for the purpose of making higher education system sustainable (Office of the President, 2013).

[9]Leading economic think tanks in Taiwan such as Taiwan Institute of Economic Research (TIER), Chung-Hua Institution for Economic Research (CIER), Taiwan Research Institute (TRI) were providing recommendations to link up Taiwan's domestic economic development with its external trade and investment policy, while the strategic think tanks such as IIR also paid attention to strategize Taiwan's networks with ASEAN-led regionalism.

Hence, in 2004, Chen assumed the chairmanship of Council of Asian Liberals and Democrats to further advance party-to-party links with Southeast Asian and regional countries (Liberal International, 2004). He combined Taiwan's presence with the promotion of an Asian democratic alliance that increased the political capacity of and international democratic supports for the economic Go South policy.

President Ma, for his part, called back the ideology of "cross-strait Taiwan" quickly after taking office, promoting diplomatic truce with Beijing, energizing cross-strait commerce and trade co-operation and institutionalizing them through the Economic Cooperation Framework Agreement (ECFA). As cross-strait policy regained its superior status in Taiwan's external relations, the expansion of Economic Co-operation Agreements (ECA) including the continuous going south efforts was reduced to being merely a means to an end. Some optimist argues that if the cross-strait relation can be well maintained, Taiwan would expect more chances to engage in multilateral activities in Southeast Asia, even to be an observer of ASEAN (Ku, 2009: 94).

Under the prerequisite that the President Chen did not harbor the ideal of realizing Taiwanese independence and the President Ma did not pursue the ideal of completing cross-strait unification, Taiwanese political elites and epistemic communities were still used to the mindset of "Taiwanese Asia" in ideological and decision-making thinking when imagining and realizing Taiwan's relationship "with" Southeast Asia. Nonetheless, "Taiwanese Asia" was never able to fend off "Cross-strait Taiwan." During Chen's time in office Taiwan's dependence on trade and investment with China continued to increase. When Ma took over, the emergence of ECFA closely tied Taiwan's overall development together with institutionalized cross-strait interaction.

An Asian Taiwan

When the DPP returned to power in 2016, marking a further democratic consolidation of Taiwan, then President-elect Tsai Ing-wen declared before her inauguration that she would promote a new southwards initiative called "New Southbound Policy". The NSP became the DPP administration's flagship policy leading domestic socio-economic transformation with regional integration. The new policy constituted a reorientation of Taiwan's linkages with Asia in two ways. One is the repositioning of Taiwan and Southeast Asia in that Southeast Asia is no longer a sub-regional southward extension of Northeast Asia/with Taiwan, but that makes Taiwan an important link in Southeast Asia's northward extension. Under this premise, Taiwan is socialized to relocate itself as a partner for the ASEAN-led community and network building process (Yang, 2017a: 5–8).

The second is a significant change of policy direction proposed by Tsai administration. Epistemic communities are paying close attention to regional dynamics of ASEAN. The strategic importance of Southeast and South Asia is highlighted in the making of Taiwan's foreign policy articulated by National Security Council and Ministry of Foreign Affairs. The NSP with its people-centered focus becomes the first official response of Taiwan to the regional integration project that the ASEAN Community developed since the 1990s. It is shaping Taiwan's "strategy for Asia" and making Taiwan as an indispensable link with the region (Hsiao and Yang, 2018). Until 2018, as Joseph Wu was appointed as Foreign Minister, from his previous post of Secretary-General of the Office of the President, the NSP remained the highest priority of Taiwan's foreign policy (Teng, 2018).

Thanks to these two reorientations, Taiwan geographically no longer belongs *only to* the cross-strait setting but *also to* the much larger Asian economic and developmental grouping. The agenda of NSP, being socialized through the concurrent regional dynamics of ASEAN integration, also changed from interest-based economic expansion to people-centered social linkages, developing robust partnerships by bringing together the stakeholders in society on both sides and nurture regional awareness (Yang, 2016). This change altered the "Taiwanese Asia" consciousness that was deeply ingrained in the mindset of Taiwanese epistemic communities, and due to the nurturing and opening of new social linkages a new "Asian Taiwan" identity is reshaping.

Admittedly, the reorientation process also involved many more stakeholders, including local governments Legislative Yuan (LY), business enterprises as well as vibrant civil society.[10] They learn to become the advocates, socializers and transnational actors that shaped the new discourse of an "Asian Taiwan". Concerning the public sectors, the *Guideline on Enhancing Economic and Trade Relations with Southeast Asia* which had still be used under Ma were replaced by the *Guidelines for the New*

[10]More involvement from different sectors and stakeholders in realizing the NSP would make "Taiwan to be recognized by the region." Interview with a leading think tanker on Southeast Asia affairs in the United States. Washington, D.C., March 23, 2018.

Southbound Policy (*xinnanxiangzhengce gangling*, 新南向政策綱領, August 2016), *Promotion Plan for the New Southbound Policy* (*xinnanxiangzhengce tuixing jihua*, 新南向推行計畫, September 2016), *Work Plan for the New Southbound Policy* (*xinnanxiangzhengce gongzuojihua*, 新南向政策工作計畫, December 2016), and *Five Flagship Programs* (*wudaqijianjihua*, 五大旗艦計畫, April and August, 2017)[11] with a broader focus on people-centered development agenda and social linkages. The institutional reinforcement of the NSP by the government looks at securing national survival of Taiwan by tying up with regional security in Southeast and South Asia.[12]

A corresponding restructure of governmental units in charge of the NSP is carried out in the beginning of 2018. Newly established special panel to strategic planning and coordination across governmental agencies is installed in National Security Council (NSC) in replace of the NSP Office, while a working group for NSP is organized in Executive Yuan to implement the policy execution (Ku and Kao, 2018).

In addition to central government, Taiwan's local governments such as Taipei, New Taipei, Kaohsiung, Taoyung, Taichung and Tainan as well as began to set up new committees and councils to take care the welfare of Southeast Asian residents in Taiwan while the LY has already set up amity associations and policy groups to strengthen ties with lawmakers from Southeast Asian countries (Yang, 2017a: 24). These endeavors reflect a careful socialization process among Taiwan's public sector in putting a stronger emphasis on what Taiwan could contribute to Southeast Asia, to its people and to the regional community. Government agencies are learning to highlight what resources should be shared between the two sides and how regional institutionalized collaboration and social linkages should be designed.

On the other hand, the private sector also hopes to deepen regional ties with Southeast Asia, building on the achievements of the past two decades and learning from the recent dynamics of and needs from ASEAN integration. *Taishang* are changing the mindset of duplicating Taiwan

---

[11]One of the programs on regional agriculture is to facilitate food security by jointly advancing sustainable development and sharing technical expertise with Southeast and South Asian counterparts.

[12]As Joseph Wu was appointed as the Secretary-General of NSC in May 2016, the rationale of "comprehensive security" was highlighted to strategize Taiwan's national security which had great impact on the formation of the NSP (Zhu, 2016).

model into Southeast Asian localities, and instead, they are socialized to take good care of the local needs and the regional trends.[13] As companies begin to attach importance to corporate social responsibility (CSR), they try to improve Taiwan's negative image as a polluter of local environment. Taiwanese-owned banks in Southeast Asia are also beginning to look beyond *Taishang* circles, providing services for local stakeholders.[14] More importantly, Taiwan's vibrant tech firms and startup enterprises, for example, Appworks, serve as a hub for liaising with the "Greater Southeast Asian" networks and incubating a new generation of startups (Chow, 2017).

Considering the supports from Taiwanese civil society, mass media coverage on Southeast Asia has been increasing since 2016, and public debates over the content and practice of the NSP are much more profuse than before, which underlines the correlation between the Policy and regional dynamics in Asia. Universities, non-governmental organizations and social enterprises have also become main socializers of the NSP in Taiwan society and transnational actors in the region. They allow Taiwan's voice and influence to come across into Southeast Asian societies and have become partners who resonate with ASEAN-led development and connectivity project in the region.

The promotion of the NSP places Taiwan within the context of ASEAN-led communities and networks. The "Taiwan" here refers not just the government or public sector, but the stakeholders and transnational actors who have maintained links with Asian societies early on. The "Taiwan" that the NSP highlights is an "Asian Taiwan." Only if Taiwan's national interests and the development concerns of individual Southeast Asian counterparts are closely connected can the regional collective awareness and identity take root in Taiwan. And only then can Taiwan's Asian neighbors find a more appropriate positioning for this island country.

To sum up, "Cross-strait Taiwan" is a structural constraint that still exists today. For a long time, Taiwan government has made efforts to overcome these restrictions. Although past Go South efforts were beholden to a "Taiwanese Asia" consciousness, it actually demonstrated Taiwan's struggle as it searched for strategic opportunities. Going south and coming into contact with Asia led to the transition from

[13] Interview with a Taiwanese businessman from Singapore in Taipei on February 12, 2018.
[14] Interview with Taiwanese bankers in Vientiane, Laos, on August 16, 2016.

"Cross-strait Taiwan" to an "Asian Taiwan." It took both the government and the society more than two decades to come to regard Taiwan as the northbound extension of Southeast Asia, to make the journey from being an outlying Asian island to becoming a partner in the making of regional community.

Socializing Taiwan in Southeast Asia

Since the 1990s, Taiwan has accumulated numerous momenta since the advancement of Going South efforts. Although it is challenging for Taiwan to bridge formal diplomatic ties with its neighbors due to political pressure from Beijing, it maintains stable informal intergovernmental collaboration and vibrant civil society links which by all means contribute to making Taiwan an indispensable link in regional networks in Asia.[15] This thanks to a process of socialization through interaction-based learning whose subjects are Taiwanese people living in Southeast Asia and immigrants to Taiwan from Southeast Asia. The former are learning to be localized and regionalized simultaneously whereas the latter come to understand, through their work and social life in Taiwan, this geographically so close yet also quite unfamiliar land and society. Of course, they are also understood by Taiwanese society as an important reference for understanding Southeast Asia.

The socialized Taishang in Southeast Asia

Contemporary interaction between Taiwan and Southeast Asia began with trade and commercial activities. This included government-supported special economic zone projects, trade and investment plans, as well as functional co-operation initiatives such as with Thailand's Royal Project Foundation in Thai mountainous north. These exchanges and projects brought Taiwanese people to Southeast Asia where they settled. In the past, the vast majority were entrepreneurs and investors, but now more diverse social exchanges are emerging. Overall, Taiwan's presence includes at least two types: commercial and social (see Table 3).

---

[15] Interview with former chairperson of Taiwanese business association in Kuala Lumpur, Malaysia, on June 4, 2015.

Table 3: Taiwanese people in Southeast Asia (Approximate Statistics)

Country	**Ethnic Chinese population**	**Ethnic Taiwanese population**	**Population of *Taishang***	***Taishang* companies**	**Number of *Taishang* association**
Brunei	40,000	23,598	30	30	1
Cambodia	140,000	3,000	4,000	300	1
Indonesia	8.48 million	201,000	10,000	2,000	9
Laos	150,000	100	100	100	1
Malaysia	6.44 million	43,000	40,000	1,800	8
Myanmar	1.23 million	400	400	200	2
Philippines	1.5 million	7,000	5,000	300	7
Singapore	2.9 million	30,000	400	200	1
Thailand	7 million	144,000	150,000	5,000	16
Vietnam	1.04 million	63,000	50,000	4,000	17

Source: Compiled by the author from the statistics provided by the Office of Trade Negotiation, 2018 (R.O.C.) and from Yang and Hsiao (2015, p. 221).

First, on the commercial side, *Taishang* account for the lion's share of residents from Taiwan in Southeast Asian countries. They arrived already in the 1980s to invest, some of them even earlier, for seeking more business opportunities at Southeast Asian localities or being involved in global production chains.[16] For decades, individual *Taishang* gradually banded together, founding friendship association-type business associations and organizations in different areas of their host countries. The highest distribution of *Taishang* is found in Thailand with some 5,000 companies registered with local chambers of commerce, followed by Vietnam, Indonesia and Malaysia. In terms of the actual number of people, Thailand and Vietnam boast the highest number of *Taishang* with the population of 150,000 and 50,000, respectively. In the earliest period,

[16]Taiwanese investment has been focusing on manufacturing industry and was facilitated by small and medium enterprises (SMEs) in Southeast Asia. Being keen to seek for overseas business interests, these private enterprises reached out to the world much earlier than Taiwan government. Interview with former chairperson, Taiwanese business association in Phnom Penh, Cambodia, on December 12, 2012; interview with former chairperson of Taiwanese business association in Kuala Lumpur, Malaysia, on June 4, 2015; interview with Taiwanese bankers in Vientiane, Laos, on August 16, 2016.

most of the Taiwan business companies chose to expand into Southeast Asia out of labor market considerations and also for the purpose of becoming a node of manufacturing chain and production network to the European and American markets. As the business communities have expanded their presence in Southeast Asia for decades, they transformed themselves from strangers to the local languages, cultural and legal systems in the beginning to be familiarized themselves with local regulations and social traits. The socialization process takes more than 10 years learning process through interacting with local governments and societies. Their successors, usually from intermarriages with locals, are more Southeast Asian in managing business and nourishing networks in the region.[17] Aside from assimilating into local society they are also able to exert their own unique political and commercial influence through local interpersonal networks.[18]

The *Taishang* experience in Vietnam and Thailand deserves further explanation. In Ho Chi Minh City of Vietnam, the development of the Phu My Hung Urban Area has attracted the greatest attention in recent years. In the very beginning, it was the CT&D Group affiliated with KMT invested in the Phu My Hung urban plan which was approved by the Vietnamese government in 1993, seen as a part of the first wave of Go South Policy. Later on, as KMT withdrew its investment, Taiwanese entrepreneur, Lawrence S. Ting, took over, using Taiwanese corporate investment to reclaim land from wetlands and develop the once desolate terrain into a modern, internationalized new urban area. Phu My Hung is not just a focal area developed by *Taishang* or the Vietnamese government in tandem with the country's overall economic development but has turned into a national-level flagship project as well. The area is an international investment hub that has attracted Korean corporations and a Japanese school among others.[19] The Ting-family-managed Phu My Hung Development Company has been awarded the first "Model New Urban

---

[17]Interview with a Taiwanese businessman based in Singapore in Taipei on February 12, 2018.

[18]Most of Taiwanese businessmen are reluctant to issues and activities with political sensitivity. Nonetheless, maintaining good relationships with local officials and political leadership is important to secure business interests in Vietnam. Interview with a Taiwanese businessman based in Hanoi, Vietnam on November 30, 2017.

[19]As Korean corporations and shops are popular in Phu My Hung area, some Vietnamese people even mistake this project as Korean investment. Interview with a Taiwanese businessman based in Singapore in Taipei on February 12, 2018.

Area" (Phu My Hung Development Company, 2018). Until 2015, the Lawrence S. Ting Memorial Fund has also been rewarded more than 65 commendations and awards from Vietnamese government in recognition of its contributions to Vietnam (Lawrence S. Ting Memorial Fund, 2018).

In Thailand, the Chairman of the Joint Foreign Chambers of Commerce (JFCCT), Stanley Kang, hails from Taiwan. As an umbrella organization, the JFCCT represents 63 foreign chambers and business organizations (JFCCT, 2018). Kang has much in common with other senior *Taishang* in that he is familiar with Thai social sentiment and the country's economic development trends. However, his socialization goes even deeper because he actively canvasses and submits suggestions from the foreign business communities regarding Thailand's national investment environment and economic policy, albeit strictly maintaining cautious neutrality on Thai internal political affairs. Thanks to his successful socialization, Kang quickly became a policy advisor to Thailand's economic sector and the development of ASEAN Economic Community (AEC) (*CNN*, 2014).

These two examples represent the success stories of *Taishang* or Taiwanese business leaders as transnational actors of international socialization in Southeast Asia. Their experience based upon interaction-based learning process provides important reference that helps Taiwan learn how to become/to be socialized as part of Southeast Asian economic and social integration project and enable Southeast Asia to corroborate Taiwan's unique experience. Ting's experience tells the story of how a large corporation's long-term investment and cultivation of business ties became a bright spot in Vietnamese urban rebuilding efforts for it had studied the growth dynamics of national socio-economic development. Kang, for his part, did not only study Thai social customs, but his interaction with Thai communities and socialization process also directly contributed to Thailand's national growth policy. Indeed, Taiwan's corporate governance model and development experience is being consulted for the development of Southeast Asian economies.

After the implementation of the NSP, trade and investment remain a link in Taiwan's overall regional presence. Nonetheless, Taiwan is further strengthening bidirectional exchanges, not only encouraging *Taishang* to invest in Southeast Asia, but also inviting *Taishang* and large corporations from Southeast Asia to invest in Taiwan. Backed by policy guidance and introduced by Taiwan's Representatives (ambassadors) in Southeast Asia, outstanding *Taishang* have repeatedly visited Taiwan to explore investment and over-the-counter (OTC) market listing opportunities (*CNA*, 2017). Through the interaction-based learning process activated by the NSP, Taiwan would be fully socialized to be a regional counterpart of Southeast Asia through a deeper and more diverse bidirectional social networks.

Nourishing new networks for regional partnership

Apart from *Taishang* networks, in recent years Taiwan has developed more diverse networks for seeking partnership in Southeast Asia. These include exchanges at the institutional, social and personal level that have brought about interaction-based learning endeavors in different fields. Since 2016, the NSP concentrates national budget on education programs, regional agriculture, innovative industries and young talent training projects, all echoing the people-centered agenda of ASEAN Community.[20]

Regarding the institutional networks, universities and research centers in Taiwan are learning to be regionalized with counterparts in Southeast Asia for the purpose of increasing common interests and professional exchanges and strengthening Taiwan's visibility and contributions in the region. Some new institutions are set up with *Taishang* associations in Southeast Asian localities, while others are seeking for institutional ties with leading academic institutions and think tanks in Southeast Asia (see Tables 4–6).

These institutions are mostly sponsored by the Ministry of Education (for example, Regional Resources Centers, Academic Alliance for the NSP and Taiwan Connection) and Ministry of Science and Technology (for example, STIC) becoming transnational actors to implement the NSP in Southeast Asian countries. Training programs and young talents cultivation projects on students and faculties either in Southeast Asia or in Taiwan are facilitated by these newly established networks.

For instance, new research centers on Southeast Asian (development) studies are established right after 2016 in Taiwan. Among them, the

[20]The United States and Japan both engaged with young leaders in Southeast Asia for years through the Young Southeast Asian Leader Initiatives (YSEALI) and the Ship for Southeast Asian and Japanese Youth Program (SSEAYP). It is important for Taiwan to participate in a region-wide network of young talents cultivation through joint efforts with YSEALI and SSEAYP. Interview with a leading think tanker on Southeast Asia affairs in Washington, D.C., the United States on March 22, 2018.

Table 4: Taiwan's regional resource centers in Southeast and South Asia under the NSP

Institutions	Coordinator
Regional Resource Centers in Malaysia/Singapore	National Cheng Kung University
Regional Resource Centers in Indonesia	Chung Yuan Christian University
Regional Resource Centers in Vietnam	National Taiwan Ocean University
Regional Resource Centers in Myanmar	National Chi Nan University
Regional Resource Centers in the Philippines	National Sun Yet-sun University
Regional Resource Centers in India	National Tsing Hua University

Source: Compiled by the author.

Table 5: Taiwan's overseas Science and Technology Innovation Centers (STIC) in Southeast and South Asia under the NSP

Institutions	Coordinator
STIC in the Philippines (water quality)	National Cheng Kung University
STIC in Thailand (medical)	Pingtung Christian Hospital
STIC in Laos (plan resources and conservation)	National Tsing Hua University
STIC in Vietnam (agriculture)	National Chung Hsing University
STIC in Indonesia (Austronesian cultures and societies)	National Taitung University
STIC in Malaysia (project management and information technology)	Tamkang University

Source: Compiled by the author.

Table 6: Taiwan's academic alliances for the NSP

Networks and Fields	Coordinator
Business and Social Sciences	National Chengchi University
Medical	National Cheng Kung University
Agriculture	National Chung Hsing University
Education and Humanities	National Taiwan Normal University
Engineering	National Tsing Hua University

Source: Compiled by the author.

Center for Southeast Asian Studies (CSEAS) at National Chengchi University, which was established in partnership with CSEAS at Kyoto University in Japan, is one of the leading institutions promoting Taiwan in the academic regionalization process. CSEAS also assumed the secretariat of the Consortium of Southeast Asian Studies in Asia (SEASIA) since 2018, which will facilitate the joint efforts between Taiwanese epistemic communities with 13 East and Southeast Asian member institutions to promote Southeast Asian studies and young professionals cultivation in the region.

For the new social network, new media in Taiwan specific focus on Southeast Asia dynamics and currents have become a channel for Taiwanese people to be familiarized with particular customs and the economic and social context in the neighboring countries.[21] Exchanges between museums and artists encourage those involved to learn from each other's societies and cultures in a fresh light. NGOs are even more active in providing capacity building programs to empower Southeast Asian migrant workers in Taiwan[22] and executing partnership program in international development in Southeast and South Asia. Taiwan Alliance in International Development (Taiwan Aid, 2015: 7–10) acts as the network and platform for twenty-five grass root NGOs in Taiwan to activate and pursue international projects with their global counterparts. In Southeast Asia, Taiwan Aid continuously carried out sixty-nine development projects including those in Cambodia (12), the Philippines (12), Thailand (12), Vietnam (12), Myanmar (10), Indonesia (5), Laos (4), Brunei (1) and Malaysia (1). These projects contribute to education, medical care, community development, environment, public health and nutrition, infrastructure construction and disaster management at different localities.

With regard to individual socializer or socializee, a growing number of Taiwanese young people take up permanent residence in Southeast Asia, be it out of personal interest, due to work, travel, or marriage. Some Taiwanese staff in local enterprises have also begun to learn Southeast

[21] In particular, new social media such as the News Lens, the ASEAN Plus Journal, and the Facebook platform of Southeast Asia Youth Researchers in Taiwan (SEAYRT) are utilizing internet to organize workshops, lectures and even public surveys on Taiwan–Southeast Asian relations. Interestingly, most of these activities are initiated by Taiwanese young talents and students in partnership with counterparts from Southeast Asia.

[22] One-Forty, for instance, is the leading grass root NGO promoting capacity building projects for migrant workers in Taiwan (Hsiao and Yang, 2018: 3).

Asian languages, gaining better cultural understanding, and have chosen to start a business and live in the region. They are both socializers of Taiwanese stories to the region as well as socializee to learn from neighboring societies. In recent years, Southeast Asia has become increasingly attractive for the Taiwanese.[23] For the people of Taiwan, the region is not only a strategic alternative that counterbalances the westwards trend but also an important framework for Taiwan's inclusion into the regional economic and social grouping.

Even though these projects were initiated and, some of which are sponsored, by the government, many more were spontaneously initiated and activated by civil society groups. They do not only enable Taiwan to learn the vision and roadmap of ASEAN-led community building project, but the deepening of local networks through socialization and interaction-based learning also allows Southeast Asian countries and societies to better understand Taiwan as a partner for regional growth.

Southeast Asian residents create a better Taiwan

In the recent past, the number of Southeast Asian residents settled in Taiwan has seen a steady increase. In 2018, about 600,000 Southeast Asian people live in Taiwan, most of whom are technical workers. The lion's share of Indonesian migrant workers are caregivers in private homes, whereas most Philippine and Thai migrants work in infrastructure construction and industry. Another 149,000 Southeast Asians are married to Taiwanese spouses and already 114,000 children from such families, so-called second-generation new immigrants, are attending local primary and secondary schools, quite sizable numbers (see Table 7). In total, more than 860,000 new immigrants and economic partners from Southeast Asia, whose number is likely to swell to more than one million in the near future, are currently putting down roots in Taiwan in an interaction-based learning process, and they are already excelling in many fields. Primary schools are going to include Southeast Asian languages among their elective subjects which shows that the new socialization process already begins in childhood.

[23] Thailand and Singapore are the most popular tourist destination for Taiwan. There are increasing numbers of guesthouses in Bangkok managed by Taiwanese people. Interview with a Taiwanese businessman based in Singapore in Taipei on February 12, 2018.

Table 7: Population of the second-generation new immigrants in Taiwan enrolled in secondary and primary schools (2016)

Country	Secondary school	Primary school	Total	Share (%)
All Countries	120,284	75,894	196,178	100
Vietnam	32,715	47,169	79,884	40.72
Indonesia	9,191	9,962	19,153	9.76
Cambodia	1,801	2,360	4,161	2.21
The Philippines	1,588	2,596	4,184	2.13
Thailand	1,324	2,158	3,482	1.77
Myanmar	621	1,146	1,767	0.90
Malaysia	466	970	1,436	0.73
Singapore	64	116	180	0.09

Source: Compiled by the author from Ministry of Education (R.O.C.) (2017, p. 4).

In the realm of public affairs, the role and capacity of new residents from Southeast Asia is growing more important as they enlighten Taiwanese society with a new understanding of ethnic diversity and equality. Meanwhile, Taiwan's LY also boasts its first legislator from Cambodian descent.[24] On top of that, the Chairwoman of the DPP's New Immigrant's Committee, Tran Thi Hoang Phuong, is a successful representative for the Vietnamese immigrant in Taiwan. She works as a lecturer teaching Vietnamese language in various universities and is a Golden Bell Awardee of the best education and cultural radio program in Taiwan. Moreover, increasing NGOs, such as TransAsia Sisters Association, Taiwan (TASAT), are concerned with the rights and empowerment of new immigrants in Taiwan and working closely with like-minded civil society organizations.

In the social realm, many stories about the unfair treatment of Southeast Asian migrant workers were going around in Taiwanese society in the past. But more recently such disputes have decreased as people from all walks of life attach great importance to migrant rights. Lately, Taiwanese labor groups have also conducted a simulated migrant workers referendum with a total of 388 Taiwanese citizens and 2,109 migrant

[24]Ms. Lin Li-Chan is a KMT Legislator sitting in the committee of internal administration of LY, see the Legislative Yuan (2018).

workers participating in the exercise. More than 90% of the participants supported the view that family caregivers should enjoy protection under Taiwanese labor laws, that migrant workers should be allowed to freely change employers, and that the private broker system should be abolished in favor of a compulsory government-to-government labor importation mechanism (Lai, 2018). This simulated referendum, a pioneering activity in Asia, drew massive attention in local society. It made its Southeast Asian neighbors understand that Taiwanese society attaches importance to migrant workers and their labor rights. On the other hand, people in Taiwan learned about and came to better understand migrant worker issues through the referendum and the social campaign around it.

Interestingly, the daily life of Southeast Asian communities in Taiwan is gradually creating new urban landmarks. On weekends, migrant workers from Indonesia and the Philippines gather at Taipei Main Station and St. Christopher's Church in Taipei's Da-an District for cultural and economic activities. For them, these places constitute a new living sphere and religious center. The stores in this commercial district do not only sell the Pilipino food or goods but also have a strong nostalgic appeal for homesick migrants.[25] Apart from this, many inhabitants of Huaxin Street in New Taipei's Yonghe District are second-generation immigrants from Myanmar. When strolling through this distinctly different neighborhood one feels like having traveled to different localities of Southeast Asia.[26] Such clusters of Southeast Asian communities right in the middle of a large metropolis have become important space for interaction-based learning by Taiwanese society. They are also successfully creating social dynamics for *a new Taiwan with Southeast Asian characteristics*.

Taiwan's NSP emphasizes a people-centered ideal. It does not only respond to the development needs of the ASEAN Community but is also an important measure in response to the diverse culture of Taiwan's immigrant society. The NSP's bidirectional transformation plan does not only place Taiwan back into the network of regional integration and regional community building process through linkages with diverse stakeholders

---

[25] Even the commercial banks are operating on the weekend providing financial services for the Philippine workers. Fieldwork conducted in St. Christopher's Church in Taipei, Taiwan on July 10, 2016 and in Taipei Main Station in Taipei, Taiwan on April 9, 2017.

[26] In recent years, the New Taipei City government has organized the New Taipei Water Festival to feature the New Year with fun-packed activities. Fieldwork conducted in Huaxin Street, New Taipei City, Taiwan, on April 15, 2018.

and partnerships but also helps Taiwanese society develop a sense of community awareness and regional identity of being situated in Asia.

Conclusion: Becoming Asia by Reinvigorating Taiwan

As Taiwan becomes more democratic, turning back to its authoritarian past, more international supports are needed to secure its state survival. Going south and becoming a part of Asia pragmatically facilitate the paradigmatic shift from the "Cross-strait Taiwan" to an "Asian Taiwan." The first wave of the Go South Policy established preliminary institutional basis for bilateral interaction between Taiwan and individual Southeast Asian countries, the promotion of the NSP would contribute to deepening the existing foundation while initiating new framing networks and learning process.

It is also true that the shift from an *interest-oriented* to a *people-centered* ideal, learning from ASEAN experiences, helps Taiwan cast off its marginal role as an outlying island in Asia. The self-transformed learning process of "becoming Asia" enables more transnational social linkages from scratch to highlight, through concrete achievements, that Taiwan is an indispensable link in ASEAN-led integration.

This process hinges on the bidirectional socialization of epistemic communities and transnational actors both in Taiwan and Southeast Asia. More stakeholders are included in the NSP than the previous Go South efforts which leads to a new partnership shaped by public and civilian sectors. Through policy reinforcement by epistemic communities and an even closer exchanges fostered by Taiwanese people in Southeast Asia and Southeast Asian immigrants in Taiwan, international socialization is not just a tool for exploring international space but the very root of reinvigorating the Asian awareness and identity in Taiwan.

In pursuit of further international socialization of the NSP, Taiwan needs to carefully tackle with the following challenges. First, it is imperative to contextualize the NSP with national and regional development agenda of ASEAN Community and its member states. Only by tying interests and common concerns of both sides through interaction-bases learning process can the NSP gain more domestic support either in Taiwan or to be recognized in the region.

Second, major powers such as the United States, Japan, India and Korea are respectively developing regional strategies to reinforce relationships with Southeast Asia countries. It is vital for Taiwan's NSP to actively seek partnerships with paralleled regional strategies to jointly realize the community awareness of regional integration.

Third, Beijing attempts to impede Taiwan's NSP with numerous enhanced incentives through the practice of Belt & Road Initiatives (BRI). The intervention of China factors requesting Southeast Asian countries to avoid government-to-government collaboration with Taiwan may undermine the practice of the NSP. Despite this, political intervention would not discourage the connectivity bridged by epistemic communities and transnational actors in Taiwan and Southeast Asia. The perpetuation of the NSP as the corner stone of Taiwan's regional strategy for Asia would allow this island country to deepen its tie with Asia and truly become the indispensable part of the regional community.

According to *The Diplomat*'s most recent issue, Taiwan's NSP to date has been a "relative success."[27] Inaugurated in 2016 as President Tsai Ing-wen's signature foreign policy to expand relations with South Asia, Southeast Asia, Australia and New Zealand, it has already scored results on several fronts: on the tourism front, visitors from the 18 targeted countries rose 6.8% to over 2.77 million last year, now accounting for 23% of total inbound tourists. The number of students from NSP countries studying in Taiwan also increased to 53,099 last year, while bilateral trade volume continues to stand strong at US$111.9 billion. It, however, is not yet a concluded story.

In 2020, While whether "deglobalization" is the case still waits to be seen, the pandemic's challenge for supply chains, business models, food security and even international stability is already evident. COVID-19 has stirred and exacerbated existent challenges for the region's outlook, which warrants the need for Taiwan to continue its comprehensive and constructive engagement with the region through the NSP. Good foundations have been set, but they need to be followed up and explore a new momentum of collaboration. The NSP's multifaceted engagement with the region in the areas of talent incubation, medical and public health, and agriculture have already been rewarded with some early results, and we anticipate the government's NSP to level up its efforts in the coming years, to lead Taiwan and the region toward a promising future.

---

[27] https://thediplomat.com/2020/04/tsai-ing-wen-2-0/.

References

Acharya, A. (1997). Ideas, Identity, and Institution-Building: From the "ASEAN Way" to the "Asia-Pacific Way". *Pacific Review*, 10(3): 319–346.

Alderson, K. (2001). Making Sense of State Socialization. *Review of International Studies*, 27: 415–433.

Beeson, M. (2014). *Regionalism and Globalization in East Asia: Politics, Security and Economic Development*. Houndmills, Palgrave Macmillan.

Blackwill, R. D. and Harris, J. M. (2016). *War by Other Means: Geoeconomics and Statecraft*. Cambridge, The Belknap Press of Harvard University Press.

Calder, K. and Min Ye (2010). *The Making of Northeast Asia*. California, Stanford University Press.

Checkel, J. T. (2003). "Going Native" in Europe? Theorizing Social Interaction in European Institutions. *Comparative Political Studies*, 36(1/2): 209–231.

Chen, J. (2002). *Foreign Policy of the New Taiwan: Pragmatic Diplomacy in Southeast Asia*. Cheltenham, Edward Elgar.

Chen, K.-H. (2010). *Asia as Method: Toward Deimperialization*. Durham and London, Duke University Press.

Chow, J. (2017). Taiwanese Tech Firms Eye Online Market in ASEAN. *The Straits Times*, March 6, 2017, http://www.straitstimes.com/asia/east-asia/taiwanese-tech-firms-eye-online-market-in-asean.

CNA (2017). Realizing the New Southbound Policy, Chen-Yuan Tung Leads Overseas Thai Business Group to Visit Taiwan. (落實新南向 童振源與泰僑商回台參訪), Central News Agency, October 15, 2017, http://www.cna.com.tw/news/afe/201710150186-1.aspx.

CNN (2014). JFCCT Chairman Stanley Kang on Thailand and the AEC. *CNNireport*, February 12, 2014, http://ireport.cnn.com/docs/DOC-1083084.

Combes, P.-P., Mayer, T. and Thisse, J.-F. (2008). *Economic Geography: The Integration of Regions and Nations*. Princeton, Princeton University Press.

Cooper, J. F. (2015). *Historical Dictionary of Taiwan (Republic of China)*. Maryland, Rowman and Littlefield.

de Lisle, J. (2016). Taiwan's Quest for International Space: Ma's Legacy Tsai's Options, China's Choices and U.S. Policy. *Orbis*, 60(4): 550–574.

Dent, C. M. (2016). *East Asian Regionalism*. New York, Routledge.

Easton, I. (2017). *The Chinese Invasion Threat: Taiwan's Defense and American Strategy in Asia*. Arlington, The Project 2049 Institute.

Eko Saputro (2017). *Indonesia and ASEAN Plus Three Financial Cooperation: Domestic Politics, Power Relations, and Regulatory Regionalism*. Singapore, Palgrave.

Fithra Faisal Hastiadi (2016). *Trade Strategy in East Asia: From Regionalization to Regionalism*. Hampshire, Palgrave Macmillan.

Flockhart, T. (2006). "Complex Socialization": A Framework for the Study of State Socialization. *European Journal of International Relations*, 12(1): 89–118.

Glaser, B. S., S. Kennedy, D. Mitchell and M. P. Funaiole (2018). *The New Southbound Policy: Deepening Taiwan's Regional Integration*. Washington, D.C., Center for Strategic and International Studies.

Greenhill, B. (2010). The Company You Keep: International Socialization and the Diffusion of Human Rights Norms. *International Studies Quarterly*, 54: 127–145.

Haas, P. M. (1992). Introduction: Epistemic Communities and International Policy Coordination. *International Organization*, 46(1): 1–35.

Hatch, W. F. (2010). *Asia's Flying Geese: How Regionalization Shapes Japan*. Ithaca, Cornell University Press.

Hobson, J. M. (2000). *The State and International Relations*. Cambridge, Cambridge University Press.

Hsiao, H. H. M. and Yang, A. H. (2018). Repositioning Taiwan in Southeast Asia: Strategies to Enhance People-to-People Connectivity. *NBR Brief*, 2018(1): 1–5.

Hsu, T.-T. K. (2017). A Review of Taiwan's Old and New Go South Policy: An Economic Perspective. *Prospect Journal*, 18: 63–87.

Huang, J. and Xiaoting Li (2010). *Inseparable Separation: The Making of China's Taiwan Policy*. Singapore, World Scientific.

Hurrell, A. (1995). Regionalism in Theoretical Perspective. In Louise Fawcett and Andrew Hurrell (eds.). *Regionalism in World Politics: Regional Organization and International Order*. Oxford, Oxford University Press.

Ikenberry, G. J. and C. A. Kupchan (1990). Socialization and Hegemonic Power. *International Organization*, 44(3): 283–315.

Investment Promotion Agency of MOFCOM. 1988. Provisions of the State Council Concerning the Encouragement of Investments by Compatriots from Taiwan. Invest in China, July 3, 1988, www.fdi.gov.cn/1800000121_39_3295_0_7.html.

JFCCT (2018). The Umbrella Organisation for the Foreign Business Community in Thailand. the Joint Foreign Chambers of Commerce in Thailand, http://www.jfcct.org/.

Johnston, A. I. (2003). Socialization in International Institutions: The ASEAN Way and International Relations Theory. In G. John Ikenberry and Michael Mastanduno (eds.). *International Relations Theory and the Asia-Pacific*. New York, Columbia University Press, pp. 107–162.

Klecha-Tylec, K. (2017). *The Theoretical and Practical Dimensions of Regionalism in East Asia*. Singapore, Palgrave.

Ku, C. and E. Kao (2018). Premier Approves Formation of New Southbound Policy Task Force. *Focus Taiwan*, January 28, 2018, http://focustaiwan.tw/news/aipl/201801280007.aspx.

Ku, S. C. Y. (2009). Taiwan and Southeast Asia since Ma Ying-jeou's Presidency. *East Asian Policy*, 1(4): 87–95.

Lai, J. (2018). Hundreds of Migrant Workers to March in Taipei on Sunday. *Taiwan News*, January 6, 2018. https://www.taiwannews.com.tw/en/news/3335419.

Lawrence, S. Ting Memorial Fund (2018). Commendations and Awards for Lawrence S. Ting Memorial Fund. Lawrence S. Ting Memorial Fund, http://www.lawrencestingfund.org/khenthuong.

Legislative Yuan (2018). "9th Legislator: Lin Li-Chan." *Legislative Yuan (R.O.C.)*, https://www.ly.gov.tw/EngPages/List.aspx?nodeid=12102.

Liberal International (2004). "Remarks by President Chen Shui-bian of Taiwan." *Liberal International*. March 4, 2004, https://liberal-international.org/what-we-do/events/executive-committee-meetings/kaohsiung-2004/remarks-by-president-chen-shui-bian-of-taiwan-kaohsiung-2004/.

Makarychev, A. (2017). Russia's Engagement with Asia Pacific: International Socialization, Multipolarity and Regionalism. *Rising Power Quarterly*, 2(1): 105–119.

Mansfield, E. D. and H. V. Milner, eds. (1997). *The Political Economy of Regionalism*. New York, Columbia University Press.

Miller, A. L. and R. Wich (2011). *Becoming Asia: Change and Continuity in Asian International Relations Since World War II*. California, Stanford University Press.

Ministry of Education (R.O.C.) (2017). *The Analysis of the Distribution of the Second Generation of New Residents Studying in Secondary and Primary Schools in Taiwan (the Academic Year of 2016)* (新住民子女就讀國中小人數分布概況統計). Taipei, the Ministry of Education.

MOEAIC (1990). Regulations on Managing Indirect Investment or Technological Cooperation in the Mainland Area. The Investment Commission, Ministry of Economic Affairs, https://www.moeaic.gov.tw/download-file.jsp?do=BP&id=aet2BUo1QFs=.

Morin, J.-F. and E. R. Gold (2016). International Socialization at the State and Individual Levels: Mixed Evidence from Intellectual Property. *Cambridge Review of International Affairs*, 29(4): 1375–1395.

Ngeow, C. B. (2017). Taiwan's Go South Policy: Déjà vu All Over Again? *Contemporary Southeast Asia*, 39(1): 96–126.

Office of the President (2013). President Ma Attends Forum with Higher Education Groups. Office of the President (R.O.C.), November 28, 2013, http://english.president.gov.tw/NEWS/4305.

Office of the President (2017a). President Tsai Delivers 2017 National Day Address. Office of the President (R.O.C.), October 10, 2017, http://english.president.gov.tw/NEWS/5231.

Office of the President (2017b). President Tsai's Remarks at Yushan Forum: Asian Dialogue for Innovation and Progress. Office of the President (R.O.C.), October 11, 2017, http://english.president.gov.tw/NEWS/5232.

Office of Trade Negotiation (R.O.C.) (2018). Statistics of Taiwanese People and Business Firms in Southeast Asia.

Phu My Hung Development Company (2018). Award and Achievement. Phu My Hung Development Company, http://www.saigonsouth.com/contents.aspx?lang=en&siteid=25&system_id=123.

Reuters (2013). Taiwan Says China Could Launch Successful Invasion by 2020. *Reuters*, October 9, 2013, https://www.reuters.com/article/us-taiwan-china/taiwan-says-china-could-launch-successful-invasion-by-2020-idUSBRE99809020131009.

Rowe, E. D. (2017). What is the Likelihood of Cross-Strait Conflict? *The Diplomat*, October 13, 2017, https://thediplomat.com/2017/10/what-is-the-likelihood-of-cross-strait-conflict/.

Schimmelfennig, F. (2000). International Socialization in the New Europe: Rational Action in an Institutional Environment. *European Journal of International Relations*, 6(1): 109–139.

Severino, R. C. (2009). *The ASEAN Regional Forum*. Singapore, Institute of Southeast Asian Studies.

Shambough, D. (2013). *China Goes Global: The Partial Power*. Oxford, Oxford University Press.

Söderbaum, F. (2016). *Rethinking Regionalism*. Houndmills, Palgrave Macmillan.

Sudo, S. (2015). *Japan's ASEAN Policy*. Singapore, Institute of Southeast Asian Studies.

Taiwan Aid (2015). *The Map of Taiwan NGOs' International Development Programs*. Taipei, Taiwan Aid.

Teng, P.-j. (2018). "Taiwan's Foreign Minister to Seek New Era for Country's Diplomacy," Taiwan News, March 10, 2018, https://www.taiwannews.com.tw/en/news/3381100.

Terhalle, M. (2011). Reciprocal Socialization: Rising Powers and the West. *International Studies Perspectives*, 12: 341–361.

The National Institute for Defense Studies (2017). *East Asian Strategic Review 2017*. Tokyo, The Japan Times, Ltd.

Weber, T. (2016). Coming to Terms with Asianism: Historical Reconciliation and Asianist History Politics in Contemporary China and Japan. In Marc Frey and Nicola Spakowski, (eds.), *Asianisms: Regionalist Interactions and Asian Integration*. Singapore, NUS Press, pp. 181–208.

Yang, A. H. (2016). Contextualizing Taiwan's New Southbound Policy in ASEAN Community: The Need to Prioritize Mutual Interest. *Prospect Journal*, 16: 25–48.

Yang, A. H. (2017a). Strategic Appraisal of Taiwan's New People-Centered Southbound Policy: The 4Rs Approach. *Prospect Journal*, 18: 1–34.

Yang, A. H. (2017b). Winning the Heart, not only Making Profits: Taiwan's Southbound Practices vs. China's Belt & Road Proximity. *China Policy Institute: Analysis*, September 15, 2017, https://cpianalysis.org/2017/09/15/winning%E2%80%8B-the-heart-not-only-making-profits-taiwans-southbound-practices-vs-chinas-belt-road-proximity/.

Yang, A. H. and Hsin-Huang Michael Hsiao (2015). Tai-shang (Taiwan Business) in Southeast Asia: Profile and Issues. In Young-Chan Kim (ed.), *Chinese Global Production Network in ASEAN*. Switzerland, Springer, pp. 213–229.

Zhu, P.-C. (2016). Joseph Wu Announced Chen Chun-lin, York Chen and Other Senior Advisors of NSC. *Taiwan People News*, May 13, 2016, http://www.peoplenews.tw/news/48ec82a2-6146-4709-9551-5501b5da2715.

https://doi.org/10.1142/9789811250668_0003

Chapter 3

China's Financial Statecraft in Southeast Asia: Aid Fungibility and the Authoritarian Donor's Dilemma

Chia-Chien Chang

Assistant Professor, Institute of China and Asia-Pacific Studies, National Sun Yat-sen University

Introduction: China's Global Ambition under the Decline of Liberal Order

Since the global financial crisis of 2007–2008 and European debt crisis, the "international liberal order", characterized as three components — diffusion of liberal democracy, economic interdependence and international multilateral institutions (Ikenberry, 2011: 61–66), has undergone a series of huge challenges. It started with the 2015 Greek referendum that signaled the resentment toward the European Union (EU) and rejected EU's controversial bail-out package with the "austerity" requirement. This ignited strong waves of euroskepticism and anti-globalization all over Europe, which culminated in the shocking 2016 "Brexit"— Britain's decision of exiting the EU. Such rejections of multilateral institutions, together with UN's inability to deal with the Syrian refugee crisis and continuing stalemate in the WTO Doha negotiation, indicate the loss of legitimacy of international liberal order as well as the incoming change of

Figure 1: The top 1% wealth share in the United States, 1913–2014

Source: World inequality database.

global governance. Perhaps the most significant transformation comes from the founder/leader of the current system — United States. Due to record high domestic economic inequality (see Figures 1 and 2; also check Alvaredo *et al*., 2013) and uneven unemployment across the country, US has gradually changed its policy focus to national issues at the expense of its global leadership. Correspondingly, US foreign policy orientation has also shifted from rule-based multilateralism to hierarchy-based (power asymmetry) bilateralism. For example, the US Congress kept blocking the IMF quota reform since the second term of Obama administration until December 2015 (*The Wall Street Journal*, 2015a). The Trump administration goes further to distance from engaging in international multilateral institutions, including withdrawing from the Trans Pacific Partnership (TPP) and the Paris Climate Agreement. The US has also forced Canada and Mexico to replace the North American Free Trade Agreement (NAFTA) with a new deal — the USMCA that includes the provisions of prohibiting exchange rate manipulation and countering unfair and non-market trade practices. The US President Trump also threatened to withdraw from the World Trade Organization (WTO) if it does not enact structural reforms (*The Washington Post*, 2017). The Trump administration also cut the funding to UN's climate change programs (*NPR*, 2017).

Figure 2: Shares of the top 1% income share in different countries

Source: World inequality database.

Trump also criticized the World Health Organization (WHO) as being under China's sway and failing to respond adequately to the COVID-19 pandemic. Trump then ordered the US federal government to suspend the funding to the WHO and start the withdrawal from the WHO (*The Wall Street Journal*, 2020).

The US strategic shift toward bilateralism might pose no surprise to International Relations scholars. For multilateralism — building international institutions and following international law — to work, it usually requires the "hegemon" (most dominant power in the international system) to bear disproportionate burdens because other countries tend to exploit the benefits without paying the costs (Lake, 2013; Thompson and Verdier, 2014).[1] In contrast, bilateral agreements tend to make it

[1] This is a classic "collective action problem" associated with public goods (Olson, 1965). When actors can enjoy public goods with paying the associated costs (either because the goods are non-rivalry or non-exclusive or both), actors tend to "free ride." This problem is especially common in international environmental governance, financial governance, and so on.

easier for dominant states to translate their power into favorable agreements than multilateral rules and institutions (Ikenberry, 2011: 115–116). In a sense, US policy shift signals its domestic discontent about multilateral institutions and an attempt to pursue national interest through power asymmetry.

As US and Western liberal democracies become more and more skeptical about multilateralism and globalization, emerging economies are facing a severe challenge. The US and Western liberal democracies used to be the main donor and capital providers for the developing world. However, the 2007/08 global financial meltdown and the Euro-debt crisis forced Western capitals to pull back. As Figure 3 shows, OECD countries' outbound direct investment toward the whole world has dropped substantially after 2008. Moreover, as Figure 4 indicates, OECD countries' aid toward Asia also declined sharply between 2008 and 2012. Their aid recovered slightly in 2013 but has stagnated ever since.

The global financial crisis as well as the change of global capital flows caused a deep concern to the developing world, and Southeast Asian countries were especially worried. Southeast Asian shared the traumatic

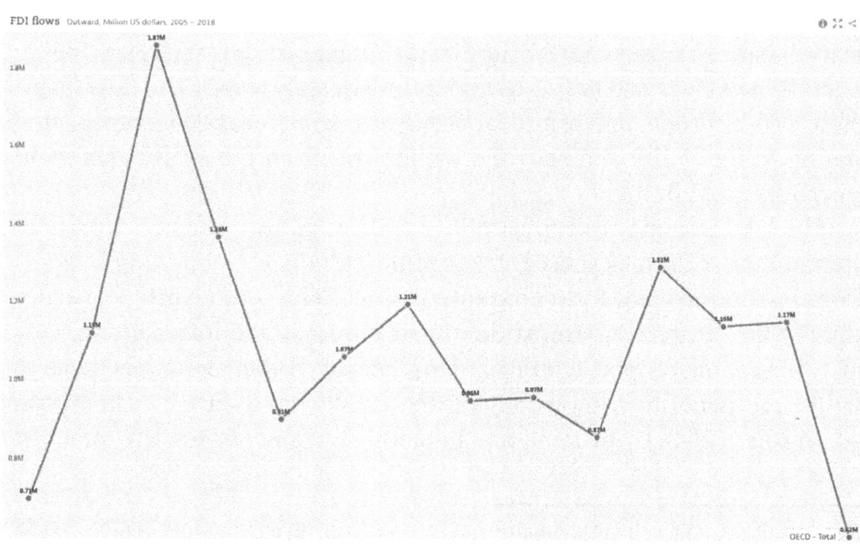

Figure 3: OECD countries' outbound direct investment, 2005–2018

Source: OECD database.

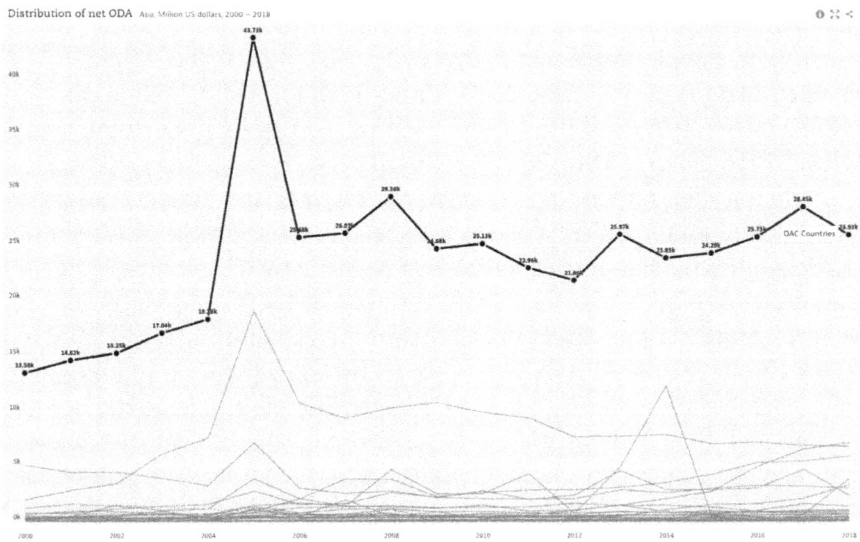

Figure 4: OECD countries' foreign aid toward Asia, 2000–2018

Source: OECD database.

memory of the 1997/1998 Asian Financial Crisis and learned that attracting stable global capital is crucially important for state survival. Therefore, since May 2000, member countries of the Association of Southeast Asian Nations (ASEAN) and Japan, China and South Korea has constructed a regional safety net, the Chiang Mai Initiative (CMI), which consists of multiple bilateral currency swap agreements. These bilateral currency swap agreements, signed bilaterally by the central bankers of the ASEAN-Plus-Three (APT) countries, allow the APT countries to seek emergency lending from other members during currency crises.

In addition, in 2009 the Asian Development Bank (ADB) and the Asian Development Bank Institute (ADBI) released a report, led by Masahiro Kawai (Japanese) and Rajat M. Nag (Indo-Canadian), indicating that there was an "$8 trillion funding gap" in Asia and proposed the initiative for an "Asian infrastructure fund" (ADB and ADBI, 2009). Later, the ADB changed its stance, instead advocating a "public–private partnership" supported jointly by the ADB and the World Bank (ADB, 2012).

In order to manage the problem of infrastructure funding shortage, the ASEAN has sought a regional solution to attract global capital. Specifically, the ASEAN sped up its process of integration and construction of interconnectivity within the ASEAN community, including physical, institutional and people-to-people connectivity. Since 2010 the ASEAN has launched two mega plans: the 2010 Master Plan on ASEAN Connectivity (MPAC 2010–2015) and the Master Plan on ASEAN Connectivity 2025 (MPAC 2016–2025) (ASEAN, 2011, 2016).

Noticing the retreat of Western capital and the urgent need for infrastructure funding, China seems to ascend to the guardian of economic interdependence, and its leader becomes the new "Davos man" (*The Economist*, 2017).[2] In October 2013, China's leader Xi Jinping proposed the establishment of an Asian Infrastructure Investment Bank (AIIB) during his trip to Southeast Asia. "In order to fill the $8 trillion funding gap in the Asian infrastructure market",[3] Chinese officials emphasized, "a new international financial institution is needed to 'supplement' the World Bank and the Asian Development Bank (ADB)." Since then, China has dedicated significant efforts to ensuring a successful launch of the institution. In October 2014, a *Memorandum of Understanding* on the establishment of AIIB was signed by 21 Asian countries. By April 2015, despite US objections, 57 countries from all over the world have joined as founding members of the China-led AIIB, including the UK and Western European countries, the United States' closest allies (*The Economist*, 2014a). The AIIB has launched its operations since 2016 and already approved 115 projects so far.

More important, during the same trip to Southeast Asia when the AIIB was introduced in 2013, Xi Jinping proposed the initiative of the "One Belt, One Road, OBOR (Belt and Road Initiative, *BRI*)" (*yí dài, yí lù*) as its 21st century grand strategy. The OBOR (BRI) initiative can be broadly understood as a grand investment strategy to strengthen the economic interdependence in Asia (and some parts of Eurasia) through two components: (1) the "Silk Road Economic Belt" aimed at connecting Central

---

[2] "Davos" is host to the World Economic Forum (WEF), an annual meeting of global political and business elites who promote the importance of globalization.

[3] Actually, China is not the pioneer in this issue. It was the ADB that originally pointed out the "$8 trillion funding gap" problem and proposed the initiative for an "Asian infrastructure fund" in 2009. Such policy suggestions came from one joint report of ADB and the Asian Development Bank institute, and the report was under the guidance of Masahiro Kawai (Japanese) and Rajat M. Nag (Indo-Canadian) (ADB and ADBI, 2009). However, ADB's latter report retreated from such a policy stance, instead advocating a "public–private partnership" supported by the ADB and the World bank (ADB, 2012).

Asian neighbors; and (2) the "21st Century Maritime Silk Road" aimed at connecting East Asian (including Southeast Asian), South Asian, West Asian (Middle East) and African countries.[4] To fulfill the strategy, China already launched a US$40 billion "Silk Road Fund" (*Xinhuanet*, 2014). During the OBOR/*BRI* summit in May 2017, China further promised to contribute an additional US$14.5 billion to the Silk Road Fund to fund OBOR-related projects. The Silk Road Fund already funded several overseas projects including Russia's largest petrochemicals company and hydropower projects in Pakistan (as part of the "China–Pakistan Economic Corridor initiative") (*The Wall Street Journal*, 2015b; *Financial Times*, 2016).

China's strategy raises some concerns. For some "Redback" alarmists, China is using its financial statecraft to further China's strategic interests that erode international liberal order. It is a "Marshall Plan with Chinese characteristics" (Tiezzi, 2014; *The Economist*, 2014a). To other more skeptical observers, the worldwide acceptance of AIIB or OBOR is nothing more than "a symbolic victory" that would neither advance the influence of the Renminbi (RMB) nor cause a significant change to the extant global financial governance (Pettis, 2015). Still other skeptics suggest that China is still far behind US in terms of almost all crucial aspects of comprehensive national capabilities (Brooks and Wohlforth, 2016), including technological level, military capability, GDP per capita (Beckley,

---

[4]The "One Belt — the Silk Road Economic Belt" begins in Xi'an in central China before stretching west through Lanzhou (Gansu province), Urumqi (Xinjiang), and Khorgas (Xinjiang), which is near the border with Kazakhstan. The Silk Road then runs southwest from Central Asia to northern Iran before swinging west through Iraq, Syria and Turkey. From Istanbul, the Silk Road crosses the Bosporus Strait and heads northwest through Europe, including Bulgaria, Romania, the Czech Republic and Germany. Reaching Duisburg in Germany, it swings north to Rotterdam in the Netherlands. From Rotterdam, the path runs south to Venice, Italy.

The "One Road — The 21st Century Maritime Silk Road" will begin in Quanzhou in Fujian, a province in southeast China, and also hit Guangzhou (Guangdong province), Beihai (Guangxi) and Haikou (Hainan) before heading south to the Malacca Strait. From Kuala Lumpur, the Maritime Silk Road heads to Kolkata, India, then crosses the rest of the Indian Ocean to Nairobi, Kenya. From Nairobi, the Maritime Silk Road goes north around the Horn of Africa and moves through the Red Sea into the Mediterranean, with a stop in Athens before meeting the land-based Silk Road in Venice (information quoted from Tiezzi, 2014; *Xinhuanet*, "China's Initiatives on Building Silk Road Economic Belt and 21st Century Maritime Silk Road").

2011), monetary and financial power (Cohen, 2015). Who is right about the impact of Chinese financial statecraft?

A relevant but more intriguing question is China's emphasis on multilateralism in the use of financial statecraft. China heavily relies on two international institutions — the AIIB and the BRICS New Development Bank (NDB, jointly established by Brazil, Russia, India, China and South Africa) — to control its funding when engaging international co-operation and projects (*The Economist*, 2014b). Even for its own grand strategy — the OBOR initiative, China still allows international forces to make decisions on the use of its financial resources. This raises an interesting question: Why does China want to incur self-constraints on its dominance and financial statecraft?

China's shift toward multilateralism under the decline of current international liberal order is puzzling and cannot be well explained by extant theories. For the paradigm of political realism that includes Hegemonic Stability theory and Power Transition theory, it suggests that establishing international institutions is either the Hegemon's privilege or responsibility (Kindleberger, 1973; Gilpin, 1981; Mearsheimer, 1995), and a state is more likely to resort to multilateralism when it ascends to the top. Logically speaking, when a hegemon declines (or just becomes not as dominant as it used to be), it might retreat to bilateralism or even unilateralism. The realist paradigm might be able to explain current US strategic shift caused by the slippage in its economic position. However, it fails to explain China's pursuit of multilateralism. As mentioned earlier, China has not become powerful enough to shoulder disproportionate burdens or to rewrite its own rules.

Liberalism, an alternative paradigm that focuses on economic interdependence, might be able to tell us about the benefits of international regimes and institutions. However, it fails to capture the strategic rationale and power considerations behind actor behaviors. In academic terms, it fails to explain the "demand-side story" — China's strategic preference behind its pursuit of multilateralism. Another liberal variant — democratic peace theory based on audience cost reasoning or the *selectorate theory* — might also be very hard to offer a plausible explanation of China's behaviors since those theories usually imply that liberal democracies are more likely to co-operate successfully (Fearon, 1994; Bueno de Mesquita *et al.*, 2003), or multilateralism could strengthen constitutional democracy (Keohane *et al.*, 2009).

This chapter argues that in order to better understand and evaluate China's grand strategy, we need to understand the strengths and constraints of "financial statecraft". For China, a particularly important constraint of financial statecraft is the *fungibility* problem: China fears that the use of Chinese financial resources is inconsistent with its national interests. However, as an authoritarian regime, Chinese leaders need to preserve the international norm of *non-interference* in a country's internal affairs for their own political survival. This leaves China few *ex-post* instruments and little legitimacy to monitor behaviors of aid-receiving countries after disbursing the funds. Therefore, China needs to rely on informal institutions (Chinese state-owned enterprises) and private relationships with local agents in the recipient country to govern its aid. Accordingly, China's aid is susceptible to corruption and tends to provoke local grievance. For example, several BRI projects caused scandals, backlashes and resistance all over the world, especially in Southeast Asia. Therefore, multilateral regimes become potential and less controversial insurance mechanisms for China. This chapter further argues that the previous two unreconciled opinions, "Redback" alarmists vs. skeptics, are both incorrect. The "Redback" alarmists are wrong because they over-exaggerate China's leadership in a discordant world in which states with divergent preferences all seek to prioritize their own agenda. The skeptics are wrong because they underestimate the potential benefits generated by multilateral regimes, including the creation of a credible mechanism for contract enforcement and internationalization of RMB.

The following sections are organized as follows: the next section briefly revisits the strategic rationale behind financial statecraft, and the associated strengths and weaknesses. This sets the stage for the analysis of China's financial statecraft. The third section articulates the rationale behind China's financial statecraft. I argue that one of the major goals behind China's outbound capital, including foreign aid and state-directed investment, is to solve domestic problems, such as an overcapacity problem, debt problem, economic inequality and lack of social safety net. I further show how the fungibility problem and authoritarian characteristics incentivize China to rely on informal strategy to govern its financial resource overseas, including policy banks, SOEs, and patronage–client relationships. In the fourth section, I present several cases to show the problems China's financial statecraft has caused to Southeast Asian countries, including corruption, socio-economic shock, and lack of contributions to local employment. These negative consequences have brought increasing local resistance. In the fifth section, I indicate that the governing weakness has led China to turn to a less controversial mechanism to protect its aid: multilateralism. I show that multilateral institutions have the potential to create the associated strategic benefits for China. However, I also point out the constraints of China's grand strategy by studying the institutional settlements and projects of two important multilateral institutions, the BRICS NDB and AIIB. The final section concludes the main points.

Financial Statecraft, Multilateralism and Bilateralism

As Harold Lasswell's classic book suggests, the central theme of politics is always about *Who get What, When, and How* (Lasswell, 1936). In the international system in which power politics is still the fundamental rule, scholars pay a special attention to what great powers want through which means (Morgenthau, 1956; Waltz, 1979; Mearsheimer, 2001). Traditionally, IR scholars emphasize hard power such as military capability. With the rise of complex interdependence and economic globalization (Keohane and Nye, 1977), scholars become more and more interested in how the use of economic tools can achieve policy goals, as well as soft power — influence through attraction (Nye, 2004). It is against this backdrop that the use of economic and financial statecraft by great power becomes quintessential to understanding international politics.

So, what do great powers (dominant states) want? The realist paradigm suggests that great powers want to establish their own "international orders" to further their own interests. The most straightforward way is to build a hierarchical relationship in which a great power exercises political power, command and authority over a subordinate actor (Lake, 2009). A great power can profit from its own hierarchy through two sources: (1) it has the privilege of writing its own rules; and (2) stability created by the hierarchy (Lake, 2013: 82–87). The second source of benefit can be understood in terms of C. Kindleberger's notion of Hegemonic Stability Theory: "for the world economy to be stabilized, there must be a stabilizer, one stabilizer" (Kindleberger, 1973). The benefit of stability also creates an incentive for weaker states to accept the hierarchy. However, in a hierarchic relationship, a weaker state confronts two risks: first, it is likely to lose too much autonomy; second, it risks being dominated and exploited by the greater power. Such risks could very likely prompt weaker states to shirk or resist commands from the greater power. Even worse, weaker states may seek protection in countervailing coalitions, a classic strategy of balance of power (checking and balancing the greater power). For a great power to successfully create its order, as suggested by Ikenberry (1999, 2011), it must not only provide benefits but also engage a strategy of "strategic restraint/constraint", meaning it needs to self-constrain its power to some extent to attract weaker states.

Economic and financial statecraft

What are the tools for great powers? Conventionally, states rely on military and diplomatic statecrafts to create their own orders. In a world of economic interdependence and globalization, economic statecraft becomes a major technique. Based on Baldwin (1985), economic statecraft refers to influence attempts relying primarily on resources that have a reasonable semblance of a market price in terms of money (Table 1). Conceptually, there are two types of economic statecraft: (1) *negative sanction* that relies on threat and punishment to change other's behaviors; (2) positive inducement that relies on promises and rewards. In the international system, great powers constantly use economic statecrafts to defend national interests and create their own orders. For example, US has imposed financial sanctions on Iran since 2006 to force Iran to give up its nuclear program. The EU also imposed sanctions against Russia over the Ukraine crisis of 2014. China is not unfamiliar with economic statecraft. Some reports show China banned rare earth metals exports to Japan from 2011–2012 in response to Japan's actions toward a disputed island, the Senkaku (in Japanese)/ Diaoyu (in Chinese). To respond to Philippines' action toward another disputed island in South China sea, the Scarborough Shoal, China constantly imposed bans on Philippine's banana imports (Reilly, 2012: 129–130). The use of negative sanctions is blunt exercise of coercive power. Therefore, it is more likely to incite resistance. Scholars thus find the use of negative sanctions rarely succeed in changing actor behaviors (Pape, 1997),[5] and find that negative sanctions actually increase the likelihood of military conflict (Lektzian and Sprecher, 2007).

---

[5] Scholars find that for negative sanctions to work, they usually work at the stage of being threatened (to use), not at the stage of actually being used (Drezner, 1999a, 2003).

Table 1: Examples of economic and financial statecraft

Economic statecraft		**Financial statecraft**	
Sanction	**Inducement**	**Sanction**	**Inducement**
• Export Control • Boycott (State-led & Citizen-mobilized) • Travel Ban • Dumping, Market Control, & Monopoly • Punitive Tariff • Market License Suspension & Denial • Non-Tariff-Barrier (Health, Environmental, & Labor) • Blacklist	• Discriminative Preferential Trade Agreement • Committed Purchase • Granting Licenses • Market Access • Tax Incentives • Franchise • Information Flow • Travel and Work Permit	• Investment Suspension • Comprehensive Financial Transaction Ban • Targeted Sanction (Individuals, Banks, Central Bank, etc) • Asset Freezing • "SWIFT Ban" (Ban from the Society for Worldwide Interbank Financial Telecommunication) • Aid Conditionalities & Suspension • Financial Blacklist	• Debt Relief • Special Loans • Committed Aid (conditional or unconditional) • Investment Guarantees • Explicit and Implicit Capital & Financial Support • Investment & Capital Incentives

Source: Created by the author based on Baldwin (1985: 41–42) and various other sources.

Positive inducement is another story. Unlike other coercive means, positive promises and rewards are less likely to provoke outright repellence. As Nincic (2010) indicates, there are two channels for positive inducement to affect state behaviors. The first one is *quid pro quo*: the great power can use financial incentives (e.g., aid) in exchange for the weaker state's support. The second one is preference shaping: once weaker states become dependent or even addicted to the given inducements, they are more likely to internalize the greater power's national interest. The impact of dollarization is a notable case. After World War II, US utilized the Marshall Plan and Bretton Woods system to revitalize the global economy, and the dollar became the most dominant currency. Under such a circumstance, countries that use the dollar as national currency (formal dollarization) or major foreign reserves always pay special attention to the US Fed's policies. This is also a critical reason behind China's internationalization of Renminbi (Cohen, 2015). Therefore, positive economic and financial statecraft is one of the necessary strategies for a great power to build its own order.

However, there is an inherent constraint: the *fungibility* problem of positive inducements. This problem is basically the same as the *fungibility* problem of international aid: aid-receiving countries cannot credibly commit themselves to honoring their agreements after aid has been delivered

(Drezner 1999b). For example, almost all country leaders promised that they would use aid from international organizations to develop domestic welfare. But, once receiving the aid, many of them used it to develop patron–client relationships or crony capitalism. In international system, great powers confront the risk that their financial resources will not be used in a way consistent with their national goals. Put it another way, great powers are worried that the weaker states would free-ride the benefits without complying to their commands.

Multilateralism and bilateralism

To deal with the *fungibility* problem of financial statecraft, great powers as well as international organizations usually develop "conditionalities" tied to aid/inducements and mechanisms for enforcing the contract. Conceptually, there are two potential strategies: multilateralism and bilateralism.

First, great powers/leading states can adopt multilateralism: create rule-based international regimes and institutions to handle the *fungibility* problem and monitor actors' free-riding behaviors. Defined as "a set of implicit or explicit principles, norms, rules and decision-making procedures that guide state behaviors and expectations" (Krasner, 1983; Keohane, 1984), international regimes/institutions are considered more useful in facilitating co-operation among states by reducing uncertainty and "transaction cost" (associated costs of state interaction in the process of international co-operation). The central reason is that international institutions are usually characterized as generalized principles of conduct that apply to everyone. In principle, they are designed to treat every member uniformly and distribute responsibilities equally (Thompson and Verdier, 2014; Ruggie, 1992). This creates an additional solution for great powers to handle the *fungibility* problem of financial statecraft and free riding. If a great power can get other states to buy into a set of rules and institutions, it does not need to spend its resources constantly to coerce other states into following them. This is because every member state more or less becomes an "institutional stakeholder", and has an incentive to monitor each state's behavior and enforce the rules (Ikenberry, 2011: 102–109). The downside of multilateralism for great powers/leading states, of course, is that they also need to be constrained to some extent. Even though great powers can still enjoy some privileges derived from power asymmetry, they are no longer able to dominate as much as they used to. This is especially the case when different states possess heterogeneous priorities and preferences. However, it is precisely such a restraint on great powers that renders legitimacy to international institutions, and the great power's order as well (Ikenberry, 1999, 2011).

Second, great powers can choose an alternative approach: bilateralism based on a hierarchical power relationship. Bilateral negotiation, as Ikenberry put it (2011: 114–116), are far more receptive to exceptional rules for powerful states. Bilateral agreements are more likely to be tailored in accordance with great power interest. With clear power asymmetry in a bilateral relationship, a dominant state can very effectively enforce the rule, punish free-riding behaviors of weaker state, and solve the *fungibility* problem (Lake, 2009; 2013). The downside of bilateralism for great powers is that such an approach is more likely to provoke resentment and opposition toward the great powers' commands and order.

To sum up, the *fungibility* problem of financial statecraft creates a difficult choice between multilateralism and bilateralism for great powers/dominant states. A great power can avoid direct confrontation and outright counterbalance by partially surrendering its power to multilateral institutions, but it risks being constrained and even giving up its priorities. In contrast, a great power can resort to a bilateral patron–client relationship to exploit power asymmetry, but it needs to be capable and willing to enforce rules and punish defection. The consequence is usually the legitimate loss of the patron–client relationship, and potential strategy of counterbalance. Below, I argue that China's strategic use of financial statecraft actually reflects such a dilemma in dealing with the *fungibility* problem.

Strategic Rationale behind China's Financial Statecraft

Why would China be willing to offer its financial resources to other countries? China's economic challenges and its policy responses illuminate the underlying rationale. After decades of rapid economic growth, China's investment-led developmental strategy seems to have reached its limit in its domestic market. In order to stimulate the domestic economy, China's central bank, the People's Bank of China (PBOC), constantly cuts interest rates, lowers the reserve requirement ratio for all banks, and plans to launch its own version of quantitative easing — "pledged supplementary lending" (*The Economist*, 2015). However, the expected effect is not very promising because of the domestic overcapacity problem: it becomes extremely hard to find high-returns and productive investments domestically. As a result, the Dragon naturally turns its eyes to the neighbors. The "8 trillion" Asian infrastructure market offers profitable opportunities to re-boost China's economy. China plans to channel its massive foreign reserves from low-return US treasuries to higher-return assets in neighboring countries, including transportation, energy facilities and other public facilities. The infrastructure investments not only help China earn more profits but also create new export markets for Chinese companies.

The crucial importance of the Asian market is evident for China's economic adjustment (*zài píng héng*, "Rebalancing" in Chinese). This is why China's leader Xi Jinping proposed the OBOR initiative (*BRI*) as its 21st century grand strategy during Xi's trip to Southeast Asia in October 2013, the same occasion the AIIB was introduced.

China has attempted to utilize financial leverage to further its strategic interests since the global financial crisis of 2007–2009. The constant setbacks of China's financial statecraft actually indicate its inherent weakness. Despite its US$3.8 trillion in foreign reserves and the status of the second largest creditor to the US,[6] China has been unable to compel the US to concede in various issues. Two notable examples Drezner points out are: (1) the (failing) reform of IMF governance; and (2) the establishment of global regulatory regime for the sovereign wealth funds (SWFs). In both cases, it was China, not the United States, that was forced to make concessions (Drezner, 2009).

The above failure may be excused as indicative of the special status of US dollar as the world's reserve currency. However, the record of China's financial power in other capital-starved countries is equally unpromising. The constraint primarily results from the *fungibility* problem of financial statecraft. But it becomes even more serious due to the opacity of China's "checkbook diplomacy." It is widely acknowledged that China's lending and investment to a country tend to boom following the Chinese leaders' visit, and contract-enforcement is usually ensured mainly by informal commitment between the Chinese leaders and the leader of recipient country. If local political conditions in the recipient country change, China's loans could easily become targets of criticism. As a

[6]China became the largest holder of US Treasuries since the global financial crisis. However, at the end of January, 2015 Japan reclaimed the status as the largest foreign creditor to the US (owning US$1.2244 trillion), surpassing China's US$1.2237 trillion (*The Wall Street Journal*, 2015d).

consequence, it increases the risks of default and expropriation of Chinese companies' property. For example, in Sri Lanka, the newly elected President, Maithripala Sirisensa, informed Beijing in February 2015 that the country would review and renegotiate the terms of Chinese loans. Sri Lanka's new leader also criticized the lax transparency and high costs on a series of Chinese-funded projects under the former president, who developed close ties with the leader of China, Xi Jinping. In Myanmar, an old ally of China, the switch from a military junta to a nominally civilian government in 2011 led to the suspension on the US$3.6 billion Myistone Dam project and the US$20 billion railway project, both financed by China (Kynge and Wildau, 2015).

Furthermore, the profit-driven nature of China's loans is on the verge of causing political backlashes in loan-recipient countries. According to a 2013 RAND Corporation report (Wolf *et al.*, 2013), China's bilateral loans to developing countries during 2001–2011, mostly concentrating on infrastructure projects and resource-development projects, are commonly tied to conditions that support the activities of Chinese companies.[7] Those conditions include purchase of Chinese goods, procurement of equipment and technical services imported from China and guaranteed supply of natural resources. In other words, China's overseas financial assistance in these areas resembles economic strategies designed to spur its domestic development. Such a strategy raises concerns of exploitation and could easily trigger local resentment. In 2013, Lamido Sanusi, Nigeria's Central Banker, accused China of attempting "a new form of imperialism" (Sanusi, 2013). In Africa, the second-largest region China has invested in,[8] opposition parties in many countries, especially in southern Africa, frequently campaign on anti-China platforms. For example, the anti-China opposition party won the Zambian election in 2011 due to unrest of copper mining workers (*The Economist*, 2011).

Domestic politics in loan-receiving countries increases uncertainty of repayment. Without a credible mechanism to ensure contract-enforcement, Chinese leaders as well as companies usually need to develop

---

[7]The 2013 Rand Corporation report estimates that the total size of China's foreign loans is US$671 billion for the period of 2001–2011. The natural-resource-development projects amount to 42% of total loans, and the infrastructure projects amount to 40% (Wolf *et al.*, 2013: xiv–xv; 47).

[8]According to the 2013 Rand Corporation report, the region that receives the largest size of China's lending is Latin America (Wolf *et al.*, 2013).

close relationships with the incumbent governments. Very often, such a strategy puts China into a disadvantageous position in the bargaining of debt-repayment: because China heavily relies on the incumbent governments of loan-receiving countries to enforce contracts, China inevitably has to support the survival of incumbent leaders. This creates opportunities for incumbent leaders to make excessive demands on China, including bigger loans, looser terms of contracts, and more debt extension. A notable example is Venezuela, the largest country China has lent to in the world. China has lent US$56.3 billion to Venezuela, of which about 20 billion is still outstanding (*Financial Times*, 2015). However, the meltdown of Venezuela's economy forces the incumbent president Nicolas Maduro, Hugo Chavez's successor, to ask for more loans from China. The risk of Venezuela's default on its debts had already skyrocketed because of the combination of recent drops in oil prices and continuing imprudent fiscal policies. China initially refused, but eventually granted a new loan of US$5 billion during April 2015 (Tiezzi, 2015). Similar challenges perturb China in the cases of loans to Zimbabwe and Ukraine (Kynge and Wildau, 2015).

In short, due to the lack of credible enforcement to solve the fungibility problem, China's financial statecraft in capital-starved countries faces a classic "Principal-Agent problem:" China has to heavily invest in the incumbent leaders to make them loyal agents for securing China's privileges. Those "loyal agents" can thus make opportunistic demands for excessive "political commissions." Other domestic opposition forces in capital-starved countries are also able to take advantage of anti-China resentment. All of these situations increase the risk of China's investment. Very often, China is forced to compromise its profit-driven, privilege-seeking purpose and allow others to free-ride on its financial contributions without gaining sufficient returns.

One of the crucial strategies China commonly uses is to rely on state-owned banks and state-owned enterprises (SOEs) to deliver financial resources. For example, when China promised to help fund infrastructure projects in Southeast Asia, the Chinese government constantly authorized state-owned banks to jointly fund the projects. On the surface, China's foreign aid is managed by the China International Development Cooperation Agency (CIDCA) under the State Council of China. In fact, there are two additional state-owned policy banks that invest ambitiously in international markets: China Development Bank and the Export-Import Bank of China (China Ex-Im Bank). These two banks are under direct control by the State Council. In recent years, the four big state-owned banks have become aggressive in overseas lending. They are Bank of China, Agriculture Bank of China, Industrial and Commercial Bank, and China Construction Bank, which are supervised and controlled by the Chinese Ministry of Finance and the "Central Huijin Investment Company." The Central Huijin Investment Company is a majority shareholder of the four banks (the Chinese Ministry of Finance is the other majority shareholder). The Central Huijin Investment Company is owned by the China Investment Corporation, a Sovereign-Wealth Fund under direct control by the Chinese State Council. Lastly, China's central bank, the PBOC, manages China's foreign reserves through the administrative agency — the State Administration of Foreign Exchange (SAFE). Perhaps not surprisingly, the SAFE is also a major player in China's financial statecraft. For example, the SAFE contributed to 60% of funding for the Silk Road Fund, one of the major aiding agencies for the *BRI* (Horn *et al.*, 2020).

In addition, the Chinese government also encouraged Chinese SOEs to use their international subsidiaries to compete for infrastructure project contracts. In many cases, the Chinese SOEs were implicitly granted exclusive privilege or priority to get the project contracts.

Resorting to state-owned banks and enterprises to manage foreign infrastructure aid projects serves China several benefits. First, since these state-owned entities tend to disguise their connections with the Chinese government in international markets, they face less public scrutiny. Second, they can use commercial or profit-driven excuses to cover the actual pursuit of China's national interests. For example, when Chinese state-owned banks provided the funding for some infrastructure projects in the recipient countries, they usually have some leverage to decide which companies can get the project contract. Very often they can successfully persuade the recipient countries to choose the Chinese state-owned enterprises as project contractors. In doing so, the Chinese state-owned entities can create informal mechanisms to monitor and protect their investment. Furthermore, the Chinese state-owned entities can nudge the recipient countries to choose certain policies that serve China's interest. For example, the Chinese SOEs could request to hire more Chinese workers or to adopt the China's industrial standards and rules. When such policies raise public concerns, suspicions or criticisms, the Chinese state-owned entities can always use commercial reasons to justify those policy choices. More important, the Chinese government can shirk the blame for interfering in other countries' domestic affairs while still maintaining control over the use of China's financial leverage.

Although China could escape the authoritarian donor's dilemma through the patronage–client relationships and the informal networks of state-owned entities, such strategies have caused different problems for China. First, relying on Chinese state-owned entities to deliver and manage China's financial resources may provoke local social discontent because those entities tend to emphasize Chinese interest more than pursuing the local development of aid- and loan-receiving countries. Second, making local politicians, including either incumbent leaders or local factions, as informal contract enforcers may increase the risk of corruption since their actions are usually opaque. Together, these problems sow the seed of local resistance against Chinese financial statecraft. In the next section, I offer several cases of China's financial statecraft in Southeast Asia and the local resistance it provoked.

China's Financial Statecraft in Southeast Asia: Its Discontents and Local Resistance

Vietnam

Although China is Vietnam's biggest trading partner, the bilateral relationship between Vietnam and China has been strenuous due to territory disputes, historical legacy and domestic issues. In the recent decade, the South China Sea territory dispute and the deep-rooted anti-China sentiments in the Vietnamese society have caused tensions between Vietnam and China. The leaders on both sides have sought to enhance bilateral economic co-operation to ease the tension. For example, in 2004, China and Vietnam agreed to launch the "Two Corridors, One Belt" (TCOB) framework to improve connectivity between Yunnan and Guangxi (in South China) and provinces in North Vietnam. The initiative also aimed to enhance the Sino-Vietnamese economic co-operation around the Tonkin Gulf. However, it did not make too much progress. After Chinese leader Xi Jinping launched the *BRI* in 2013, China and Vietnam went through lengthy negotiations about how to expand the Sino-Vietnamese co-operation under *BRI*. One of the main issues is that Vietnam is worried about losing autonomy under the China-led *BRI*. In 2017, the two countries finally agree to sign a memorandum on "Strengthening the OBOR Initiative and TCOB Project" during Xi Jin-Ping's visit to Hanoi. However, as Vietnamese scholar Le Hong Hiep points out, Vietnam remains cautious about China's potential dominance. For example, the title of such a memorandum implies that the TCOB, equally led by both countries, is independent from the *BRI*. This strategy suggests that Vietnam is determined to retain its own control when engaging co-operation with China. Furthermore, during Vietnamese President Tran Dai Quang's visit to the first Belt and Road Forum for International Cooperation in Beijing in 2017, he emphasized that co-operation must be based on the principles of consensus, equality and "compliance with the UN Charter and international law" (Le, 2018: 4).

Why is Vietnam so cautious about China's financial statecraft? As indicated earlier, China tends to rely on its state-owned entities to govern and deliver its aid. As a result, it not only opens the opportunity for Chinese companies to exploit but it also causes the threat of debt problem in the local society. For example, the Line 2A of Hanoi MRT (Cát Linh–Hà Đông Line) project, constructed by the Chinese state-owned enterprise China Railway Sixth Bureau (a subsidiary of China Railway Group), started its construction in 2011. Mainly funded by the Export-Import Bank of China, the project was supposed to be completed by 2013. However, the project has been delayed due to several problem including industrial accidents, frequent design changes and increasing safety concerns during the construction period. Due to continuous delays, the cost of the project has exceeded original expectations. The original estimated cost was US$552 million, and the Chinese side provided a loan of US$419 million. Later, the total cost was increased to US$891 million. After the Sino-Vietnamese negotiations, China promised to provide an additional US$250 million in loans in 2017, bringing in the financial source of BRI to this project (*VnExpress*, 2019). As of December 12, 2020, the line is still not officially opened, making the Vietnamese highly question the efficiency and benefits of Chinese capital. The Ministry of Transport of Vietnam therefore issued a report stating that many foreign companies investing in Vietnam not only lack competitiveness, but are of low quality. These companies include China Guangxi Road and Bridge Group, ZTE Corporation, China Railway Sixth Bureau and South Korean companies, etc. The Ministry of Investment and Planning of Vietnam even recommended to avoid accepting Chinese aid and investment plans, because these Chinese-funded projects usually cannot meet local needs, and the construction process is usually delayed, the cost exceeds the original budget, and the loan interest rate is higher than that provided by other countries (*Nikkei Asian Review*, 2018).

Therefore, it is China's state-dictated financial statecraft, the threat of debt trap, together with the thorny South China Sea dispute, that cause Vietnam's systematic distrust of China. Vietnam's vigilance is also significant in its pandemic prevention policy in the face of COVID-19. For example, when China was trying to cover up the pandemic situation during the very early stage, Vietnam was highly suspicious of China's propaganda. Vietnam was also among the first countries to impose travel ban on China (Bac and Murray, 2020).

Malaysia

Malaysia has long been one of the major investment destinations for Chinese capital. The bilateral economic and investment relationships have blossomed especially under former Prime Minister Najib Razak (in office from 2009 to May 2018). When Chinese leader Xi Jinping launched the *BRI* in 2013, the Najib administration highly welcomed the initiative and was eager to participate in associated programs. To show his support, Najib himself also took part in the first Belt and Road Summit in Beijing in May 2017 (*The Strait Times*, 2017a). With Najib's full endorsement, China was set to launch several projects in Malaysia.

One of the famous China-backed projects in Malaysia is the Malaysia East Coast Rail Link (ECRL). With a project value worth US$18.2 billion, the ECRL is widely seen as *BRI* flagship project in Southeast Asia. It is a two-track railway project aiming to connect the Port Klang on the Straits of Malacca with the East Coast Special Economic Zone. The project is mainly financed by the Export-Import Bank of China. China Communications Construction Corporation (CCCC) is the main contractor for the construction. The ECRL will be owned by the Malaysia Rail Link Sdn Bhd (MRLSB), which is wholly-owned by the Malaysian Minister of Finance Incorporated (MOF Inc.). However, under the MOU for the ECRL, the MRLSB and CCCC will form a 50:50 joint venture to manage, operate and maintain the rail network jointly (Malaysia Rail Link Sdn Bhd (MRL), 2020).

The project received full support from the former Najib government. In fact, Najib himself played a crucial role in paving the way for the China-led project. The China–Malaysia co-operation deal was made during Najib's visit to Beijing in late 2016. During the week-long visit, Najib met Chinese President Xi Jinping and Premier Li Keqiang, and he secured a soft loan from the Export-Import Bank of China. In return, Najib endorsed the agreement that the CCCC, a famous Chinese state-owned enterprise, would be awarded the contract for the construction of the ECRL (Liu and Lim, 2019). Then, the CCCC started to send a large number of Chinese workers to Malaysia to conduct the project. While some raised concerns that China's financial capital and statecraft would not benefit local business and employment, Najib still touted the ECRL as a game changer that would spur the momentum for Malaysia's economic development (*The Strait Times*, 2017b; *The South China Morning Post*, 2016). In addition, the Najib government had also approved several co-operative projects. For example, the Najib government agreed to sign a contract to allow the China Petroleum Pipeline Bureau (CPPB), a subsidiary of state-owned China National Petroleum Corporation (CNPC), to develop the Multi-Product Pipeline in Kedah and the Trans-Sabah Natural Gas Pipeline in Sabah (*The Star*, 2018).

China's BRI projects in Malaysia indicate how aid fungibility and authoritarian dilemma affect China's execution of its financial statecraft. Being constrained by its authoritarian foreign policy orientation — non-interventionism — China is short of enforcement mechanisms to guarantee Chinese interests when delivering its aid and financial capital. Therefore, China heavily relies on its state-owned entities to manage and execute its financial statecraft. This strategy may also create overseas job opportunities for Chinese workers. However, it tends to incite local resentment because of its disproportionate emphasis on China's own strategic benefits. Therefore, China usually needs to develop close informal relationships with local political agents, who are reliable clients that can be count on to shield China's financial statecraft from local resistance. Such informal enforcement mechanisms, while useful in dealing with aid fungibility problem, may create too much discretionary power for the local agent. As a result, it is likely to generate opportunities for corruption. This explains how BRI projects got involved in the "1MDB" scandal.

According to the *Wall Street Journal* report (*Wall Street Journal*, 2019), when the Najib government and China began negotiations in 2016, the Malaysian sovereign wealth fund "1MDB" was already on the verge of bankruptcy. The US Department of Justice also began investigating the fund's illegal investments in the United States and freezing its assets. Seizing the chance that China was seeking investment target for its *BRI*, Najib turned to China in the hope that China would provide funds to repay the 1MDB debt. In return, the Najib government promised to offer

China the contracts to construct the ECRL and the Sabah Natural Gas Pipeline Development Project. The Najib government was also willing to tout the two projects as flagship programs of the China-backed BRI. Furthermore, Malaysia also promised to offer construction contracts with higher premiums than market price to Chinese SOEs. Take the Sabah Natural Gas Pipeline Project as an example, the Najib government took a loan from the Export-Import Bank of China, and then paid the loan to the China Petroleum Pipeline Corporation for construction. Such an arrangement eventually allowed most of Chinese financial resources to circle back to China. However, the arrangement actually increased Malaysia's debt to China. Moreover, a contract design like this made it difficult for the Malaysian government to monitor the project. When the construction of project only reached 11.4%, the Malaysian government had already made 87.2% payment. Furthermore, during the negotiation of the ERCL project, the Najib government had repeatedly asked the CCCC to assume part of the 1MDB debt as soon as possible in exchange for the approval of the project. In addition, reports show that Chinese officials even said that they were trying to tap the *Wall Street Journal*'s Hong Kong office and assist the Najib government to find out the "whistleblower" who leaked the information about the corruption of 1MDB (*The Wall Street Journal*, 2019).

After the 1MDB's corruption case was disclosed by the international media, it triggered full-scale resistance and demonstrations in Malaysian society, believing that China's investment plan is an important cause of domestic corruption and debt traps. Public support for the Najib government dropped sharply. In the general election of 2018, all major societal groups formed a united resistance coalition — Pakatan Harapan (PH) with the leader of Mahathir Mohamad. And the PH then ousted the long-ruling UMNO from power. Mahathir returned as prime minister at the age of 93. After taking office, Mahathir immediately stopped the ECRL project and the Sabah Natural Gas Pipeline Project on the grounds of anti-corruption and budget control. During Mahathir's visit to China in late 2018, Mahathir met with Chinese Premier Li Keqiang and told him directly: "You don't want a situation where there's a new version of colonialism happening…" (Martin and Raghu, 2018). Then during an interview in 2019, Mahathir warned the risk of debt trap by Chinese capital: "if you borrow huge sums of money from China, and then you cannot pay, you are under the control of the lender. So, we have to be very careful about that." In the same interview, Mahathir also warned that letting in a huge number of Chinese workers could disturb the political and societal orders (*The Strait Times*, 2019). After that, China was finally willing to drastically reduce the manufacturing cost of East Rail, and the Malaysian government agreed to the plan to resume it (*Reuters*, 2019).

Solving the Authoritarian Donor's Dilemma: China's Strategic Turn to Multilateralism — Benefit, Challenge and Long-Term Goal

The benefit: A credible mechanism for contract-enforcement

As indicated previously, China's authoritarian foreign policy orientation causes difficulties in dealing with the aid fungibility problem when wielding its financial statecraft. China usually needs to rely on local political agents to manage and execute its financial statecraft. This creates opportunities for those agents to make opportunistic demands, forcing China to make more concessions or breed the seed of corruption.

Multilateralism offers a solution. A multilateral regime could help solve those problems because of three institutional advantages: multiple veto players, higher transparency and the linkage with other financing entities. This is why China established the AIIB, and co-operated with other BRICS countries to form the NDB.

Due to the multilateral nature of AIIB, other member states could have a voice in the decision-making process or even serve as veto players to reject reckless bailouts. In addition, as potential stakeholders/co-financiers, other member states should have incentives to increase the transparency of AIIB to better monitor those funding programs. As a consequence, China's arbitrary behaviors in delivering loans or debt-renegotiation could be checked and counterbalanced. I have already pointed out in the last section that China's opaque and discretionary financial diplomacy actually puts China into a disadvantaged position: because China could not credibly commit itself to punishing default, the borrowing states tend to exploit such a loophole by opportunism. The AIIB could preempt those opportunistic behaviors by "tying China's hands" in the first place. Lastly, every lending decision made by the AIIB would potentially have a linkage effect: it would easily trigger multilateral responses. Assuming a scenario in which a borrowing country is contemplating defaulting on AIIB's loans, it would confront the risk of being sanctioned by every other possible financing entity, including the IMF or other creditor states. This risk should be high enough to deter opportunistic borrowers.

Why would China be willing to self-restrain its dominion just for providing such a seemingly public good? China's economic challenges are the main reasons. As indicated previously, China has suffered an overcapacity problem domestically after several decades of rapid economic booms. In addition, China's investment-led, export-oriented developmental strategy has created a large and persistent amount of trade surplus with the US, causing the risk of trade war. In order to stabilize its currency as well as the domestic economy, China has continued to redirect its surplus toward the low-return US treasuries in the US financial markets. This strategy hardly serves China's long-term economic and strategic interests. Therefore, China is confronting substantial pressure for readjusting its model.

The crucial importance of the Asian market is evident for China's economic adjustment (*zài píng héng*, "Rebalancing" in Chinese) or Xi Jinping's "Dual Circulation" strategy (*Reuters*, 2020).[9] However, China's ambitious bilateral initiatives, the *BRI* for example, all suffer commitment problems and principal-agent problems. If China wants to protect its investments by making credible threats or conditionality, it could easily draw sharp criticisms of "new imperialism." Therefore, for China, the AIIB becomes a "blessing". China could rely on the AIIB as a gatekeeper to safeguard its assets. When criticisms arise, China could potentially shirk the responsibilities by diverting those criticisms toward the multilateral nature of AIIB. Paradoxically, in order to realize such a strategic benefit, China must surrender its power in the first place to make the AIIB truly multilateral.

The challenge: Difficulties in coordinating with other competing powers

Although China could take advantage of multilateralism to solve an authoritarian donor's dilemma, China still faces a thorny challenge — the

[9]During May 2020, Chinese President Xi Jinping indicated that China will rely mainly on "internal circulation" — the domestic cycle of production, distribution, and consumption — for its development, supported by innovation and upgrades in the economy. Xi also said "internal circulation" will be supported by "external circulation." Jointly, the internal circulation and external circulation strategies form the "dual circulation" (*Reuters*, 2020).

difficulties in coordinating with other competing powers. Since every major power has its own agenda and unique national interests, China tends to pursue a cautious balancing strategy to navigate power conflicts when forming or initiating new multilateral regimes in order to co-operate with such a diversified group of countries.

The institutional design of the NDB adequately illustrates China's cautious approach in engaging global financial governance. Founded by the BRICS countries (Brazil, Russia, India, China and South Africa) in 2014,[10] the NDB is widely thought to serve as a countervailing power to the US-led IMF and World Bank (*The Economist*, 2014b; *The Deutsche Welle*, 2014). However, a closer look at the internal arrangement of NDB shows that maintaining an "internal balance" is the priority within a group of diversified emerging powers. First, despite the resource discrepancy among founding members, the NDB adopts a framework of equal voting rights and capital contributions: each of the BRICS countries is given an equal vote and none have veto power. Each founding member is required to contribute exactly the same amount of capital to form the multilateral bank.[11] Second, the governing structure of the NDB includes three-tiers: a Board of Governors, a Board of Directors, and a President. Again, an elegant balance has been maintained: the first president and the chairman of Board of Governors were from India. There are four vice presidents, each from Russia, China, Brazil, South Africa. The first chairman of the Board of Directors was from Brazil. Those governing positions continue to rotate. Currently, the president of NDB is from Brazil. The chairpersons of the Board of Governors and the Board of Directors are from Russia. The vice chairman of the Board of Directors is from India (New Development Bank, 2020).

The NDB has its headquarters in Shanghai, China. The first regional office was in Johannesburg, South Africa (*The BRICS Fortaleza Declaration,*

---

[10]The NDB was initially proposed during the 4th BRICS summit in 2012. After the agreement among BRICS leaders in 2013 (the 5th summit), the institutional arrangements of NDB were negotiated and established during the 6th summit in Brazil in 2014. The BRICS countries agree to complete the ratification process (Russia has ratified and India is under the process) and have the NDB fully functioning by the end of 2015.

[11]The initial authorized capital of NDB is US$100 billion (the same size as the AIIB), and the startup capital is US$50 billion equally shared by the five founding members (Arts. 6, 7). It is worth noting that the funding projects NDB plans to target are similar to that of the AIIB: infrastructure lending in emergent markets. See the *Agreement on the BRICS New Development Bank (NDB)* in http://brics6.itamaraty.gov.br/agreements.

2014). Thereafter, it opened three other regional offices in Russia, India, and Brazil (NDB, 2020).

Third, along with the creation of the NDB, the BRICS countries also established a US$ 100 billion "Contingency Reserve Arrangement" (CRA), arguably aimed at replacing the "infamous" IMF conditionality-lending in international short-term liquidity crises. China has committed to an amount of US$41 billion, the lion's share of the CRA. However, all the founding members agreed on the principle of decision-making based on consensus rule, including China.[12]

The experience of launching the NDB indicates the critical constraint of China's financial power: because China cannot credibly commit not to exploit the regime for its own sake, and because the distributional problem is equally thorny among emerging powers, China tends to pursue a cautious balancing strategy to navigate power conflicts. Such a strategy usually entails self-restraint.

The NDB is not the first multilateral financial regime in which China has utilized such a balancing approach. The East Asian Chiang Mai Initiative Multilateralization (CMIM) is another salient example of regional balance between China (with Hong Kong) and Japan, with no member state controlling veto power. In the case of the AIIB, in which founding members are even more diverse, any action by China to create rules that benefit exclusively itself could trigger a countervailing move from the other members. Therefore, China actually strategically delegates the governing power and emulates the extant multilateral regimes. It is thus no coincidence that the first president of AIIB, Jin Liqun, is highly experienced in working within international financial organizations (Jin once served as the vice president of ADB). There was also evidence indicating that Jin tried very hard to persuade Japan to join by guaranteeing

[12]The shares of committed resources: China: US$41 billion; Russia: US$18 billion; India: US$18 billion; Brazil: US$18 billion; South Africa: US$5 billion (Arts. 2, 3(b), 3(d)). While the BRICS countries all commit to the consensus rule in decision-making, they accept simple majority of weighted voting of providing parties in an executive-level situation: the Standing Committee can use such rule to approve requests for support or for renewals of support through the liquidity or precautionary instruments. Except for that situation, all other decisions of the Standing Committee shall be taken by consensus. (Art. 3(d)). See the *Treaty for The Establishment of a BRICS Contingency Reserve Arrangement (CRA)* in http://brics6.itamaraty.gov.br/agreements.

Japan high governing positions.[13] The major reason, according to some analysts, is to minimize the concerns of Chinese dominance by accommodating another potential balancer (*Nikkei*, 2015).

In fact, the institutional structure of AIIB shows China's strategic balance and restrain. Although China enjoys veto power based on its quota shares, China indicates its willingness to accept future expansion of other countries' quota and relinquishment of its veto power. More important, the AIIB also establishes five vice presidents, each from UK, Russia, India, Germany, Indonesia. Furthermore, the leadership of AIIB remains a close relationship with current international organizations. For example, in addition to Jin's previous experience with the ADB, many of the AIIB former and current vice presidents had abundant experiences in working with the World Bank, the ADB, or other international institutions. Needless to say, they are also experienced in international financial co-operation. Furthermore, a cursory look at the AIIB approved projects indicates that a large number of them are co-financed projects, with the World Bank or ADB as the largest financers (AIIB, 2020).

The long-term strategic goal: Internationalization of RMB and global financial governance

Although China's multilateral financial statecraft faces a thorny challenge, it still has the potential to serve its long-term strategic goals — namely internationalizing the RMB and the reform of global financial governance.

It is no secret that China wants to promote a "much-more-fair" international economic order. Put more precisely, China hopes to have more say in global financial and monetary governance. However, the extant global currency system is still predominated by the US dollar, putting China (and any other country) in a disadvantageous bargaining position in international economic affairs. Therefore, in spite of potential costs and risks, internationalization of the RMB is a crucial strategy for China to "exit and/or voice." In light of the strategic view, the AIIB could facilitate the international usage of RMB and increase China's leverage within the IMF.

[13]The Japanese news media points out that Jin directly contacted Takehiko Nakao, the president of the ADB, to persuade Japan's participation by offering "a top-ranking vice president" and the post of a director representing only Japan (*Nikkei*, 2015).

In fact, China's ambition dates back to decades ago, when the devastating experience of the 1997 Asian financial crisis still lingered. It was during this time that the United States started to criticize China as an "exchange-rate manipulator" and began requesting an appreciation of RMB. The Asian financial crisis taught China a lesson: without a stronger say in the IMF, the extant paradigm of international financial governance may push against China's own national interest. The pressure to appreciate the RMB also led China to realize that the reserve currency status would render great power to the issuing state to deflect costs of adjustment. However, China's pursuit of that ambition had to wait until the Global Financial Crisis of 2007, a potential "window of opportunities." Since then, China has eagerly promoted the international uses of RMB through various policies. For example, China has signed many RMB-denominated bilateral currency swap agreements (BSAs) to facilitate trade or to rescue short-term liquidity crises (Eichengreen and Kawai, 2014: 9). In addition, China has tried to incrementally relax capital controls, such as fostering the growth of an offshore RMB-denominated bond market in Hong Kong, allowing qualified foreign institutional investors (QFII) and RQFII to invest in the onshore interbank bond market (the so-called "panda bond market") and equity market, and permitting qualified domestic institutional investors (QDII) and non-financial institutions to invest or issue RMB bonds in the Hong Kong offshore market (the so-called "dim sum bond market").

China's effort has had some success. According to the Society for Worldwide Interbank Financial Telecommunication (SWIFT), in 2015 the RMB was the 5th most-used currency for international payments (*The Wall Street Journal*, 2015c).[14] There are also more than 37 central banks that have added the RMB to their reserve portfolio since 2010 (Liao and McDowell, 2015). It is evident that those achievements are a result of China's bilateral or unilateral policies. The question then becomes: Why does China bother to add a multilateral approach?

An immediate benefit is that the AIIB is likely to increase additional credible channels for RMB internationalization, such as issuing RMB-denominated bonds or approving RMB-denominated loans. In fact, co-operating with multilateral institutions has always been a major strategy

[14]The RMB declined to the 7th position during February 2015 but then bounced back in March (Bloomberg, 2015). In 2017, it declined to 6th position (1–5: Dollar, Euro, Sterling, Yen, Canadian Dollar).

for China in experimenting with deregulation of capital account. In 2005, the ADB and the International Finance Corporation (a member of the World Bank Group) became the first two issuers of "Panda bonds", the RMB-denominated bond designed for non-Chinese issuers in the onshore market. In 2010, the ADB issued the "Dim sum bond", the RMB-denominated bond designed to be traded in the offshore market in Hong Kong. The ADB's bond is the longest-dated (10-year maturity) and highest-rated (triple A) bond denominated in the RMB ever sold to international investors (*Financial Times*, 2010).

Internationalization of the RMB through the multilateral institutions is beneficial for China since those bonds or loans tend to have longer maturity, and they are usually designed to invest in productivity. This is consistent with China's preference toward financial liberalization: China wants to avoid short-term speculative capital flows in the process of deregulation.

In addition, the AIIB could promote and approve projects that use the local currencies other than the dollar to finance the operations, just as the BRICS NDB has managed to achieve. According to Article 24, the NDB's operations could be financed through the local currency of the country in which the operations takes place. In addition to the NDB, the BRICS countries also signed two agreements to extend credit in its own currency to the four others.[15] Those multilateral agreements could not only help further trade relationships among members but also create the incentive structure that may encourage member states to decrease somewhat the size of dollar assets in their reserve portfolio. The AIIB, along with the BRICS NDB, would very likely to contribute to furthering the internationalization of RMB.

Why would multilateralism be more useful than bilateralism for China to advance the reserve currency status of RMB? It is because China, as every rising power does, confronts a commitment problem: it is not entirely clear whether China would be a benign and responsible leader forever. Would China be seduced to exploit the seigniorage and impose its will on others recklessly once the RMB becomes the major reserve currency? The AIIB has the potential to solve the problem because of its multilateral nature: since member states could voice their opinions,

[15]The agreements are (1) the Master Agreement in Extending Credit Facility in Local Currencies; and (2) the BRICS Multilateral Letter of Credit Confirmation Facility Agreement. They were signed in 2012 (BRICS Information Centre, 2012).

monitor the decisions, or even form veto power by coalition, and they would be more likely to support the AIIB's policies even if those policies may be in favor of China's strategic interest. Of course, as noted earlier, in order to make the AIIB a credible solution, China has to restrain its privileged power in the first place. This is why the AIIB chooses to co-operate closely with the World Bank and ADB without eagerly pursuing its own project. Furthermore, for fear of potential critics and resistance, the scope of RMB internationalization through the AIIB would probably be limited in the beginning, centering on Southeast Asian countries or countries in conflict with the US (e.g., Iran or Russia).

A Contender with the IMF and World Bank?

Lastly but perhaps most importantly, we should not ignore the potential impact of the AIIB on the governance of the IMF. The establishment of the AIIB is strategically important for China because it is very likely to increase China's leverage within the IMF. Before articulating this point, I need to make clear first that such a scenario is different from the prediction made by the "Redback" alarmists or optimists — that the economic rise of China would eventually lead China-led institutions to overtake the IMF or World Bank. This prediction, I argue, is plain unrealistic. China's influence could grow not because the AIIB is going to challenge the IMF. On the contrary, it is precisely the potential "partnership" between the AIIB and the IMF that would provide China strategic leverage in international financial and monetary governance. The AIIB seeks to co-operate with the IMF or World Bank. By doing so, it could create opportunities for persuading the IMF to further accommodate the rise of China.

In fact, after the Global Financial Crisis and the Eurozone Debt Crisis, the importance of regional financial co-operation has been recognized by the IMF. In the 2013 G20-IMF meeting, the IMF met with senior managers of the four regional financial arrangements (RFAs) and discussed ways of potential co-operation.[16] The IMF also published a report to elaborate how to incorporate the RFAs into the global financial safety net (IMF,

[16]The four RFAs are: Anti-Crisis Fund of the Eurasian Economic Community (ACF); CMIM; European Stability Mechanism (ESM); and Latin American Reserves Fund (FLAR) (G20, 2013).

2013). Since then, the IMF regularly holds meetings with RFAs.[17] The IMF's constant accommodation of the RFAs opens up another channel for China to exercise its influence: instead of directly confronting with the US, the only veto power, in the issue of IMF governance reform, China can affect the IMF by consistently interacting with the IMF staff and other member states in the bail-out programs.

The experience of the "troika governance"[18] in the Eurozone Debt Crisis and the Greek Crisis demonstrates how creditor countries can leverage their power through the co-operation between the IMF and RFAs. In essence, two ways stand out: the first is the direct power-exercise through co-financing. When the IMF adopts a co-financing strategy with other organizations to conduct its program, it is natural for the IMF to take into account the preferences of those funding partners. The second is normative persuasion through constant interactions during operation. The IMF usually seeks advice and local knowledge from bureaucrats of regional organizations. Those bureaucrats usually come from creditor countries, which may be able to persuade the IMF of their agenda. If those bureaucrats can help the IMF more effectively conduct the bail-out programs without arousing strong grievances, the legitimacy of those countries in international economic governance can increase. This would be very likely to encourage the IMF to accept more voice and leverage from those "rising powers." Evidently, after the successful campaign of AIIB during 2015–2016, the IMF finally approved and included RMB into its "international reserve currency basket" that backs up the special drawing rights (SDR) — The IMF's reserve currency. RMB is alongside the dollar, euro, British pound and Japanese yen (*The Wall Street Journal*, 2016).

Because co-operating with the IMF and World Bank is more strategically beneficial, China is unlikely to make the AIIB a contender in international monetary governance. This is why China keeps emphasizing the supplementary role the AIIB could serve. In fact, this is also the common

---

[17]For example, in 2014 the IMF held a meeting with the ASEAN+3 Macroeconomic Research Office (AMRO), the permanent surveillance unit of the CMIM, to discuss the recent progress of the CMIM and necessary assistance (IMF, 2014); the IMF also met with the Arab Monetary Fund (AMF) and signed a Memorandum of Understanding (MOU) of cooperation in April, 2015 (IMF, 2015).

[18]In dealing with European Sovereign Debt Crisis, the IMF, the European Commission (EC) and the European Central Bank (ECB) worked together in all major rescue programs. The governing body of them has been widely called the "Troika."

standpoint shared by all other rising powers. Again, the BRICS, NDB illustrates this point very well. Despite BRICS countries' sharp criticisms of the IMF (mostly from Russia), the NDB actually is ready to co-operate with the IMF. Its articles already indicate the principle of co-operating with international financial institutions.[19] It also allows the possibility of accepting international financial institutions as observers at the meetings of the Board of Governors.[20] Furthermore, the BRICS CRA has already designed methods of incorporating the IMF in bail-out operation. The rules include: (1) every member state's access to the BRICS CRA has the "IMF-linked portion:" 70% of each member state's maximum access should subject to the existence of an on-track arrangement between the IMF and the requesting member state that involves a commitment of the IMF to provide financing based on conditionality; and (2) the record of a member state's compliance with the IMF conditionality is critical for the approval and renewal of the CRA bail-out package.[21] Such rules suggest an important implication: although those emerging powers are not totally satisfied with the IMF, they recognize its crucial role in international economic governance. Instead of overthrowing or substituting the IMF, they are more willing to promote changes within the institution by engaging and co-operating with the IMF through other supplementary organizational networks.

Conclusion

After the global financial crisis of 2008 and the Euro-Debt crisis, the world has witnessed a sharp decline in international aid and investment from the Western liberal democracies and United States. In the meantime, China has launched ambitious bilateral and multilateral financial statecraft, including the BRI and the establishment of the AIIB and the NDB. However, China's financial statecraft has raised several concerns in the recipient countries especially in Southeast Asia, including corruption, resource monopoly, and environmental unsustainability. Built on the literature on foreign aid and authoritarian foreign policy, this article develops a theory — authoritarian donor's dilemma — to explain China's

---

[19]BRICS NDB Arts. 3(ii), 19(b).

[20]BRICS NDB Arts. 5(d).

[21]BRICS CRA Arts. 5(d), 5(e), 14(b.v).

choice of financial statecraft, its governance problem, and its consequences on the recipient countries in Southeast Asia.

This chapter argues that the governing weakness of China's aid is rooted in a dilemma authoritarian regimes commonly face when wielding their financial power globally. That is, authoritarian regimes need to solve the *fungibility* problem of aid without losing the legitimacy of *non-interference* foreign policy doctrine. On one hand, China wants to make sure that the use of its financial resources is consistent with its national interests. One of the major goals behind Chinese outbound capitals is to solve its domestic problems, from an overcapacity problem and overcoming obstacles to rebalancing domestic socio-economic order. On the other hand, as an authoritarian regime, Chinese leaders need to preserve the international norm of *non-interference* in a country's internal affairs for their own political survival. This leaves China few *ex-post* instruments and little legitimacy to monitor behaviors of aid-receiving countries after disbursing the funds. Therefore, China needs to rely on informal institutions (Chinese state-owned enterprises) and private relationships with local agents in the recipient country to govern its aid. Accordingly, China's aid is susceptible to corruption and tends to provoke local grievance.

I conduct several case studies of China's financial statecraft in Vietnam and Malaysia to show how authoritarian donor's dilemma affects the execution of China's financial statecraft, and how China's strategy has provoked local discontent as well as resistance in Southeast Asia. I show that one of the major goals behind China's outbound capital in Southeast Asia, including foreign aid and state-directed investment, is to solve domestic problems, such as an overcapacity problem, debt problem, economic inequality and lack of social safety net. In both the Vietnam and Malaysia cases, the authoritarian donor's dilemma incentivized China to rely on informal strategy to govern its financial resource overseas, including policy banks, SOEs, and patronage–client relationships. This created opportunities for many local political agents to make opportunistic demands, forcing China to make more concessions or breed the seed of corruption. As a consequence, China's financial statecraft has caused several problems to local societies, including corruption, socio-economic shock, lack of contributions to local employment, and the threat of debt trap. These negative consequences have brought increasing local resistance.

Because the authoritarian donor's dilemma creates a substantial constraint on China's bilateral financial statecraft, China strategically turns to a less controversial mechanism to protect its aid — multilateralism. Resorting to the AIIB and the NDB to govern part of its financial statecraft is likely to allow China to outsource the responsibilities of monitoring and aid contract enforcement while preserving China's interest. However, there is a thorny challenge to China, namely the difficulties in coordinating competing powers, because every major power has its own agenda and unique national interests. In order to co-operate with such a diversified group of countries, China has to pursue a cautious balancing strategy to navigate power conflicts when engaging in multilateralism. The institutional arrangements and the approved projects of the AIIB and the NDB illustrate how China is maintaining a delicate balance among rising powers. While facing great challenges, China-led multilateral financial statecraft still has the potential to achieve its long-term strategic goals, that is, creating additional channels for further internationalizing the RMB and promoting the reforms of global financial governance as well as regional governance in Southeast Asia.

References

AIIB (2020). Project Overview, https://www.aiib.org/en/projects/list/index.html.

Alvaredo, F., A. B. Atkinson, T. Piketty and E. Saez (2013). The Top 1 Percent in International and Historical Perspective. *Journal of Economic Perspectives*, 27(3): 320.

ASEAN (2011). Master Plan on ASEAN Connectivity, https://www.usasean.org/system/files/downloads/MPAC.pdf.

ASEAN (2016). Master Plan on ASEAN Connectivity 2025, https://asean.org/wp-content/uploads/2018/01/47.-December-2017-MPAC2025-2nd-Reprint-.pdf.

Asian Development Bank (ADB) and Asian Development Bank Institute (ABDI) (2009). Infrastructure for a Seamless Asia. Tokyo, Asian Development Bank Institute, http://www.adbi.org/files/2009.08.31.book.infrastructure.seamless.asia.pdf.

Asian Development Bank (ADB) (2012). Infrastructure for Supporting Inclusive Growth and Poverty Reduction in Asia, http://www.adb.org/sites/default/files/publication/29823/infrastructure-supporting-inclusive-growth.pdf.

Bac, P. and B. Murray (2020). Behind Vietnam's COVID-19 Response, Deep Distrust of China. *The Diplomat*, https://thediplomat.com/2020/05/behind-vietnams-covid-19-response-deep-distrust-of-china.

Baldwin, D. A. (1985). *Economic Statecraft*. Princeton, N.J, Princeton University Press.

Beckley, M. (2011). China's Century: Why America's Edge Will Endure? *International Security*, 36: 41–78.

Bloomberg (2015). Yuan Regains Fifth Place in Global Payments Rankings, Swift Says. April 30, 2015, http://www.bloomberg.com/news/articles/2015-04-30/china-s-yuan-regains-fifth-ranking-in-global-payments-swift.

BRICS Contingency Reserve Arrangement (CRA). *The Treaty for The Establishment of a BRICS Contingent Reserve Arrangement (CRA)*, http://brics6.itamaraty.gov.br/agreements.

BRICS Fortaleza Declaration (2014). Fortaleza Declaration and Action Plan, http://brics6.itamaraty.gov.br/category-english/21-documents/223-sixth-summit-declaration-and-action-plan.

BRICS Information Centre (2012). Agreements between BRICS Development Banks. Agreements Signed on March 29, 2012 in New Delhi, India, http://www.brics.utoronto.ca/docs/120329-devbank-agreement.pdf.

BRICS New Development Bank (NDB). *The Agreement on the BRICS New Development Bank (NDB)*, http://brics6.itamaraty.gov.br/agreements.

Brooks, S. G. and W. C. Wohlforth (2016). The Once and Future Superpower: Why China Won't Overtake the United States. *Foreign Affairs*, https://www.foreignaffairs.com/articles/united-states/2016-04-13/once-and-future-superpower.

Bueno de Mesquita, B. *et al.* (2003). *The Logic of Political Survival*. Cambridge, Mass, MIT Press.

Cohen, B. J. (2015). *Currency Power: Understanding Monetary Rivalry*. New Jersey, Princeton University Press.

Drezner, D. W. (1999a). The Trouble with Carrots: Transaction Costs, Conflict Expectations, and Economic Inducements. *Security Studies*, 9(1–2): 188–218.

Drezner, D. W. (1999b). *The Sanctions Paradox*. Cambridge, Cambridge University Press.

Drezner, D. W. (2003). The Hidden Hand of Economic Coercion. *International Organization*, 57(3): 643–659.

Drezner, D. (2009). Bad Debts: Assessing China's Financial Influence in Great Power Politics. *International Security*, 34(2): 7–45.

Eichengreen, B. and Masahiro Kawai (2014). Issues for Renminbi Internationalization: An Overview. *ADBI Working Paper Series* 454, http://www.adbi.org/files/2014.01.20.wp454.issues.renminbi.internationalization.overview.pdf.

Fearon, J. (1994). Domestic Political Audiences and the Escalation of International Disputes. *American Political Science Review*, 88(3): 577–592.

Financial Times (2010). ADB Issues Landmark Renminbi Bond, October 19, 2010, http://www.ft.com/intl/cms/s/0/5ca536cc-db7a-11df-ae99-00144feabdc0.html#axzz3ZPXfOffA.

Financial Times (2015). Venezuela Offers China Tough Lending Lessons: Crisis Holds Mirror to Beijing's State-To-State Financing Model, January 25, 2015, http://www.ft.com/intl/cms/s/0/ae3a606a-a2fa-11e4-ac1c-00144feab7de.html#axzz3YlioXEOu.

Financial Times (2016). China Fund to Buy 10% Stake in Russia's Largest Petrochemicals Group, December 14, 2016, https://www.ft.com/content/a9ac0b64-2b86-37b4-8883-e0b9f4898799.

G20 (2013). G20 and IMF Discussed the RFA's Role in International Financial Architecture. Meeting held at Washington D.C., April 17, 2013, http://en.g20russia.ru/news/20130417/781294747.html.

Gilpin, R. (1981). *War and Change in World Politics*. Cambridge, Cambridge University Press.

Horn, S., C. M. Reinhart and C. Trebesch (2020). China's Overseas Lending. *NBER Working Papers* 26050, https://www.nber.org/papers/w26050.

Ikenberry, G. J. (1999). Institutions, Strategic Restraint, and the Persistence of American Postwar Order. *International Security*, 33(3): 43–78.

Ikenberry, G. J. (2011). *Liberal Leviathan: The Origins, Crisis, and Transformation of the Order*. New Jersey, Princeton University Press.

IMF (2013). Stocktaking the Fund's Engagement with Regional Financing Arrangements. *IMF Survey: Policy*, http://www.imf.org/external/np/pp/eng/2013/041113b.pdf.

IMF (2014). First AMRO-IMF Joint Seminar. Meeting held on January 23, 2014 in Tokyo, Japan, http://www.imf.org/external/np/sec/pr/2014/pr1421.htm.

IMF (2015). The International Monetary Fund (IMF) and the Arab Monetary Fund (AMF) Enhance Cooperation. Meeting held April 19, 2015 in Washington D.C., http://www.imf.org/external/np/sec/pr/2015/pr15171.htm.

Keohane, R. O. (1984). *After Hegemony*. New Jersey, Princeton University Press.

Keohane, R. O. and J. S. Nye (1977). *Power and Interdependence: World Politics in Transition*, Boston, Little, Brown.

Keohane, R. O., S. Macedo and A. Moravcsik (2009). Democracy-Enhancing Multilateralism, *International Organization*, 63(Winter): 1–31.

Kindleberger, C. (1973). *The World in Depression, 1929–1939*. London, Allen.

Krasner, S. D. ed. (1983). *International Regimes*. Ithaca and London, Cornell University Press.

Kynge, J. and G. Wildau (2015). China: With friends like these Financial Times, March 17, 2015, In https://www.ft.com/content/2bb4028a-cbf0-11e4-aeb5-00144feab7de.

Lake, D. A. (2009). *Hierarchy in International Relations*. Ithaca, Cornell University Press.

Lake, D. A. (2013). Legitimating Power: The Domestic Politics of US International Hierarchy. *International Security*, 38(2): 74–111.

Lasswell, H. D. (1936). *Politics; Who Gets What, When, How*. New York, Whittlesey House.

Le, H. H. (2018). The Belt and Road Initiative in Vietnam: Challenges and Prospects. *ISEAS Perspective Issue*, 18: 3–5.

Lektzian, D. J. and C. M. Sprecher (2007). Sanctions, Signals, and Militarized Conflict. *American Journal of Political Science*, 51(2): 415–431.

Liao, S. and D. E. McDowell (2015). No Reservations: International Order and Demand for the Renminbi as a Reserve Currency. Presented at the 2014 American Political Science Association Annual meeting. Washington D.C., https://dl.dropboxusercontent.com/u/11479754/reserve/reserve.pdf.

Liu, H. and G. Lim (2019). The Political Economy of a Rising China in Southeast Asia: Malaysia's Response to the Belt and Road Initiative. *Journal of Contemporary China*, 28(116): 216–231.

Malaysia Rail Link Sdn Bhd (MRL) (2020). FAQ for 2019 ECRL, http://www.mrl.com.my/en/faq/.

Martin, P. and A. Raghu (2018). Mahathir Warns Against New "Colonialism" During Visit to China. *The Bloomberg*, August 20, 2018, https://www.bloomberg.com/news/articles/2018-08-20/mahathir-warns-against-new-colonialism-during-visit-to-china.

Mearsheimer, J. J. (1995). The False Promise of International Institutions, *International Security*, 19(3): 5–49.

Mearsheimer, J. J. (2001). *The Tragedy of Great Power Politics*. New York, W.W. Norton & Company.

Morgenthau, H. (1956). *Politics Among Nations*. New York, Alfred A. Knopf.

New Development Bank (NDB) (2020). Organization, https://www.ndb.int/about-us/organisation/members/.

Nikkei (2015). China Offered Japan No. 2 Post at New Bank, April 15, 2015, http://asia.nikkei.com/Japan-Update/China-offered-Japan-No.-2-post-at-new-bank.

Nikkei Asian Review (2018). Vietnam Ministry Wants Government to Avoid Chinese-AidedProjects,https://asia.nikkei.com/Economy/Vietnam-ministry-wants-government-to-avoid-Chinese-aided-projects.

Nincic, M. (2010). Getting What You Want: Positive Inducements in International Relations. *International Security*, 35(1): 138–183.

NPR (2017). Trump's Budget Slashes Climate Change Funding, http://www.npr.org/sections/thetwo-way/2017/03/16/520399205/trumps-budget-slashes-climate-change-funding.

Nye, J. S. (2004). *Soft Power: The Means to Success in World Politics*. New York, Public Affairs.

Olson, M. (1965). *The Logic of Collective Action: Public Goods and the Theory of Groups*. Cambridge, Harvard University Press.

Pape, R. (1997). Why Economic Sanctions Do Not Work. *International Security*, 22(2): 90–136.

Pettis, M. (2015). Will the AIIB One Day Matter?" http://blog.mpettis.com/2015/04/will-the-aiib-one-day-matter/.

Reilly, J. (2012). China's Unilateral Sanctions. *Washington Quarterly*, 35(4): 121–133, https://csis.org/files/publication/twq12FallReilly.pdf.

Reuters (2019). China, Malaysia Restart Massive "Belt and Road" Project after Hiccups, July 25, 2019, https://www.reuters.com/article/us-china-silkroad-malaysia-idUSKCN1UK0DG.

Reuters (2020). What We Know about China's "Dual Circulation" Economic Strategy, September 6, 2020, https://www.reuters.com/article/china-economy-transformation-explainer-idUSKBN2600B5.

Ruggie, J. G. (1992). Multilateralism: The Anatomy of an Institution, *International Organization*, 46: 561–598.

Sanusi, L. (2013). Africa Must Get Real about Chinese Ties, *Financial Times*, March 11, 2013, http://www.ft.com/intl/cms/s/0/562692b0-898c-11e2-ad3f-00144feabdc0.html#axzz3ZD6Dnvnu.

The Deutsche Welle (2014). BRICS Launch New Bank and Monetary Fund, July 16, 2014, http://www.dw.de/brics-launch-new-bank-and-monetary-fund/a-17789608.

The Economist (2011). The Chinese in Africa: Trying to Pull Together, April 20, 2011, http://www.economist.com/node/18586448.

The Economist (2014a). Why China is Creating a New "World Bank" for Asia., November 11, 2014, http://www.economist.com/blogs/economist-explains/2014/11/economist-explains-6.

The Economist (2014b). The BRICS Bank: An Acronym with Capital, July 19, 2014, http://www.economist.com/news/finance-and-economics/21607851-setting-up-rivals-imf-and-world-bank-easier-running-them-acronym.

The Economist (2015). China's Monetary Policy: The Flawed Analogy of Chinese QE, April 28, 2015, http://www.economist.com/blogs/freeexchange/2015/04/chinas-monetary-policy.

The Economist (2017). The New Davos Man: Xi Jinping Portrays China as a Rock of Stability, http://www.economist.com/news/china/21715035-does-he-really-want-be-global-leader-xi-jinping-portrays-china-rock-stability.

The South China Morning Post (2016). What has Malaysian leader Najib Razak's China Trip Got To Do with 1MDB? October 29, 2016, https://www.scmp.com/week-asia/geopolitics/article/2040709/what-has-malaysian-leader-najib-razaks-china-trip-got-do-1mdb.

The Star (2018). 1MDB Scandal May Involve Money Laundering to China Companies, Tony Pua Tells BBC, July 17, 2018, https://www.thestar.com.my/news/nation/2018/07/17/1mdb-scandal-may-involve-money-laundering-to-china-companies-tony-pua-tells-bbc/.

The Straits Times (2017a). Beijing–KL Relationship at Its Best Ever, says Xi Jinping, May 14, 2017, https://www.straitstimes.com/asia/east-asia/beijing-kl-relationship-at-its-best-ever-says-xi.

The Straits Times (2017b). Malaysia's PM Najib Hails East Coast Rail Link as "Game-Changer", August 9, 2017, https://www.straitstimes.com/asia/se-asia/malaysias-pm-najib-hails-east-coast-rail-link-as-game-changer.

The Straits Times (2019). Beware of China "Debt Trap": Said Mahathir Mohamad, March 8, 2019, https://www.straitstimes.com/asia/beware-of-china-debt-trap-mahathir.

The Wall Street Journal (2015a). Congress Set to Approve Overhaul of IMF's Governance, https://www.wsj.com/articles/congress-set-to-approve-imf-governance-overhaul-1450280799.

The Wall Street Journal (2015b). China Readies $46 Billion for Pakistan Trade Route, April 16, 2015, http://www.wsj.com/articles/china-to-unveil-billions-of-dollars-in-pakistan-investment-1429214705?mod=trending_now_3.

The Wall Street Journal (2015c). Yuan is World's Fifth Payments Currency, January 15, 2015, http://www.wsj.com/articles/yuan-is-worlds-fifth-payments-currency-1422431603.

The Wall Street Journal (2015d). Japan Overtakes China as Largest U.S. Bondholder, April 15, 2015, http://www.wsj.com/articles/japan-overtakes-china-as-largest-u-s-bondholder-1429129765.

The Wall Street Journal (2016). Why the Yuan Still Has Long Way to Go to Supplant U.S. Dollar, September 30, 2016, https://www.wsj.com/articles/BL-MBB-53945.

The Wall Street Journal (2019). China Offered to Bail Out Troubled Malaysian Fund in Return for Deals, https://www.wsj.com/articles/how-china-flexes-its-political-muscle-to-expand-power-overseas-11546890449.

The Wall Street Journal (2020). Trump Moves to Pull U.S. Out of World Health Organization in Midst of Covid-19 Pandemic, July 7, 2020, https://www.wsj.com/articles/white-house-says-u-s-has-pulled-out-of-the-world-health-organization-11594150928.

The Washington Post (2017). Trump Suggests Ignoring World Trade Organization in Major Policy Shift, https://www.washingtonpost.com/news/wonk/wp/2017/03/01/trump-may-ignore-wto-in-major-shift-of-u-s-trade-policy/?utm_term=.ad79700215e4.

Thompson, A. and D. Verdier (2014). Multilateralism, Bilateralism, and Regime Design. *International Studies Quarterly*, 58(1): 15–28.

Tiezzi, S. (2014). China's "New Silk Road" Vision Revealed. *The Diplomat*, May 9, 2014, http://thediplomat.com/2014/11/the-new-silk-road-chinas-marshall-plan/.

Tiezzi, S. (2015). Maduro: China Gives $5 Billion Loan to Venezuela. *The Diplomat*, April 21, 2015, http://thediplomat.com/2014/11/the-new-silk-road-chinas-marshall-plan/.

VN Express International (2019). Hanoi Metro Inauguration Delayed Yet Again. https://e.vnexpress.net/news/news/hanoi-metro-inauguration-delayed-yet-again-3916746.html.

Waltz, K. (1979). *Theory of International Politics*. New York, McGraw-Hill.

Wolf, C., Xiao Wang and E. Warner (2013). *China's Foreign Aid and Government-Sponsored Investment Activities: Scale, Content, Destinations, and Implications*. Santa Monica, CA, RAND Corporation, http://www.rand.org/pubs/research_reports/RR118.

Xinhuanet (2014). China Pledges 40 Bln USD for Silk Road Fund, November 8, 2014, http://news.xinhuanet.com/english/china/2014-11/08/c_133774993.htm.

Xinhuanet. China's Initiatives on Building Silk Road Economic Belt and 21st Century Maritime Silk Road, https://english.news.cn/20211015/C99FC9852A90000116FA7F0015841911/c.html.

https://doi.org/10.1142/9789811250668_0004

Chapter 4

Historical Change of the International Trade of Southeast Asia and Its Relations with Japan

Hiroyoshi Kano

Emeritus Professor, The University of Tokyo, Japan

Introduction

Relations with East Asia, particularly with Japan and China, have played an important role in the development and structural change of Southeast Asian economies in the 20th and 21st centuries, even when most of them were under the Western colonial rule before the Second World War. The principal purpose of this chapter is to make a survey of the historical change in economic relations between Southeast Asia and East Asia for the last 100 years from the 1910s to the 2010s, with special attention to the Japanese position and role in the international trade and foreign direct investment among the major Southeast Asian countries by resorting to the official statistical data.

Under the colonial regime that was established at the end of the 19th century, the production of primary commodities for export had developed as the pivotal sector of economy in Southeast Asian countries. Even though these countries have attained the national independence after the end of the Second World War, such economic structure was sustained for a good while. Since the 1960s, import-substituting industrialization has started in several Southeast Asian countries. Nevertheless, primary commodities such as rubber, sugar, rice and petroleum had held the principal position of export items until the 1970s. After the start-up of export-oriented industrialization in the 1980s, they were gradually replaced by manufactured goods. At the end of the 2010s, manufactured goods already hold the principal position of export items in most of ASEAN countries. In parallel with such transformation, the economic relations between Southeast Asia and Japan through international trade and direct investment has also underwent different phases of historical change since the beginning of the 20th century until the present day. This chapter examines such historical change by presenting the statistical data on the international trade and the direct investment of each phase.

Colonial Age before the Second World War

After the annexation of Burma into British India in 1886 and the formation of French Indochina by uniting Vietnam, Laos and Cambodia in 1887, the whole area of Southeast Asia except Thailand (Siam as it was known then) came under the Western colonial rule. In parallel with the deepening of colonial rule, the production of primary commodities for export to the world market had developed as key industry of the regional economy, such as cane sugar in Dutch East Indies (What is now Indonesia) and the Philippines, natural rubber and tin in British Malaya (What is now a part of Malaysia) together with Dutch East Indies, and rice in Burma, Siam and French Indochina. The colonial regime endured until the 1950s when most of the Southeast Asian countries had attained the national independence.

Table 1 shows the major destination of export from six Southeast Asian countries in the 3 years of 1913, 1929 and 1937 all before the Second World War. On the other hand, Table 2 shows the major origin of import to these countries in the same years. In 1913, a year before the outbreak of the First World War, the most important destination of export from Dutch East Indies, British Malaya and the Philippines were their suzerain states, namely the Netherlands, the United Kingdom and the United States. In case of French Indochina and Siam whose top export commodity was rice, the principal destination of export was the ports of transit to the adjacent Asian consumer market of rice, that is, Hong Kong and Singapore (comprised in British Malaya). Both ports were then under the British rule. In the meantime, France as the suzerain of Indochina, also held the second place among its destination of export. At the same time, the principal origins of import

Table 1: Major destination of export from six Southeast Asian countries before the Second World War
(Top five countries, % in value)

Country	Year	1		2		3		4		5	
Dutch East Indies	1913	Netherlands	28.1	British Malaya	21.0	British India	14.5	Japan	5.8	Hong Kong	5.6
	1929	British Malaya	22.9	Netherlands	16.0	USA	11.5	British India	9.9	UK	8.8
	1937	Netherlands	20.1	British Malaya	20.1	USA	18.7	UK	5.3	Japan	4.5
British Malaya[a]	1913	UK	28.8	Dutch East Indies	16.6	USA	14.2	British India	7.9	Germany	5.7
	1929	USA	42.2	UK	14.3	Dutch East Indies	9.4	Japan	4.2	France	4.1
	1937	USA	44.2	UK	11.1	France	7.7	Japan	6.7	Dutch East Indies	3.9
Philippines	1913	USA	36.8	UK	16.9	Japan	7.1	Hong Kong	5.7	Spain	4.5
	1929	USA	75.7	Japan	4.3	UK	4.3	China	1.9	France	1.4
	1937	USA	9.8	Japan	6.6	UK	4.1	Germany	1.2	Netherlands	0.7
French Indochina	1913	Hong Kong	32.7	France	26.3	Singapore	11.1	Dutch East Indies	7.0	Japan	6.1
	1929	Hong Kong	32.1	France	22.1	British Malaya	10.8	Dutch East Indies	9.8	China	7.2
	1937	France	46.1	Hong Kong	11.4	British Malaya	7.6	USA	6.9	China	5.4
Siam[b]	1913	British Malaya	38.7	Hong Kong	32.2	Netherlands	7.2	Germany	6.4	UK	5.0
	1929	British Malaya	55.4	Hong Kong	16.8	Japan	7.3	Dutch East Indies	4.8	UK	1.5
	1937	British Malaya	66.5	Hong Kong	12.5	Japan	3.5	British India	2.5	UK	1.6
Burma[c]	1937	British India	50.9	UK	16.9	British Malaya	6.9	Germany	3.8	Japan	2.8

Note: [a]Before the Second World War Singapore was a part of British Malaya.
[b]Siam was renamed to Thailand in 1939.
[c]Burma was separated from British India in 1937.
Sources: Calculated from the statistical data contained in Taiwan Government-General Secretariat (1935) and Nan-yo Kyokai (1934).

Table 2: Major origin of import to six Southeast Asian countries before the Second World War (Top five countries, % in value)

Country	Year	1		2		3		4		5	
Dutch East Indies	1913	Netherlands	33.3	British Malaya	18.7	UK	17.5	Germany	6.6	British India	6.2
	1929	Netherlands	19.6	USA	12.0	British Malaya	11.8	UK	10.8	Germany	10.7
	1937	Japan	25.4	Netherlands	19.1	USA	10.2	Germany	8.5	UK	8.3
British Malaya[a]	1913	Dutch East Indies	19.2	British India	14.9	UK	14.5	Siam	12.8	Hong Kong	11.6
	1929	Dutch East Indies	30.4	UK	16.5	Siam	11.0	British India	8.2	China	4.6
	1937	Dutch East Indies	32.4	UK	15.6	Siam	13.6	Japan	5.8	Burma	4.2
Philippines	1913	USA	46.5	UK	10.0	Australia	5.0	Japan	4.9	Germany	4.9
	1929	USA	62.9	Japan	8.1	China	4.8	UK	4.1	French Indochina	3.9
	1937	USA	59.1	Japan	14.8	China	3.0	UK	2.4	British India	2.2
French Indochina	1913	France	30.1	Hong Kong	19.4	Singapore	6.2	China	5.9	UK	1.2
	1929	France	47.2	Hong Kong	15.9	Dutch East Indies	7.3	China	6.7	USA	5.2
	1937	France	53.5	China	9.2	Hong Kong	8.7	Dutch East Indies	4.4	British Malaya	3.7
Siam[b]	1913	UK	21.6	British Malaya	17.1	Hong Kong	16.0	British India	10.3	China	9.7
	1929	British Malaya	16.9	UK	16.5	Hong Kong	14.9	Dutch East Indies	8.6	Japan	8.1
	1937	British Malaya	27.2	Japan	19.8	UK	12.2	Hong Kong	7.6	Dutch East Indies	5.0
Burma[c]	1937	British India	49.2	Japan	8.8	USA	4.3	British Malaya	2.6	UK	2.0

Note: [a]Before the Second World War Singapore was a part of British Malaya.
[b]Siam was renamed to Thailand in 1939.
[c]Burma was separated from British India in 1937.
Sources: Calculated from the statistical data contained in Taiwan Government-General Secretariat (1935) and Nan-yo Kyokai (1934).

to Dutch East Indies, British Malaya, the Philippines and French Indochina were also their suzerain states, as indicated by Table 2. On the other hand, more than half of export from Siam was in total bound for the United Kingdom, Malaya and Hong Kong. All of them were within the British territory. In other words, the international trade of Southeast Asia in this period was firmly connected with the areas dominated by Western colonial powers. Southeast Asia exported primary commodities and imported manufactured goods. In such circumstances, the Japanese presence in the international trade of Southeast Asia was still minor. It merely held the third and fourth positions as the destination of export from the Philippines and Dutch East Indies.

Such situation began to change during the First World War. The trade with Europe via Suez Canal and the Mediterranean Sea was blocked and the substitutional import of manufactured goods from Japan and the United States temporarily increased. Even though the trade with Europe had restored after the war. the United States became the significant destination of export from British Malaya and Dutch East Indies in the 1920s as evidenced by the data for the year 1929 of Table 1. The rapidly growing automobile industry in the United States demanded the large amount of natural rubber produced in Southeast Asia as the major raw materials of tire. On the other hand, the economic development of Japan had also conduced the growth of its import from Southeast Asia. As a result, in 1929 Japan advanced to the second, third and fourth ranked destination of export respectively from the Philippines, Siam and British Malaya.

In the time of Great Depression after 1929, the origin of import to Southeast Asia had significantly changed. In 1937, Japan had achieved the top position as the origin of import to Dutch East Indies as shown by Table 2. Also in Siam, Burma and the Philippines, it had jumped to the second position as the origin of import. Even in British Malaya, Japan had emerged as the fourth ranked origin of its import. Cotton textiles and sundry goods from Japan flooded the consumer market in Southeast Asia.

Even before 1929, Japan was an important destination of cane sugar export from Java, as the core region of Dutch East Indies. In the 1920s, Java was the second ranked exporter of cane sugar after Cuba in the world and sugar was a most important export commodity of Dutch East Indies together with natural rubber that was mainly produced in Sumatra. Table 3 shows the destination of Javanese sugar export from 1890 to 1923. In the 1890s, Europe and the United States were the most important destination of sugar export from Java. The situation had changed

Table 3: Destination of sugar export from Java (1890–1924)

		1890–1894	1895–1899	1900–1904	1905–1909	1910–1914	1915–1919	1920–1923
Area / Country		**Average**	**Average**	**Average**	**Average**	**Average**	**Average**	**Average**
[Unit: 1,000 tons]								
Asia		148.9	175.4	369.5	611.3	907.6	911.1	1.036.6
	British India	5.3	7.6	52.4	251.9	467.3	389.8	444.9
	China and Hong Kong	122.6	137.9	191.6	173.8	207.2	215.7	276.0
	Japan and Taiwan	—	8.7	85.1	145.7	153.6	188.5	247.8
	Others	21.0	21.2	40.4	39.9	79.5	117.1	67.9
Outside Asia		313.4	436.9	468.0	395.2	385.4	539.5	529.3
	Europe	164.0	142.7	62.3	16.0	156.0	432.9	235.9
	Port Said and Suez[a]	—	—	225.4	254.3	168.6	51.6	182.9
	USA	106.7	277.7	115.7	89.5	28.6	10.8	72.5
	Others	42.7	16.5	64.6	35.4	32.2	44.2	38.0
Total		462.3	612.3	837.5	1,006.7	1,293.4	1,451.3	1579.4
[Unit: %]								
Asia		32.2	28.6	44.1	60.7	70.2	62.8	65.6
	British India	1.1	1.2	6.3	25.0	36.1	26.9	28.2
	China and Hong Kong	26.5	22.5	22.9	17.3	16.0	14.9	17.5
	Japan and Taiwan	—	1.4	10.2	14.5	11.9	13.0	15.7
	Others	4.5	3.5	4.8	4.0	6.1	8.1	4.3
Outside Asia		67.8	71.4	55.9	39.3	29.8	37.2	33.5
	Europe	35.5	23.3	7.4	1.6	12.1	29.8	14.9
	Port Said and Suez[a]	—	—	26.9	25.3	13.0	3.6	11.6
	USA	23.1	45.4	13.8	8.9	2.2	0.7	4.6
	Others	9.2	2.7	7.7	3.5	2.5	3.0	2.4
Total		100.0	100.0	100.0	100.0	100.0	100.0	100.0

Note: [a]Including the re-export to Europe.
Source: Geerligs (1924), pp. 182–183.

however, since the end of the 19th century. By the increase of beet sugar production in Europe and the takeover of the Philippines (another cane sugar exporter in Southeast Asia) by the United States from Spain, the proportion of sugar export to the West from Java began to decline remarkably. Since the latter half of the 1900s, the export to Asia. held more than 60% of the total amount of sugar export from Java. In Asia, Japan (including Taiwan) became the third ranked destination after British India and China (including Hong Kong). Even after the annexation of Taiwan in 1895 and the development of modern sugar industry there, Japan constantly imported raw sugar from Java and refined it chiefly for the export to China.

As evidenced by Table 4, Japanese trading corporations were deeply involved in business for the sugar export from Java in the 1920s, not only to Japan but also to other countries in Asia. In addition, among Japanese citizens who pursued sugar trade in Java were included Chinese merchants who had acquired Japanese citizenship as *Taiwan sekimin* (台湾籍民), meaning "persons registered in Taiwan". Kwik Djoen Eng (郭春秧) was the most prominent and successful one among such merchants (Claver, 2014: 289–299; Kudo, 2005).

Rise of the Trade with Japan from the Late 1950s to the 1970s

In the last month of 1941, Japan declared war against the United States and the United Kingdom. From March 1942 to August 1945, the nearly whole area of Southeast Asia was under the Japanese control. Nonetheless, Japan was unsuccessful in creating a self-reliant economic bloc that comprised Southeast Asia and Japan because of its insufficient industrial capacity and the military attack of the Allied Forces against the maritime transportation route.

From August 1945 to April 1952, Japan was under the rule of General Headquarters of Allied Forces set up in Tokyo. After recovering the sovereignty, the Japanese government began to restore the diplomatic relations with other countries. In Southeast Asia, the national independence was attained by most countries before the 1950s. In the latter half of the 1950s, Japan established economic relations officially with Burma, the Philippines, Indonesia and South Vietnam by concluding the wartime reparation

Table 4: Purchase amount of Javanese export sugar classified by kinds of buyers

Harvest year	European buyers		Japanese buyers		Chinese buyers		Other buyers		Total	
of sugar cane	1,000 pikuls	(%)	1,000 pikuls	(%)	1,000 pikuls	(%)	1,000 pikuls	(%)	1,000 pikuls	(%)
1920	10,874	48.8	6,597	29.6	3,957	17.8	848	3.8	22,276	100.0
1921	8,623	35.5	7,147	29.4	7,253	29.9	1,264	5.2	24,287	100.0
1922	7,568	29.2	9,992	38.5	7,023	27.1	1,351	5.2	25,934	100.0
1923	7,894	30.6	9,924	38.5	5,293	20.5	2,683	10.4	25,794	100.0
1924	8,953	31.0	10,383	35.9	8,658	29.9	932	3.2	28,926	100.0
1925	11,470	34.5	11,502	34.6	9,456	28.4	834	2.5	33,262	100.0
1926	9,209	31.0	11,506	38.8	7,514	25.3	1,460	4.9	29,689	100.0
1927	8,150	26.9	14,575	48.1	6,700	22.1	887	2.9	30,312	100.0

Source: Mandere (1928), p. 95.

agreements. The high economic growth in Japan after 1955 enabled the rapid expansion of international trade with Southeast Asia.

Table 5 shows the details of international trade of five Southeast Asian countries in 1960. Major items of their export were still primary commodities such as natural rubber, petroleum (categorized as mineral fuels), copra, rice and sugar. The United States and the United Kingdom maintained the pivotal position as the trade partners of Southeast Asia. On the other hand, Japan had already emerged as an important destination of export from Thailand, the Philippines and Malaya. Japan also held the high position as origin of import to Indonesia, Thailand and the Philippines.

Since the late 1960s the direct investment of Japanese manufacturing enterprises in Southeast Asia started to expand. International trade with Japan had also rapidly increased. Table 6 shows the details of international trade of five countries in 1970.[1] The principal items of their export were still primary commodities as in 1960. The top position as the origin of import was now held by Japan for all of them. Japan had become the major supplier of manufactured goods for Southeast Asia. Japanese position as the destination of export was also rising and stood on a par with the United States. In contrast, the United Kingdom had lost its position as a trade partner.

Massive inflow of Japanese manufacturing enterprises in Southeast Asia triggered the anti-Japanese demonstrations in Thailand and Indonesia when the Japanese prime minister made a round of visit to Southeast Asia in January 1974. Despite such accidents, economic exchanges between Southeast Asia and Japan steadily expanded through the 1970s. Table 7 shows the details of international trade of five Southeast Asian countries in 1980. Japan kept the dominant position as partner of their trade. Primary commodities such as petroleum, rubber and sugar still made up the most important part of export items in Indonesia, Malaysia and the Philippines. In contrast, primary commodities were giving way to manufactured goods as the export items of Singapore and Thailand. Waves of industrialization in Southeast Asia began to spread in this period.

---

[1] Malaysia was founded in 1963 by uniting Federation of Malaya, Singapore, North Borneo (Sabah) and Sarawak. But, Singapore withdrew from Malaysia and became an independent nation in 1965. Then, five countries in Table 6 jointly founded Association of Southeast Asian Nations (ASEAN) in 1967.

Table 5: Details of international trade of five Southeast Asian countries (1960)

	Amount of trade (million US$)									
	Indonesia		**Singapore**		**Federation of Malaya**		**Philippines**		**Thailand**	
	Export	840	Export	1,136	Export	956	Export	560	Export	399
	Import	574	Import	1,332	Import	703	Import	604	Import	453
	Indonesia	**(%)**	**Singapore**	**(%)**	**Federation of Malaya**	**(%)**	**Philippines**	**(%)**	**Thailand**	**(%)**
	Major export items (proportion to the total amount of export)									
No. 1	Natural rubber	45.0	Natural rubber	41.0	Natural rubber	61.2	Copra	24.7	Crude rubber	30.6
No. 2	Mineral fuels[a]	26.3	Mineral fuels[a]	11.3	Tin[c]	17.3	Sugar	23.8	Rice	30.5
No. 3	Tin ore	6.0	Textile[b]	4.1	Iron ore[d]	4.8	Cork and woods	16.4	Maize (unmilled)	6.5
	Major origin import items (proportion to the total amount of import)									
No. 1	Japan	16.1	Indonesia	24.5	Indonesia	21.5	USA	42.3	Japan	25.8
No. 2	USA	15.6	Fed. of Malaya	20.9	Fed. Of Malaya	15.1	Japan	26.4	USA	16.8
No. 3	China	9.9	China	8.9	UK	11.6	Indonesia	4.8	UK	9.9
	Major destination export items (proportion to the total amount of export)									
No. 1	Singapore	23.1	Fed. of Malaya	24.2	Singapore	21.7	USA	50.7	Japan	18.1
No. 2	USA	23.1	UK	8.2	UK	13.1	Japan	23.5	Fed. of Malaya	16.0
No. 3	UK	10.9	USA	7.0	Japan	12.6	Netherlands	8.3	USA	14.2

Note: [a]Mineral fuels, lubricants and related materials (SITC 3).
[b]Textile yarn, fabrics and made-up articles (SITC 65).
[c]Tin and tin alloys, unwrought (SITC 687 01).
[d]Iron ore and concentrates (SITC 281).
Source: United Nations. *International Trade Statistics Yearbook 1961*.

Table 6: Details of international trade of five ASEAN countries (1970)

	Amount of trade (million US$)									
	Indonesia		**Singapore**		**Malaysia**		**Philippines**		**Thailand**	
	Export	1,055	Export	1,554	Export	1,764	Export	1,060	Export	710
	Import	892	Import	2,461	Import	1,489	Import	1,210	Import	1,293
	Indonesia	**(%)**	**Singapore**	**(%)**	**Malaysia**	**(%)**	**Philippines**	**(%)**	**Thailand**	**(%)**
	Major export items (proportion to the total amount of export)									
No. 1	Petroleum[a]	32.8	Rubber	24.7	Rubber	32.0	Wood[b]	23.8	Rice	17.0
No. 2	Rubber	23.6	Petroleum[a]	23.1	Basic Manu.[d]	22.7	Sugar[e]	18.7	Rubber	15.2
No. 3	Wood[b]	10.0	Machines[c]	11.0	Wood[b]	15.8	Copper[f]	18.0	Fruit and vegetables	11.0
	Major origin import items (proportion to the total amount of import)									
No. 1	Japan	29.5	Japan	19.4	Japan	16.6	Japan	30.5	Japan	37.6
No. 2	USA	17.7	Malaysia	18.6	UK	12.8	UK	29.3	USA	14.9
No. 3	West Germany	9.5	USA	10.8	USA	8.2	USA	5.7	UK	8.5
	Major destination export items (proportion to the total amount of export)									
No. 1	Japan	33.3	Malaysia	21.9	Singapore	20.6	USA	41.7	Japan	25.5
No. 2	Singapore	15.8	USA	11.1	Japan	17.5	Japan	39.6	USA	13.4
No. 3	USA	14.0	Japan	7.6	USA	12.4	Netherlands	4.1	Netherlands	8.6

Note: [a] Petroleum and products (SITC 33).
[b] Wood, lumber and cork (SITC 24).
[c] Machines, transport equipment (SITC 7).
[d] Basic Manufactures (SITC 6).
[e] Sugar and preparations, honey (SITC 06).
[f] Copper ores, concentrate (SITC 283 1).
Source: United Nations. *International Trade Statistics Yearbook 1974*.

Table 7: Details of international trade of five ASEAN countries (1980)

	Amount of trade (million US$)									
	Indonesia		**Singapore**		**Malaysia**		**Philippines**		**Thailand**	
	Export	21,909	Export	19,375	Export	12,939	Export	5,788	Export	6,505
	Import	10,834	Import	24,003	Import	10,735	Import	8,295	Import	9,450
	Indonesia	**(%)**	**Singapore**	**(%)**	**Malaysia**	**(%)**	**Philippines**	**(%)**	**Thailand**	**(%)**
	Major export items (proportion to the total amount of export)									
No. 1	Petroleum[a]	58.7	Petroleum[a]	28.5	Petroleum[a]	24.7	Sugar[f]	11.4	Basic Manu.[e]	21.7
No. 2	Natural gas[b]	13.2	Machines[d]	26.8	Crude rubber	16.4	Coconut (copra) oil	9.8	Rice	14.7
No. 3	Cork and wood[c]	8.9	Basic Manu.[e]	8.3	Cork and wood[c]	14.2	Copper ore[g]	9.4	Crude rubber	9.3
	Major origin import (proportion to the total amount of import)									
No. 1	Japan	31.5	Japan	17.8	Japan	23.0	USA	23.6	Japan	20.7
No. 2	USA	13.0	USA	14.1	USA	15.0	Japan	19.9	USA	16.6
No. 3	Saudi Arabia	8.9	Malaysia	13.9	Singapore	11.7	USA	10.0	Saudi Arabia	9.9
	Major destination export (proportion to the total amount of export)									
No. 1	Japan	49.3	Malaysia	15.0	Japan	22.8	USA	27.5	Japan	15.1
No. 2	USA	19.6	USA	12.7	Singapore	19.1	Japan	26.6	USA	13,2
No. 3	Singapore	11.3	Japan	8.1	USA	16.3	Netherlands	6.3	Netherlands	12.7

Note: [a] Petroleum and products (SITC 33).
[b] Gas, natural and manufactured (SITC 341).
[c] SITC 24.
[d] Machines, transport equipment (SITC 7).
[e] Basic Manufactures (SITC 6).
[f] Sugar and preparations, honey (SITC 06).
[g] Copper ores, concentrate (SITC 283 1).
Source: United Nations. *International Trade Statistics Yearbook 1983*.

Two Decades at the End of the 20th Century

On account of the high economic growth and technological innovation, the international competitiveness of Japanese manufacturing industries had rapidly risen since the 1960s. The principal destination of Japanese export of manufactured goods was the United States. As a result, the trade surplus with the United States had increased rapidly after 1965 and had triggered off the chronic trade conflict between the United States and Japan. Major export items from Japan that conduced to the trade surplus had changed with the times. Since the latter half of the 1960s until the beginning of the 1970s, they were textile products. Then, in the latter half of the 1970s steel products became the primary factor of the trade surplus. Finally, automobiles and semiconductors became the focus of the conflict in the 1980s.

The United States decided to make a breakthrough by the devaluation of US dollar against the currencies of other advanced countries, especially Japanese yen. In September 1985, a joint-agreement called the Plaza Accord was signed at the Plaza Hotel in New York between France, West Germany, Japan, the United Kingdom and the United States, to depreciate the US dollar in relation to yen and German mark by intervening in currency markets. After the Plaza Accord, the rise in the yen's value drastically accelerated. The US dollar exchange rate in Tokyo currency market was more than 240 yen before the Plaza Accord. Then, it had declined to less than 200 yen at the end of 1985, further to 128 yen at the beginning of 1988.

In the long run, the appreciation of yen brought the gradual decline of competitiveness of Japanese export industries. To avoid this disadvantage, the overseas transfer of manufacturing production sites from Japan by foreign direct investment was given a strong impetus. On the other hand, a low-interest policy was continuously maintained within Japan for the purpose of preventing the economic slump. Such trend had induced to the soaring asset prices and the outbreak of bubble economy. The collapse of the bubble economy at the end of the 1980s in Japan brought about the prolonged stagnation, which also prompted the overseas transfer of production bases by direct investment.

For the nearly 10 years after 1985, the principal destination of Japanese foreign direct investment was North America. From the end of the 1990s, Asia became the main target of the direct investment. China and ASEAN were the most important destination. Thus, the foreign direct investment of Japan has developed in parallel with the accelerated industrialization of neighboring Asian countries. Such structural change was also reflected in the international trade between ASEAN countries and Japan after the 1980s.

Table 8 shows the details of international trade of five ASEAN countries in 1990. Machinery and transport equipment had become the principal export item in Singapore and Malaysia, while it had also risen to the second-ranked item of export in the Philippines and Thailand. Even in Indonesia, manufactured goods had already become the second-ranked item of export. In other words, the industrialization of Southeast Asia had entered the further stage of development. Even in this year, Japan held the dominant position as the origin of import to these countries. On the contrary, as the destination of export its position had fallen behind the United States, except in Indonesia.

Besides its five founding members, Brunei, Vietnam, Laos together with Myanmar, and Cambodia joined ASEAN respectively in 1984, 1995, 1997 and 1999. As a result, ASEAN now covered the whole area of Southeast Asia. Despite the 1997 Asian financial crisis that started in Thailand and spread over most of Southeast Asia, ASEAN economies had returned to the normal track of development before 2000. As demonstrated by Table 9, manufactured goods represented by machinery had already made up more than 60% of the total amount of export from Singapore, Malaysia, the Philippines and Thailand. Even in Indonesia, the proportion of manufactured goods surpassed that of mineral fuels in their total amount of export. In this year, Japan steadily held the top position as the origin of import to all these countries. In contrast, the proportion of export to Japan showed the sign of gradual decline in all of them.

Structural Change in the 21st Century

For nearly 30 years since the end of the 1970s, the industrialization of leading ASEAN countries proceeded rapidly and the international relationship of manufacturing production among them became closer. Accordingly, the amount of intra-ASEAN international trade had also fairly expanded in this period. On the other hand, the major focus of Japanese interests in the economic exchange with Southeast Asia had gradually shifted from the expansion of trade to the deepening of investment. As a result, the Japanese share as a major trade partner of ASEAN has gradually declined for the first two decades of the 21st century. Figure 1 clearly shows the change of major trade partners of ASEAN for the three decades from 1980 to 2010. The

Table 8: Details of international trade of five ASEAN countries (1990)

	Amount of trade (million US$)									
	Indonesia		**Singapore**		**Malaysia**		**Philippines**		**Thailand**	
	Export	25,553	Export	52,627	Export	29,446	Export	8,186	Export	23,067
	Import	21,837	Import	60,647	Import	27,841	Import	13,040	Import	33,129
	Indonesia	**(%)**	**Singapore**	**(%)**	**Malaysia**	**(%)**	**Philippines**	**(%)**	**Thailand**	**(%)**
	Major export items (proportion to the total amount of export)									
No. 1	Petroleum[a]	24.3	Machines[d]	50.2	Machines[d]	35.7	Misc. Manu.[e]	16.4	Misc. Manu.[e]	26.1
No. 2	Basic Manu.[b]	11.5	Petroleum[a]	18.1	Petroleum[a]	14.9	Machines[d]	12.5	Machines[d]	22.0
No. 3	Natural gas[c]	6.9	Misc. Manu.[e]	9.0	Cork and wood[f]	9.6	Basic Manu.[b]	9.3	Basic Manu.[b]	13.7
	Major origin of import (proportion to the total amount of import)									
No. 1	Japan	25.9	Japan	20.1	Japan	25.3	USA	19.5	Japan	30.6
No. 2	USA	15.3	USA	16.0	USA	17.6	Japan	18.4	USA	10.9
No. 3	Saudi Arabia	14.6	Germany	13.7	Malaysia	14.6	Saudi Arabia	4.4	Germany	7.5
	Major destination of export (proportion to the total amount of export)									
No. 1	Japan	42.7	USA	21.3	Singapore	22.8	USA	37.9	USA	22.7
No. 2	USA	13.2	Malaysia	13.0	USA	16.9	Japan	19.8	Japan	17.2
No. 3	Singapore	7.1	Japan	8.7	Japan	15.8	Germany	4.8	Singapore	7.3

Note: [a]Petroleum and products (SITC 33).

[b]Basic manufactured goods (SITC 6).

[c]Gas, natural and manufactured (SITC 341).

[d]Machinery and transport equipment (SITC 7).

[e]Miscellaneous manufactured goods (SITC 8).

[f]SITC 24.

Source: United Nations. *International Trade Statistics Yearbook 1993*.

Table 9: Details of international trade of five ASEAN countries (2000)

	Amount of trade (million US$)									
	Indonesia		**Singapore**		**Malaysia**		**Philippines**		**Thailand**	
	Export	62,124	Export	137,806	Export	98,230	Export	38,078	Export	68,787
	Import	33,515	Import	134,546	Import	81,290	Import	31,694	Import	61,451
	Indonesia	**(%)**	**Singapore**	**(%)**	**Malaysia**	**(%)**	**Philippines**	**(%)**	**Thailand**	**(%)**
	Major export items (proportion to the total amount of export)									
No. 1	Petroleum[a]	25.2	Machines[c]	67.4	Machines[c]	62.5	Machines[c]	36.9	Machines[c]	43.7
No. 2	Basic Manu.[b]	19.9	Petroleum[a]	9.7	Petroleum[a]	9.6	Misc. Manu.[d]	7.0	Basic Manu.[b]	15.4
No. 3	Machines[c]	17.3	Misc. Manu.[e]	8.1	Misc. Manu.[d]	8.0	Food[e]	3.4	Food[e]	14.1
	Major origin of import (proportion to the total amount of import)									
No. 1	Japan	16.1	Japan	17.2	Japan	21.2	Japan	20.4	Japan	24.9
No. 2	Singapore	11.3	Malaysia	17.0	USA	16.8	USA	18.0	USA	10.6
No. 3	USA	10.1	USA	15.1	Singapore	14.5	South Korea	7.8	Singapore	5.5
	Major destination of export (proportion to the total amount of export)									
No. 1	Japan	23.2	Malaysia	18.2	USA	20.5	USA	30.0	USA	21.4
No. 2	USA	13.7	USA	17.3	Singapore	18.4	Japan	14.7	Japan	14.8
No. 3	Singapore	10.6	Hong Kong	7.9	Japan	13.1	Singapore	8.2	Singapore	8.7

Note: [a]Mineral fuels, lubricants and related materials (SITC 3).
[b]Manufactured goods classified chiefly by materials (SITC 6).
[c]Machinery and transport equipment (SITC 7).
[d]Miscellaneous manufactured articles (SITC 8).
[e]Food and live animals (SITC 0).
Source: United Nations. *International Trade Statistics Yearbook 2000.*

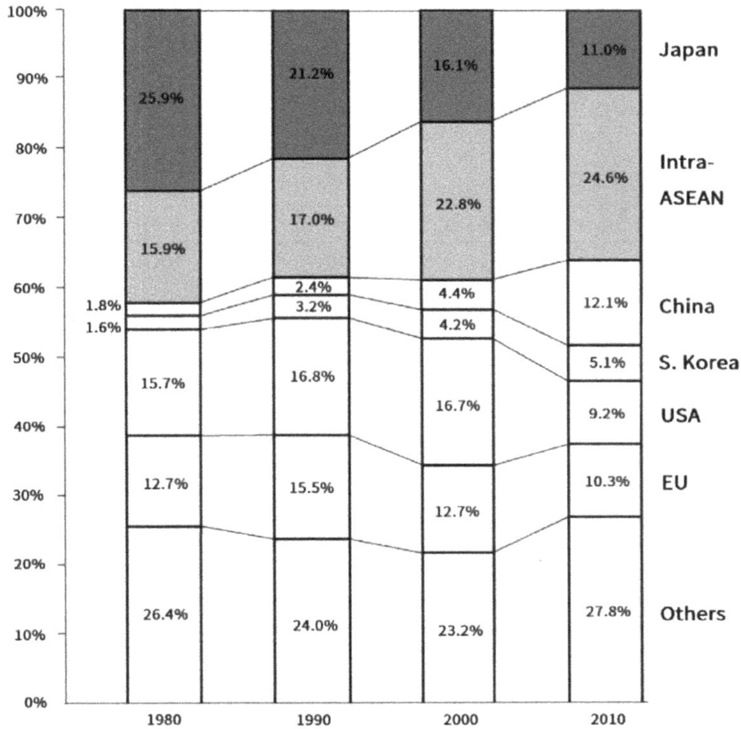

Figure 1: Major Trade partners of ASEAN (Percentage in the value of the total amount of export and import).

Source: Quoted from the website of Japan–ASEAN Centre in August 2012.

Japanese share in the total amount of international trade (export and import) of ASEAN has declined from 25.9% in 1980 to 11% in 2010, whereas the share of the intra-ASEAN trade has risen from 15.9% to 24.6% for the same period.

On the other hand, Table 10 shows the details of international trade of six ASEAN countries in 2010. The Japanese position as an origin of import has distinctly retreated in Singapore and Indonesia, while it still held the top position in Thailand, the Philippines and Malaysia. As a destination of export, Japan maintained the high-ranking position, though its share as indicated by the figures of percentage has rather declined, except in the Philippines. With regard to the major export items, the proportion of machinery and other manufactured goods was constantly high in Singapore, Malaysia, the Philippines and Thailand. In contrast, the proportion of primary commodities categorized as mineral fuels and crude

Table 10: Details of international trade of six ASEAN countries (2010)

			Amount of trade (million US$)			
	Indonesia		**Singapore**		**Malaysia**	
	Export	157,779	Export	351,867	Export	198,791
	Import	135,663	Import	310,791	Import	164,586
			Major export items (proportion to the total amount of export)			
	Indonesia	(%)	Singapore	(%)	Malaysia	(%)
No. 1	Mineral fuels[a]	29.6	Machinery[d]	51.1	Machinery[d]	43.9
No. 2	Manufactured[b]	13.9	Mineral fuels[a]	16.1	Mineral fuels[a]	15.8
No. 3	Crude materials[c]	12.8	Chemicals[e]	11.3	Manufactured[b]	8.8
			Major origin of import (proportion to the total amount of import)			
	Indonesia	(%)	Singapore	(%)	Malaysia	(%)
No. 1	China	15.1	Malaysia	11.7	Japan	12.6
No. 2	Singapore	14.9	USA	11.5	China	12.6
No. 3	Japan	12.5	China	10.8	Singapore	11.4
			Major destination of export (proportion to the total amount of export)			
	Indonesia	(%)	Singapore	(%)	Malaysia	(%)
No. 1	Japan	16.3	Malaysia	11.9	Singapore	13.4
No. 2	China	9.9	Hong Kong	11.7	China	12.6
No. 3	USA	9.1	China	10.3	Japan	10.4
			Amount of trade (million US$)			
	Philippines	(%)	Thailand	(%)	Vietnam*	(%)
	Export	51,432	Export	195,312	Export	57,096
	Import	58,229	Import	182,393	Import	69,949
			Major export items (proportion to the total amount of export)			
	Philippines	(%)	Thailand	(%)	Vietnam*	(%)
No. 1	Machinery[d]	70.2	Machinery[d]	42.2	Misc. Manu.[f]	34.8
No. 2	Misc. Manu.[f]	7.5	Food and animals[g]	12.3	Food and animals[g]	20.1
No. 3	Manufactured[b]	6.5	Manufactured[b]	12.2	Mineral fuels[a]	14.9
			Major origin of import (proportion to the total amount of import)			
	Philippines	(%)	Thailand	(%)	Vietnam*	(%)
No. 1	Japan	12.5	Japan	20.8	China	23.8
No. 2	USA	10.8	China	13.3	Japan	10.7
No. 3	Singapore	9.3	USA	5.9	South Korea	10.0

(*Continued*)

Table 10: (*Continued*)

	Major destination of export (proportion to the total amount of export)					
	Philippines	(%)	Thailand	(%)	Vietnam*	(%)
No. 1	Japan	15.2	China	11.0	USA	20.0
No. 2	USA	14.7	Japan	10.5	Japan	11.1
No. 3	Singapore	14.3	USA	10.4	China	9.5

Notes: *As to Vietnam, the data in 2009 is shown.
[a] Mineral fuels, lubricants and related materials (SITC 3).
[b] Manufactured goods classified chiefly by materials (SITC 6).
[c] Crude materials, inedible, except fuels (SITC 2).
[d] Machinery and transport equipment (SITC 7).
[e] Chemicals and related products (SITC 5).
[f] Miscellaneous manufactured articles (SITC 8).
[g] Food and live animals (SITC 0).
Source: United Nations. *International Trade Statistics Yearbook 2010* (legacy version).

materials became dominant again in the export of Indonesia. In case of Vietnam, the percentage of miscellaneous manufactured articles was almost on a par with primary commodities (food and animals plus mineral fuels).

After 2010, a remarkable change has taken place in the composition of ASEAN trade partners as evidenced by Table 11. Japanese share in the amount of ASEAN international trade has continuously declined, both in export and in import. On the contrary, Chinese share has rapidly increased. The share of the United States has also increased as the destination of export, though its share as the origin of import has slightly declined. In contrast to the preceding three decades, the proportion of the intra-ASEAN trade tends to decline in this period despite the establishment of ASEAN Economic Community (AEC) at the end of 2015.

In accordance with the formation of AEC, the statistics on major items of international trade has been provided aggregately for the whole ASEAN that consists of ten countries. Table 12 shows top ten items among the total amount of ASEAN international trade in 2018. Unlike the old days, electrical machinery and equipment now holds the top position. Such change reflects the latest stage of development of ASEAN economies. Nevertheless, mineral fuels, etc., also hold the second position

Table 11: Partners of ASEAN international trade (2010–2018)

	Value (million US$)			Share (%)		
	2010	**2015**	**2018**	**2010**	**2015**	**2018**
Export (of goods)						
Intra-ASEAN	264,398	287,106	346,462	25.3	24.5	24.1
Australia	37,960	35,791	39,211	3.6	3.1	2.7
China	112,512	145,291	198,956	10.8	12.4	13.9
EU-28	114,229	127,387	160,937	10.9	10.9	11.2
India	37,076	40,553	50,737	3.5	3.5	3.5
Japan	102,901	101,941	114,834	9.8	8.7	8.0
South Korea	45,011	45,421	60,490	4.3	3.9	4.2
USA	97,984	125,443	160,284	9.4	10.7	11.2
Others	233,459	262,800	304,507	22.3	22.4	21.2
Total	1,045,531	1,171,734	1,436,415	100.0	100.0	100.0
Import (of goods)						
Intra-ASEAN	238,466	248,274	304,267	25.1	22.5	21.9
Australia	19,439	21,702	26,959	2.0	2.0	1.9
China	121,783	218,205	284,809	12.8	19.8	20.5
EU-28	88,571	103,268	127,289	9.3	9.4	9.2
India	19,590	19,612	30,330	2.1	1.8	2.2
Japan	115,799	100,859	116,882	12.2	9.2	8.4
South Korea	56,733	75,146	101,025	6.0	6.8	7.3
USA	81,236	85,140	102,740	8.6	7.7	7.4
Others	207,684	228,922	294,549	21.9	20.8	21.2
Total	949,301	1,101,128	1,388,848	100.0	100.0	100.0

Source: ASEAN Secretariat. *ASEAN Statistical Yearbook 2019*.

among the international trade items. The above-mentioned two items hold almost equal position in the intra-ASEAN trade, as indicated by Table 13. Meanwhile, Table 14 provides the major items of trade between ASEAN and Japan in 2017. Both in export and import, electrical machinery and equipment also holds the top position. In case of export from ASEAN, the second position is occupied by the traditional item of mineral fuels, etc., which predominantly consists of natural gas and petroleum from Indonesia,

Table 12: Top 10 items of ASEAN international trade by 2-digit HS code (2018)

Export (of goods)				Import (of goods)			
HS	Commodities	Value (mil. US$)	Share (%)	HS	Commodities	Value (mil. US $)	Share (%)
85	Electrical machinery and equipment[a]	377,596	26.3	85	Electrical machinery and equipment[a]	321,586	23.2
27	Mineral fuels[b]	161,038	11.2	27	Mineral fuels[b]	223,813	16.1
84	Nuclear reactors, boilers, machinery[c]	152,651	10.6	84	Nuclear reactors, boilers, machinery[c]	166,653	12.0
39	Plastics and articles thereof	47,375	3.3	39	Plastics and articles thereof	55,686	4.0
87	Vehicles[d]	46,989	3.3	72	Iron and steel	49,251	3.5
90	Optical instruments[e]	44,238	3.1	87	Vehicles[d]	45,610	3.3
71	Precious stones and metals[f]	40,981	2.9	71	Precious stones and metals[f]	40,933	2.9
40	Rubber and articles thereof	35,891	2.5	90	Optical instruments[e]	36,467	2.6
15	Animal or vegetable fats and oils[g]	34,697	2.4	29	Organic chemicals	28,340	2.0
29	Organic chemicals	31,901	2.2	73	Iron or steel articles	24,107	1.7
	Others	463,058	32.2		Others	396,403	28.5
	TOTAL	1,436,415	100.0		TOTAL	1,388,848	100.0

Note: [a]Electrical machinery and equipment and parts thereof; sound recorders and reproducers; television image and sound recorders and reproducers, parts and accessories of such articles.

[b]Mineral fuels, mineral oils and products of their distillation; bituminous substances; mineral waxes.

[c]Nuclear reactors, boilers, machinery and mechanical appliances; parts thereof.

[d]Vehicles; other than railway or tramway rolling stock, and parts and accessories thereof.

[e]Optical, photographic, cinematographic, measuring, checking, medical or surgical instruments and apparatus; parts and accessories.

[f]Natural, cultured pearls; precious, semi-precious stones; precious metals, metals clad with precious metal, and articles thereof; imitation jewelry; coin.

[g]Animal or vegetable fats and oils and their cleavage products; prepared animal fats; animal or vegetable waxes.

Source: ASEAN Secretariat. *ASEAN Statistical Yearbook 2019*.

Table 13: Top 10 items of intra-ASEAN trade by 2-digit HS code (2018)

Export (of goods)				Import (of goods)			
HS	Commodities	Value (mil. US$)	Share (%)	HS	Commodities	Value (mil. US$)	Share (%)
85	Electrical machinery and equipment[a]	77,958	22.5	27	Mineral fuels[b]	74,353	24.4
27	Mineral fuels[b]	70,489	20.3	85	Electrical machinery and equipment[a]	66,541	21.9
84	Nuclear reactors, boilers, machinery[c]	38,290	11.1	84	Nuclear reactors, boilers, machinery[c]	29,031	9.5
87	Vehicles[d]	15,704	4.5	87	Vehicles[d]	15,992	5.3
39	Plastics and articles thereof	14,964	4.3	39	Plastics and articles thereof	12,762	4.2
71	Precious stones and metals[e]	13,764	4.0	71	Precious stones and metals[e]	7,244	2.4
90	Optical instruments[f]	6,792	2.0	29	Organic chemicals	6,412	2.1
29	Organic chemicals	6,739	1.9	90	Optical instruments[f]	5,303	1.7
72	Iron and steel	5,714	1.6	72	Iron and steel	4,469	1.5
73	Iron or steel articles	4,894	1.4	15	Animal or vegetable fats and oils[g]	4,111	1.4
	Others	91,154	26.3		Others	78,050	25.7
	TOTAL	346,462	100.0		TOTAL	304,267	100.0

Note: [a] Electrical machinery and equipment and parts thereof; sound recorders and reproducers; television image and sound recorders and reproducers, parts and accessories of such articles.

[b] Mineral fuels, mineral oils and products of their distillation; bituminous substances; mineral waxes.

[c] Nuclear reactors, boilers, machinery and mechanical appliances; parts thereof.

[d] Vehicles; other than railway or tramway rolling stock, and parts and accessories thereof.

[e] Natural, cultured pearls; precious, semi-precious stones; precious metals, metals clad with precious metal, and articles thereof; imitation jewelry; coin.

[f] Optical, photographic, cinematographic, measuring, checking, medical or surgical instruments and apparatus; parts and accessories.

[g] Animal or vegetable fats and oils and their cleavage products; prepared animal fats; animal or vegetable waxes.

Source: ASEAN Secretariat. *ASEAN Statistical Yearbook 2019*.

Table 14: Top 10 items of ASEAN international trade with Japan by 2-digit HS code (2017*)

Export (of goods)				Import (of goods)			
HS	Commodities	Value (mil. US$)	Share (%)	HS	Commodities	Value (mil. US$)	Share (%)
85	Electrical machinery and equipment[a]	24,663	23.3	85	Electrical machinery and equipment[a]	25,204	22.3
27	Mineral fuels[b]	14,336	13.5	84	Nuclear reactors, boilers, machinery[c]	23,019	20.4
84	Nuclear reactors, boilers, machinery[c]	10,020	9.5	87	Vehicles[i]	11,833	10.5
39	Plastics and articles thereo[f]	4,077	3.8	72	Iron and steel	9,127	8.1
44	Wood and articles of wood[d]	3,623	3.4	39	Plastics and articles thereof	5,693	5.0
90	Optical instruments[e]	3,560	3.4	90	Optical instruments[e]	4,420	3.9
62	Apparel; not knitted[f]	2,837	2.7	71	Precious stones and metals[j]	3,952	3.5
61	Apparel; knitted[g]	2,778	2.6	73	Iron or steel articles	3,826	3.4
16	Meat, fish, etc.[h]	2,738	2.6	74	Copper and articles thereof	2,291	2.0

(Continued)

Table 14: (*Continued*)

Export (of goods)				Import (of goods)			
		Value	Share			Value	Share
HS	Commodities	(mil. US$)	(%)	HS	Commodities	(mil. US$)	(%)
40	Rubber and articles thereof[f]	2,576	2.4	27	Mineral fuels[b]	2,263	2.0
	Others	34,731	32.8		Others	21,234	18.8
	TOTAL	105,938	100.0		TOTAL	112,860	100.0

Note: [a]Electrical machinery and equipment and parts thereof; sound recorders and reproducers; television image and sound recorders and reproducers, parts and accessories of such articles.

[b]Mineral fuels, mineral oils and products of their distillation; bituminous substances; mineral waxes.

[c]Nuclear reactors, boilers, machinery and mechanical appliances; parts thereof.

[d]Wood and articles of wood; wood charcoal.

[e]Optical, photographic, cinematographic, measuring, checking, medical or surgical instruments and apparatus; parts and accessories.

[f]Apparel and clothing accessories; not knitted or crocheted.

[g]Apparel and clothing accessories; knitted or crocheted.

[h]Meat, fish or crustaceans, mollusks or other aquatic invertebrates; preparations thereof.

[i]Vehicles; other than railway or tramway rolling stock, and parts and accessories thereof.

[j]Natural, cultured pearls; precious, semi-precious stones; precious metals, metals clad with precious metal, and articles thereof; imitation jewelry; coin.

*The year 2017 is selected because the export data for 2018 in the same source are apparently incorrect.

Source: ASEAN Secretariat. *ASEAN Statistical Yearbook 2019*.

Malaysia and Brunei. On the other hand, the second position of items imported from Japan is occupied by goods categorized as "nuclear reactors, boilers, machinery etc.", which in fact consist of various kinds of non-nuclear machinery.

Foreign Direct Investment (FDI) of Japan and Southeast Asia

As explained in the previous section, since the 1980s principal focus of Japanese concern about the economic relations with Southeast Asia has gradually shifted from the expansion of international trade to the direct investment. Table 15 demonstrates the change of geographical target of foreign direct investment (FDI) from Japan since 1995. In the 21st century, the amount of Japanese FDI in Asia has surpassed on average that in North America and Europe. Within Asia, the amount of direct investment to ASEAN has exceeded the investment to China in the 2010s, and has reached to more than half of the total investment in Asia.

In the meantime, Table 16 classifies the Japanese FDI in ASEAN by nationality for the same period. Thailand and Indonesia were its most

Table 15: Destination of foreign direct investment (FDI) from Japan

	(Balance of payments basis, net, flow; million US$)							
	Asia				North			
Year	China	ASEAN	Others	Total	America	EU	Others	World Total
1995	3,183	3,987	1,277	8,447	9,411	3,230	1,562	22,651
2005	6,575	5,002	4,611	16,188	13,168	7,832	8,232	45,461
2010	7,252	8,930	5,950	22,131	9,016	8,359	17,717	57,223
2015	10,011	20,920	4,125	35,057	51,451	35,785	16,136	138,428
2019	14,063	34,628	11,589	60,279	51,375	45,884	89,242	246,780
	(Balance of payments basis, net, flow; %)							
1995	14.1	17.6	5.6	37.3	41.5	14.3	6.9	100.0
2005	14.5	11.0	10.1	35.6	29.0	17.3	18.1	100.0
2010	12.7	15.6	10.4	38.7	15.8	14.6	31.0	100.0
2015	7.2	15.1	3.0	25.3	37.2	25.9	11.7	100.0
2019	5.7	14.0	4.7	24,4	20.8	18.6	36.2	100.0

Source: JETRO. https://www.jetro.go.jp/world/japan/stats/fdi.html (Retrieved on April 9, 2020).

Table 16: Destination of foreign direct investment (FDI) from Japan to ASEAN

Year	Singapore	Thailand	Indonesia	Malaysia	Philippines	Vietnam	Others	ASEAN total
	(Balance of payments basis, net, flow; million US$)							
1995	676	935	946	371	1,061	n.a.	n.a.	3,987
2005	557	2,125	1,185	524	442	154	15	5,002
2010	3,845	2,248	490	1,058	514	748	26	8,930
2015	7,010	4,057	3,213	2,918	1,531	1,446	746	20,920
2019	15,686	5,094	8,242	560	1,763	2,654	629	34,628
	(Balance of payments basis, net, flow; %)							
1995	16.9	23.4	23.7	9.3	26.6	n.a.	n.a.	100.0
2005	11.1	42.5	23.7	10.5	8.8	3.1	0.3	100.0
2010	43.1	25.2	5.5	11.9	5.8	8.4	0.3	100.0
2015	33.5	19.4	15.4	13.9	7.3	6.9	3.6	100.0
2019	45.3	14.7	23.8	1.6	5.1	7.7	1.8	100.0

Source: JETRO. https://www.jetro.go.jp/world/japan/stats/fdi.html (Retrieved on April 9, 2020).

important targets in 2005, while the investment in Singapore has become dominant since 2015. In this relation, we must keep in mind that Singapore also plays the role of stepping-stone for further investment to other ASEAN countries.

On the other hand, Table 17 shows the classification of FDI inward to ASEAN (as a whole) in 2010 and 2017 by host and source countries. Similarly, with FDI from Japan, Singapore has become the top host country followed by Indonesia, Vietnam, the Philippines and Thailand. Among the source countries, Japan, EU and the United States have been equally major. The intra-ASEAN transfer of capital is also important, though most of them actually consists of indirect investment through Singapore by other sources including Japan. The investment from China is also growing rapidly and its amount is coming close to the Japanese one. Nevertheless, it seems that the major target of investment from China is physical infrastructure development, thus rather different with the fields of Japanese investment.

Although it is difficult to statistically classify the Japanese FDI in Southeast Asia by kind of industry, Table 18 suggests the general trend of change in Japanese FDI from manufacturing industries to non-manufacturing

Table 17: Foreign direct investment (FDI) inward flows to ASEAN

(2010 and 2017, million US$)

By host country	2010	2017	By source country	2010	2017
Brunei	625	460	Intra-ASEAN	16,306	25,474
Cambodia	783	2,732	Australia	3,959	1,313
Indonesia	13,770	20,579	China	3,489	13,701
Laos	333	1,695	EU-28	21,145	14,916
Malaysia	9,156	9,296	Japan	12,987	16,149
Myanmar[a]	2,249	4,002	South Korea	4,319	4,535
Philippines	1,298	10,256	USA	13,682	24,891
Singapore	57,214	75,735	Others	32,287	46,106
Thailand	14,747	8,229			
Vietnam	8,000	14,100			
TOTAL	108,174	147,085	TOTAL	108,174	147,085

Note: [a]Myanmar: Figures in each fiscal year which ends in March of the following calendar year.
Source: ASEAN Secretariat. *ASEAN Statistical Yearbook 2019*.

Table 18: Foreign direct investment (FDI) of Japan by kind of industry

(Balance of payments basis, net, flow; million US$)

Kind of industry	**2006**	**2009**	**2012**	**2015**	**2018**
Manufacturing	34,513	32,934	49,250	51,027	54,874
Chemical and medical	4,413	7,407	6,494	8,830	14,312
Iron and non-ferrous metals	1,795	3,738	4,206	2,484	3,675
General machinery and equipment	1,663	4,411	7,979	7,962	6,206
Electric machinery and equipment	7,041	2,505	6,707	8,497	8,141
Transport machinery and equipment	8,597	566	10,465	10,465	10,465
Others					
Non-manufacturing	15,652	41,717	73,102	85,237	88,331
Mining	1,577	6,482	20,934	4,812	7,814
Telecommunication	–3,368	3,870	7,208	11,806	38,964
Wholesale and retail trade	5,483	8,418	18,372	13,598	14,043
Finance and insurance	5,562	15,463	14,210	34,613	24,944
Others	6,398	7,484	12,378	20,408	2,566
Total	50,165	74,651	122,352	136,264	143,205

Source: JETRO. https://www.jetro.go.jp/world/japan/stats/fdi.html (Retrieved on April 9, 2020).

activities. Finance, trade and telecommunication seem to be the most important fields of recent Japanese FDI. Such observation would also be applicable to the recent Japanese FDI in Southeast Asia.

Conclusion

After the Second World War, Japan restarted the economic exchange with Southeast Asian countries that had achieved their national independence. In the 1960s and the 1970s, the heyday of rapid economic growth in postwar Japan, international trade with Japan and Japanese direct investment toward the import-substituting manufacturing industries in Southeast Asia rapidly expanded. Although the major export items of Southeast Asia in this period were still traditional primary commodities such as natural rubber, copra, rice and petroleum, the export-oriented industrialization also started in some Southeast Asian countries in the latter half of the 1970s.

The year 1985 became a remarkable turning point in the history of the international economic relations in East and Southeast Asia. The appreciation of Japanese yen brought about by the so-called Plaza Accord in this year urged Japanese manufacturing enterprises to relocate their production sites to the neighboring Asian nations, at first mainly to China, then to Southeast Asia. In parallel with this trend, the industrialization of Southeast Asian countries was accelerated and their major export items have changed to manufactured goods from primary commodities.

For the initial two decades of the 21st century, the proportion of trade with Japan in the total value of international trade of Southeast Asia has fairly declined, while the intra-regional trade and the trade with China has remarkably advanced. However, in the scope of foreign direct investment (including the roundabout investment via Singapore) to Southeast Asia, Japan maintains its important role and position. In addition, its field of expertise seems to be shifting from manufacturing to service industries.

Whatever may be the case, in any period of the past ten decades, the proportion of trade with a particular single nation (including Japan) has never exceeded 30 precent of the total value of international trade of Southeast Asia. This proposition will probably hold true concerning the future international trade of Southeast Asia. Southeast Asian economies can subsist only through the international exchange with plural partners, particularly with East Asian neighbors, the United States and the European nations. Keeping the optimal balance in the relations with them will be consistently essential for the stable economic development of Southeast Asia.

References

ASEAN Secretariat (2019). *ASEAN Statistical Yearbook 2019*. Jakarta: ASEAN Secretariat.

Claver, A. (2014). *Dutch Commerce and Chinese Merchants in Java: Colonial Relationships in Trade and Finance, 1800-1942*. Leiden & Boston: Brill.

Geerligs, H. C. Prinsen (1924). *Handboek ten dienste van de suikerrietcultuur en de rietsuiker-fabricage op Java. deel IV (De rietsuiker industrie in de verschillende landen van productie)*. Amsterdam: J. H. de Bussy.

JETRO. https://www.jetro.go.jp/world/japan/stats/fdi.html (Retrieved on April 9, 2020).

Kudo, Y. (2005). Taiwan Sekimin in Java: Commercial Activities of Kwik Djoen Eng (ジャワの台湾籍民ー郭春秧の商業活動をめぐって). *History and Folklore* (歴史民俗) 3, 22-38. Tokyo: Second School of Humanities and Social Sciences, Waseda University.

Mandere, H. Ch. G. J. van der (1928). *De Javasuikerindustrie in heden en verleden: Gezien in het bijzonder in hare sociaal-economische beteekens.* Amsterdam: Uitgave Bureau Industria.

Nan-yo Kyokai 南洋協会 (1934) ed. *Statistical Tables of International Trade in Southern Areas* (南方圏貿易統計表). Tokyo, Nihon Hyoron-sha (日本評論社).

Taiwan Government-General Secretariat, Foreign Affairs Office 台湾総督官房外事課 (1935) ed. *Overview of the International Trade of South China and Southeast Asia* (南支南洋貿易概観). Taipei: Taiwan Government-General.

United Nations (1962). *International Trade Statistics Yearbook 1961*. New York: Department of Economic and Social Affairs, Statistical Office, United Nations.

United Nations (1975). *International Trade Statistics Yearbook 1974*. New York: Department of Economic and Social Affairs, Statistical Office, United Nations.

United Nations (1984). *International Trade Statistics Yearbook 1983*. New York: Department of Economic and Social Affairs, Statistical Office, United Nations.

United Nations (1994). *International Trade Statistics Yearbook 1993*. New York: Department of Economic and Social Affairs, Statistical Office, United Nations.

United Nations (2001). *International Trade Statistics Yearbook 2000*. New York: Department of Economic and Social Affairs, Statistical Office, United Nations.

United Nations (2011). *International Trade Statistics Yearbook 2010 (legacy version)*. New York: Department of Economic and Social Affairs, Statistical Division, United Nations.

Part 2

Economic Flows of Capital & People

https://doi.org/10.1142/9789811250668_0005

Chapter 5

The Role of Hakka Merchants in Asia: Focusing on the Family Network between Kobe, Batavia, Hong Kong and Meixian in Early 20th Century

Laixing Chen

School of Economics and Management, University of Hyogo, Japan

Hakka in Dutch Indies and Japan in Early 20th Century

Hakka, also rendered Kejia, is one of the major groups of Chinese who speak varieties of unique Hakka dialect. They live in the southern part of China, mainly in the boundary area of southwest Fujian, southern Jiangxi and northeast Guangdong. They also live in Sichuan, Taiwan, Hong Kong and Southeast Asia.

Meixian, the capital county of Meizhou (Jiayingzhou), has been considered to be an important core of Hakka intellectuals who insisted on their identities early in the 20th century. Meixian dialect (Moiyen) has also been taken as the standard of Hakka dialect in the People's Republic of China. Meizhou (Jiayingzhou) Hakka is composed of those from Dapu, Fengshun, Xingning, Wuhua, Jiaoling, Pingyuan and Meixian counties.

Hakka in Batavia

According to *Annals of Meizhou Overseas Chinese* published in 2001, the country with the largest Meizhou Hakka population was Indonesia, followed by Thailand, Hong Kong and Malaysia. Around 66.3% of the total 656,446 Hakka of Meizhou origin in Indonesia were from the central Meixian county, while in Thailand only 18.9% of the total 639,652 Meizhou Hakka population were from the Meixian county. In Hong Kong, over half of the total 435,242 Meizhou Hakka were from Xingning and Wuhua counties near Hong Kong (Guangdong Province Meizhoushi Huaqiaozhi Editorial Committee and Society of Meizhoushi Overseas Chinese History, 2001). That is to say, Hakka from central Meizhou is a typical image of Indonesian Hakka.

Hakka in Dutch East Indies were considered to be latecomers, Totok. Most of them immigrated to the outer islands as workers after the 19th century. Chinese communities in early days developed mainly in Java island. Hokkien people as Peranakan Tionghoa were the majority of them. Batavia was an exception. Hakka merchants as well as miscellaneous city workers and manufacturers established a presence in the early 20th century in Batavia. According to the report issued by Bank of Taiwan on the remittance by Chinese living in Batavia in 1914, the remittance by Hokkien people was 350,000 guilders, the remittance by Cantonese was 30,000 a month. Remittance by Hakka who "came here comparatively later than Hokkien people" amounted to 500,000 guilders (Bank of Taiwan, 1914).

According to the 1930 census, the number of male Hakka was recorded 38,542 in west Java, while male Hokkien people was 77,624. During this time, Hakka population already accounted for almost half of Hokkien people there. In other districts like central and east Java, Hakka had little power, though (Research Division of Bank of Kanan, 1942: 14–15).

Hakka in Japan

When several ports of Japan were first opened for foreigners in 1859, Chinese were attracted and gathered to the foreign settlement of Yokohama because it was a major trading port on the north American steamship line starting from Hong Kong and Shanghai. This is the reason why the structure of Yokohama Chinese community was mainly composed of Cantonese, similar to those of San Francisco and Victoria, Canada. The list of directors of Yokohama Chinese Chamber of Commerce of 1910 tells us there were 59 Cantonese out of total 78 directors, supervisors and staffs.[1] Those from the counties along the delta region of the Pearl River, Xiangshan, Nanhai, Panyu, Xinhui, Shunde, Gaoming, Sanshui were the main constituents. We cannot find even a name of Jiayingzhou (Hakka) origin nor of Chaozhou origin in the list.

Kobe and Osaka in Kansai area whose ports were opened in 1868, nine years later than Yokohama, gradually became important international trading ports at the turn of the century according as the intra-Asian trade, mainly Sino-Japanese trade, increased rapidly. The structure of Chinese communities of Kansai area underwent a considerable change. In Osaka, Chinese from northern provinces like Shandong and Hebei came to take the initiative of Chinese society, while Cantonese were dominant in preceding Yokohama China Town. In Kobe, Chinese merchants from around Shanghai and Fujian also came to stand out in the Chinese society at the competitive level with Cantonese, reflecting the tendency of varieties of trading merchants in Kobe. The Kobe and Osaka Chinese Consolidated Benevolent Association hall was built in 1893 and registered in local Kobe (Hyogo) government in 1904.[2]

After the Russo-Japanese War, Hakka merchants came to distinguish themselves and made a prominent figure after World War I. After Taiwan was liberated from Japanese control after WWII, Hakka of Taiwan origin became to be the majority of the Hakka in post-war Japan. They were powerful in organizing groups and networking each other.[3] The latter tells us quite a different story, though. This would be the first research examining the old Hakka network in Japan, if I can safely call the Hakka via Taiwan to Japan mainly after the WWII the new Hakka network.

This chapter will focus on how Hakka directly came before the Second World War from the Hakka region of China and properly established themselves in Japan and what roles they played. The purpose of this chapter is to evaluate the role of old Hakka elite merchants, collating mutual relations of important families in China, Japan and Indonesia.

---

[1] *A List of Directors and Staffs of Yokohama Chinese Chamber of Commerce, 1910 (Hengbin Zhonghua Shangwu Zonghui 1910 nian zhiyuan yilan biao)* Yokohama, Japan, Yokohama Chuka shoumu Soukai, owned by Suzhoushi Archives, I14-01-0067-002008.

[2] Chinese Consolidated Benevolent Association (2013) explains about the Chinese Society in Kobe in early days.

[3] As for the post-war Hakka in Japan, please refer to Chang (2015).

Pan Family Originated in Qiaoxiang Village of Nankou, Meixian

The first Hakka merchant Pan Zhiwo (潘植我) who left his name on overseas Chinese history in Japan came to Kobe just after the Russo-Japanese War of 1904–1905. Pan Zhiwo was born in Qiaoxiang village of Nankouzhen in Meixian county in 1885. He was chosen as a dispatched student to Japan to master textile dyeing technique for his village by Pan Lizhai (潘立斋) and Pan Xiangchu (潘祥初). Pan Lizhai, famous as the owner of Dexingtang (德馨堂) mansion, settled in Batavia, and Pan Xiangchu, famous as the owner of Nanhuayoulu (南華又廬) mansion, first settled in Batavia and then succeeded in Hong Kong. Another character in this chapter from Qiaoxiang village of the Pan family's is Pan Junmian (潘君勉), who was just 3 years elder than Pan Zhiwo. Junmian settled in Hong Kong being promoted as a manager of Wantonganji (萬通安記) by its founder Pan Xiangchu. When Zhiwo established his own trading company Derenhe (得人和) in Kobe in 1914, Junmian became a shareholder and was appointed as vice-president. Junmian was a closer relative of Zhiwo, while Lizhai and Xiangchu belonging to the elder generation were distant relatives of his. Zhiwo's company enjoyed prosperity during the first world war by exporting Japanese textile goods. Finally he became the most successful Chinese merchant, undertaking chairman of Kobe Chinese Chamber of Commerce and chairman of board of directors of Kobe Tongwen Overseas Chinese School during the last years of his stay in Kobe until 1939 (Chen, 2016b).[4] It was in 1919 when he started the construction of his traditional Hakka style Donghualu (東華廬) and Donghuayoulu (東華又廬) mansions with honor (Pan, 2016: 75). Pan Junmian, also famous for his acquaintance and interchange with Sun Yat-sen (孫逸仙) and Ye Jianying (葉剣英), gained a reputation in Hong Kong as a successful businessman too, being the first president of Jiaying Hakka Association in Hong Kong (旅港嘉属商会) established in 1916 (Serizawa, 2016). Junmian also started the construction of Yinhualu (蔭華廬 , Figure 2) in his hometown just next to Donghuayoulu in 1919.

The following four, Lizhai, Xiangchu, Junmian and Zhiwo, are considered to be the "Four Sages" who made a great contribution to the education of their hometown. Their lives and achievements are precisely

[4]Please refer to my recent paper on Pan Zhiwo written in Japanese (Chen 2016b).

Figure 1: Four sages for Anren School

Source: Photo by Laixing Chen in September 2013.

described in the display case settled inside the gate of Anren Elementary School in Nankou-zhen (Figure 1).

Pan Zhiwo and his important human networks in Japan: Wu Zhiyuan and Liao Daoming

When Pan Zhiwo landed on Kobe in 1906 as a dispatched student who was to do an internship at Yoshida Textile Dyeing Factory in Osaka, he lodged at Yong An Xiang (永安祥) company in Kobe. Later, he joined an advance party of five youngsters from Meixian-county, three Liaos, one Qiu and one Liang who were respectively dispatched by successful Meixian Hakka merchants, Liao Yiguang (廖煜光), Qiu Xieting (丘燮亭), Liang Yingxing (梁映星), who had already taken root in Batavia. After mastering the dyeing technique, they decided to ask Qiu Xieting who was visiting Japan at that time on business, to let them go to Tokyo and study further for the future need of operating their own factories at home. Thus, these five pupils went for study in Tokyo except Zhiwo. Pan Zhiwo was retained by the owner Liao Daoming (廖道明) to work at his trading company Yong An Xiang in Kobe.

Wu Zhiyuan (1863–1914) in Yokohama

Let me explain the relation of Pan Zhiwo with Wu Zhiyuan (吳植垣) first, because Zhiwo respected him as the elder Chinese community leader so much as to take one character from Wu's name in his own name (Pan Zhiwo, 2002). Wu Zhiyuan, originally from Nanhai county of Guangdong, was a famous leader in Yokohama Chinese community. He was not only appointed as chairman of Yokohama Chinese Chamber of Commerce, representative of Chinese petition campaign for mixed residence of foreigners in 1899, known as an activist when they first established their Chinese school in 1897, etc. (Li, 1914: 645–646), but also had many friends in Japanese high society. Wu was the president of Yong An He (永安和) trading company in Yokohama, and was a shareholder of Yong An Xiang of Kobe as a vice-president. This was the reason why Pan Zhiwo got acquainted with him. Wu often took senior officials and big names to Kyoto, and asked Zhiwo to accompany him. Wu Zhiyuan's evaluation of Zhiwo was as follows. Zhiwo is "somewhat different from other employees. He is not a person who is always working under some other's direction. Someday, he will surely set up business on his own. Since there are so many Hakka traders in the Southeast Asia, Zhiwo's future business will be more promising than Yong An Xiang" (Pan, 2002). That is to say, when Wu Zhiyuan was a joint partner with Liao Daoming to operate Yong An Xiang of Kobe, Wu Zhiyuan already had a perspective that Hakka business network would expand in the near future in Japan. Yong An Xiang's main shareholders were Liao's family, supposedly Daoming's uncles in Batavia. After Wu Zhiyuan died in 1914, Liao Daoming became known as the president of Guang Xing Chang (廣興昌) trading company. Daoming's business seemed to be concentrated in the trade between Hakka merchants in the South Sea, specifically the Dutch East Indies.

Liao Daoming (1881–?) in Kobe

Liao Daoming was born in Guangzhou in 1881. His father was a medical doctor who took on the chairman of street association, and one of his uncles was working as a teacher of the famous traditional school Yuexiu Shuyuan (粵秀書院) after quitting the job of civil service. The other two uncles went into business in the Dutch Indies. According to his memoirs written in 1947, his ancestors originally came from Fujian by way of Meixian and settled in Nanhai county a hundred years before. Although he was the third generation born in Guangzhou, Nanhai county, Liao family's relatives were still living in Meixian and had their tombs there (Liao Daoming, 1947: 32–34). We cannot confirm now whether he spoke Hakka dialect or not, but his business style was surely based upon Hakka network. It would be better to call him an "invisible Hakka".

Liao Daoming was known as a keyperson who exported Japanese matches made in Kobe and Osaka to the Hakka traders in Batavia. There were Liao family's stockshares in Lian Xing (聯興 ***Lian Hien***) and Zeng Xing (増興 ***Tjeng Hien***), famous Chinese Hakka traders operated at Glodok (China town) area in North Batavia. Liao's new company Guang Xing Chang (廣興昌) had the same Chinese character "Xing" with these two companies. Another Hakka trader in Batavia Lun Chang (綸昌 ***Loen Tjiang***), neighboring Zeng Xing, imported matches from Liao Daoming's Guang Xing Chang in Kobe. As for how their capital were shared, I would discuss more in detail. Anyway, they were closely connected with each other. Daoming was once sent to the South Sea to work for his uncles. However, he had his pigtail cut there. Because of this incident, he was pulled back to Guangzhou and then sent to Yokohama for study. Soon, he was instructed to be in charge of the newly established trading company Yong An Xiang at Kobe. It was not until after the Russo-Japanese war that he came to Kobe. About 6 years later, when Wuchang Xinhai revolution succeeded, Chinese in Kobe soon established the association Qiaoshang Tongyi Lianhehui (僑商統一聯合会) to support the new government. Liao Daoming, only 30 years old, was elected as representative from Guangdong group (Chinese Consolidated Benevolent Association, 2013: 134). This might be because he was regarded to be a member of a distinguished family, who was even associated with famous political refugees Kang Youwei (康有為) and Liang Qichao (梁啓超) in Kobe at that time. Daoming had already been acquainted with them when he was in Guangzhou.

Pan Junmian (1882–1968) in Hong Kong

Wan Tong An Ji (萬通安記), originally established by Pan Xiangchu and later mainly operated by Pan Junmian, was one of the biggest and oldest trading companies in Hong Kong. They not only exported Chinese goods from Guangzhou, Foshan and Hong Kong to Hakka merchants in the ports of the Dutch Indies but also operated remittance service. Wang Tong An Ji was situated on the main street of Hong Kong island. The second floor was used as an office, the third and fourth floors were used as lodging house where Meixian people going back and forth to the Dutch Indies stayed. Thousands of Meixian people and hundreds of recruiters were the customers. They also helped these countrymen to get official documents at the Dutch Consulate in Hong Kong or helped them buy steamship tickets. Handling remittance service was also their important business. They were supposed to have direct connections with Hakka remittance agencies in Batavia usually running trade companies simultaneously.

According to the memoirs written by Junmian's third son Pan Maoxian (懋賢), Junmian helped his nephew, Zhiwo, to establish De Ren He trading company in Kobe. They exported Japanese goods to the ports of Jakarta, Surabaya, Macassar, Jogjakarta, Bangkok and Singapore, where "Hakka" importers and wholesale dealers were responsible with selling goods. In accordance with the boom of Japan's South Sea trade, they enjoyed continuing prosperity after 1914. In 1931, Junmian decided to withdraw his stocks from De Ren He and let his elder son Maoduan (懋端) establish another trading company Dong Ming (東明) of their own in Kobe using one-third of the capital. The rest of the withdrawn capital amounting 160,000 Hong Kong dollar was sent to Hong Kong. The second son Maoqun (懋群) purchased a land at Yuan Lang (元朗) and began the construction of traditional Hakka style Yin Hua Lu (Figure 3) there, that was completed 3 years later (Pan, 1989).

Pan Junmian's family rooted in Hong Kong even after the closure of Wan Tong An Ji in late 1920s. Wan Tong (萬通) of Hong Kong was succeeded by the second son Maoqun, and Wan Tong of Shanghai and Jiulong Nanyang Textile Company (九龍南洋織業公司) were operated by the third son Maoxian. They mostly engaged in trade, like exporting goods from Kobe, Shanghai, Hong Kong to South Sea areas. Pan Junmian also opened Zhong Tian National Goods Department Store (中天國貨百貨公司) in the 1950s.[5]

Pan Lizhai (1854–1926) in Batavia

Pan Lizhai, Jieying (捷潁) was born in Qiaoxiang village in 1854. He left home at the age of 19. He stayed in Guangzhou, Hainan island and

[5]Li and Lin (2015). As for the trend of opening of national goods department stores in Hong Kong by Indonesian Hakka in the 1950s, please refer to Serizawa (2011).

Figure 2: Yinhualu in Nankou constructed in 1919

Source: Photo by Laixing Chen in September 2013.

Figure 3: Yinhualu in Yuanlang, Hong Kong constructed in 1931

Source: Photo by Laixing Chen in November 2015.

Wuzhou before he got to Batavia when he was 21 years old. Later, he established Zeng Xing (增興) trading company in Batavia and a branch in Surabaya with his friend Xiao Yu Zhai (蕭郁斎), who was from Long Wen zhen (隆文鎮) near Nankou zhen, Meixian. He also invested in Wan Tong Wan Ji in Hong Kong with his clan relative Pan Xiang Chu, who is actually a nephew 2 years older than him. Lizhai also established Lun Chang (綸昌), and invested in Xing Long (興隆), Fu Tong (阜通) and Yuan Tong (遠通) of Batavia, Xing Chang (興昌) of Macassar, Huiqun (滙群) of Semarang, Tong Chang (通昌) of Macao and Guang Xing Chang (廣興昌) of Kobe.

Pan Lizhai was known as *Phoa Lip Tjay* in Batavia Chinese community. When Hakka merchants began to take root in Batavia in the middle of 19th century, situation surrounding Chinese in the Dutch Indies underwent a great change. The tax collection contract system as a whole was gradually suspended. Strict regulations applied to Chinese merchants also became more relaxed. New European immigrants increased and comparatively better business circumstances was provided (Erkelens, 2013). Hakka as newcomers grasped the opportunity in the business and city job field, among whom the new local leaders were born riding on the rise of *Kaoem moeda* movement.

Well known in Batavia Chinese History, active community leaders established the first Chinese consolidated association Tiong Hoa Hwe Koan, THHK, in March 1900 and started managing the Chinese school next year. Among these activists, there were at least three important Hakka merchants from Meixian. Qiu Xieting (丘燮亭), known as *Khoe A Fan* (丘亞恒), took up the position of the first vice-president till 1908 and again in 1917–1918. He was described as one of the important persons who played a "transboarder" role especially with Japan (Kwartanada, 2012: 31–33). Pan Lizhai known as *Phoa Lip Tjay* (潘立斎) and Liang Yingtang (梁映堂) known as *Nio Hoey Own* (梁輝運) were included in these 20 founders and assumed the position of directors of the first term. Liang Yingtang also took up the position of vice-president during 1905–1915. Another important Hakka leader was Liao Yiguang (廖煜光), known as *Lieuw A Yoeng* (廖亞榮), who was also elected as vice-president during 1911–1915 (Nio, 1940: 241–243).

The newest wooden tablet made in 1918 to the memory of contributors owned by Leiden University now was originally hung inside Kong Kuan, Chinese Council building in Batavia (Figure 4). It shows that Liang Yingtang was bestowed the rank as Kapitan, while Qiu Xieting and Liao

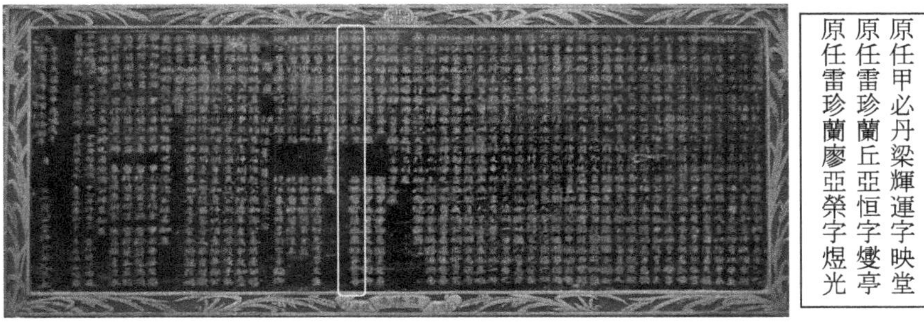

Figure 4: Wooden tablet of 1918 used to be hung inside Kong Kuan

Source: Photo by Laixing Chen in Leiden University in September 2010.

Yiguang were qualified as Liutenant. This means they were not only the enthusiastic members to lead the Chinese community to new direction but also were regarded as respectable Chinese by the Dutch colonial government.

Family Network Connecting Three Important Ports and Their Hometown

Panzhiwo and important Hakka families in Batavia

Please recall the reason and process how Pan Zhiwo came to Kobe and how his employer Liao Daoming came to Kobe via Yokohama. Before Zhiwo arrived at Kobe, three youngsters from Liao family, one from Qiu family and one from Liang family were there and studied together. Qiu Xieting was always going back and forth between Japan and Batavia. This is the reason why they asked uncle Qiu to allow them to study further.

Figure 5 shows that Pan Zhiwo was certainly a family member of Pan Lizhai at Nankou. Zhiwo's memoirs tells us Qiu Maorong was from Qiu Xieting's shop and Liang Zhengcheng (梁正成) was from Liang Yingxing's (梁映星) shop (Pan Zhiwo, 2002: 4). I would assume Liang Yingxing should be Liang Yingtang's family member. If not, Pan Zhiwo might have mistaken Yingxing for Yingtang when he wrote down his autobiography. There was no explanation in his memoirs about who sent Liao Youde (友德), Liao Xianglan (湘瀾) and Liao Guoyi (國義) to Kobe. I would imagine it was Liao Yiguang that sent his young family members there. Taking into consideration that Liao Daoming was from a family of good

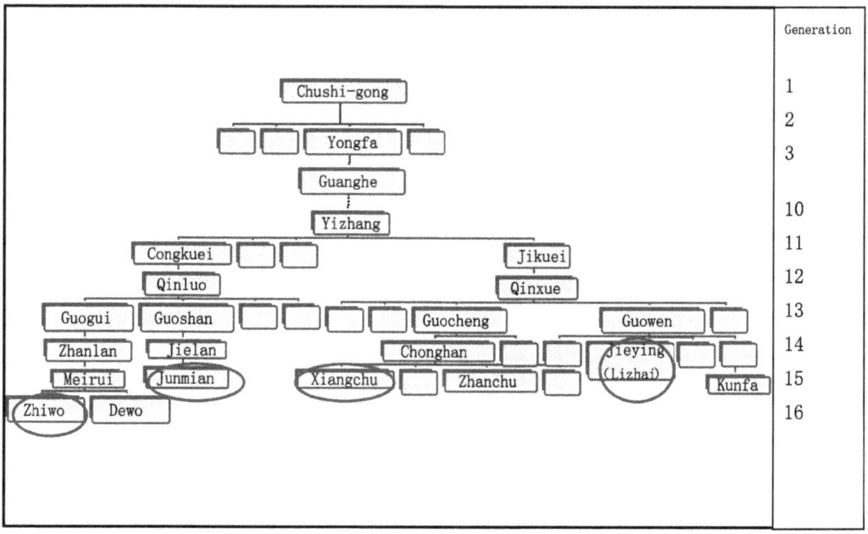

Figure 5: Pan family genealogy at qiaoxiang village of Nankou, Meixian

Source: Chen and Li (2007).

reputation, I assume one of his uncles where he was sent to study business before his visit to Japan was Liao Yiguang, namely *Lieuw A Yoeng*, the future Liutenant of Batavia Chinese Council.

Liao's family was from Songkou zhen (松口鎮), Meixian, the same hometown as Liang Yingtang's. These four important Hakka families in Batavia, Liang (*Nio* 梁), Liao (*Lieuw* 廖), Qiu (*Khoe* 丘), Pan (*Phoa* 潘) were also closely linked together in business. To see how the stocks were shared would explain how they co-operated in their business. Lian Xing (*Lian Hien*) company was owned by Liao Yiguang and Qiu Xieting. Zeng Xing (*Tjeng Hien*) was owned by Pan Lizhai and his friend Xiao Yuzhai (蕭郁斋) known as *Siauw A Hien*.[6] According to the memoirs of Pan

[6]As for the capital and shareholders, please refer to the Figures 3-6 in the third chapter of the doctoral thesis by Kudo (2016). When they were first registered, Lian Xing was capitalized at 125,000 guilders. Respectively *Liauw A Yoeng* held 23 stocks, *Liauw To Beng* held 2 stocks, *Khoe A Fan* held 23 stocks and *Khoe Sim Yoeng* held 2 stocks. Zeng Xing was capitalized at 100,000 guilders. *Siauw A Hien* held 24 stocks, *Siauw Phoe Tjaij* had 1 stock, *Phoa Liep Tjaij* had 23 stocks, *Phoe Tek Tjhoe* had 1 stock and *Phoa Kie Hoat* kept 1stock. From this, we can safely say *Liao To Beng* should be Liao Daoming and *Liauw A Yoen*'s close family member.

Zhiwo, Pan's family was sharing the stocks with Lian Xing and Zeng Xing (Pan, 2002: 3). Zeng Xing's next door Lun Chang (*LoenTjiang*) owned by Liaos, Pans and Xiaos was importing Japanese matches from Kobe with the Java style labels. Trade mark holder of this match who registered at the trademark office in Japan was Liao Daoming.[7] According to the research done in Indonesia, Qiu Xieting invested in the trading companies Yong An Xiang, Guang Xing Chang in Kobe and Yong An He in Yokohama mentioned above.[8] Liao Daoming was a key person at the nodal point Kobe. It is amazing to see how Hakka network was mutually related and extended.

Hakka of early days in Batavia

There is an old Chinese style ancestral hall called Baishi Zong Yici (百氏總義祠) (Figure 6), Consolidated Mausoleum for a Hundred Families,

Figure 6: Baishi Zong Yici

Source: Photo by Yuko Kudo and Laixing Chen in September 2017.

[7]Thanks to Yuko, Kudo who told and showed me the proof of registration.

[8]Kwartanada (2012), p. 32. I suppose *Wing On Chong* and *Kwang Wing On* of Kobe in Didi's paper should be Yong An Xiang and Guang Xing Chang. *Wing On Who* of Yokohama there should be Yong An He.

Figure 7: Relief of Qiu Xieting

Source: Photo by Yuko Kudo and Laixing Chen in September 2017.

within the block just across Jembatan Batu street at the back side of Kota Station. This mausoleum building was built in 1876, and Yi Cheng (義成) Elementary School was operated there in 1906. It was once called Hakka Consolidated Mausoleum (客属總義祠 Keshu Zong Yici), later Hakka Association (客属總會 Keshu Zonghui) in 1937 and then Overseas Chinese Association (華僑公会 Huaqiao Gonghui) in 1939 (Zhu, 1948: 2–3). On the wall of the light side facing the ancestral temple, the relief of Qiu Xieting is embedded and his contribution to the Chinese society is explained on it by the name of Overseas Chinese Association at the time of 1939 (Figure 7). After his death, his family donated 10,000 guilders from his inheritance to set up a fund for the local Chinese junior high school. His nephew Qiu Yuanrong's (丘元榮) contribution was also recorded on the stone tablet.

Hakka as newcomers Totok came to Batavia in the late 19th century and started to make a living around today's Glodok Chinatown area. Hakka gradually settled in Pintu Besar Selatan and some moved to the north, while Hokkien people were concentrated in Pintu Kecil of Glodok. The early Hakka traders shops like Zeng Xing and Lun Chang were situated along Pintu Besar Selatan Street. Along Jembatan Batu street near the

Kota Station are San Yuan Gong temple settled by Hakka and the ancestral halls of several Hakka families like Zhang's, Chen's and Liang's just next door to the former Overseas Chinese Association building and the Consolidated Mausoleum for a Hundred Families.

Family network strengthened

These four families strengthened the mutual trust through marriage. Pan Zhiwo's third son Qiaoyuan (潘翹元) got married with a daughter of Qiu Yuanrong (丘元榮), who assumed the position of chairman of Batavia Chinese Chamber of Commerce in the 1930s. Yuanrong was a nephew of Qiu Xieting as mentioned above. Liang Yingtang's great grandson is Shizhen (梁世禎), very well known as Soetjipto Nagaria, chairman of Sumarecon Group. His mother Pan Shurong is also from the Pan family, a granddaughter of Pan Xiangchu. Another famous business leader of Chinese origin Pandji Wisaksana (潘萬鑫), chairman of Pioneer Plastics Ltd., is also from these three natural villages in Nankou, Siqian (寺前), Tangdu (塘肚) and Gaotian (高田). They were integrated and called Qiaoxiang village administratively. According to Pan Zhenchong, Benny Suwandy, a grandson of Pan Lizhai's elder brother, who was the former chairman of Pan Family Association of Indonesia, there are about 200 Pan family members in Indonesia now and most of them were originally from Nankou.[9]

The report made by Bank of Taiwan on the remittance by Chinese in Batavia in 1914 recorded eight Hakka remittance shops as follows (Bank of Taiwan, 1914: 122):

> Lian Xing 聯興、Nan Mao 南茂、Lun Chang 綸昌、Gong Yuan 恭源、Chang Shun 長順、Zeng Xing 增興、De Yu Long 德裕隆、Yuan Xing 元興

As already pointed out, Lian Xing was managed by Qiu and Liao, Zeng Xing was managed by Pan and Xiao, Lun Chang was owned by Liao, Pan, and Xiao. In addition to this, Nan Mao was founded by Liang Yingtang's father Caichen (梁采臣). Qiu and Liao held two-thirds of the stocks of De Yu Long. Like this, five out of eight remittance shops were closely related with five Hakka families mentioned above including Xiao. Their families were always going back and forth between hometown and

[9]Interview on September 28, 2017 at Benny's office on Gunung Sahari Raya Street.

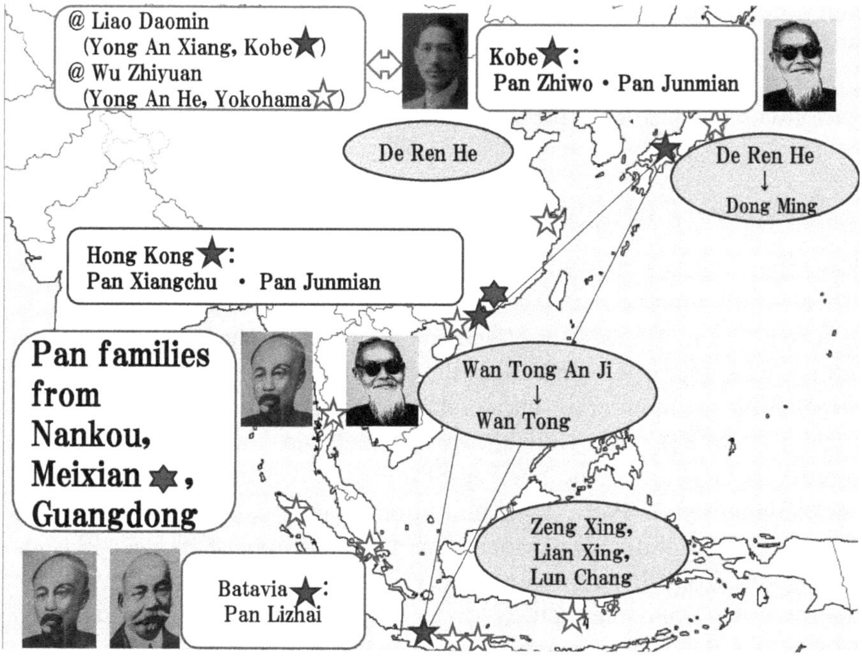

Figure 8: Pan family network

Batavia via Hong Kong. The families were also linked tightly by remittance. Figure 8 shows the Pan family network mentioned above so far. By the success of Pan Zhiwo, the Pan family network could extend to Kobe, Japan and Shanghai became their important nodal port.

Conclusion

In the previous study (Chen, 2016b), I made it clear how Pan Zhiwo was able to make a tremendous success in the competitive business world. World War I provided Chinese merchants in Japan a chance to handle Japanese goods to the South Seas. During the War, exports from Japan to Dutch Indies showed a rapid increase as quick as over 10 times in volume in 5 years. As one of the very few Hakka merchants, Pan Zhiwo grasped a chance, and finally became the top Chinese exporter of Japan to the South Seas in the 1930s (Chen, 2017). In the process of completion of the chapter, I came to notice that Pan family along with Liao family had set up an intimate family-based commercial network with their homeland, Hong Kong, Guangzhou and Batavia. The most active "trans-boarder" Hakka Totok Qiu Xieting in Batavia was a key person who sent young people to learn the technique in Japan. Liao Yiguang, Liang Yingtang and Pan Lizhai followed. These people proved to be highly important Hakka Chinese in Batavia. The purpose of this chapter was to collate mutual relations of important families and evaluate the role of Hakka merchants.

Next, there certainly existed a big trend or passion by Meixian Hakka people to introduce new knowledge and technique. It might have come from a particular background at a particular time. Taiwanese Hakka Qiu Fengjia's (丘逢甲) retreat from Japanese conquest of Taiwan to homeland in 1895, Huang Zunxian's (黄遵憲) retirement from the central political world to homeland Meixian in 1898, establishment of Department of Commerce by the central government and the promulgation of Chinese Chamber of Commerce Regulation in 1904 and Japan's victory over Russia in 1905 were the backgrounds of Hakka's extension outward. Both Pan Zhiwo and Liao Daoming were dispatched to Japan after the Russo-Japanese War. Japan's victory over Russia actually cheered up Chinese. Treatment for Japanese had been improved in Dutch East Indies in 1899 and Japanese Consulate was established there in 1908. In other words, the political status of Japanese as foreigners in the Dutch East Indies was pulled up to the level of Western people. On the other hand, Chinese status there remained unchanged. Almost at the same time, Dutch nationality law was put in force to let Chinese born in the East Indies acquire Dutch citizenship as colonial population. The system of gathering together as members of Chinese chambers of commerce prevailing worldwide was timely provided for the Chinese there. They began to appeal to overseas Chinese asking for the promulgation of nationality law under paternal blood line theory together, utilizing the chambers of commerce network (Chen, 2016a). Thus, Chinese nationalism came to gain power. THHK, Chinese school and Chinese Chamber of Commerce into which Hakka could well be devoted were starting to come into shape.

Trans-national networking ability based upon their newly built family bases in new ports like Hong Kong and Kobe was their superiority. In other words, Japan factor was crucial in every point when Hakka tried to assert themselves in Batavia. By strengthening the family networks through marriage, they made their business strategy more effective later.

References

Bank of Taiwan (1914). *Nanyo ni Okeru Kakyo: Shina Yijyu Min Fu Kawase Kankei* 『南洋に於ける華僑:支那移住民,附為替係』(Overseas Chinese in the South Seas: Their Foreign Exchange and Remittance),(pp. 121–122). Taipei, Bank of Taiwan.

Chang, W., ed. (2015). 『東瀛客縱; 日本客家研究初探』 (A Preliminary Study on Hakka in Japan). Taiwan Hakka Culture Development Center.

Chen, L. (2016a). Kindai Chugoku no Soshokai Seido — Tsunagaru Kajin No Sekai 『近代中国の総商会制度:繋がる華人の世界」(Chinese Chambers of Commerce in the First Half of Twentieth Century: Connecting Chinese Societies). Kyoto, Kyoto University Academic Press.

Chen, L. (2016b). 20 Seiki Shotou ni Okeru Hakkakei Kashou no Taitou: Kobe to Honkon ni Shinshutsu Shita Meixian Nankou-zhen no Pan Shi Ichizoku「20世紀初頭における客家系華商の台頭:神戸と香港に進出した梅縣南口鎮の潘氏一族」 (The Rise of Hakka Merchants in the Early Twentieth Century: Pan's Family Advancing into Kobe and Hong Kong from Nankou-zhen of Meixian), Murakami Ei (ed.), Kindai Chugoku ni Okeru Shakai Keizai Seido no Saihen『近代中国における社会経済制度の再編』 (Reconstruction of Socio-Economic System of Modern China), (pp. 53–82). Kyoto, Institute for Research in Humanities, Kyoto University. http://www.zinbun.kyoto-u.ac.jp/~rcmcc/02_chen.

Chen, L. (2017). 『十九世紀末到二戰前後為主東亞華僑史中客家商人與客家精英的定位:梅縣－香港－神戶－巴達維亞』 (The Evaluation on Hakka Merchants and Hakka Elites in East Asia from the End of the 19th Century to the Second World War: Meixian, Hong Kong, Kobe and Batavia). Chang Weian 張維安(Ed.), 在地、南向與全球客家 (Hakka: Locality, Southbound and Globalization), (pp. 533–565). Taoyuan, National Chiao Tung University Press.

Chen, Z. and Li, Q. (2007). *Meixian Sancun*『梅縣三村』 (Three Village in Meixian). Beijing, Qinghua University Press.

Chinese Consolidated Benevolent Association, ed. (2013). Rakuchi Seikon: Kobe Kakyo to Kamisaka Chuka Kaikan no Hyakunen [Zoutei Ban] 『落地生根:神戸華僑と神阪中華会館の百年[増訂版]』(Roots in a New Chinese Homeland: A Hundred History of Overseas Chinese in Kobe and the Chinese Consolidated Benevolent Association of Kobe and Osaka [Revised version]). Tokyo, Kenbun Shuppansha.

Erkelens, M. (2013). *The Decline of the Chinese Council of Batavia: The Loss of Prestige and Authority of the Traditional Elite amongst the Chinese Community from the End of the Nineteenth Century until 1942.* Dissertation submitted to Leiden University. https://openaccess.leidenuniv.nl/bitstream/handle/1887/21954/FulltextDEZEGEBRUIKEN.pdf?sequence=19.

Guangdong Province Meizhoushi Huaqiaozhi Editorial Committee and Society of Meizhoushi Overseas Chinese History, ed. (2001). *Meizhou Shi Huaqiao Zhi* 『梅州市華僑志』(Annals of Meizhou Overseas Chinese). Shenzhen, Editorial Committee.

Kudo, Y. (2016). *Chinese Economic Activity in the Netherlands Indies: A Study of Merchants in Semarang, 1900–1930*. Dissertation submitted to the University of Tokyo.

Kwartanada, D. (2012). The Tiong How Hwee Koan School: A Tranborder Project of Modernity in Batavia, c. 1900s. In Siew-Min Sai, Chang-Yau Hoon (eds.), *Chinese Indonesians Reassessed: History, Religion and Belonging*. London, Routledge.

Li, M. and Lin, D. (2015). 「壹幢古宅」(An Old Traditional Mansion), *Yi Zhou Kan* 『壹週刊』 June 25, 2015, Hong Kong, Yi Zhou Kan.

Li, W. (1914). 「呉植垣傳」 (Biography of Wu Zhiyuan), 『中國實業雑誌』 (Chinese Industrial Review), Tokyo, Chinese Industrial Review, 5(7).

Nio, J. 梁友蘭 (1940). *Riwajat 40 Taon Dari Tiong Hoa Hwee Koan Batavia (1900–1939)*. Jakarta, Tiong Hoa Hwee Koan Batavia.

Pan, M. (1989). *Xianfu Junmian Gong Shengping Shiji Jianjie Zhi San* (A Profile of the Biography of my Father Junmian, No. 3), written on April 10, 1989, owned by the successor of Yinhualu of Qiaoxiang village, Nankou-zhen, Meixian.

Pan, S., ed. (2016). 『廣東省梅縣南口鎮僑鄉村縣志』 (Annals of Qiaoxiang Village, Nankou-zhen of Meixian-County in Guangdong). Guangzhou, Nanfang Chuban Chuanmei and Xinshiji Chubanshe.

Pan, Z. (2002). Memoirs by Pan Zhiwo, provided by Pan Ganyuan, Zhiwo's eldest son, digitized in *Shantou Wenshi,* Shantou, China: Shantou Wenshi Ziliao Yanjiu Weiyuanhui, No. 17, 6.

Research Division of Bank of Kanan (1942). Ranryo Indo shogyo kai ni okeru kakyo, *Kagin-chosyo No. 89* 「蘭領印度商業界にける於ける華僑」(Overseas Chinese in the Business Circles of Dutch East Indies), 『華銀調書 89』. Taipei, Bank of Kanan.

Serizawa, S. (2011). Kokka Kousi: Reisen Jidai Ni Okeru Honkon Syakai No Ichimen 「「国貨公司」：冷戦時代における香港社会の一面」(The Department Store for Chinese Products: An Aspect of Hong Kong Society in the Cold-War Era), Sogo *Kenkyuusyo Syoho* (Bulletin of Research Institute), 19: 45–65.

Serizawa, S. (2016). Honkon Indonesia Kajin Gaisetsu「香港インドネシア華人概説」(An Introduction to the Study of the Chinese Indonesian in Hong Kong), Kitamura Yumi (ed.), *20 Seiki Ajia no Kokusai kankei to Indonesia Kajin no Ido* (Chinese Indonesian on the Move within the International

Relations of 20th Century Asia), (pp. 127–143). Kyoto, Kyoto University Library.

Zhu. C. (1948). *A Brief History of Overseas Chinese Association, The Tenth Anniversary of Overseas Chinese Association* 『華僑公会十週年紀念刊』. Jakarta, Overseas Chinese Association.

https://doi.org/10.1142/9789811250668_0006

Chapter 6

Proving "Japaneseness": Passport and Identification Problems of Japanese in the Dutch East Indies*

Makoto Yoshida

Professor, Nanzan University, Japan

Introduction

With Taiwan ceded to Japan by the Treaty of Shimonoseki concluded with the Qing dynasty in 1895, establishing control over the island became an urgent issue for the Japanese government. Besides a series of military operations to suppress armed resistance against Japanese rule, one of the first attempts by Japan to establish effective rule over Taiwan was to grant Taiwanese residents Japanese nationality. For this purpose, the colonial government in Taiwan took two measures in 1897: making people residing in Taiwan Japanese subjects and institutionalizing passports.

The Governor-General of Taiwan set a deadline of May 8, 1897 for granting Japanese nationality to the Taiwanese. Local people who failed to depart from Taiwan before that date were treated as Japanese subjects. In other words, they were considered to have chosen Japanese nationality and automatically given up their status as Qing subjects. Prior to this

*The research for this chapter was generously supported by JSPS KAKENHI Grant Numbers JP20H04406, JP18K11820, JP16H00740, JP16H03501 and Nanzan University Pache Research Subsidy I-A-2 for the 2021 academic year.

measure, a passport regulation was enacted in January. This regulation was adopted from Ministry of Foreign Affairs Ordinance No. 1 (外務省令第1号) of 1878. The preamble to this ordinance clearly stated that "A passport is a means to prove Japanese nationality…" (Keishicho, 1893: 122). Thus, introducing a modern passport system in Taiwan was a logical means for the Japanese government to link the Taiwanese to Japanese nationality. In April 1899, when the Japanese government legislated the 1899 Nationality Act, the Governor-General of Taiwan declared that the Act should be applied to Taiwan.

With this series of measures to "embrace" the people of Taiwan as Japanese subjects, the Japanese government affirmed its sovereignty over Taiwan.[1] Taiwanese who became Japanese subjects were called *Taiwan sekimin* 台湾籍民 and formed part of a group of people called *gaichijin* 外地人 (Japanese from the colonies). *Gaichijin* possessed Japanese nationality, but their rights differed from those of *naichijin* 内地人 (Japanese from the mainland). A distinction was made between Japanese–Japanese and Taiwanese–Japanese subjects based on the family register system, or *koseki* 戸籍, which was adopted from mainland Japan.

While the family register system in Taiwan functioned in a similar way to that of mainland Japan — for example, passports were issued based on the family register records — it was given a different name: *koko* 戸口. It was basically impossible for a Taiwanese to be registered in a *koseki* even after moving to mainland Japan.[2] Taiwanese were required to carry a passport when they went abroad and were to be treated as Japanese subjects at immigration control outside Japanese territory. However, problems arose for the Governor-General of Taiwan after these measures were undertaken due to the emergence of *gisō sekimin* 偽装籍民 or "pseudo-Japanese," people who had obtained Japanese passports illegally.

This chapter deals with the problems of national identity and passports that became a diplomatic concern for the Japanese and the Dutch governments at the turn of the twentieth century by examining the

---

[1] Torpey uses the verb "embrace" instead of "govern" or "rule" in the process of state formation. See Torpey (2000).

[2] The family register system in Taiwan was legislated in 1905. However, as several studies have pointed out, this legislation did not follow the Japanese family register system. It differentiated between Japanese from mainland Japan (*naichi* 内地) and Japanese from the colony (*gaichi* 外地). The latter were not entitled to full citizenship. For details, see Endō (2010), Oguma (1998), and Kurihara (2000, 2002, 2004).

movement of people between empires, specifically the movement of people from Taiwan to the Dutch East Indies. The movement of Taiwanese during the colonial period has mainly been discussed in relation to Mainland China, where the problem of *gisō sekimin* became an issue as a result of the extraterritoriality that Japan exercised in China.

A number of studies have focused on the way the Japanese colonial government attempted to establish sovereignty over Taiwan by controlling the movement of people between Taiwan and Mainland China (Kurihara 2000, 2002; Nakamura 1980; Wu 2018). Although there are several studies on *Taiwan sekimin*, these are mostly concerned with their commercial activities in the Dutch East Indies (Claver, 2014; Kudo, 2005; Post, 1993, 1995). Studies concerning legal or political aspects of *Taiwan sekimin* provide only a partial view of the subject, based on either Japanese documents (Goto, 2012) or Dutch documents (Lohanda, 2002; Tjiook-Liem, 2009).

Institutionalization of the passport played a critical role in defining Japanese nationals. Using archival documents from Japan, the Netherlands and Taiwan, this chapter reveals how the passport, an official document used to prove nationality and identity, became a major source of concern for the Japanese and Dutch authorities, and how they worked to resolve passport-related problems.

Movement of Taiwanese People and the Origin of *gisō sekimin*

In 1897, the Governor-General of Taiwan issued passports for the first time (Kurihara, 2000). Passport applications were filed at local issuing authorities in Taiwan from this time onward. Applicants had to fill in the following information: name, social status, registered domicile, address, age, and purpose of travel and destination (Keishicho 1900: 40–41). According to the 1897 records, Amoy (present-day Xiamen), on the coast of southeastern China, was the place most people visited, and their main purpose of travel was business. Other travel purposes such as visiting ancestral graves or reunions with relatives followed a decade later. These patterns continued through the colonial period. As Table 1 shows, not so many people traveled from Taiwan to the Dutch East Indies.

After Japan established sovereignty over Taiwan, the Governor-General of Taiwan gave priority to economic development of the sugar

Table 1: Statistical data from passport records issued in Taiwan

	Qing (until 1912), China (after 1913)	**Hong Kong**	**Straits settlements**	**The East Indies (until 1915), The Dutch East Indies (after 1916)**	**Java (after 1915)**	**Borneo**
1906	3564/280	62/4	3/2	3		
1907	3030/298	36/1	1	4	1	
1908	2364/231	17	2		7	
1909	2206/242	18		1/1	8	
1913	1571/182	69/4			26/1	
1914	1747/526	66/2	13		36/6	
1915	2196/399	399/47	23		40	
1916	2921/614	614/68	38/9	73/9		10/2
1917	2643/695	75/18	35/4	61/17		737/46
1918	2488/626	72/5	28/9	72/8		242/30
1919	2153/529	88/8	16/7	83/8		4/2
1920	1633/407	104/20	36/6	79/17		11/3

Source: Gaimushō Tsūshō Kyoku. *Ryoken Kahusū oyobi Imin Tōkei* (Passport Issuance Number and Migration Data), 1921.

industry in the colony. At that time Taiwan was also already known for tea production. Therefore, it is not difficult to guess the reasons Taiwanese traveled to the Dutch East Indies: many of them went there for commercial purposes, such as tea trading, inspecting sugar factories and running small businesses. The most common route was to embark at Keelung, stopping by Amoy or Hong Kong, and then transferring for Batavia in Singapore.

If applicants filled in Batavia as their destination, it is almost certain that they visited the East Indies. However, there were a great number of people whose journeys cannot be tracked. In 1897, a Japanese consul at Amoy reported to the Governor-General of Taiwan that many Chinese had applied for Japanese passports claiming that they were Taiwanese (Kurihara, 2002: 24). This consul also mentioned similar cases of Chinese applying to other Japanese consulates in China for passports. Because people continued to move between Taiwan and Mainland China without passports even after May 8, 1897, the effective control of peoples' movement by the Japanese authorities came into question. This issue concerned Japanese sovereignty over Taiwan. If Chinese left for the Dutch East

Indies with Japanese passports from Mainland China, it was almost impossible to track their footsteps.

As the purpose-of-travel records suggest, many Taiwanese were originally from Mainland China and maintained kinship and the practice of regularly visiting their ancestors' graves. Some continued living in Amoy, Swatow or Hong Kong after being registered as Japanese subjects in Taiwan. Their frequent comings and goings between Taiwan and Mainland China caused serious concern among Japanese officials over the problem of *gisō sekimin*.

A *gisō sekimin* was a person who obtained a Japanese passport illegally, and then pretended to be a Japanese subject. Once regarded as a Japanese subject, such a person was able to exercise extraterritorial rights in the Chinese cities mentioned above. Due to this privilege attached to it, the Japanese passport attracted not just merchants but criminals as well, including opium dealers and procurers of prostitution. Whereas the Japanese consul often urged wealthy Chinese merchants to acquire Japanese passports, expecting that they would make economic contributions to Taiwan, many of the "merchants" who obtained Japanese passports were opium dealers.

Dispatches issued by the Japanese consulate estimated that only 1–2% of the total number of "Taiwanese" in Fujian were true Taiwanese (Nakamura, 1980: 66–67). Despite frequent requests from the Japanese consulates to find a solution to the problem of *gisō sekimin*, the issue had still not been resolved by the time the Second Sino-Japanese War broke out in 1937 (Kurihara, 2000, 2002). Although the number of *gisō sekimin* in the Dutch East Indies was small, the Japanese government viewed them as a serious diplomatic concern.

Japanese Subjects in the Dutch East Indies

To understand the *gisō sekimin* issue in the Dutch East Indies, it is necessary to grasp the socio-legal context, which is different from that of *gisō sekimin* in China. In 1854, the Dutch parliament enacted a general administrative law, the *Regerings-reglement*, to govern the East Indies. Article 109 of this law defined the legal status of persons living in the Dutch East Indies, creating two classes of citizens: Europeans and indigenous people (*Inlanders*). Europeans were subject to Dutch law whereas indigenous people were subject to customary law or *adat* (Yoshida, 2002). Rights and duties with regard to taxation, freedom of movement and residence, land rights, unpaid labor for public works, etc., were different for the two groups. The criterion for categorizing a person as European or indigenous was race (*rascriterium*).

On this legal basis, Japanese were classified into a sub-category of indigenous people called Foreign Orientals (*Vreemde Oosterlingen*). Foreign Orientals, whose category became independent next to European and indigenous with the reform of *Regerings-reglement* in 1925, included most Asians other than natives of the Dutch East Indies, primarily Chinese. In fact, Japanese were regarded as Chinese by the Dutch authorities. Diplomatic records reveal that Japanese were treated as Chinese by local authorities in the Dutch East Indies. In 1897, a Japanese consul in Singapore, Fujita Toshio, sent a series of dispatches to Vice-Minister for Foreign Affairs Komura Jutarō describing the situation of Japanese in the Dutch East Indies as follows:

> Japanese have always been regarded as Chinese in Java and other Dutch-controlled islands. Japanese are provided with a travel pass with a note that the pass holder is Chinese. They stay in a Chinese district or settle down there and are levied the same amount of tax as the Chinese pay. All the petitions to the Dutch authorities must be submitted via the Chinese representative of each district (these men are called Captain or Major). In other words, Japanese are equal to Chinese.[3]

Chinese, who had emigrated to the Dutch East Indies since the 10th century, played a major role in commercial activities (South Manchuria Railway, 1940; Tai, 2014: 42). Despite their leading role in business, however, there were several restrictions on their economic freedom. They were only allowed to stay in a designated area (*Chineesche wijk*), and permission from local authorities was needed in order to go out of this "ghetto" (Tjiook-Liem, 2009: 297–300). A travel pass was also required to visit other towns, cities and districts even within the island of Java (Figure 1). Because many Chinese earned their living by peddling, these restrictions on freedom of movement constituted a major obstacle to carrying out their economic activities (South Manchuria Railway, 1940: 81).

Although Japanese were regarded as Chinese, the legal status of Japanese changed when the Japanese and Dutch governments revised the

[3]Public No. 19, April 5, 1897 (Diplomatic Archives: 3.8.2.72).

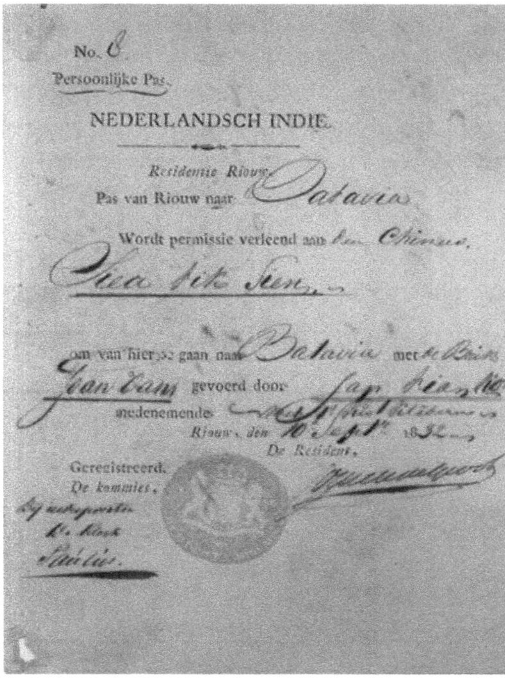
No. 8
Persoonlijke Pas.
NEDERLANDSCH INDIE.
Residentie Riouw.
Pas van Riouw naar Batavia.
Wordt permissie verleend aan den Chinees,
Siea Tin Sien,
om van hier te gaan naar Batavia met de
gevoerd door
medenemende
Riouw, den 10 Sept. 1832
De Resident,
Geregistreerd.
De kommies,

Figure 1: A personal pass for a trip from Riau to Batavia, issued for a Chinese, Siea Tin Sien, on September 10, 1832. Endangered Archives Programme, British Library, EAP 153/3/12 (https://eap.bl.uk/archive-file/EAP153-3-12)

unequal Treaty of Amity and Commerce between the Netherlands and Japan, which had been signed in 1859. The 1896 Japan–Netherlands Treaty of Commerce and Navigation granted "most-favored nation" treatment to both countries. Based on this, the Japanese government asked the Dutch government to extend most-favored nation treatment to the Dutch East Indies so that Japanese subjects there could be entitled to the same legal rights as Europeans. This meant that Article 109 of the *Regeringsreglement* had to be revised.

In 1899, when the revised treaty came into effect, the Dutch parliament passed a law to revise Article 109. Known as the "Japanese law" (Lijnkamp, 1938; Tjiook-Liem, 2009: 260–266; Yoshida, 2008), this changed the legal status of the Japanese from Foreign Orientals to Europeans. With this revision, the unequal treatment of Japanese in the Dutch East Indies ended, at least legally. But in reality, mistreatment of Japanese by the Dutch officials continued for several reasons. Although the Dutch colonial government notified local authorities in 1903 that Japanese, including *Taiwan sekimin*, should be treated as Europeans, these authorities found it difficult to distinguish Japanese subjects, especially *Taiwan sekimin*, from Chinese on the basis of their appearance and customs. Another problem that arose with the change in legal status of the Japanese was the issue of *gisō sekimin* in the East Indies.

The Impact of the "Japanese law" and Requests for Japanese Nationality via Naturalization

As mentioned earlier, the legal status of people living in the Dutch East Indies had a great impact on their lives. The revision of the legal status of Japanese affected not only Japanese but also Chinese residing in the Dutch East Indies. The Chinese were well aware that the law had been revised and that Japanese now had legal status equal to that of Europeans, and this discriminatory classification generated in them a strong sense of unfairness, or simply anger.[4]

Japanese who had immigrated to the Dutch East Indies following the end of Japan's long-standing isolationist policy under the Tokugawa shogunate were mostly women, and many were engaged in prostitution, or at best, household work. Prostitution was called *shūgyō* 醜業, literally "dirty work," and the social reputation of the Japanese in the Dutch East Indies was accordingly quite negative, not only among all population groups in the East Indies but in Holland as well. In the parliamentary session held in the Netherlands to discuss revision of Article 109, some politicians questioned whether the Japanese in the Dutch East Indies, considering their professions and education, were civilized enough to be regarded as Europeans and given equal status (Yoshida, 2008: 13–15).

It is quite understandable that the Chinese community in the Dutch East Indies felt insulted upon learning that the Japanese had acquired legal status superior to their own. This sense of unfairness reinforced in the East Indies the Chinese nationalist sentiment that was being disseminated from China at the beginning of the twentieth century. Chinese demanded that the Dutch colonial government also grant them rights equal to those of Europeans. The growing number of immigrants from China as well as

[4]National Archive 2.05.03 inv.40.

their nationalistic tendencies were seen by the Dutch colonial government as a major threat to their secure governance.[5]

Not all Chinese joined the Chinese nationalism movement, however. Some, instead of demanding status equal to that of Europeans, tried to become Japanese subjects either through naturalization or by obtaining Japanese passports. Japan's victory in the Russo-Japanese War and emergence as a modern nation state based on Western models attracted some Chinese. A Chinese person residing in Palembang sent a petition for naturalization to the Imperial Household Agency in January of 1906. Besides maltreatment by local Dutch officials, one of his reasons for desiring Japanese nationality was Japan's military victory over Russia. This petitioner also noted that he had his queue, worn by male subjects of China's Qing dynasty, cut off, by which he showed himself wholeheartedly ready to become a Japanese subject.[6]

Another petition asking for naturalization, sent to Japan's Foreign Ministry in 1906 by Tan Sioe Liem (陳秀林), a Chinese merchant living in Semarang, Java, stated the reasons for wanting to become a Japanese subject as follows:

> Owing to my commercial business I have to travel about very much and moreover as I intend commencing an Import and Commission business that would oblige me to visit Japan, China, Europe and several other countries. Being a Chinaman and subject to the Dutch Laws, which do not allow Chinese people to travel about, even in this country, without being provided with a pass, it would be very difficult for me to travel. The obtaining and counter-signing of such a pass requires much time and is accompanied with great difficulties, for a Chinaman in the Dutch East Indies is treated as a Native of the country. Being a Japanese subject means being equal to Europeans and no obstacles whatever are placed before them. Europeans are free to travel about without a permit and are not thwarted about in any way."[7]

---

[5]According to the 1930 census, the number of Chinese residing in the Dutch East Indies was 221,438 in 1860; 461,089 in 1890; 537,316 in 1900; 809,039 in 1920; and 1,233,214 in 1930 (Volkstelling, 1930; Deel IV, 39). For the reasons for this rapid increase, see Tai 2014, 42.

[6]Diplomatic Archives: 3.9.5.3.

[7]Petition from Tan Sioe Liem, February 1906 (Diplomatic Archives: 3.9.5.3). Original text in English.

The Foreign Ministry of Japan replied to Tan Sioe Liem that his petition was not accepted. As a Japanese consul in Batavia pointed out in a report to the Ministry of Foreign Affairs, Chinese in the Dutch East Indies, especially wealthy Chinese, frequently tried to obtain Japanese nationality through naturalization, especially after the Russo-Japanese War. Their efforts were in vain, however; the rules and conditions for naturalization in the Japanese Nationality Act were so strict that not a single petition for Japanese nationality succeeded.[8]

Nationality, Passports and *giso sekimin*

Besides naturalization, there was another way Chinese could attempt to become Japanese subjects in the Dutch East Indies: to be registered in a family register in Japan. Japanese nationality was granted based on the family register system, or *koseki*. Hence, once registered as a Taiwanese, it was possible for a person to apply for a Japanese passport to the Governor-General of Taiwan. As several previous studies have pointed out, it took several years for the family register system to function properly in Taiwan due to a lack of skilled officers and know-how. Because of this, identity checks at the registration office were often arbitrary, depending on the knowledge and skill of the officer in charge (Endō, 2010; Kurihara, 2004; Oguma, 1998; Sato, 2012). This created a chance for some Chinese from Mainland China to claim they were from Taiwan and be successfully registered as Taiwanese.

On November 11, 1904, a report was sent by a Dutch official in Surabaya to the Governor-General of the Dutch East Indies which said that a wealthy Chinese man named Kwik Hong Biauw (郭洪淼), a cousin and a business partner of famous tea trader Kwik Djoen Eng (郭春秧), had visited Taiwan, purchased land there, and applied to the Japanese authorities for a travel pass. Prior to this, Kwik Hong Biauw had been sentenced to hard labor for violating the opium monopoly by the Dutch colonial government. He had sent a petition to the local court in the Dutch East Indies claiming that he was originally from Taiwan and therefore,

[8]For example, Goh Kim Chim, a wealthy Chinese businessman, applied for naturalization to the Japanese government but was rejected because he had not resided in Japan for a required period of time (South Manchuria Railway East Asiatic Economic Investigation Bureau 1940: Appendix 15).

based on the "Japanese Law", should be treated as a European. He argued that Dutch criminal law should be applied in his case rather than criminal regulations intended for the indigenous population.

Kwik Hong Biauw's petition was rejected by the Governor-General of the Dutch East Indies. After finishing his prison term, he immediately left the Dutch East Indies for Taiwan via Singapore, purchased land in Taiwan, and applied to the Japanese authorities for a travel pass (*reispas*).[9] Once the pass was issued, he returned to the East Indies with it where he asked the local authorities to treat him as a Japanese subject, based on his travel pass which had been issued by the Japanese authorities. He also had his queue cut off while he was in Taiwan. He was granted status equal to that of a Japanese, and therefore equal to that of a European. This case had a great impact on the Chinese community, the report said.[10]

The report by the Dutch official in Surabaya does not tell us what kind of pass Kwik Hong Biauw was issued by the Governor-General of Taiwan nor by what procedure he was granted status as a Japanese after his return to the Dutch East Indies.[11] However, a document filed at the Diplomatic Archives in Tokyo reveals that a Japanese passport was properly issued to Kwik Hong Biauw on March 16, 1904 (Figure 2). The report from Surabaya also indicates that a travel pass, or *reispas*, was viewed as a Japanese passport, and was accepted as proof of Japanese nationality by the Dutch authorities. The story of Kwik Hong Biauw suggests that the Chinese community in the East Indies already knew at this time that the Japanese had been recognized as equal in status to Europeans.

---

[9]Claver points out that Kwik Hong Biauw obtained a Japanese passport with his cousin Kwik Djoen Eng (Claver, 2014: 302–304). However, archival records in Tokyo and Taiwan show that Kwik Djoen Eng repeatedly visited the Dutch East Indies with a Japanese passport before Kwik Hong Biauw reportedly applied for his travel pass. The earliest record of Kwik Djoen Eng's visiting Java is from 1901 (Taiwan Sōtokufu Archive, The Archives of Institute of Taiwan History, Academia Sinica: 619–613). Therefore, it is reasonable to suppose that Kwik Djoen Eng had already obtained Japanese nationality before Kwik Hong Biauw applied for it in 1903–1904, and that he may have advised Kwik Hong Biauw to apply.

[10]Nationaal Archief: geheim in V.16.08.1906-29/inv.399. See also Post 1995, 271–273; Tjiook-Liem, 2009: 261–262.

[11]Post mentions that Chinese could apply for a Japanese passport by submitting proof of land purchase to the Japanese consulate in Singapore (Post, 1995: 271–272). But he does not mention from which archival documents he found this "loophole" procedure. Claver makes the same argument as Post (Claver, 2014: 304).

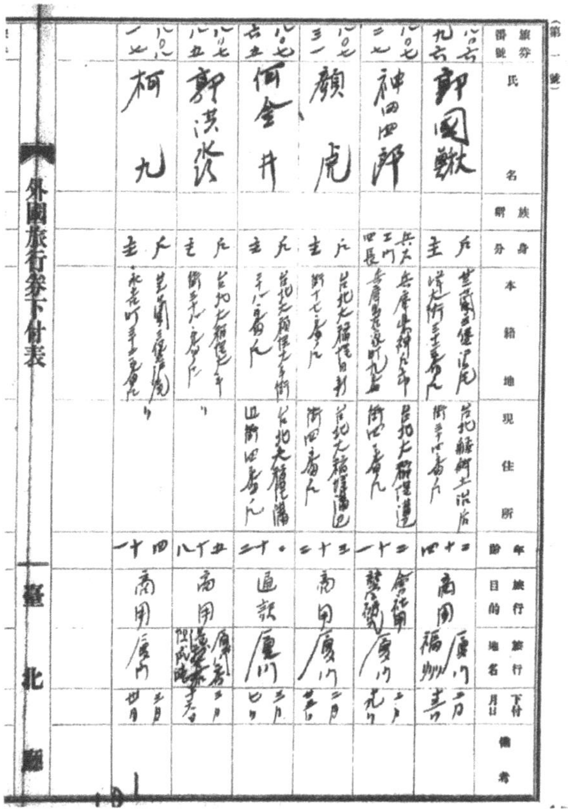

Figure 2: Record of passport issuance to Kwik Hong Biauw. Second from the left. From the top: passport number, name, social status, place of family register, address, age, purpose of trip, destination and date of issue (Diplomatic Archives: Kaigai Ryoken Kafu Hyo, Ryo 35)

Another case is a report about a group of 15 "so-called Chinese Japanese (*zogenaamde Chineesche Japanners*)" who landed at the port of Semarang on October 15, 1907.[12] The Governor-General of the Dutch East Indies ordered a Dutch Resident in Semarang to investigate this group after he read an article about their arrival in a local newspaper. An interview with a leader of the group named Soe Ing Soei (薛允瑞)

[12]Reports from Semarang, No. 317/68 November 9, 1907 and No. 332/68 November 18, 1907 (Nationaal Archief: 2.19.36.94 inv. 536).

provides a rare glimpse into the motives and process by which one Chinese person became a Japanese subject by obtaining a Japanese passport:

Question: What is your name, how old are you, what is your occupation and where do you live?

Answer: My actual name is Sie Oen Soei. Japanese read this name, written in Chinese character, as Soe Ing Soei. I am 46 years old, I was born in Taiwan, and I am a tobacco trader. I am currently residing in the district of Parakan, department of Temanggoeng, residence of Kedoe.

Question: Have you been living in Parakan for a long time?

Answer: Yes, I have been living in Parakan about 30 years.

Question: How did you come to Parakan?

Answer: I came with my father when I was 15 or 16 years old. My father, Si Gé, alias Sie Kie, is also from Taiwan. He had settled in Parakan, but went back to his native land where he had a house and owned land and traded. I with my father lived in Parakan about 10 years. Afterwards he returned to Formosa, to the city of Tai Pik, where he died. I stayed in Parakan. As I inherited my father's business along with his other properties with a brother of mine, I went to Formosa on a regular basis, to check the situation. How long I stayed there depended on what I found to do. Once I stayed there for 3 years. It was May or June of 1906 that I visited Taiwan for last time before I came back to Java. I arrived again in Semarang on October 15, 1907.

Question: Did you and your family members ask for a travel pass that is valid for Europeans upon your return to Semarang in October?

Answer: The last time I was in Formosa, I applied for land from the Japanese Government there, and received it for development for agricultural or other use. When I wanted to return to Parakan, the Japanese Government asked me what my nationality was. I stated that I was from Formosa, but had been a resident of Parakan in the Dutch East Indies for many years, for which I had a permanent residence permit. Then I was told that only Japanese nationals of Formosa were allowed to develop land issued by the Government. If I did not wish to assert my rights as a Japanese subject in the Dutch East Indies, the land would

> be taken back by the Government and handed over to others. Since I had already invested a great deal of money into that land, I complied with the wishes of the Japanese Government and returned to the Dutch East Indies with my family's Japanese passports. I strongly deny that I have been to Formosa for the purpose of obtaining documents required to be regarded as Japanese and equal to "Europeans".

The testimony of Soe Ing Soei reveals how and why he returned to the Dutch East Indies after becoming a Japanese subject by acquiring a Japanese passport. Though he had settled down in the Dutch East Indies before Taiwan was colonized by Japan, he maintained his strong ties with Taiwan, and frequently visited Taiwan where his father owned land and ran a business. This case illustrates the early form of migration between Taiwan and the Dutch East Indies, before the modern nation state system controlled the free movement of people.

The cases of Kwik Hong Biauw and Soe Ing Soei share similarities. Both men had settled in the Dutch East Indies before Japan colonized Taiwan, and both visited Taiwan and stayed there for several months before applying for a passport. Although there was no stipulation that land ownership was required for a passport application, both of their passports seem to have been issued based on their possession of real estate in Taiwan. Soe Ing Soei's statements in particular seem to confirm this.[13] However, few records exist of the acquisition of Japanese nationality by Chinese in the Dutch East Indies who were registered in a family register in Taiwan.[14]

Another means of acquiring Japanese nationality was to obtain a Japanese passport illegally, or at least through deception. Dutch diplomatic records do not report any cases of forged Japanese passports being held by Chinese residing in the East Indies. But the Japanese Diplomatic Archives have records of forged or counterfeit passports.[15] These include passports created by submitting a copy of a different person's family register, replacing the original passport photo with a different one, or bribing an officer to issue a passport. A report from the colonial government in Taiwan dated June 21, 1905 mentions that an officer in the passport

[13]Lohanda, quoting an article from a newspaper, notes that it was possible to acquire Japanese nationality by purchasing land in Taiwan valued at the equivalent of 500 yen in 1916 (Lohanda, 2002: 101).

[14]See Kurihara (2002, 2004).

[15]Diplomatic Archives: 3.8.5.19.

division issued dozens of passports illegally without leaving any records.[16] It turned out that this officer meant to pay off his debts by illegally issuing passports. In cases such as these, it was quite difficult to check the authenticity of the passports, since no copies or records existed other than the original passports themselves.

Surveillance Activities by the Dutch Authorities in the Dutch East Indies

It is not clear from official Dutch documents how the Dutch authorities investigated the illegal use of passports by Chinese. However, it is clear that they were cautious and issued warnings to the concerned authorities. Strict immigration control upon arrival in the Dutch East Indies was a result of this caution. Immigration officers interrogated those who fell under suspicion and some were deported, despite complaints by the Japanese Consulate General at Batavia. In addition to tight immigration control at the border, officers also practiced daily surveillance activities inside the Dutch East Indies.

A Taiwanese tea merchant named Liu Yuan（劉元）was refused permission to enter the Dutch East Indies by an immigration officer upon landing at the port of Surabaya in March of 1909. Although Liu had a Japanese passport with him, the Dutch officer identified him as Chinese and insisted that he would be admitted only if he followed the entrance procedure applied to Chinese persons. Despite his claim to be a Japanese subject and to be therefore entitled to freely enter the Dutch East Indies based on the most-favored nation clause in the treaty between the two countries, Liu was fined 100 guilders and forced to leave the Dutch East Indies. The Japanese consulate at Batavia made an inquiry to the colonial government in Taiwan about Liu Yuan's nationality and learned that Liu Yuan had been properly registered in a family register and was therefore clearly a Japanese subject.[17]

Although Liu Yuan had already been deported back to Taiwan, the Japanese consulate at Batavia lodged a protest against this measure and asked the Governor-General of the Dutch East Indies to reimburse the 100 guilder fine paid by Liu Yuan. This was agreed to. Being refused permission to enter the East Indies at immigration control points was something that

[16]Report No. 2670-2, June 21, 1905 (Diplomatic Archives: 3.8.5.19.3).

[17]Report No. 12, March 12, 1909 (Diplomatic Archives: 3.8.2.254).

often happened not only to Taiwanese but also to Japanese from mainland Japan, though the reasons differed. The entry of Japanese from mainland Japan was refused mostly for financial reasons, namely, lack of the required amount to cover living expenses,[18] whereas the refusal of entry to Taiwanese was often due to failure to show proper proof of identity.

Another form of surveillance activity conducted by the Dutch authorities in the East Indies involved the confiscation of Japanese passports. In October 1908, three Japanese subjects, two of whom were Taiwanese, visited Bagansiapiapi, a town in Sumatra, to explore the possibility of funding a primary school for local people, mostly Chinese children. The local Dutch authorities confiscated their passports and refused to return them, despite their protests. Facing deportation, these Japanese subjects asked the Japanese consulate for help. The Japanese consulate attempted to intervene on their behalf but was rebuffed by the local Dutch authorities, who expressed serious doubts as to whether the Japanese passports were authentic or had been forged.[19]

On June 8, 1909, the office of the Governor-General of Taiwan gave notice that any Taiwanese who wished to travel to the Dutch East Indies should have a passport with a visa endorsed at the Dutch consulate. At the same time, the office requested that the Dutch authorities treat Taiwanese as Japanese, and thus as Europeans by law, even though the Dutch colonial authorities were still highly suspicious of claims of Taiwanese nationality, "...especially in cases when Chinese (in appearance) claimed admission as Europeans, pretending to be the Japanese subjects and therefore equaled[sic] with Europeans. Such pretention in itself is not at all unacceptable[sic], as in Formosa, as a part of the Japanese Empire, there are lots of Japanese subjects, who are Chinese both by appearance and origin."[20] Such suspicions were backed by another fact, that "most Taiwanese speak only Chinese or Malay".

---

[18]A letter from the Dutch colonial government to the Japanese consul at Batavia included an attached report about the number of and reasons for cases of refusal of entry. From 1912 to 1914, 17 Japanese subjects were refused entry by the Dutch authorities. The reasons were insufficient financial means (13 cases), prostitution (3 cases), and procurer (1 case). Included were two Taiwanese and two Koreans. Public No. 218, October 7, 1915 (Diplomatic Archives: 3.8.2.254).

[19]Confidential report No. 10, December 21, 1908 (Diplomatic Archives: 3.8.2.254).

[20]Circular No. 3858. Department of Justice, March 30, 1910 (Diplomatic Archives: 3.8.2.254).

Considering the wave of immigration from Mainland China to the Dutch East Indies at the beginning of the twentieth century, the concern of the Dutch authorities is understandable. More than half of the Chinese immigrants in the Dutch East Indies were from Fujian, and a large number were from Kwangtung as well. Fujian, which faced Taiwan across the channel and was where the important cities of Amoy and Swatow were located, had historically been closely connected to Taiwan. The people spoke the same language and shared the same customs. In March of 1910, a Japanese consul at Batavia reported that "Taiwanese residing in Java ... usually arrived via Amoy and Swatow ...."[21] It was therefore an almost impossible task for the Dutch authorities in the East Indies to distinguish between Taiwanese and Chinese when they landed at a port in the East Indies on a ship which had departed from one of the port cities in Mainland China. Thus, for the Dutch authorities, and to a certain extent for the Japanese authorities as well, there was no means available to identify a Taiwanese person other than by a Japanese passport.

The Quest for "Perfect Proof"

The Japanese consul at Batavia, the Governor-General of Taiwan and the Ministry of Foreign Affairs all took the Taiwanese–Japanese nationality question seriously. This was not just a matter of the illegal use of passports by *gisō sekimin* or the inability of the Dutch authorities to recognize who was Chinese and who was Taiwanese at a glance. This was a matter of sovereignty over Taiwan by Japan, the first non-Western power to possess a colony in the age of imperialism. As long as this nationality question remained unresolved, it meant that Japan's efforts to institutionalize its colonial administration of Taiwan would be seen as a failure. Institutionalizing passports symbolized effective colonial governance.

The Japanese Foreign Ministry discussed several measures with the Japanese consulate at Batavia and other concerned consulates to "prevent misdeeds by Chinese who tried to arrogate our nationality."[22] Stricter procedures for issuing passports were implemented. Changes were made concerning identity checks and passport format. Local police were required to check the identity of an applicant once a passport application

[21]Public No. 31, March 29, 1910 (Diplomatic Archives: 3.8.2.254).

[22]No. 38, June 21, 1910 (Diplomatic Archives: 3.8.2.254).

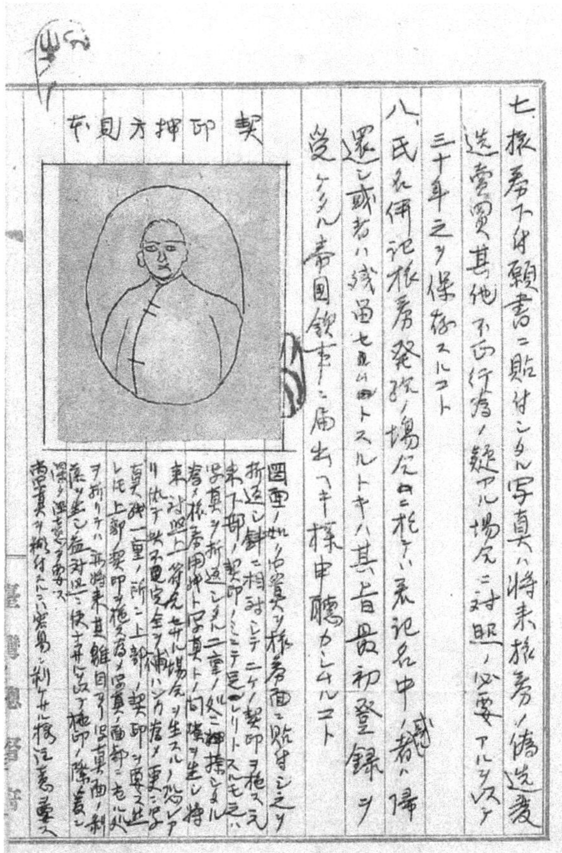
七、旅券下付願書ニ貼付シタル写真ハ将来旅券ノ偽造変
造売買其他不正行為ノ疑アル場合ニ対照ノ必要アルニ因ス
三十年之ヲ保存スルコト
八、氏名併記旅券発給ノ場合ニ於テハ記名中ノ一名ハ帰
還シ或者ハ残留セムトスルトキハ其旨最初登録ヲ
受ケタル帝国領事ニ届出ヘキ様申聴カシムルコト
契印押方見本

Figure 3: Circular of instructions on passports issued in Taiwan, October 10, 1907. Detailed instructions on photo attachment are described. Issuing authorities were required to store the photograph for 30 years (Diplomatic Archives: 3.8.2.254)

was submitted. Passport applications were accepted in Taiwan only; the issuing of passports at the Japanese consulates in Chinese cities such as Amoy, Fujian, Swatow, Hong Kong and Kwantung was no longer authorized. Two photos of the applicant were to be submitted with the application form, one to be attached to the passport with the official stamp on it (Figure 3) and the other to be stored by the issuing authorities for 30 years. A passport used for travel to the Dutch East Indies had to be issued with a visa endorsed by the Dutch consulate before the traveler left Taiwan. In addition to these new requirements, passport holders were required to carry with them a transcript of their family register as a supporting document. Finally, identity checks of Taiwanese–Japanese residing in the East Indies were to be undertaken by the Japanese consul at Batavia. These guidelines were circulated to Japanese consulates in Amoy, Fujian, Swatow, Hong Kong and Kwantung.

Based on these guidelines, in 1910 the Japanese authorities negotiated intensively with the Dutch authorities to settle the proof-of-nationality matter. On behalf of the Japanese government, a Japanese consul, Seisyo Someya, sent a letter to the Governor-General of the Dutch East Indies on August 6, summing up four instructions to be enforced: (1) Taiwanese residing in Mainland China must return to Taiwan for passport application; (2) Japanese consuls "at Amoy, Swatow, Foochow, Hongkong, and Kwantung (all in China) shall abstain in future from issuing passports"; (3) Passport and identity checks on Taiwanese residing in the Dutch East Indies will be enforced by the Japanese consulate at Batavia; and (4) "all the passports carried by Formosans, being Japanese subjects, shall bear their photograph and the Japanese Government's stamp."[23]

The Governor-General of the Dutch East Indies accepted these administrative rules proposed by the Japanese authorities, and sent a circular letter, dated March 17, 1911, to the concerned authorities in the East Indies stating that a Japanese passport should be accepted *unconditionally* as proof of Japanese nationality if it fulfilled the following conditions: it was issued in Japan (including Taiwan) and it was endorsed either by the Japanese consulate or by a Dutch consular officer.

The Final Blow

The issue of Japanese passports and proper proof of identification of *Taiwan sekimin* seemed to be settled as the Japanese government established measures to eliminate *gisō sekimin* in the East Indies. But it was at exactly this moment that another concern arose. A Taiwanese man, Li Jin Tong（李金周), visited a Japanese consul at Batavia to register his newborn baby in his family register in Taiwan. This application was sent to a local office in Taipei

---

[23] In 1897, Sen'ichi Ueno, a Japanese consul at Amoy, recommended to the Governor-General of Taiwan that a photograph of the applicant must be attached to a passport. Twenty years later, in 1917, regulations for passports changed in line with Ueno's advice (Kurihara, 2002: 22–23).

where his family register was supposed to be stored, but the officer in the Taipei office replied that no registration of Li Jin Tong could be found. Further inquiry revealed that Li Jin Tong had stayed in Taipei for only two months, and that he had obtained his passport during that period. The reason that local authorities issued a passport to him is not mentioned.

The Japanese consul, Someya, having received this unexpected reply, feared that this would spoil all the efforts the government had made to resolve passport problems in the East Indies. Even though Li Jin Tong's passport had been issued in 1905, 5 years before the *Taiwan sekimin* identification problem had been settled with the Dutch authorities, this meant that there had been a lack of proper checks by the Japanese officials, even after the Dutch authorities had repeatedly demanded improvement of the system. The Ministry of Foreign Affairs of Japan shared the consul's concern, considering this case to be "a matter of national prestige". The Ministry feared that if this case became known to the Dutch authorities, not only would it create obstacles for the entry of Taiwanese to the East Indies, it would also cause Japan's ability to govern its colony to be doubted by the Dutch.[24]

Someya summoned Li Jin Tong to the Japanese consulate for an interview to find out how he had obtained a passport. His passport was issued in Taipei in May of 1905 with his photo and signature. Someya checked the passport in question and confirmed it was not counterfeit. He also collected information about Li Jin Tong's family and discovered that none of them were recorded in the family register in Taiwan. The solution of the Foreign Ministry of Japan to this issue was to secretly create a family register for Li Jin Tong, regardless of whether he possessed Japanese nationality or not, based on information about Li's family that Someya provided.

After these various diplomatic concerns had been settled with the Governor-General of the Dutch East Indies in 1910, the rules for applying for passports issued by both countries changed. The Treaty of Commerce and Navigation between the Netherlands and Japan was revised in 1912, and Article 1 of this treaty guaranteed nationals of both countries complete freedom of movement as long as it did not conflict with domestic law in either country. Based on the idea of most-favored nation treatment, the treaty included a rule not to require passports to enter each country. This rule did not function well, however. In 1913, a notice to passengers

---

[24] Secret No. 953, March 24, 1911 (Diplomatic Archives: 3.8.2.254).

sailing to Java warned that Japanese traveling to Java were still sometimes misidentified as Chinese by the Dutch local authorities.

The Dutch authorities demanded another official document from the Japanese government stating that a passport was not required to enter the Dutch East Indies. In 1916, a "certificate of nationality" was introduced to replace the passport as proof of Japanese nationality. The Japanese authorities, however, continued to advise Japanese nationals to carry a Japanese passport in case of inspection in the East Indies.[25] The nationality problem of Taiwanese was thus settled at the governmental level, though it rearose sporadically through the 1920s.

Concluding Remarks

The issue of *Taiwan sekimin* arose during the early period of institutionalizing passports. When Japan colonized Taiwan as its first colony in 1895, the Japanese government was not prepared to institutionalize a modern passport system. Although passport regulations were legislated in 1897, it was not until 1899 that Japan's first Nationality Act was enacted.

In spite of this legislation, effective control over Taiwan had not yet been achieved: the Governor-General of Taiwan was not successful in controlling the movement of people between Taiwan and Mainland China. *Gisō sekimin*, or "pseudo-Japanese," appeared, demonstrating that the link between nationality and passport had not been reliably established. A structural inequality created by international politics facilitated the appearance of *gisō sekimin*. In Mainland China, extraterritoriality was exercised by the Japanese, whereas in the Dutch East Indies, there were different population groups with differing rights. Chinese were treated as natives, but *Taiwan sekimin*, despite sharing the same ethnicity, language and customs as Chinese, were regarded as Europeans.

The identification problem of *Taiwan sekimin* was not only a matter of the passport system, it was also a matter of sovereignty for the Japanese government. The issue gave rise to a series of negotiations between the Japanese and the Dutch authorities, and although it was solved temporarily, the quest for a "perfect" proof of identity persisted. From a governmental point of view, there was no room for *gisō sekimin* to exist. But from a human point of view, *gisō sekimin* can be described as those who

[25]Public No. 164, July 13, 1916 (Diplomatic Archives: 3.8.2.254).

tried to evade or resist monopolization of their identity by the state and sought the ability to cross borders and exercise rights.

References

Claver, A. (2014). *Dutch Commerce and Chinese Merchants in Java: Colonial Relationships in Trade and Finance, 1800–1942*. Leiden, KITLV Press.

Endō, M. (2010). *Kindai Nihon no Shokuminch Tōchi ni okeru Kokuseki to Koseki: Manshū, Chōsen, Taiwan* (Nationality and Family Registration System in Colonies of Modern Japan: Manchuria, Korea, Taiwan). Tokyo, Akashi Shoten.

Gaimushō Tsūshō Kyoku (1921). *Ryoken Kahusū Oyobi Imin Tōkei* (Passport Issuance Number and Migration Data). Tokyo, Gaimushō Tsūshō Kyoku.

Goto, K. (2012). *Tōnan Ajia Kara Mita Kin-Gendai Nihon: "Nanshin," Senryō, Datsu Shokuminnchika wo Meguru Rekishi Ninshiki* (Modern Japan Observed through Southeast Asia: Debate over History of "Nanshin," Occupation, Decolonization). Tokyo, Iwanami Shoten.

Keishicho (1893). *Gaikokujin Toriatsukai Rēki Tsūsan* (Foreigners' Regulations and Samples). Tokyo, Kēshi-chō.

Keishicho (1900). *Keisatsu Yōmu* (Handbook for Police). Tokyo, Keishi-chō.

Kudo, Y. (2005). Taiwan Sekimin in Java: On the Commercial Activities of Kwik Djoen Eng. *Rekishi Minzoku*, 3: 22–38.

Kurihara, J. (2000). Taiwan Sekimin to Kokuseki Mondai. In Taiwanshō Bunken-Iinkai Seirikumi (Ed.), *Taiwan Bunkenshiryō-seiri Gakujutu Kentokai Ronbunsyū* (pp. 451–476). Nantōshi, Shō Bunken-kai.

Kurihara, J. (2002). Citizenship Issues of Taiwan Residents, as Seen in the Public Documents of the Governor General of Taiwan's Office. *Annals of the Institute for Comparative Studies of Culture*, 63: 19–40.

Kurihara, J. (2004). The National Census, Family Registrations and the Extraordinary Taiwan Census of 1905. *Annals of the Institute for Comparative Studies of Culture*, 65: 33–77.

Lijnkamp, H. A. F. (1938). *De "Japannerwet": Onderzoek Naar de Wording*. Utrecht, Oosthoek.

Lohanda, M. (2002). *Growing Pains: The Chinese and the Dutch in Colonial Java, 1890–1942*. Jakarta, Yayasan Cipta Loka Caraka.

Nakamura, T. (1980). Formosans of Japanese Nationality in Fukien. *South East Asian Studies*, 18(3): 422–445.

Oguma, E. (1998). *"Nihonjin" no Kyōkai — Okinawa, Ainu, Taiwan, Chōsen: Shokuminchi Sihai kara Hukki Undō Made* (Border of the Japanese — Okinawa, Ainu, Taiwan, Korea: From Colonial Rule to Repatriation Movement). Tokyo, Shinyōsha.

Post, P. (1993). Tai-Ran'in Keizai Kakuchō to Oranda no Taiō (Japan's Economic Expansion into Prewar Indonesia and the Dutch Reaction). In Ōe Shinobu (ed.), *Kindai Nihon to Shokuminchi 3: Shokuminchika to Sangyōka* (Modern Japan and Colonies: Colonization and Industrialization) (pp. 51–73). Tokyo, Iwanami Shoten.

Post, P. (1995). Chinese Business Networks and Japanese Capital in South East Asia, 1880–1940: Some Preliminary Observations. In Rajeswary Ampalavanar Brown (ed.), *Chinese Business Enterprise in Asia* (pp. 259–290). London, Routledge.

Ryokenhō Kenkyu-kai (1999). *Chikujō Kaisetsu Ryokenhō* (A Commentary on Passport Law). Tokyo, Ministry of Finance Printing Bureau.

Sato Masahiro (2012). *Teikoku Nihon to Tōkei Chōsa: Tōchi Shoki Taiwan no Senmonka Shūdan* (Imperial Japan and Statistics: Trained Groups in the Early Period of Taiwan Governance). Tokyo, Iwanami Shoten.

South Manchuria Railway East Asiatic Economic Investigation Bureau (1940). *Ranryō Indo ni Okeru Kakyō* (Chinese in the Dutch East Indies). Tokyo, Kaimeidō.

Tai, Y. W. (2014). The Chinese Community in the Dutch East Indonesia: Population and Socio-Economic Characteristics. *Malaysian Journal of Chinese Studies*, 3(2): 41–66.

Tjiook-Liem, P. (2009). *De Rechtspositie der Chinezen in Nederlandsch-Indië 1848–1942*. Leiden, Leiden University Press.

Torpey, J. (2000). *The Invention of the Passport: Surveillance, Citizenship and the State*. Cambridge, Cambridge University Press.

Volkstelling (1930). Department van Landbouw, Nijverheid en Handel (Nederlandsch-Indie), Batavia, Landsdrukkerij.

Wu, L. (2018). The Immigration Policy in Taiwan under the Japanese Empire: Focusing on the Grace Period for Selection of Nationality between May 8th, 1895 and May 8th, 1897. *Social Systems: Political, Legal and Economic Studies*, 21: 1–21.

Yoshida, M. (2002). Colonialism and the Rule of Law: The Creation of *European* and *Inlander* in the Dutch East Indies. *South East Asian Studies*, 40(2): 115–140.

Yoshida, M. (2008). Civilization, Law, and Race: The Drafting Process of the "Japanese Law" and the Debate over Civilization. *South East Asia: History and Culture*, 37: 3–27.

Diplomatic Records

Nationaalarchief, Den Haag.

Diplomatic Archives of the Ministry of Foreign Affairs of Japan.

Endangered Archives Programme, British Library, https://eap.bl.uk/.

Taiwan Sōtokufu Archive, The Archives of Institute of Taiwan History, Academia Sinica.

https://doi.org/10.1142/9789811250668_0007

Chapter 7

Entangled Mobility: Hui Migration, Religious Identity and Cultural Capital in Malaysia*

Hew Wai Weng

Fellow, Institute of Malaysian and International Studies,
National University of Malaysia, Malaysia

Contemporary Hui Mobility

"We share a language with the local Chinese, and we share a religion with Malay Muslims. We get along well with both communities" — this is a popular saying of many overseas Hui I met in Malaysia. By capitalizing on both Chinese and Islamic identity, despite being non-citizens, many contemporary Hui migrants enjoy relatively well-off livelihoods in Malaysia, a Muslim majority country with a considerable number of ethnic Chinese. For example, the encounter of an *imam* from China, Abu Bakar Siddiq, known as Imam Yu in Malaysia clearly exemplifies how the ability of speaking Chinese and mastering Islamic knowledge allow him

*Entangled Mobility: Hui Migration, Religious Identity and Cultural Capital in Malaysia, HEW WAI WENG, Issues & Studies, Vol. 54, No. 01, 1840001 (2018). Copyright @ 2018 Issues and Studies and World Scientific Publishing Co. Pte. Ltd. https://www.world scientific.com/doi/abs/10.1142/S1013251118400015.

to move around different places as well as to build good relations with religious leaders and to make a living in Malaysia.

As I will further illustrate later, Imam Yu's experience in Malaysia shows how cultural capital (speaking Chinese and mastering Islamic knowledge) are turned into social capital (networking with religious leaders) and economic capital (working as an Imam and running a part-time business). His case exemplifies various entanglements between spatial and social mobility, between religious and economic aspiration, between Islamic practices and Chinese culture, and between transnational connections and local adaptions amidst Hui mobility in Malaysia today. By describing the social encounters of a few Hui migrants living in Malaysia, this chapter examines how Hui mobility is intertwined with religious aspiration, educational opportunity and business prospect, as well as intersected with the accumulation and circulation of various forms of capital associated to their Chineseness and Muslimness.

Muslims from China have long traveled and lived in Southeast Asia (Ma, 2010; C. B. Tan, 1991). The most well-known cases in Malaysia and Indonesia, include the visit of Admiral Zheng He in 15th and 16th centuries, and more recently the arrival of Ibrahim Ma Tian Ying and his families in the mid-20th century. Yet, the recent presence and visibility of Hui in both countries, especially in Malaysia, began in the 1980s, as a result of student mobility. Although there are no official figures of Hui migrants in Malaysia, Wong (2013) estimates that there are about 2,000 Hui students studying and 50 Hui families living in Malaysia, most of whom would have first come as students and later engaged in business activities. My research experience suggests the exact number of Hui in Malaysia would be slightly higher than this estimation.

There are arguably two waves of contemporary Hui migrations in Malaysia — the first one beginning in the 1980s, was mainly motivated by educational purposes; the second one began in the 2000s and is driven by multiple reasons. Since 1980s, many Hui came to Malaysia to pursue their studies (of both religious and modern subjects) at public universities and private colleges. In a survey of 888 mainland Chinese students in various universities and colleges in Malaysia, about 13.9% were Hui (Wong and Ooi, 2013). This figure is high compared with their 2.5% share of China's total population. Many of them are from the northwestern region of China, especially Gansu Province, while others come from various provinces such as Yunnan, Henan, Qinghai and Ningxia. Kuala Lumpur and Selangor have the highest concentration of Hui students, with a high proportion registered at the International Islamic University of Malaysia (IIUM). Gombak and Wangsa Waju, two suburbs of Kuala Lumpur adjacent to IIUM, are places where many Hui live and, in some cases, also run their businesses. I have also met some Hui who are studying and living in Johor, Penang, Kelantan and Perak.

Hui students frequently visit China, keep close connection with families and friends back home, and quite often also persuade more Hui to join them in Malaysia. After the completion of their studies, some of them stay in Malaysia to develop their careers and business activities, while others, upon their return to China, move from the Muslim heartland in the northwest to the country's commercial coastal cities such as Guangzhou and Shanghai, where they are largely engaged in the import–export trade and service industries (Wong, 2013).

In addition to students, there has been a growing number of religiously motivated and economically driven Hui migrants, especially since year 2000. They come to Malaysia aspiring to learn about Islam, to act as an *imam* (religious leader) or simply to live in a Muslim-majority environment, as well as to seek job opportunities or expand their business networks. The recent mushrooming of Hui-established restaurants and travel agencies, as well as the visibility of Hui *imams* are clear evidence of their presence. Although in fewer numbers, some Hui make their way to Indonesia, for example, to study at Saudi-funded Islamic institutions and to run restaurants. For many Hui, mobility, business interests and religious activities go hand in hand (Hew, 2017). As Wong (2013, 2015) points out, religion plays a critical role in the mobility decisions and migration patterns of Hui Muslims, as they navigate their minority lives through the spaces of the Chinese nation-state and the transnational Islamic world.

The increase of contemporary Hui mobility is in response to two current trends noticed among the Hui in China. First, there has been a religious revival and increasing aspiration for Islamic education among segments of Hui Muslims (Armijo-Hussein, 1999; Stewart, 2016), leading some of them to further their studies in Muslim-majority countries such as Malaysia, Indonesia and Saudi Arabia. Second, there has been an increasing number of Hui businesspeople who are eager to build business networks in Muslim-majority countries. In many cases, both religious motivation and economic aspiration co-exist. At the same time, there are some middle-class Muslims in cities such as those in Xi'an, who prefer to purchase Malaysian *halal*-certified products and view Malaysia as their favorable Muslim-friendly travel destination (Yang, in press).

Recently as China embarked on its ambitious strategy of "the Belt and Road Initiative" (BRI), some Hui businessmen tap into such initiative to invest in *halal* industries in Muslim-majorities countries. In addition, there are also increasing numbers of Hui traveling to Malaysia and Indonesia for holidays. It is important to note that many overseas Hui keep their Chinese citizenship, strategically use their both Chinese and Islamic identity to navigate their life in Malaysia. For many reasons, Malaysia stands out as a strategic and favorable country for Hui to study, to live or to invest. It is perceived as a multilingual modern Muslim country with sizable Chinese-speaking population, comprehensive Islamic education system in English and Arabic language as well as growing numbers of middle-class Muslims — offering Hui migrants "cultural affinity", "religious authenticity", "educational mobility" and "business opportunity" (Hew, 2021).

At the same time, there are increasing demands for cultural diversity within Islamic framework among urban middle-class Malay Muslims. Various cultural and aesthetic forms — be it Arabic or Western, be it Korean or Chinese — have been adopted and appropriated in contemporary Islamic expressions in Malaysia and Indonesia today (Hew, 2016). Together with local Chinese converts, overseas Hui can offer them Chinese-cultured Islamic expressions. For example, Chinese-style mosques, Chinese *halal* cuisine, and Chinese-style Arabic calligraphy are desirable among segments of Malay Muslims (Hew, 2014, 2018). Instead of seeing Islam as a "Malay religion", there is a growing number of pious middle-class Malay Muslims who view Islam as a religion for all mankind — therefore, appreciating Chinese culture does not only acknowledge the universality of Islam, but also becomes their subtle ways of preaching Islam among non-Muslim Chinese Malaysians (Hew, 2013).

It is important to clarify the different meaning between Chinese Muslims and Hui Muslims in this chapter. I use Hui mainly refer to Chinese-speaking born-Muslims from China, while Chinese Muslims refer to Chinese Malaysians and Indonesians (citizens) who embrace Islam. Most Chinese Muslims in Malaysia today are third or fourth generation of non-Muslim Han Chinese migrants from the southeastern regions of China; many of them are converts. Meanwhile, many contemporary Hui migrants in both countries are originally from the northwestern part of China, especially the Gansu Province. Of course, what constitute Hui, who are Hui is heavily debated and contested. The term Hui has had different meanings in different periods of China's history. Hui identities are also expressed diversely in different local contexts in China (Gillette, 2000; Gladney, 1996; Lipman, 1998). I also specifically use Hui, instead of "Muslims in China", as most of my informants are ethnically Hui (broadly defined) and there are very few Uyghur migrants in Malaysia due to their limited mobility.

In Chinese, many overseas Hui prefer to identify themselves as "中國穆斯林" (Chinese-national Muslims), while local Chinese Muslims call themselves "華人穆斯林" (ethnically Chinese Muslims). Yet, in English, the common use of "Chinese Muslims" might cause some confusion — as some Hui restaurants also names themselves as "Chinese Muslim" in English but "中國穆斯林" in Chinese. In this chapter, with the exception of the restaurant names, I use "Chinese Muslims" mainly refer to local Chinese converts. Despite different nationalities as well as religious schools of thought (most Hui Muslims follow Hanafi school, while Chinese Muslims in Malaysia follow Shafii school), the ability to speak Chinese bonds both overseas Hui and local Chinese Muslims who can speak Chinese together, prompting a possibility of "Sinophone Muslim diaspora". A Hui Imam living in Malaysia emphasized that Hui have played an important role in the changing of terms used to refer to Islam and Muslim among Chinese-speaking Malaysians (from "回教" to "伊斯蘭" for Islam, from "回教徒" to "穆斯林" for Muslim), as he suggested that phonetic translations can better reflect the universality of Islamic teaching.[1]

I have elsewhere discussed the intersection of religion, business and mobility (Hew, 2017), as well as the place-making amidst their mobility (Hew, 2021). This chapter examines the circulation of various forms of capital (cultural, social and economic) and the intersection of capitalization of "Chineseness" and "Muslimness" among Hui living in Malaysia. First, it discusses the mobility capital — in which Hui Muslims enjoy relatively freedom to move around in China and beyond China, compared to their Uyghur counterparts who have limited mobility. Second, by exploring the religious, cultural and business activities of Hui migrants, it explores how the accumulation and circulation of different forms of capital take place in mosques, in restaurants and on social media platforms. Third, it highlights that Hui mobility is not only about their physical movements from one place to another place, but also about their social mobility, business expansion and religious enhancement.

[1] Interview with Imam Yu, February 17, 2017.

Mobility Capital of Hui Muslims

Different persons and groups have different capacities, potentials and choices of mobility. A concept of "motility" or "mobility capital" (Kaufmann *et al.*, 2004) has been deployed to analyze how different groups and individuals "appropriates the field of possibilities relative to movement and uses them" (Kaufmann and Montulet, 2008: 45). According to Kaufmann *et al.* (2004: 750), spatial mobility refers to geographic movement from a site to another site, while social mobility refers to the transformation in the distribution of resources or social positions of access and the appropriation of capacities for socio-spatial mobility within a given social structure or network. Hence, motility entails both spatial and social mobility, can be defined as the capacity of entities to be mobile in both social and geographic space. Depending on context, individual actors, groups and institutions differ in access, competence and appropriation, and have thus at their disposal different motility options (Kaufmann *et al.*, 2004: 754).

In other words, Sheller (2011: 5) propose to conceptualize "mobility capital" (Kaufmann *et al.*, 2004) as the uneven distribution of these capacities and competencies, in relation to the surrounding physical, social and political affordances for movement (with the legal structures regulating who or what can and cannot move being crucial). Hui and Uyghur are the two largest Muslim-majority ethnic groups in China — Hui are scattered across different areas in China with a higher concentration in Northwestern Chinese provinces such as Ningxia and Gansu, and in Yunnan province in Southwest of China, while most Uyghurs reside in the Xinjiang province. Despite both being Muslims, these two ethnic groups have different "mobility capital" — the Chinese government gives Hui relatively freedom to move around in China and beyond China but restrict the mobility of Uyghurs (Crane, 2014).

Overall, even though Han-Hui relations are far from always harmonious, they are certainly better than Han–Uyghur relations (Friedrichs, 2017). Geopolitically speaking, there is a long-existing independence movement among Uyghurs in Xinjang, considered by the Chinese government as an act of de-stabilizing its state sovereignty. Culturally speaking, Uyghurs speak a Turkic language and are racially distinct from the Han, while the Hui have many cultural and linguistic similarities with their Han counterparts. Similarly, many Malaysians welcome Hui as students, businessmen, tourists or *imams*, but the Malaysian government has hesitated to receive Uyghur as refugees in order to maintain a good relationship with the Chinese government. Uyghur might also prefer to move to Turkey for cultural proximity, while Hui prefer Malaysia for its relatively large Chinese-speaking community.

In 2013, the Chinese President Xi Jinping launched China's BRI with the aim to interconnect major economies in Asia and Europe through infrastructure, investment, and trade. China has to familiarize itself with Islamic beliefs and cultures given that many of the core countries along the BRI are Muslim-majority: the Central Asian republics, Iran, Turkey, Indonesia, Malaysia and Middle Eastern countries among others. Muslims in China might be able to play a role in promoting intercultural exchanges and facilitating the people-to-people interactions needed to make multinational initiatives successful. However, the Chinese state is also worried that such positioning of Muslims in China might risk domestic instability and threaten national sovereignty, especially in the province of Xinjiang (Meyer, 2016). Despite such worries, cultural exchange and economic co-operation between Muslims in China and other Muslim-majority countries have intensified, reflected in the growing number of Hui migrants and tourists, the expansion of Chinese *halal* market and the mushrooming of Hui restaurants in countries such as Malaysia. It is important to note that such intensified interactions between Muslims in China and in Malaysia are not a new phenomenon after the launch of BRI. Instead of seeing BRI as a main causal factor of contemporary Hui mobility, this chapter suggests that many Hui migrants and businessmen tap into such initiative to justify and to facilitate their mobility beyond China.

Even before the launch of BRI, Ningxia Autonomous Region, with a large concentration of Muslims, was designated by the Chinese government as the production center for *halal* food products in China (Chow, 2010). Such an initiative is a key strategy for improving China's global image, especially in building strategic foreign relations and business opportunities with the Arab and Muslim world (Ho, 2012). Ho (2012: 106) suggests that Hui might be an important "asset" representing China's national interest and goodwill in the Muslim world.

In Malaysia, the state of Kelantan has been ruled since 1990 by a coalition led by the Pan-Malaysian Islamic Party (PAS). At the federal level this party is in opposition, as a result of which Kelantan does not receive full financial support from the federal government. Thus, in order to attract Chinese investment into the state, the Kelantan government has initiated various efforts to attract investment from both Hui and Han entrepreneurs from mainland China, such as organizing the 2010 Cheng Ho Expo (Kelantan–China International Trade Fair) and the 2011 Kelantan Cheng Ho International Food Festival (KELCHEF).[2] In 2011, the Kelantan state government signed a memorandum of understanding with Qinghai Yijiale Halal Supermarket to promote business collaboration between Kelantan and Qinghai ("Usahawan Kelantan", 2011).

In 2013, there has been a new collaboration between Malaysia's East Coast Economic Region Development Council (ECERDC) and China's Ningxia Light and Textile Industrial Bureau (NLTIB) to develop a regional *halal* food-manufacturing hub in Pahang, another state in Malaysia (Salama, 2013). In addition, since 2000, Hui from China have actively taken part in various *halal* food and product exhibitions in Malaysia (Hew, 2014). After the launch of China's BRI, the Malaysian government is also keen to tap opportunities to promote cross-border trade and investment, in which *halal* market has been identified as a key highlight (C. K. Tan, 2017). In addition, Malaysia is one of the most favorable destinations for Hui Muslims to further study and to travel. Some Hui in Malaysia run travel agencies to cater to tourists from China, especially Muslims. In 2017, the state of Johor also aimed to attract more Muslim tourists from China (Basri, 2017). In addition, from its inception in 2002, the Malaysia My Second Home (MM2H) scheme has approved 35,381 overseas applicants, with Chinese-nationals topping the list with 8,714 or 37% of the total applicants. MM2H is an international residency scheme enacted by the Government of Malaysia to allow foreigners to live in the country on a long-stay visa of up to 10 years. A few informants have told me some of these Chinese-national MM2H residents in Malaysia are of Hui background.

Besides some Hui MM2H residents, most Hui living in Malaysia today are mainly documented migrants holding either student, business or working visa. In contrast, on the news, Uyghurs in Malaysia have been associated with undocumented refugees or even suspected "militants", due to their alleged involvement in the Xinjiang separatist secession movement in China. Different groups of non-citizens, including foreign workers, students and refugees experience different forms of rights and belonging in Malaysia today (Khoo, 2014). Similarly, the Malaysian government has a mixed record in providing for Muslims refugees, such as Bosnian, Syrian, Cham and Rohingya asylum seekers (Hoffstaedter, 2017). Yet, in order to

---

[2]For more details on these events, see http://kelcheff.blogspot.de/ (January 8, 2015).

maintain a good relationship with the Chinese government, the Malaysian government has refused to protect Uyghur asylum seekers and has deported them back to China. In 2011 and 2013, Malaysia respectively returned 6 and 11 Uyghurs to China. In September 2017, former Deputy Prime Minister of Malaysia Ahmad Zahid Hamidi said Malaysia had since 2011 arrested 29 suspected Uyghur "militants" and deported them to China (*Bernama*, 2017). Malaysia's relationship with China has become closer in recent years under former Prime Minister Najib Razak, as Beijing has pumped billions into Malaysia over the last two years, particularly into infrastructure projects, as Najib looks to tackle massive government debt (Ananthalakshmi, 2018). Perhaps, in contemporary warming Malaysia–China relations, Hui might have advantages to position themselves as cultural brokers and trade partners, yet Uyghurs face a higher risk in their journeys to seek asylum.

Capital Accumulation and Circulation among Hui Muslims

To grasp the entanglements between the economic, cultural, religious and social dimensions of Hui mobility, this chapter uses Bourdieu's (1986) conceptualization of different forms of capital and their convertibility. In his classic article titled "The Forms of Capital", Bourdieu distinguishes three main types of capital, namely, economic, social and cultural. Economic capital includes command of economic resources; social capital refers to actual and potential resources linked to the possession of a durable network of institutionalized relationships of mutual acquaintance and recognition; while cultural capital entails a person's education, knowledge and intellectual skills that enable social mobility. These forms of capital are interlinked and convertible. Their convertibility is the basis of the strategies aimed at ensuring the reproduction of capital and the position occupied in social space.

Cultural capital, according to Bourdieu (1986), appears in three states: embodied, institutionalized and objectified. As for the case of Hui migrants, their cultural capital is embodied in practices such as speaking Chinese and reciting Qur'anic verses, institutionalized by universities and mosque committees, as well as objectified in their cuisine, mosque architectural design and calligraphic works. In his article on Indonesia's Islamic preacher economy, Slama (2017) focuses on the rise of social media and the temporality of capital accumulation. In this chapter, I emphasize the spatial aspects to explore how the physical movement from one site to another site and the place-making in a certain site entail the processes of capital accumulation and circulation. It explores where the capital exchange takes place (e.g. in the IIUM or on the social media platforms such as WeChat), and how it results in the making of certain places such as Chinese-style mosques and Hui restaurants.

Vasquez and Knott (2014) have emphasized that spatial strategies are crucial in managing the migrants' presence, visibility and invisibility. I further examine the interconnection between spatial strategies and capital accumulation among Hui migrants in Malaysia today. Economic capital provides the middle-class Hui with financial support to study at overseas universities and colleges, while cultural capital gives religiously learned Hui the ability to secure a job as an *imam* in Chinese-style mosques in Malaysia. In Malaysia, capitalizing on their Chinese and Islamic identity, many Hui enhance their social capital in "a durable network of more or less institutionalized relationships" (Bourdieu, 1986: 248) not only through education but also through their interaction with Malay Muslims and non-Muslim Chinese. Such social capital might be able to transform into an economic one, allowing some Hui to run businesses, such as opening restaurants. These restaurants can function as sites of interaction for people of different ethnic, religious and national background — exemplifying a conversion from economic capital into cultural and social capital. In return, such positioning of a socio-cultural space might attract more customers to visit the restaurant in which these forms of capital are transformed back into economic capital easily. For many Hui living in Malaysia, accumulating economic capital (money), cultural capital (being pious) and social capital (ability to mix well in Malaysian societies) are equally important. The ethnographic examples in the next section illustrate how such accumulation and circulation of such capital take place.

Looking at the localizations of "Arabness" through the lens of Bourdieu's theory on different forms of capital, Luecking (2016) suggested that "Arabness" appears to bear the potential to become a resource within economic, cultural and social dynamics in Madura, an overwhelmingly Muslim-majority island in Indonesia. As a symbol for piety and learnedness, "Arabness" acquired through cultural and religious practices among Madurese Muslims legitimizes their leadership claims and enables their participation in the management of the *hajj* — and thus offers the possibility to generate economic capital in the pilgrimage business.

In return, the business success gives them higher social status as well as more resources to invest in the accumulation of cultural capital. She suggests that such circulation of capital relies on local contexts — in which "Arabness" only becomes meaningful in the web of social relationships and values on the ground (Luecking, 2016: 20). She also suggests that there are multiple meanings and manifestation of "Arabness", be it Hadhrami Arabness, Pop Arabness and Madurese Arabness (Luecking, 2016: 21).

Similarly, "Chineseness" of Hui Muslims from China and Chinese converts in Malaysia have different connotations and configurations in China and in Malaysia. As Caroline Hau (2014) frames it, there is "an internal contestation over what 'Chinese' means, who can claim Chineseness, who counts as Chinese, and who can 'represent' it" (Hau, 2014: 310). For an example, many Hui do not celebrate Chinese New Year in Mainland China, but they endorse the Chinese New Year open house events organized by local Chinese Muslims to support their preaching activities. Similarly, some Hui I met expressed their preferences to build new mosques in pan-Islamic style, but they have no problem to join activities at Chinese-style mosques in Malaysia. To distinguish themselves from Han Chinese, Hui downplay certain aspects of their "Chineseness" in China. Yet, to make themselves appealing among Malay Muslims in Malaysia, Hui embrace their "Chineseness", which could be a resource within economic, cultural and social dynamics in Malaysia, as there is a growing demand among middle-class Malay Muslims for diverse cultural expression of Islamic identities. By doing so, the Hui presence also challenges the perceived perception that Islam and "Chineseness" are incompatible. Indeed, this case shows that migration results in "new ways of producing and re-producing (mobilizing, enacting, validating) cultural capital that builds on, rather than simply mirrors, power relations of either the country of origin or the country of migration" (Erel, 2010: 642). As Erel (2010: 642) further argues, "migrants create mechanisms of validation for their cultural capital, negotiating both ethnic majority and migrant institutions and networks." By validating their "Chineseness" and "Muslimness", Hui migrants exercise their cultural capital to navigate their life within Malaysian multi-ethnic and multi-religious contexts.

Building upon the concept of mobility capital (Kaufmann *et al.*, 2004) and capital convertibility (Bourdieu, 1986), I propose the concept of "entangled mobility" to examine the intersection between Chineseness and Muslimness, the interconnection between spatial and social mobility, the combination of religious and economic aspiration, as well as the circulation of various forms of capital among Hui amid their mobility across spaces and settlement in certain sites. For sure, Hui migrants do not hold homogenous cultural capital, instead, their cultural capital vary according to their gender, religiosity, class and educational background. In the following section, I highlight social encounters of three male *imams* — Imam Yu, Imam Ali and Imam Qin. Despite originally from different parts of China and residing in different towns in Malaysia, there share certain similarities — have religious credentials, play a role in disseminating Islamic knowledge, maintain good relation with local Chinese and Muslim leaders, as well as directly or indirectly involve in some business activities. By exploring their stories and cases studies related to them, this chapter illustrates how aspirations such as "cultural affinity", "religious authenticity", "educational mobility" and "business opportunity" drive Hui migration to Malaysia. By doing so, it examines how their spatial and social mobility are entangled with each other and with broader economic, social and religious processes.

Imam Ali: Teaching Chinese in an Islamic School

Originally from Yunnan, Imam Ali Wang left his home country in 1995, and studied in a college in Terengganu for 3 years before moving to Kelantan for work. Imam Ali, was an *imam* for the Sultan Petra Ismail Mosque, a Chinese-style mosque, which is also best known as "Beijing Mosque", because its architectural design is inspired by the Niujie Mosque, an ancient mosque in Beijing. He led Ramadan *terawih* prayers (non-obligatory prayers during the month of Ramadan) in the mosque in 2010. Today, Imam Ali is no longer an *imam* for the mosque, but he is still teaching Arabic, Chinese and Islamic subjects at Sultan Petra Ismail International Islamic College (Kolej Islam Antarabangsa Sultan Petra Ismail, KIAS), an Islamic college in Kota Bahru, the capital city of Kelantan state in Malaysia. On weekends his wife runs a small stall that sells grocery items imported from China, in a market in downtown Kota Bahru.[3]

---

[3]Interview with Imam Ali, September 17, 2011.

Imam Ali, his wife, and his two eldest sons, who were all born in China, have not obtained Malaysian citizenship. Yet, his youngest son, Badaruddin, who was born in Kelantan, has been granted such citizenship. Remarkably, Badaruddin is also the godchild of the late Nik Abdul Aziz, former Kelantan Chief Minister and spiritual leader of PAS (an Islamist party in Malaysia). Badaruddin spent a few years living together with Nik Abdul Aziz. Nik Abdul Aziz had also frequently publicly expressed his support toward Malaysian Chinese Muslims and Hui Muslims from China. He was the key proponent of building the "Beijing Mosque" to manifest the universality of Islamic teaching. He invited many *imams* from China to visit Kelantan and has appointed Imam Ali to be an *imam* for the mosque. Imam Ali's knowledge in Islamic texts and his fluency in Chinese language are his cultural capital which enable him to acquire a kind of social capital — being close to local religious leaders and respected among Malay Muslims. Such cultural and social capital give him a chance to stay in Malaysia continuously over many years, to secure a permanent job in an Islamic college and to enable his wife to run a small business in a local market, even though they have not been granted Malaysian citizenship.

Since the late 2000s, his eldest son Hassan Wang, who was raised in Yunnan followed his father and moved to Kota Bahru. Hassan Wang first studied Islam in Chiang Mai, a northern city in Thailand, before moving to study Arabic language in an Islamic college in Kota Bahru. In 2012, working together with another Hui migrant, Hassan opened a grocery shop, called Yunnan Berkat. The shop sells various grocery items, from cooking utensils to religious clothing, from decorative items to sleeping mats, all imported from China. The shop also sells its imported products to other shops in Kelantan and Terengganu. Given that both Kelantan and Terengganu are Muslim-majority states, many of the shop's customers are Malay Muslims. Naming the shop with "Yunnan" is a strategic choice as many Malays heard about Muslims in the province of Yunnan in China and that the famous Admiral Zheng He was born in Yunnan (C. B. Tan, 1991). In other words, "Yunnan" signifies the authenticity of "being a Muslim in China" and is a trademark that could attract Malay customers in Kelantan. Similarly, while preferring me to call him in his Chinese given name "Weibo", he uses his Islamic name together with Chinese surname "Hassan Wang" when interacting with local Malays.[4] In some

[4]Interview with Hassan Wang, December 9, 2012.

ways, his everyday naming practices validate his cultural capital and enables the circulation of his cultural capital into social capital (communicating with local Malays) and economic capital (to attract Muslim customers).

While many Hui study at the International Islamic University Malaysia (IIUM) and other colleges in Kuala Lumpur, there are some Hui who pursue their studies in Kota Bahru, Kelantan. Hassan explained why Malaysia has become one of the favorite educational destinations for Hui: "Malaysia is a Muslim majority country and it offers a more comprehensive religious education than China. We can also learn different languages — Malay, English and Arabic. We have no problem communicating with those local Chinese, who can speak Chinese. Moreover, the certificates issued here are acknowledged overseas, which allows graduates to further their studies in other countries."[5] He cited an example in which a few Hui students went to Jordan to further their studies after completing their courses in Kelantan.

Unsurprisingly, Hassan suggested that by sharing a language with local Chinese and a religion with Malay Muslims, Hui Muslims are able to get along with the two ethnic majority groups in Malaysia — a unique advantage for them to establish business network. He noted that many Hui entrepreneurs have visited Malaysia and Indonesia in the last few years to seek business and investment opportunities in industries such as food production, palm oil plantations and mining. In Kelantan, the PAS-led government has frequently invited *imams* from China to visit the state. As discussed earlier, the Kelantan government organized the Cheng Ho Expo several years ago, inviting businessmen from China and seeking their investment. Whenever there are Hui visiting from China, whether they be *imams* or entrepreneurs, Hassan and his friends will help the state government to welcome and assist them.

Imam Yu: Teaching Islam in a Chinese-Style Mosque

In 2013, in Seremban, a town not far from Kuala Lumpur, there was a Chinese New Year dinner celebration inside the Al-Saadah Complex, a Chinese-style mosque, mimicking the design of the Great Mosque in Xi'an. An *imam* from Mainland China, Abu Bakar Siddiq, known as

[5] Interview with Hassan Wang, December 9, 2012.

Imam Yu, recited the *du'a* (prayers) at the beginning of this event. Meanwhile, his wife set up a small stall next to the dinner venue, selling various products, mostly imported from China. At that event, Imam Yu wore *tangzhuang*,[6] a kind of Chinese traditional dress, an attire that he rarely wears when in China. He explains, "the local Chinese Muslims leaders always wear *tangzhuang* in order to manifest their Chineseness. I was asked to do the same. It is okay. It is not our tradition back home, but I understand the context in Malaysia."[7] This case shows that while Imam Yu is well equipped in Islamic knowledge and Chinese language which have given him "mobility capital" to move beyond China, the enactment of his cultural identity (e.g. wearing *tangzhuang*) is crucial to enable its transformation to social capital in the context of Malaysia.

Imam Yu, originally from Gansu, first came to Kuching in Sarawak, where he worked as a religious teacher — giving regular classes and counseling on Islam in Chinese language to new Chinese converts. He later moved to Seremban in Negeri Sembilan to serve as *imam* for the newly established mosque, Al-Saadah Mosque Complex. This mosque, built in 2011, is the first mosque in contemporary Malaysia that occasionally conducts Friday sermons in Chinese language, which is led by Imam Yu. Both cultural and religious factors are integral to Imam Yu's mobility. As he said, "not many Chinese Muslims in Malaysia who can speak good Chinese and master Islamic knowledge at the same time, that is why I am invited to be an Imam here."[8] At the same time, Imam Yu see Malaysia as an ideal place for overseas Hui, because "I can send my kids to Chinese language school and at the same time, they can grow up in a Muslim-majority environment."[9] Having said that, Imam Yu keeps his Chinese-national citizenship and maintains a close relationship with Huis in China. Being an Imam back in China, he does not think that life has become

---

[6] *Tangzhuang* refers to the Chinese jacket that originated at the end of the Qing Dynasty (1644–1911). It evolved from *magua*, a Manchurian costume, which was, in turn, adopted by the Han Chinese during the Qing Dynasty. Today, *tangzhuang* is one of the main formal costumes for Chinese men for many occasions. At the Asia-Pacific Economic Cooperation summit in Shanghai, China in November 2001, the host presented its silk *tangzhuang* jacket as the Chinese traditional national costume. Since then, some Chinese overseas have worn *tangzhuang*, either as a fashion statement or for cultural expression.

[7] Interview with Imam Yu, February 16, 2013.

[8] *Ibid.*

[9] *Ibid.*

untenable at home, instead a desire to explore opportunities abroad brings him to Malaysia. Indeed, as he says "Hui people are always traveling for a better life. In the past, we move around within China and now, we can also move beyond China, without losing our Chinese nationality."[10]

I met Imam Yu again in 2017 in the Al-Saadah Mosque after Friday prayer. At that time, he was no longer working fulltime for the mosque, but was employed in a government-sponsored convert organization.[11] Like Imam Ali in Kelantan, Imam Yu enjoys a good relationship with religious officials and leaders in Negeri Sembilan. Imam Yu introduced to me a Han convert from China. She told me why she moved to Malaysia to practice Islam, "compared to Saudi Arabia, I feel more at home in Malaysia, as culturally and linguistically speaking, there are similarities. I can get by easily by speaking Chinese. But at the same time, I can learn 'true Islam' in Malaysia, because in China, Islamic teaching and learning is censored."[12] In other words, Malaysia offers some Hui from China both "cultural affinity" and "religious authenticity", together with "business opportunity". At the same time, Hui migrants also capitalize their cultural and religious affiliations to make their life easier in Malaysia.

The relations between cultural, social, economic and mobility capital are not resulted in a simple causal–effect relationship but manifested in a circular transformation. For sure, cultural capital enables Imam Yu to move beyond China, to work as *imam* and to live a rather good life in Malaysia. Yet, at the same, his mobility and economic capital also enable him to contribute to the networking of Hui and the well-being of Muslims, both in China and beyond. In 2017, Imam Yu established a WeChat group 大馬華穆之家 (Home of Chinese Muslims in Malaysia), in which he introduces the group as a platform where Malaysian Chinese (non-Muslims), Chinese Muslims and China-national Muslims living in Malaysia interact and share information on religious, cultural and business issues. In 2016, Imam Yu also set up another Wechat page (新月國際視線) sharing news and charity information among Chinese-speaking Muslims in China and in Malaysia. Through WeChat, the popular social media platform in China, he initiated 中國穆斯林援助羅興亞穆斯林志願團 (Chinese-national Muslim Volunteer Team for Helping Rohingya Muslims) to collect donations from Hui, both in China and overseas, to help

---

[10] *Ibid.*

[11] Interview with Imam Yu, February 17, 2017.

[12] Fieldnote, February 17, 2017.

Rohingya Muslims living in Malaysia and Myanmar. To a certain extent, WeChat helps overseas Hui in overcoming the geographical barriers, bonding Hui living in China and in Malaysia, as well as connecting them to the plights of Muslims living in Myanmar (Hew, 2021).

While Imam Ali and Imam Yu are both residing in Malaysia now, there are also other Hui *imams* who frequently visit Malaysia for religious and business purposes. One of them is Imam Yahya Ma Yiping who is an Imam of the Great Mosque of Xi'an and a well-known Chinese-Arabic calligrapher. He has visited Malaysia a number of times and has run a Chinese Islamic calligraphy exhibition. In 2016, with the help of a group of Malay students who studied in Beijing, he hosted a calligraphy exhibition at Putrajaya International Islamic Arts and Cultural Festival. As I observed, his calligraphy was very popular among Malay Muslim attendants. As of 2016, his son was studying at IIUM.[13] In the same year, Imam Ma led a Friday prayer and held a calligraphy exhibition in the Al-Saadah Mosque Complex. In 2017, another Chinese-Arabic calligrapher Liu Jingyi operated a small stall selling Chinese-Arabic calligraphic artworks in a shopping complex in Johor Bahru. Together with other Islamic-themed arts, Chinese-Arabic calligraphies are popular among segments of urban middle-class Malay Muslim. Such demands for Chinese-Arabic calligraphy works have given some Hui calligraphers opportunities to convert their cultural capital into financial income in Malaysia.

Imam Qin: Selling *Halal* Cuisine at Hui Restaurants

Using Hui Muslims in Beijing as a case study, Gladney (1993) suggests that the importance of the pork taboo, the dispersion of Hui in most cities, and their important mediating socio-economic position all help to make the Hui restaurant a Hui cultural center in the city. In Beijing and other Chinese cities, Hui involvement in *halal* restaurants is crucial to both their economic survival and the maintaining of the identity. Hui restaurants in Kuala Lumpur play a similar role as sites for Hui migrants to maintain their identity, to preach Islam, and to make a living. As I will describe, as being both "Chinese" and "halal" are desirable in contemporary Muslim consumer market, these restaurants are also sites where the accumulation

[13] Interview with Imam Ma Yiping, December 3, 2016.

and circulation of various forms of capital among some Hui migrants take place.

In Kuala Lumpur, Imam Ishaq Qin runs a Hui restaurant, "Imam Qin Restaurant", with another Hui migrant. Imam Qin is also a good friend of Imam Yu in Seremban, as they studied together at the same college in China. Having earlier served as an *imam* in a mosque in his home province of Gansu, Imam Qin first visited Kuala Lumpur briefly in 2008 to attend a religious course. In 2009, he moved to Malaysia to further his studies in Arabic literature at the IIUM with a hope to deepen his knowledge and to secure a better livelihood. In order to support his living cost, he first ran a small food stall in the university canteen. In 2012, he opened a restaurant selling dishes such as Lanzhou hand-pulled noodle, Xinjiang grilled meat and dumplings, food that is popular among Muslims in China. In 2014, he renamed his restaurants to "CIQ (China Imam Qin)" Restaurant. By 2015, he had opened three branches of his restaurants.

Strategically putting "Imam" as part of the restaurant name and "China Islamic Traditional Cuisine" as the restaurant tagline, together with decorating his restaurants with Chinese-style Islamic calligraphy, Imam Qin took advantages of his religious authority and cultural authenticity to establish social network and to generate economic capital through restaurant business. By doing so, he could also convince Malay Muslims that the food his restaurants serve are *halal*, even though they were not yet officially certified by the Malaysian religious department. As he explains, "in the beginning, some Malay hesitate to visit our restaurants because they worried the food might not *halal*. But the name of my restaurants already clearly reflected: we serve Muslim cuisine from China."[14] Indeed, the term "Chinese/China Muslim" is widespread in the naming of the Hui restaurants in Malaysia. Many of them claim themselves to serve "authentic Chinese Muslim cuisine" or "authentic Muslim cuisine from China", which is mainly a mixture of Northwestern Chinese and Uyghur dishes, such Lanzhou hand-pulled noodle and Xinjiang grilled meat.

Imam Qin sees his restaurant not only as a way of making profit but also as a medium for preaching Islam (*dakwah*). As he says, "I take the opportunity to share my thoughts with my customers, both non-Muslim Chinese and Malay Muslims, about the life of Hui in China. I want my customers to understand the beauty of Islam, and to realize that converting to Islam does not mean that you have to lose your Chinese cultural

[14] Interview with Imam Qin, February 5, 2013.

identity."[15] According to Imam Qin, the restaurant also functions as a site of social interaction and religious preaching, illustrating how the economic capital is being transformed back to social and cultural capital.

CIQ Restaurant is only one of the many Hui restaurants mushrooming in Malaysia over the last few years. While CIQ Restaurant has closed in 2016 probably due to financial problem, other Hui restaurants are flourishing. The most successful and popular case is "Chinese Muslim Authentic Heritage Pulled Noodle Restaurant" chain. As of 2017, it has 33 branches and its target is rather ambitious, to have more than 100 branches across cities in Malaysia. Some of it branches have live performance of Hui making the hand-pulled noodle, a cultural magnetism that drawing customers to visit the restaurants. While most of these restaurants are profit-driven, some owners cited religious consideration in their business enterprise. For example, Yahya Liu who co-runs "Salam Noodles Restaurant" explained to me why he left China and moved to Malaysia, "In China, we ran our restaurants in Shenzhen, a city with very small Muslim population and in order to survive, we rely on non-Muslim customers and we have to serve alcohol drinks. The money we earn is not *halal*.... My brother and I decided to move to Malaysia, as it is a Muslim-majority country and we can sustain our business without serving alcoholic drinks. Malaysia is also a better place for us to learn and to practice Islam."[16]

There are at least three different categories of Hui restaurants in Malaysia. The first one is a small-scale restaurant, mainly run by student-turned-businessperson, such as "China Imam Qin Restaurant". Another example is "Hot Meal Bar" in the campus of the National University of Malaysia, operated by Yang Jing Ishak, a PhD student at IIUM. The second type is a larger-scale restaurant, mainly run by Hui migrants with some food business experience back in China, such as "Salam Noodle" and "Chinese Muslim Authentic Heritage Pulled Noodle Restaurant", both now having multiple branches in Malaysia. The third one is a branch of chained Hui restaurant in China, which expanding their business overseas such as "Amber Restaurant" and "Qingfang Restaurant". Established in 2015, tapping into the China's BRI, as a branch from Hui restaurant chain based in Gansu, "Amber Restaurant" in Kuala Lumpur claims it serves "Silk Road" Muslim cuisine, referring to *halal* Chinese cuisine

[15] *Ibid.*

[16] Interview with Yahya Liu, February 19, 2016.

from the northern parts of China. However, in this case, such trademark of "Silk Road" cuisine is much more a marketing strategy and it does not imply that the restaurant expansion is part of the China's BRI strategy. In some ways, all the restaurants are not only selling Chinese *halal* cuisine from China but also selling "Islamic culture from China" to local Malay Muslims who are searching for cultural diversity within Islamic framework.

Conclusion: Entangled Hui Mobility

The increasing visibility of Hui presence in Malaysia is in tandem with another trend — an increasing number of Malay and Chinese Muslims from Malaysia who go to China to study, to travel and to run business. These developments appropriate the meaning of "Chineseness" and "Muslimness" in Malaysia by reconciling two sets of perceived incompatible identities. Such combination of "Chineseness" and "Muslimness" enables the accumulation and circulation of different forms of capital, be it mobility, cultural, social and economic among contemporary Hui migrants. Generally speaking, as compared to Uighur, Hui in China are freer to move within and beyond China. By sharing similar language (Chinese) with Chinese Malaysians and sharing the same religion (Islam) with ethnic Malays, as well as positioning themselves as a bridge between non-Muslims Chinese and Malay Muslims, Hui Muslims acquire cultural capital in navigating their life in Malaysia even if they are non-citizens. Such cultural capital has turned into social and economic capital, allowing them to interact with people from different ethnic and religious background, as well as to attract potential customers if they run businesses. In return, such social and economic status also allow Hui to play a greater role in preaching Islam as well as promoting their unique cultural identity.

However, instead of reifying such capital as given, Hui migrants also perform their cultural capital for the Malaysian context, exemplified by practices such as using Islamic names, wearing traditional Chinese clothing and promoting so-called Muslim cuisine from China. Such enactments of cultural capital play significant role in Hui mobility across national borders and enable the circulation of their different forms of capital to take place in different sites, such as in Chinese-style mosques and Hui restaurants. Hui mobility can be conceptualized as a form of "entangled mobility" as their mobility does not only entail their physical and spatial movement but also the travel and transformation of food practices, architectural idioms and Islamic knowledges. Their spatial mobility goes hand on hand with their social mobility, and sometimes also, with piety enhancement, knowledge improvement and business expansion. By moving to Malaysia, either to study or to work, some Hui desire a movement up of the scale of their socio-economic classes, while other might think they could live a more pious lifestyle in Muslim-majority countries such as Malaysia. Such processes often entail the accumulation and circulation of different forms of capital amid Hui mobility. In other words, "entangled mobility" seeks to understand how and under what conditions, spatial and social mobilities are entangled with each other and broader economic, social and political processes.

By exploring three cases of Hui *imams* living in Malaysia, I have illustrated the intersection between Chineseness and Muslimness, the interconnection between spatial and social mobility, the combination of religious and economic aspiration, as well as the circulation of various forms of capital among Hui amid their mobility across spaces and settlement in certain sites. Here, I would like to end by reiterating a few features that underpinning contemporary Hui entangled mobility. First, Hui mobility is entangled with the cultural politics of Islam and Chineseness in China and in Malaysia. Their mobility is in some ways engage with competing discourses of what constitute "authentic Chinese culture" and "proper Islamic practices" in both countries today. Second, Hui mobility entail both spatial and social mobility as well as religious and economic aspiration. Being able to interact with both local Malay Muslims and non-Muslim Chinese in Malaysia, they appropriate and exercise their cultural capital to navigate their life in multi-ethnic and multi-religious Malaysia. Third, the relations between cultural, social, economic and mobility capital do not result in a simple cause–effect relationship but manifest in a circular transformation. I have discussed how these forms of capital are accumulated across spaces, and how their exchanges take places and contribute to place-making such as Hui restaurants. Last but not least, Hui mobility today is mediated in both online and offline spheres, shaping and shaped by material environments and digital technologies.

References

Armijo-Hussein, J. (1999). Resurgence of Islamic Education in China. *ISIM Newsletter*, 4(99): 12.

Ananthalakshmi, A. (2018). Exclusive: Uighur Thai Jail Escapees detained in Malaysia and China Wants Them Back. *Reuters*, February 8, https://www.reuters.com/article/us-malaysia-uighurs-exclusive/exclusive-uighur-thai-jail-escapees-detained-in-malaysia-and-china-wants-them-back-sources-idUSKBN1FS0TH.

Basri, N. B. (2017). Johor Targets Muslim Tourists from China. *Bernama*, August 23, http://www.bernama.com/en/general/news.php?id=1384753.

Bernama (2017). Malaysia Had Deported 29 Uighur Militants to China, September 27, http://www.bernama.com/en/general/news.php?id=1394892.

Bourdieu, P. (1986). The Forms of Capital. In J. Richardson (ed.), *Handbook of Theory and Research for the Sociology of Education* (pp. 241–258). New York, NY, Greenwood.

Chow, H. B. (2010). Huge Potential in Halal Trade. *The Star Online*, October 9, from https://www.thestar.com.my/opinion/columnists/made-in-china/2010/10/09/huge-potential-in-halal-trade/.

Crane, B. (2014). A Tale of Two Chinese Muslim Minorities. *The Diplomat*, August 22, https://thediplomat.com/2014/08/a-tale-of-two-chinese-muslim-minorities/.

Erel, U. (2010). Migrating Cultural Capital: Bourdieu in Migration Studies. *Sociology*, 44(4): 642–660.

Friedrichs, J. (2017). Sino-Muslim Relations: The Han, the Hui, and the Uyghurs. *Journal of Muslim Minority Affairs*, 31(1): 55–79.

Gillette, M. B. (2000). *Between Mecca and Beijing: Modernization and Consumption among Urban Chinese Muslim*. California, Stanford University Press.

Gladney, D. C. (1993). Hui Urban Entrepreneurialism in Beijing: State Policy, Ethnoreligious Identity and the Chinese City. In G. Guldin and A. Southall (eds.), *Urban Anthropology in China* (pp. 278–307). Leiden, Brill.

Gladney, D. C. (1996). *Muslims Chinese: Ethnic Nationalism in the People's Republic*. Cambridge, Harvard University Press.

Hau, C. (2014). The Chinese Question: Ethnicity, Nation, and Region in and beyond the Philippines. Kyoto, Kyoto University Press.

Hew, W. W. (2013). Universalising Islam in Malaysia. *New Mandala*, August 23, http://www.newmandala.org/universalising-islam-in-malaysia/.

Hew, W. W. (2014). *Identiti Cina Muslim di Malaysia: Persempadanan, Perundingan dan Kacukan Budaya* (Chinese Muslims in Malaysia: Boundary-Making, Identity Negotiation and Cultural Hybridity). Bangi, Penerbit UKM (National University of Malaysia Publisher).

Hew, W. W. (2016). Musing on the Aesthetics of Modern Muslims. *New Mandala*, May 18, http://www.newmandala.org/musing-aesthetics-modern-muslims/.

Hew, W. W. (2017). Translocal Pious Entrepreneurialism: Hui Business and Religious Activities in Malaysia and Indonesia. In P. Nyiri and D. Tan (eds.), *Chinese Encounters in Southeast Asia: How People, Money and Ideas from China are Changing a Region* (pp. 58–78). Seattle, The University of Washington Press.

Hew, W. W. (2018). *Chinese Ways of Being Muslim: Negotiating Ethnicity and Religiosity in Indonesia.* Copenhagen, NIAS Press.

Hew, W. W. (2021). Translocal Encounter: Islam, Hui Mobility and Place-Making in Malaysia and Indonesia. In R. Harris, G. Ha and M. Jaschok (eds.), *Ethnographies of Islam in China: Revivals, Identities and Mobilities* (pp. 225–244). Honolulu, The University of Hawaii Press.

Ho, W. Y. (2012). Mobilizing the Muslim Minority for China's Development: Hui Muslims, Ethnic Relations and Sino-Arab Connections. *Journal of Comparative Asian Development*, 12(1): 84–112.

Hoffstaedter, G. (2017). Refugees, Islam, and the State: The Role of Religion in Providing Sanctuary in Malaysia. *Journal of Immigrant & Refugee Studies*, 15(3): 287–304.

Kaufmann, V. and Montulet, B. (2008). Between Social and Spatial Mobilities: The Issue of Social Fluidity. In W. Canzler, V. Kaufmann and S. Kesselring (eds.), *Tracing Mobilities: Towards a Cosmopolitan Perspective* (pp. 37–56). Farnham, Ashgate.

Kaufmann, V., Bergman, M. M. and Joye, D. (2004). Motility: Mobility as Capital. *International Journal of Urban and Regional Research*, 28(4): 745–756.

Khoo, G. C. (2014). Introduction: Theorizing Different Forms of Belonging in a Cosmopolitan Malaysia. *Citizenship Studies*, 18(8): 791–806.

Lipman, J. N. (1998). *Familiar Strangers: A History of Muslims in Northwest China*. Seattle, The University of Washington Press.

Luecking, M. (2016). Beyond Islam Nusantara and "Arabization" — Capitalizing "Arabness" in Madura, East Java. *ASIEN: The German Journal on Contemporary Asia*, 2016(139): 5–24.

Ma, R. W. (2010, August 11). Chinese Muslims in Malaysia, History and Development. *The Light of Islam*, August 11, www.islamhk.com/en/?p=12&a=view&r=43.

Meyer, P. K. (2016). To Grant or Not to Grant Chinese Muslims Their Rights. *The Diplomat*, April 1, https://thediplomat.com/2016/04/to-grant-or-not-to-grant-chinese-muslims-their-rights/

Salama. (2013). Ningxia and Malaysia's ECER Reach Deal to Explore Halal Investment. *Halal Focus*, January 4, http://halalfocus.net/ningxia-malaysias-ecer-reaches-deal-to-explore-halal-investments/.

Sheller, M. (2011). Mobility. *Sociopedia.isa*, http://www.sagepub.net/isa/resources/pdf/mobility.pdf.

Slama, M. (2017). A Subtle Economy of Time: Social Media and the Transformation of Indonesia's Islamic Preacher Economy. *Economic Anthropology*, 4(1): 94–106.

Stewart, A. (2016). *Chinese Muslims and the Global Ummah: Islamic Revival and Ethnic Identity among the Hui of Qinghai Province*. London, Routledge.

Tan, C. B. (1991). A Note on the Orang Yunnan in Trengganu. *Archipel*, 42: 93–120.

Tan, C. K. (2017). Malaysia's Halal Trade Gets E-Commerce Push. *Nikkei Asian Review*, April 5, https://asia.nikkei.com/Business/Trends/Malaysia-s-halal-trade-gets-e-commerce-push.

Usahawan Kelantan Dipelawa Pasar Produk Halal di China (Halal Markets in China Welcome Kelantanese Entrepreneurs) (2011). *Buletin Darulnaim*, 2011(112): 16–31.

Vasquez, M. A. and Knott, K. (2014). Three Dimensions of Religious Place Making in Diaspora. *Global Network: A Journal of Transnational Affairs*, 14(3): 326–347.

Wong, D. [黃永寶]. (2013). Musilin de Liudong yu Zhongguo Xinyimin: Malaixiya Huizu Liudong Gean Yanjiu (穆斯林的流動與中國新移民—馬來西亞回族流動個案研究, Muslim Mobility and the New Chinese Migration: A Case-Study of Hui Mobility in Malaysia). *Huaqiao Huaren Lishi Yanjiu* (華僑華人歷史研究, Overseas Chinese History Studies), 2013(2): 13–29.

Wong, D. (2015). "We are Believers": Contemporary Hui Mobility in Transnational Islamic Space — A Malaysian Case-Study. *Chinese Southern Diaspora Studies*, 7: 88–108.

Wong, D. and Ooi, P. W. (2013). The Globalization of Tertiary Education and Intra-Asian Student Mobility: Mainland Chinese Student Mobility to Malaysia. *Asian and Pacific Migration Journal*, 22(1): 55–76.

Yang, Y. (in press). Displaying "Muslim-ness" through the Bridal Look: Wedding Photography, Wedding Dresses with Non-Chinese Origins, and the Hui in Xi'an, China. In R. Harris, G. Ha and M. Jaschok (eds.), *Ethnographies of Islam in China: Revivals, Identities and Mobilities*. Honolulu, The University of Hawaii Press.

https://doi.org/10.1142/9789811250668_0008

Chapter 8

Taiwan Investment in Southeast Asia: The Choice of Taishang and Their Response in the Changing Asia

Kristy Hsu

Director, Taiwan ASEAN Studies Center, Taiwan

Introduction

Taiwan is an outward looking economy, highly dependent on international trade as a major economic growth engine. Since the late 1980s, Taiwan began to undertake industrial upgrading and re-structuring which led to the beginning of off-shoring labor intensive manufacturing operations to Southeast Asia and China. To better manage the capital movement, since mid-1990s Taiwanese government has implemented a series of policy measures under similar guiding principles to encourage Taiwanese companies to Go South and establish manufacturing operations in the labor-abundant Southeast Asian countries. The series of policy interventions and the active response of Taishang have created significant capital outflows to Southeast Asia, building close economic and trade ties with most of the Southeast Asian countries and integrating Taiwanese business in the rising regional economy (White, 1999: 97–141).

Taishang, known as Taiwanese businesses, usually refer to Taiwanese entrepreneurs establishing overseas business and often long-term residents in the host countries. The term of Taishang was first widely used to refer to the entrepreneurs or the companies investing and operating in Southeast Asia since the 1980s (Schubert *et al.*, 2016).[1] After continuous capital outflows to Southeast Asia and intensified economic exchange for more than three decades, Taishang have not only increased in numbers and capital scale but have also expanded in economic contribution to and influence in host countries.

Furthermore, as Taishang became increasingly integrated in host society and domestic economy, Taishang organizations also underwent institutional reforms in order to play more active roles in representing Taiwanese overall interests and communicating with host governments to enhance their collective social images and protect their business interests (Schubert *et al.*, 2017: 856–884).[2] Therefore, the New Southbound Policy in 2016 has particularly highlighted the "linkage functions" of Taishang organizations to promote connections between Taiwan and the Southeast Asian countries and to play the role of economic diplomacy for Taiwan.

This chapter aims to review Taiwanese investment flows in Southeast Asia and the roles of Taishang and Taishang organizations. The chapter is divided into five parts. It first gives an overview of Taiwanese investment in Southeast Asia and its changing nature. Then it explores the current status of Taishang in Southeast Asia and introduces the Taishang organizations and their development and evolution in the region. It then analyzes the latest trend of Taishang's movement in responding to the escalating US–China trade conflicts and the COVID-19 pandemic outbreaks. It then makes conclusions in the last part.

---

[1] Since mid-1990s, the term was given different meaning. It was used to refer to the Taiwanese companies or entrepreneurs investing in China, which increased rapidly in numbers and their influence in Chinese economy. However, Taishang in Southeast Asia and China are generally two different groups, representing different business interests, development paths, relations with host governments and society and adaption to local culture, and in many cases different political orientation.

[2] Taiwanese government has developed two separate systems of Taishang organizations in Southeast Asia and China, respectively administered by OCTC and the Mainland Affairs Council (MAC). In Southeast Asia and countries excluding China, the standard names of the Taishang organizations are Taiwan Chambers of Commerce, while in China the names are Taiwan Business Associations. As of 2020, Taiwan companies in China have established 152 Taiwan Business Associations across the Mainland.

An Overview of the Taiwanese Investment in Southeast Asia

Taiwan's outbound investment flows to Southeast Asia took shape in the 1980s. After almost four decades of investment in the region, Indonesia and Thailand have the largest Taiwanese population, around 200,000 and 150,000 Taiwanese now working in the two countries respectively. While with regard of total investment value, Vietnam has received the largest accumulated investment capital from Taiwan, followed by Thailand, Indonesia, Malaysia and Singapore. In the past decade, Taiwanese investment also gradually expanded to less developed countries, including Cambodia, Laos and Myanmar and even East Timor, making footprints across the region.

A statistical review

According to historical literature, Taiwan's earliest reported outbound investment project to Southeast Asia was filed in the 1950s. Since then, Taiwanese companies began to set foot in Southeast Asia. However, in the early years, due to little international experiences and shared culture and family ties with ethnic Chinese in Southeast Asia, most of Taishang developed business partnership mainly with ethnic Chinese in the host countries.[3]

According to statistics released by Ministry of Economic Affair (MOEA), Taiwan, in the late 1980s, Indonesia, Thailand, Malaysia and the Philippines were home to a lot of Taiwan's small private businesses which had a spirit of risk-taking in overseas markets. In 1994 when President Lee Tung Huei launched the Go South policy[4] — often referred to as the first wave of Taiwan's Southern policy, the policy further encouraged medium to large-sized state-owned and KMT-owned companies and banks to go South.[5]

---

[3] The gradual appreciation of New Taiwan Dollars since mid-1980s due to a weak US dollar and increasing trade surplus toward the US encouraged another investment boom in the Southeast Asia.

[4] The formal name is Go South policy or Facing South policy.

[5] The Kuo Min Tang (KMT) was the ruling political party until 2000 when Democratic Progressive Party (DPP) won the presidential election and for the first time resulted in the change of government in Taiwan. In the 1990s and 2000s, the KMT was regarded as one

In 2000, the KMT lost the presidential election and the DPP for the first time became the ruling government. Following the Southern policy adopted in the 1990s, President Chen Shui Bian announced more policy measures. Chen's version of Southern policy aimed at strengthening economic and trade ties with Southeast Asian countries, hoping to re-orient Taiwanese investors from going to China to Southeast Asia.

It is notable that under these Southern policies, Taiwanese companies' interests gradually expanded from the traditionally popular destinations to newcomers to the regional integration.[6] In 1994, Vietnam, undertaking economic reform to allow foreign direct investment (FDI) under the *Doi Moi* since 1986 (Vuong, 2014),[7] was included together with other more developed countries in the scope of President Lee's Southern policy.[8] Lee's policy made Taiwan the first non-Socialist country which officially responded and encouraged capital flows to Vietnam before the US government "normalized" bilateral relations with the country in 1995 and ended 20-year economic sanctions (Eleanor, 2019).[9] With the government endorsement, Vietnam soon became the most popular investment destination compared with other more developed countries such as Malaysia and Thailand.

Later in 1997, the Southern policy further expanded its geographical scope to Cambodia, Laos and Myanmar (the CLM countries). The policy

---

of the richest political parties in the world. Through funding via various channels, the KMT had set up dozens of companies and non-profit organizations in Taiwan and foreign countries. Some KMT-owned companies were among the most active investors in Taiwan in acquisition of lands and estates, as well as investing overseas. For example, the earliest large investment by Taiwan in Vietnam in 1991 was made by then KMT-owned company Central Trading and Development Corporation (CT&D). The company was privatized in the 2000s and becomes a private company.

[6]Compared with the Founding Member States of ASEAN, Vietnam, Cambodia, Laos and Myanmar, joining ASEAN in the late 1990s, were all transitional economies and newly open to foreign capitals.

[7]The Vietnamese term Đổi Mới literally means "renovation" or "reconstruction", referring to the Open-Door and Innovation Policy. The Đổi Mới was officially endorsed by the 6th national congress of Vietnam in 1986.

[8]Taiwanese was the earliest foreign investor in Vietnam. The first investment projects were registered in 1989.

[9]After the Vietnam War ended in 1975, US put economic sanctions on Vietnam until then US President Bill Clinton announced formal normalization of diplomatic relations with the Socialist Republic of Vietnam on July 11, 1995.

expansion symbolized the adoption of a full-fledged external economic strategy which prioritized the Southeast Asia as Taiwan's most important economic and trading partners, while in the meantime, tried to downplay the importance of China as an investment destination and potential market. Since then, the questions of "Go West" or "Turn to China" and the questions of "Go South" or "Turn from China" have always been the center of heated policy debates between different political parties. Taiwanese business community needed to decide between "Go West" or "Go South" when they planned for overseas operations.

In the past 25 years since the first Southern policy was put in place, Taiwanese investment in Southeast Asia has continued to grow. In the 1990s and before mid-2000s, Taiwan was often or among the top three foreign investors in these countries, if not the largest one. However, after mid-2000s, Taiwanese investment outflows significantly shifted to China, regardless of the government's Southern policy.

According to the official FDI statistics released by the host governments, as of end of 2019, total amount of accumulated Taiwanese investment registered in Southeast Asian countries amounted to around US$100 billion, total number of Taiwanese companies exceeding 15,000. Among the Southeast Asian countries, Vietnam alone received around US$33 billion of investment, while Indonesia, Thailand, Singapore and Malaysia, respectively, received investment ranging from US$12 billion to 18 billion. The Philippines and Cambodia received US$3 billion and 2 billion, respectively.

On the other hand, according to statistics of approved reported outbound investment by Investment Commission, MOEA, Taiwan, as of end of 2019, total amount of accumulated Taiwan investment outflows registered in Southeast Asian countries was around US$37 billion, only about one-third of the amount registered at the host countries. The wide gap between Taiwanese data and host countries' data explained the tendency of Taishang companies not reporting to Taiwanese government of their outbound investment[10] (See Table 1).

Among the reported accumulated investment, Singapore topped other Southeast Asian countries and received around US$14.2 billion. While according to Southeast Asian governments' statistics, as of March 2020,

[10]The current regulations of MOEA, Taiwan, only require outbound investment projects exceeding NTD 50 million, approximately US$1.6 million, to report to the Investment Commission of MOEA.

Table 1: Taiwan FDI stock in Southeast Asian countries (as end of 2019)

	MOEA, Taiwan		Host governments	
Country	**No. of cases**	**Amount (US$ million)**	**No. of cases**	**Amount (US$ million)**
World (exc. China)	61,035	332,204		
Vietnam	724	10,980	2,759	33,037
Indonesia	310	1,644	3,848	18,034
Thailand	571	4,066	2,493	15,239
Malaysia	446	3,297	2,524 (2018)	12,580 (2018)
Singapore	642	14,252	615 (2018)	13,616 (2018)
Philippines	236	2,144	1,124 (As 2019.Q1)	2,626 (As 2019.Q1)
Cambodia	67	735	363 (As Dec. 2018)	1,193 (As Dec. 2018)

Source: Investment Commission, MOEA, Taiwan (2021). FDI statistics of Southeast Asian Countries.

Vietnam received around US$33 billion of registered accumulated FDI from Taiwan, making Vietnam the largest destination of Taiwanese capital investment in the region.[11]

Reviews of Taiwan's southern policy in different periods

In 1993, Taiwan's MOEA proposed a 3 year "Work Plans for Enhancing Economic Ties and Trade in Southeast Asia", laying down the groundwork for President Lee Tung Huei's Southern policy announced a year later. The Work Plans, soon approved by the Executive Yuan, became retrospectively effective from January 1, 1994, listing seven Southeast Asian countries as targeted partners, including the original six ASEAN Member States[12] and the Socialist country Vietnam.

[11] See FDI data, Foreign Investment Agency, Ministry of Planning and Investment, Vietnam, http://www.mpi.gov.vn/Pages/tinbai.aspx?idTin=46093&idcm=208.

[12] Thailand, Indonesia, Malaysia, Singapore, the Philippines and Brunei.

The Southern Policy was a key element of President Lee's Pragmatic Diplomacy to respond to the intensifying pressures from China in enforcing its One China Principle in international world. The Southern policy aimed at strengthening economic relations with Southeast Asian countries through trade and investment. The government also expected to promote trade diplomacy to enhance government to government relations, institutionalize high ranking officials' mutual visits and meetings, and finally negotiate bilateral agreements with the partner countries. Furthermore, President Lee also attempted to re-orient Taiwanese companies' investment movement from China to Southeast Asia, as he found that after 1988 Chinese governments at central and local levels provided generous investment incentives to attract "compatriots in Taiwan" to invest in "homeland China".[13] During Lee's presidency (1988–2000), he launched two waves of Southern Policy. The second was implemented in 1997 during the Asian Financial Crisis.

In 2000, the Democratic Progressive Party (DPP) won the presidential election, becoming the ruling government since the political party was established in September 1986. In August 2002, then President Chen Seui Bian reiterated the importance of continuing the Southern policy. It was also DPP's first regional policy addressing Southeast Asia,[14] regarded as Taiwan's third wave of Southern policy (Hsiao *et al.*, 2008: 1330–1151). However, in these years the rise of Chinese economy had attracted more Taiwanese companies. The admission of China to the World Trade Organization (WTO) in December 2001 further stimulated a boom of Taishang formerly operating in Southeast Asia to close their operations and move to China (Hsu, 2020: 73–105).[15] For example, it was estimated that by end of 2002, among the 300 Taishang companies in Malaysia, only

---

[13] On July 7, 1988, the State Department of China released a decree to encourage Taiwanese compatriots to invest in China. To respond to China' policy change, on May 20, 1990, President Lee Tung Huei in his inaugural speech announced a new policy to begin cross-straits academic, cultural, economic and technology exchanges based on reciprocity and equality.

[14] The "Work Plans for Enhancing Economic Ties and Trade in Southeast Asia" had continued during Chen's administration (2000–2008). Chen's policy further expanded from Southeast Asia to India, putting India for the first time in the government's Work Plans for Enhancing Economic Ties and Trade in Southeast Asia and India.

[15] China was admitted to the WTO on November 16, 2001, followed by Taiwan's admission on January 1, 2002. China's entry into the global trading system triggered huge

16 remained in operation while all others either closed business or relocated to China.[16]

In January 2002, Taiwan became a member of the WTO. In May 2008, President Ma Ying Jeou took office after KMT won the presidential election in January. President Ma then adopted the Work Plan (2008–2015) to enhance economic ties with Southeast Asian neighbors (Ma, 2008). In 2013, Taiwan and Singapore successfully signed a bilateral Economic Cooperation Agreement (ECA). However, different from President Chen, Ma never officially announced adoption of any subsequent or new Southern policies during his two terms of presidency (2008–2016).[17]

During the three waves of Southern policy, while the policy objectives and priority had varied in different years to respond to the changing external economic and geo-political environment, one common goal was to encourage off-shoring of labor-intensive manufacturing industries to Southeast Asia, while in Taiwan promoting industrial upgrading. Though it was found that many Taiwanese companies which followed the Southern policy to invest in Southeast Asia had then relocated to China, Taiwan had remained an important source of foreign capital and technology in Southeast Asia. (Chen *et al.*, 2017: 367–387).

Considering the accelerating economic integration in Southeast Asia, on May 20, 2016, President Tsai Ing Wen in her inaugural address announced launch of New Southbound Policy, the latest version of Taiwan's Southern policy (Executive Yuan, 2016). Emphasizing its distinctive nature from the previous versions, the New Southbound Policy contained a broader geographic scope of target countries and different approaches and priority areas (Hsu, 2017: 63–87). Among the 18

foreign investment capital inflows in the country and the beginning of its era of becoming the World Factory.

[16]Other notable examples are Subic Bay of the Philippines and Batum of Indonesia where were major destinations of Taishang companies during President Lee administration.

[17]President Ma in his inaugural address in May 2008 exposed that his plan was to "actively participate in Asian Pacific regional cooperation..., to fully integrate in the East Asian economic integration and to make contribution to the peace and prosperity in East Asia." According to Taiwan scholars, President Ma had restrained from launching a separate Go South policy due to concerns that it would induce China's unfavorable response.

countries, Southeast Asia remains the cornerstone of Tsai's policy.[18] Among them, six countries are identified as priority partners, including Thailand, Malaysia, Indonesia, Philippines, Vietnam and India.

As all countries' national policy carries a political agenda, all of Taiwan's Southern policies have an agenda beyond building bilateral economic and trade ties. For both KMT and DPP, the main purpose is to improve political and official relations with Southeast Asian countries through improved economic and trade ties. Though lacking comprehensive assessment, the Southern policy in the 1990s had made significant achievements in successfully signing bilateral investment agreements and double taxation agreements, and institutionalizing ministerial or vice-ministerial annual consultative meetings with trade ministers in several countries.[19] Though President Chen and President Tsai aimed to upgrade overall bilateral relations with these countries, they found it more difficult than President Lee's time due to China's increasing influence in the region (Thornton, 2017).[20]

For example, both KMT and DPP governments endeavored to increase international space and enhance "visibility" through Taiwan's trade diplomacy in Southeast Asia. In 1993, Premiere Lien Chan successfully managed to visit Malaysia and Singapore, followed by President Lee Tung-Hui who visited the Philippines, Thailand and Indonesia during the Chinese Lunar New Year Holidays in 1994. These trips were described by the media as "Vacation Diplomacy". After DPP came to power in 2000, Taishang played a more important role in the government's trade diplomacy. In May 2006, President Chen successfully visited a Taiwan-invested industrial zone in Batam island of Indonesia (Chou and Wang,

---

[18]The New Southbound Policy has targeted at 18 countries, including 10 Southeast Asian countries, 6 South Asian countries (India, Pakistan, Bangladesh, Nepal, Sri Lanka and Bhutan), and 2 Oceanic countries (Australia and New Zealand). However, as Taiwan has no representative offices in 7 countries (Cambodia, Laos, Pakistan, Bangladesh, Nepal, Sri Lanka and Bhutan), promoting exchanges with these countries is very difficult.

[19]Taiwan signed bilateral investment agreements with Philippines, Malaysia, Indonesia, Thailand, Singapore and Vietnam, and double taxation agreement with Singapore, Malaysia, Indonesia and Vietnam, all major investment destinations in the 1990s.

[20]It was reported that President Chen designated a representative to Singapore to discuss the Singapore–Taiwan FTA.

2006).[21] Before Chen's visit, Vice President Annette Lu also visited in Bali in August 2002, claiming in her "private capacity" to greet Taiwanese companies investing in the country (Office of the President, Republic of China (Taiwan), 2002). To Southeast Asian countries, maintaining good relations with Taiwanese government could encourage more Taiwanese investment. To Taiwan, all these ground breaking presidential, vice-presidential and premiere-level visits made diplomatic milestones in Taiwan's pursuit of international space.

In May 2016, when President Tsai announced the New Southbound Policy (NSP), one of her strategic considerations is to continue the trade diplomacy of previous administrations while further expanding bilateral exchanges to "soft power" areas which she considered were not sufficiently addressed in previous policy, including culture, education, tourism and people to people exchanges.[22] In this regard, it is sometimes recognized that Tsai successfully took a step further in adopting soft power diplomacy which helped to counter the increasing sharp power diplomacy of China under its Belt and Road Initiative (BRI). However, while making some achievements, Tsai's soft power diplomacy was also criticized to have limited and temporary effects and did not significantly change Taiwan's isolation from international community.

Taishang and Taishang Organizations in Southeast Asia

The Constitution of Republic of China (ROC Taiwan) lists overseas compatriot affairs among the nation's "fundamental national policies" and stipulates that the nation should protect and assist overseas compatriots in their business development and promote Taiwan economy globally.[23] For decades, Taiwanese government has identified overseas compatriot

---

[21] On May 11, 2006, President Chen, in his second term of presidency, on his return trip from Latin America back to Taiwan, managed to visit Batam island of Indonesia, where he met with Taiwanese companies located in an industrial zone developed by a Taiwanese enterprise on the island, and was received by Ismeth Abdullah, governor of Riau of Indonesia.

[22] See the official New Southbound Policy website, https://www.newsouthboundpolicy.tw/index.aspx.

[23] Article 151 reads, "With respect to Chinese citizens residing abroad, the State shall foster and protect the development of their economic enterprises."

Table 2: Numbers of overseas Taiwanese worldwide

(Unit: 10,000 people)

Year	Total	Asia	Americas	Europe	Oceania	Africa
2010	178.1	58.1	111.8	3.3	3.8	1.1
2011	179.5	59.0	112.2	3.3	3.9	1.1
2012	180.7	59.3	113.1	3.4	4.0	1.0
2013	182.2	59.8	113.8	3.5	4.1	1.0
2014	183.7	59.9	114.6	3.7	4.3	1.0
2015	187.1	59.8	118.0	3.9	4.4	1.0
2016	191.1	61.3	120.2	4.2	4.3	1.0
2017	197.1	62.6	123.5	4.4	5.6	1.0
2018	198.1	60.9	125.0	4.6	6.5	1.0

Source: OCAC, Taiwan (2018). Annual Statistics Book.

businesses all over the world as "an extension of national power". Therefore, southern policies adopted by different administration meets the national policy goals to promote overseas economic activities.

The Overseas Community Affairs Council (OCAC) is the administrative organ responsible for handling Taiwan's overseas community and ethnic Chinese affairs under the Executive Yuan. According to OCAC, as of end of 2018, there are 1.98 million overseas Taiwanese across the globe in 91 countries, increasing by 0.51% as compared with 2018.[24] In 2019, Taiwanese population in Asia was 609,000, increased by 4% compared with the number in 2010 (see Table 2).

One major goal of the OCAC under its Department of Business Affairs, is to provide assistance to Taiwanese business community in foreign countries by facilitating and assisting the establishment of overseas Taiwan Chambers of Commerce in host countries.[25] In the past years, Taishang organizations in Southeast Asia have gradually evolved and

[24] Overseas Taiwanese refer to the Taiwanese emigrated from Republic of China (ROC), Taiwan and their descendants. In contrast, in 2019 the total number of Overseas Chinese, referring to the Chinese originated from Mainland China and their descendants, is 48.69 million, increased by 2.52% as compared with 2018.

[25] The OCAC supports their activities and conferences by providing funds and assistance and sending senior executives to participate, in the hope of interacting with the chambers and helping them achieve better development.

played a more active role to respond to the changing role of Taishang and the policy guidance under the Southern policy.

The development of Taishang organizations in Southeast Asia

In the early 1990s, there were already various groups and associations established by Taishang in several Southeast Asian countries. Most of these associations were loosely structured sodalities aimed at social networking and distributing business matching opportunities among the members. In July 1993, under guidance of Lee's administration, the Asia Taiwanese Chambers of Commerce (ASTCC) was established. The ASTCC was the first institutionalized Taiwan Chambers of Commerce representing overseas Taishang and Taishang companies.[26] A year later, in September 1994, the World Taiwanese Chambers of Commerce (WTCC) was established, under which six continental Chambers of Commerce were also created, including the ASTCC, and the Chambers of Commerce in North America, Latin America, Europe, Africa and Oceania.[27]

To provide assistance to the increasing number of overseas Taishang and to promote institutionalization of the overseas Taishang organizations, the OCAC also underwent structural and policy changes. On policy level, the OCAC was originally established to serve overseas compatriots, it then established a special division to handle Taishang related affairs.[28] Since then, Taishang, usually referred to as the "new compatriots" *vis-á-vis* the traditional "old compatriots" in host society, become a new policy focus under the Southern policy.

The Chambers of Commerce were further re-structured after 2010. For example, they set up a Junior Chapter to invite second generation of

[26]Being the first overseas Taiwan Chambers of Commerce, the ASTCC also has the largest membership compared with other continental Chambers of Commerce. It currently has 17 country-level Chambers of Commerce and 74 district-level Chambers of Commerce across Asia.

[27]They are ASTCC, Taiwanese Chambers of Commerce of North America (TCCNA), Taiwanese Chambers of Commerce in Latin America (TCCLA), Taiwanese Chamber of Commerce in Europe (ETCC), African Taiwanese Chambers of Commerce (ATCC), Taiwanese Chambers of Commerce in Oceania (TCCO), with more than 40,000 company members across 75 countries in 6 continents.

[28]According to OCAC, this is because overseas compatriots and Taishang usually have different needs and requirement of assistance.

Taishang to participate in the business networking. In President Tsai's New Southbound Policy, the second generation of Taishang, or young Taishang, is a highlight of the evolution of the Taishang in Southeast Asia. The OCAC provides training, business consultation and assistance to upgrade these young Taishang to develop their own business and enhance influence in Southeast Asia.

Among the Southeast Asian countries, Malaysia's ethnic Chinese population made it more attractive to Taiwan compared with other Southeast Asian countries in early years. In 1990, Taiwan became the country's largest source of FDI. The Association of Republic of China Business Investing in Malaysia was established in 1990, which was reorganized later in 2005 and renamed as the Council of Taiwan Chambers of Commerce in Malaysia.[29] There are currently 1,700 Taiwanese companies in Malaysia, including 450 company members from the Council and 1,250 companies not registered under the Council.

Thailand, the second largest economy in Southeast Asia, was the most important destination for Taiwanese companies before Vietnam replaced it in the mid-2000s. Thailand Business Association was established in 1992 and registered to Thai government in April 1993, later changed to the Council of Taiwan Chambers of Commerce in Thailand. It has currently around 3,000 company members registered in its 15 district-level Chambers of Commerce, the largest number of company members in Southeast Asia. If including Taishang not registered with the Council, total Taishang companies in Thailand would exceed 5,000.[30]

Indonesia as the largest economy in Southeast Asia has been a very important destination to Taiwanese investment since the 1990s. The Indonesia Taiwan Chambers of Commerce was established in 1990s. Currently there are around 2,000 companies and around 200,000 Taiwanese working in Indonesia.

During Lee's presidency, Taiwan already developed close business ties with ethnic Chinese entrepreneurs in the Philippines. Taiwanese investment in the Philippines were widely spread in different clusters which established separate organizations to serve their separate needs. The first Taiwanese business group was the Overseas Republic of China

---

[29] The Council has 7 district-level Chambers of Commerce across Malaysia, including Kuala Lumpur, Penang, Negeri Kedah, Perak, etc.

[30] Many Taishang companies in Thailand are not reported in Thailand because they are not registered as Taiwan capitals or have Taiwan's share less than 49%.

Taiwanese Business Association, established in March 1988, which was also the first ever Taiwanese overseas business group legally registered in the host country.[31] The Taiwan Association Inc. in the Philippines is a member of ASTCC.

Taiwanese investment in Singapore is different from those in other Southeast Asian countries. As Taiwanese investment in Singapore focuses in services industries, the Council of Taiwan Chamber of Commerce in Singapore has more members in services sector than in manufacturing sector.

Taiwan was the first foreign investor when Vietnam opened its door to foreign direct investment in 1986. In these early years, Taiwan's small companies managed to run business in Vietnam doing simple assembly or food processing.[32] In June 1994, two business associations were established — the Club of Taiwanese companies in South Vietnam and the Association of Taiwan Business in North Vietnam, the two then merged as the Council of Taiwanese Chambers of Commerce in Vietnam. The Council was approved by Vietnamese government in October, 1997.

The Council currently has around 1,600 members under its 15 district-level councils. It also developed several industrial sectoral chapters, including textile and garment, bicycle, furniture, and footwear, to provide more specific services to their members. It is estimated that there are around 4,100 Taiwanese companies in Vietnam, including around 2,500 companies not registered to the Council. For many years, Taiwan maintained the largest foreign investor in Vietnam until it was replaced by Republic of Korea after early 2010s. Taiwan also fell behind Singapore and Japan after 2010s.

Taishang's footprints in Cambodia can be traced back to 1989 when the country first opened to foreign investment. Currently there are around 200 Taishang companies, mostly small and medium-sized companies. Among these companies, more than 50 are in garment and appeals sector. Taiwan Commercial Association in Cambodia was established in

[31] In 2005, it was renamed as Taiwan Chamber of Commerce in Philippines, in May 2010 renamed as Taiwan Chamber of Commerce and Industry in the Philippines. In the Philippines, there are more than 10 Taiwan compatriots or business associations outside the ASOCC system.

[32] A lot of these small companies invested in Vietnam through connections from their Vietnamese spouses and their relatives in Vietnam.

September 1996. Taishang in garment sector also established an Association of Taiwan Companies in Garment in Cambodia.

Compared with the early entry of Taiwanese investors in Vietnam and Cambodia, most Taiwanese investors entered into Myanmar only after 2014,[33] when the Myanmar government officially lifted the ban prohibiting direct investment from Taiwan.[34] Before the ban was removed, Taishang companies established an informal association under the name of Taiwan Charity Golf Club. In 2016, under Myanmar government's approval, the Club changed its name to Taiwan Chamber of Commerce in Myanmar. It has around 250 members now.[35]

The three smallest Chambers of Commerce in Southeast Asia are the Taiwan Business Association in Brunei Darussalam, which has around 35 members, the Council of Taiwan Chambers of Commerce in Laos, and the Timor-Leste Taiwan Chamber of Commerce. The latter was established in February 2017 in the youngest Southeast Asian country, marking it the 11th Taiwan Chambers of Commerce in the region.

According to OCAC, after three decades of investment in Southeast Asia and continuous implementation of the Southern policy, there are currently around 15,000 Taiwanese companies investing across the Southeast Asia, and around 550,000 Taiwanese work or live in the region (see Table 3).

The evolving role of the Taishang organizations in Southeast Asia

Over the decades, Taiwanese government has struggled to build official relations with the Southeast Asian countries. Despite frequent exchanges between private sectors from two sides, including industries and business

---

[33] There were more than 200 Taiwanese companies investing in Myanmar in the early 1990s, mostly in garment sector. Most of them had closed operations when Myanmar were sanctioned in 2007 and moved to China.

[34] The Myanmar government had prohibited direct trade with and investment from Taiwan due to the country's One China policy. Taiwanese investment therefore was made by companies registered in a third country, usually Singapore, to apply for investment license. In 2014, the ban was removed to allow direct trade links and FDI from Taiwan. In 2015, the Ministry of Commerce of Myanmar established a Myanmar Trade Office in Taipei. In 2016, Taipei Economic and Cultural Office (TECO) was established in Yangon.

[35] Some companies organized another group — Taiwan Business Association, outside the ASTCC system.

Table 3: Taiwanese compatriots and Taiwanese companies in Southeast Asia

Country	**Thai**	**VN**	**IR**	**Msia**	**Ph**	**S'por**	**Cam**	**Laos**	**MY**	**BR**
Ethnic Chinese (10,000)	733	101	824	658	143	285	14	15	116	4
Taiwanese Compatriots (1,000)	142	61	209	43	4	31	30	1	0.2	22
Taiwanese companies (1,000)	5	4	2	1.75	0.5	0.4	0.2	0.2	0.2	0.04

Source: OCAC statistics, compiled by author.

associations, it is still difficult to move forward co-operation in areas where the host governments consider politically sensitive and may thus violate the countries' One China policy. As a result, Taishang and Taishang organizations become an important constituency to play trade diplomacy, facilitate two-way communications between Taiwan and the host governments, and promote Taiwan's overall images. This "linkage" or "agency" role is particularly vital when there are no effective communications channels, or when host governments hold a more restrictive stance on One China policy.

Since the overseas Chambers of Commerce in Southeast Asia were established in the 1990s and early 2000s, their major tasks were to network with ethnic Chinese groups and other local business communities and to share business opportunities. Sometimes they also represented specific positions or interests of Taishang and Taishang companies as an interest group (Hsiao *et al*., 2008: 1330–1151).

As such, Taishang and Taishang organizations have played an important role by bridging Taiwan and the host countries as an intermediator through their non-governmental channels and non-official nature. Furthermore, being a significant economic contributor and a major source of capital, technology and management skills, Taishang have developed their own networks where host government officials can trustfully solicit their advice on specific economic policy and business issues. This advisory function of Taishang is especially appreciated when host governments draft economic plans or trade-related legislation or are in need of feedback from private sectors.

When President Tsai launched the New Southbound Policy, she deliberately differentiated her version from previous ones by emphasizing the "soft power" elements in the policy's objectives in order to develop co-operation in education, tourism, and people to people exchanges. Therefore, Taishang and Taishang networks are an important part of the soft power diplomacy. To further take advantage of the Taishang networks, the New Southbound Policy has highlighted the roles of Taishang organizations. Since 2016, the government has held frequent meetings and dialogues with the World Chambers of Commerce, Asia Chambers of Commerce, and Councils of Chambers of Commerce in individual country.

President Tsai and Vice President Chen Chien Jen also gave high profile receptions for representatives of the Chambers of Commerce, and created advisory or honorary positions for Taishang leaders or representatives, for example, the National Policy Advisor to the President, and increased financial support for overseas Taishang activities. The OCAC is also re-structured to establish a specific division to serve Taishang and a separate Overseas Taishang Service Center to support overseas Taishang activities.

In September 2017, the Councils of Taiwan Chambers of Commerce in Vietnam formally submitted a White Paper of Taiwan Chambers of Commerce in Vietnam to Vietnam Chamber of Commerce and Industry (VCCI), representing Vietnamese authorities, to deliver Taiwanese investors' views and policy recommendations to Vietnamese government (Ku and Hsu, 2017). Being the earliest and among the top foreign investors in Vietnam, Taishang's economic contribution to the rise of Vietnamese economy has long been recognized in Vietnam. Taishang's advice may have significant implications on Vietnam's trade and investment policy. Therefore, the submission of the first Taiwan's White Paper not only demonstrated Taiwan's strong economic presence in Vietnam but also led to more institutionalized policy dialogues between Taiwan and Vietnamese authorities.

Following the White Paper submitted in Vietnam, the Councils of Taiwan Chambers of Commerce in Thailand and in the Philippines respectively submitted their first White Paper in May and December 2018 (Yeh, 2018). According to the OCAC, the White Papers submitted by Taishang organizations have successfully increased Taishang's visibility, helped two-way communications and elicited positive response of the host governments to address issues raised in the White Papers. The OCAF in joint efforts with Ministry of Foreign Affair (MOFA) will further facilitate the successful models to continue in other partner countries under the New Southbound policy in order to raise visibility of Taiwan and Taishang.

In addition to government-funded and supported programs and activities, Taishang and Taishang organizations in Southeast Asia find it increasingly important to promote Taishang's collective corporate images, especially when in some countries or districts where some Taishang companies were constantly challenged or questioned by local environmental organizations or labor unions of their corporate governance in these fields. To promote good images, Taishang organizations have promoted corporate governance and corporate social responsibility (CSR) among Taishang companies. They also organize or sponsor charity activities or other public programs to demonstrate they are socially responsible enterprises.

In December 2019, a non-profit organization established under the New Southbound Policy, Taiwan-Asia Exchange Foundation (TAEF), released a Taiwan image survey report in Vietnam entitled "the Image of Taiwan and Taishang Companies in Vietnam". Being the first systematic survey conducted by a Taiwanese entity, the survey investigated how Vietnamese business leaders perceived Taiwan and Taishang image. It found that among Vietnam's top 10 foreign investors, Taiwan ranked in the second place in collective corporate images perceived by Vietnamese business leaders (Taiwan-Asia Exchange Foundation, 2019).[36] However, despite the good image of being a contributor to Vietnamese economy, Taishang in Vietnam were found wanting in several aspects, namely "need to improve treatments to employees", "need to improve environmental friendly measures",[37] "need to provide equal promotion opportunities for employees" and "need to treat employees well" (Tong, 2016).

The survey results reflected some of the general perceptions of Taishang companies in Vietnam and other Southeast Asian countries, good business

[36]The survey investigated 120 Vietnamese business leaders who have business contacts with Taishang. According to the survey, among those top 10 foreign investors in Vietnam, Taiwan ranks behind Japan while have better images than the US (third) and China (ninth).

[37]The perception of Taiwan companies' poor performance in implementing environment-friendly measures resulted from the serious environmental incident caused by a Taiwan-invested steel plant in Tỉnh Hà Tĩnh, Vietnam. The incident led to the riots on May 13, 2014 when hundreds of thousand Vietnamese went to streets to protest against the steel plant. It was the most disastrous incident to Taiwan-Vietnam economic relations in past decades.

partners with important economic contribution to host countries but poor performance in protecting environment and workers' rights. The New Southbound Policy should prioritize the improvement of Taishang images in all partner countries so they can better play the role of "soft power" diplomacy. One possible approach is to have the Taishang organizations to organize and implement a series of activities to improve their images. They should also work with local business communities to jointly promote environment protection and corporate social responsibility.

The Latest Trend — From "Going West" to "Going South"

It is undeniable that all Taiwan's Southern policies, including the current New Southbound Policy, share one common policy objective: to reduce Taiwan's over dependence in Chinese market by re-orienting Taiwanese investment from China to other destinations. While encouraging Taiwanese companies to 'Go South", policy makers also found that since 2010, Taiwanese investment in China has demonstrated two different trends — the growth rate in China continued to decline while more Taiwanese companies, including Taishang operating in China, showed increasing interests in Southeast Asia.

Why Taiwanese companies chose to "Go West" or to "Go South"? The decisions were affected by two factors: the "push" effects of the deteriorating Chinese investment environment and the "pull" effect of the economic growth and accelerating integration in the Southeast Asia.

China — The fading world factory?

According to recent annual survey of the "Perceptions of Chinese Investment Environments and Investment Risks" conducted by Taiwan Electrical and Electronic Manufacturers' Association (TEEMA) for its company members' views on Chinese investment environment and their willingness to expand investment in China,[38] a growing proportion of the

[38] Founded in 1948, TEEMA currently has more than 3,000 company members and is among the eight largest national industrial trade groups in Taiwan. TEEMA has carried out the survey on "Perceptions of Chinese Investment Environments and Investment Risks" since 2011 to collect responses from its member companies operating in China.

responding Taiwanese electronics producers operating in China felt pessimistic about Chinese economic outlook and decreasing business profits in China. The survey in 2018, compared with TEEMA's previous surveys, revealed a continued sentiment since 2011: Chinese investment environment was deteriorating which made Taishang either suspend their expansion plans in China or consider to move to other markets or return to Taiwan (CNA, 2018).

The same survey by TEEMA in 2011 found that about 50.95% of the respondents considered an expansion plan in China. In 2017, the proportion went down to 32.46%, further down to 29.08% in 2018, showing a downward trend for 8 consecutive years. These survey results delivered the same signals as did the outbound investment statistics in the past years. According to Investment Commission, MOEA, Taiwan, between 1990 and 2019, the amount of Taiwanese investment outflows to China reached a peak in 2010, registered at US$14.62 billion. However, the amounts continued to decline in the following years. In 2019, total amount of investment outflows to China declined to US$4.17 billion, the lowest since 2002.

On the other hand, before 2001 when China was admitted to the WTO, Taiwanese companies had more diversified investment plans in international markets. While after 2002, China had been the major destination and absorbed most of Taiwan's capital outflows. The trend has continued for 14 years until in 2016 investment amounts (US$12.12 billion) in the world (excluding China) surpassed the amounts of investment (US$9.67 billion) in China. The gap between capital flows in the world (excluding China) and in China became even wider after the US–China trade conflicts in 2018, meaning Taiwanese outbound investment are more diversified outside China than ever and that investment amounts in China, dropping to its lowest point since 2002, may very likely continue its low levels (see Figure 1, Table 4).

In 1990, the output of China's manufacturing industry accounted for only 3% of the world's total manufacturing capacity. In 2019, it accounts for more than half of the global market. In 1990, China's exports accounted for only 2% of the world's exports, while in 2019 the share increased to around 15%, a six-fold growth. When Taishang, and many other multinational corporations, are leaving China or downsized their export-oriented manufacturing operations in the country, China's role as the "World Factory" will be severely undermined. The continuous relocation and re-configuration of the China-centered supply chains also change the economic landscape of Southeast Asia.

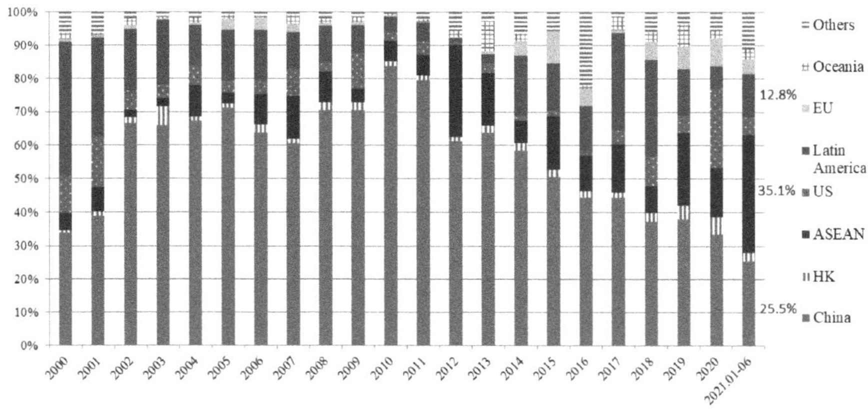

Figure 1: Taiwanese Outbound FDI to China and the World (excluding China) (2000–2021)

Source: Investment Commission, MOEA, Taiwan, compiled by author.

Table 4: Taiwan FDI in the world and in China (1980–2020)

(Unit: US$1,000)

Year	World (excl. China)	China	Year	World (excl. China)	China
1980	42,105	—	2001	4,391,654	2,784,147
1981	10,764	—	2002	3,370,046	6,723,058
1982	11,632	—	2003	3,968,588	7,698,784
1983	10,563	—	2004	3,382,022	6,940,663
1984	39,263	—	2005	2,447,449	6,006,953
1985	41,334	—	2006	4,315,426	7,642,335
1986	56,911	—	2007	6,469,978	9,970,545
1987	102,751	—	2008	4,466,491	10,691,390
1988	218,736	—	2009	3,005,554	7,142,593
1989	930,986	—	2010	2,823,451	14,617,872
1990	1,552,206	—	2011	3,696,827	14,376,624
1991	1,656,231	174,158	2012	8,098,641	12,792,077
1992	887,259	246,992	2013	5,232,266	9,190,090
1993	1,661,046	3,168,411	2014	7,293,683	10,276,570
1994	1,616,844	962,209	2015	10,745,195	10,965,485

(*Continued*)

Table 4: (*Continued*)

Year	World (excl. China)	China	Year	World (excl. China)	China
1995	1,356,878	1,092,713	2016	12,123,094	9,670,732
1996	2,165,404	1,229,241	2017	11,573,208	9,248,862
1997	2,893,826	4,334,313	2018	14,294,562	8,497,730
1998	3,296,302	2,034,621	2019	6,851,155	4,173,090
1999	3,269,013	1,252,780	2020	11,805,105	5,906,489
2000	5,077,062	2,607,142			

Source: Investment Commission, MOEA, Taiwan.

Taishang's Choice — Participation in the regional economic integration

Since mid-2010s, economic integration in Southeast Asia has accelerated its once very slow pace. In December 2015, ASEAN Leaders announced the establishment of the ASEAN Economic Community (AEC). To further the ASEAN-centric integration, since 2012 Southeast Asian leaders have started trade negotiations to develop the Regional Comprehensive Economic Partnership (RCEP), the world's largest free trade area if successfully accomplished among the 10 ASEAN Member States and its 6 FTA partner countries — China, Japan, South Korea, Australia, New Zealand and India. The RCEP is also the most populous Free Trade Area in the world, covering a population of 3.5 billion.

However, in November 2019, India announced its decision to withdraw from current negotiations due to rising domestic criticism that India will not benefit from the trade agreement. Amid the pessimistic atmosphere of economic outlook in the region, the rest 15 RCEP members expressed their strong political will to conclude trade negotiations and sign the mega FTA as "RCEP will provide a more stable and predictable economic environment to support the much-needed recovery of trade and investment in the region, which has been adversely affected by the COVID-19 pandemic" (ASEAN, 2020). The RCEP will also help the Southeast Asian countries to counter impacts brought by increasing trade protectionism and reap benefits from the US–China trade conflicts. On December 15, 2020, 15 members successfully signed the agreement, which later came into force on January 1, 2022.

Besides the RCEP, the Comprehensive Progressive Trans Pacific Partnership (CPTPP) has entered into force in December 2018. Currently 8 of its 11 signatories have ratified the agreement and implemented tariff reductions toward other members. The AEC, RCEP and CPTPP provide Southeast Asian countries with considerable preferential market access to major markets. The preferential tariffs, cheap labor cost (compared with China), and current status as "Safe Haven" from US–China trade conflicts all make Taiwanese companies believe Southeast Asia a better destination for export-oriented manufacturing operations in the future (Pesek, 2019).

Among the Southeast Asian countries, Vietnam is particularly "attractive" to Taiwan's export-oriented manufacturers because of its RCEP and CPTPP membership and bilateral FTAs with major economies, including Japan and the European Union.[39] Total amount of Taiwanese investment in Vietnam already reached US$32 billion, making up around 35% of Taiwanese investment in the Southeast Asia. Taiwan's first investment projects in Vietnam in the early 1990s were apparently encouraged by President Lee's Southern policy. However, Taiwanese capital flows into the country after early 2000s were mainly driven by market force and Taishang's business decisions. For example, the first investment boom took place when Vietnam completed its accession negotiations to the WTO and became a member in January 2007. The second investment boom was targeting Vietnam's TPP membership. The recent third boom was registered in 2019 when Taiwanese companies in China relocated their manufacturing capacities to Vietnam or expand their existing production lines there.[40]

According to a study of the Chung Hua Institution of Economic Research (CIER), Taiwan, the reasons Vietnam became the most popular destination in Southeast Asia are its abundant labor force and comparatively low labor cost, stable political environment and policy consistency, and most of all, its foundations of industrial clusters making supply chains possible and FTA networks. The study explains the priority considerations when Taishang make business decisions to invest in Vietnam. It is

[39]The Agreement between Japan and the Socialist Republic of *Vietnam* for an Economic Partnership entered into force in October 2009. The Vietnam–EU FTA was signed in 2019, will enter into force in 2020.

[40]A lot of these investments were not made from Taiwan directly, so they were not included in the Taiwan FDI released by Vietnamese government.

expected that Taiwanese investment in Vietnam will continue its growth trend.

Besides heavy investment in Vietnam, some Taiwanese companies have explored business opportunities in other less developed countries, mainly Cambodia and Myanmar. Taiwanese investments in Cambodia, Laos and Myanmar (the CLM countries) are mainly in manufacturing industry, ranging from textile and garment, footwear, food processing, bicycles to electronics and automobile parts (*CNAIC*, 2016). Since 2019, the US–China trade conflicts have also provided unexpected opportunities to these countries, but quite different from Vietnam, Taishang in these countries find it challenging in terms of having more stable and coherent policy environment and quality labor force.

The global COVID-19 pandemic — More opportunities and challenges for Taishang in Southeast Asia

The US–China trade conflicts triggered by former US President Donald Trump's America First policy which imposed 301 tariffs on Chinese imports after a series of 301 investigation against China since mid-2017 have, unexpectedly, aroused rapidly growing interests of Taiwanese business communities in the Southeast Asia. According to media reports in Taiwan, since mid-2018, Taishang in different provinces in China have visited Thailand, Malaysia, Indonesia, Vietnam, Philippines, Cambodia and Myanmar in search of lands in industrial zones in order to build or transfer their production lines from China.

Most Taishang operating in China believe that, though the US–China trade conflicts may temporarily ease after two sides reached an agreement,[41] the long-term prospects of the US–China bilateral relations are still bleak (USTR, 2020). To diversify risks of over dependence on Chinese supply chains, Taishang review their global business strategies in order to make responsive decisions to relocate to and expand operations in countries outside China but still adjacent to the Greater China supply chains. All these considerations lead to increasing investment in Southeast Asia.

---

[41] US and China signed the Economic and Trade Agreement Between the Government of the United States and the Government of the People's Republic of China, or referred to as the First Phase Trade Agreement, on January 15, 2020.

Further to the US–China trade conflicts, the COVID-19 pandemic spreading across the globe further arouse attention on the issues of supply chains management and resilience. To stop virus spreading, supply chains are disrupted with factories shut down in China and lockdowns in other countries. In the aftermath of the pandemic, it is widely expected that Taiwanese companies will follow their earlier decisions to diversify away from China.

As the movement toward diversification will continue in the future, it is notable that in the past decades, Taishang in East Asia have evolved into two different systems — the China-based and Southeast Asia-based Taishang, which have cultivated different business culture, networks and relations with local governments and communities. Take Vietnam for example, in 2019 when an increasing number of China-based Taishang moved in, these new comers have acquired lands and facilities as well as brought different business culture and behaviors, which may impact Taishang operating in Vietnam.[42] Whether these Taishang will collaborate or compete in the same markets will remain to be observed.

Conclusions — The Prospects and Challenges in a New International Order

Taiwan has been investing in Southeast Asia since the 1980s, building manufacturing operations and business networks which led to closer economic and trade ties between Taiwan and the host countries. Taishang and Taishang organizations, as the key players and center of the bilateral economic relations, underwent business expansion and evolution of structures and functions. The Southern policies adopted by Taiwanese governments since the 1990s have successfully encouraged Taiwanese companies to "Look South" and "Go South". Though a lot of Taishang operating in Southeast Asia relocated to China in the early 2000s, the deteriorating Chinese business climate and the US–China trade conflicts and the COVID-19 pandemic have further changed, unexpectedly, the trends from "Go West" to "Go South". It is widely believed that more Taiwanese companies, including Taishang operating in China, will review their China-based supply chains and adjust their business decisions to expand their

[42] For example, it was reported that since end of 2018, rapidly increasing investment in Vietnam has pushed up land prices and wages to hit new height.

operations in Southeast Asia after the COVID-19 pandemic in the region is better controlled.

Taishang in Southeast Asia have important "linkage" functions between Taiwan and Southeast Asian countries and thus play an important role in connecting Taiwan and the host governments and society. Under the current New Southbound Policy, Taishang organizations, namely Taiwanese Chambers of Commerce in various Southeast Asian countries, are institutionalized and strengthened in their functions and resources in order to play more important roles of trade diplomacy and demonstrating Taiwan's "soft power".

On the other hand, Taishang in Southeast Asia face increasingly complicated challenges to their business prospects and daily operation. These include more competition in the Southeast Asian markets. Taiwan used to be the top or among the top three foreign investors in most of the Southeast Asian countries. Taiwan's ranking fell in the past years as more countries also adopted various policies to encourage their business to "Go South". Taishang also need to face issues related to upgrading collective Taishang images in the host society, as was reflected by TAEF's survey of Taiwan and Taishang Images in Vietnam. Last but not least, as the US–China trade conflicts and COVID-19 pandemic have raised the issue of supply chains diversification and resilience, Taishang in China as well as in Southeast Asia will need to investigate their operations with better risk management and diversification plans.

References

ASEAN (2020). Joint Statement of the 29th Regional Comprehensive Economic Partnership.

Chen, S.-H., Pei-Chang, W. and Meng-Chun, L. (2017). Late Development Through and Beyond Deep Integration: The Evolution of Taiwan's Economic Links with Southeast Asia. *Journal of Southeast Asian Economies*, 34(2): 367–387.

Chou, Y.-L. and Pin-Yu, W. (2006). President Chen visited Batam of Indonesia (in Chinese), *The Liberty Times,* May 12, 2006, https://news.ltn.com.tw/news/focus/paper/71286.

CNA (2018). TEEMA Survey: Taishang's Investment Interests in China Declined. *Central News Agency (CNA)*, August 31, 2018, https://www.storm.mg/article/484464.

CNAIC (2016). *Exploring Business Opportunities in Cambodia and Laos (in Chinese)*. Taipei, The Chinese National Association of Industry and Commerce (CNAIC).

Eleanor, A. (2019). The Evolution of U.S.–Vietnam Ties. Council on Foreign Affairs, US, cfr.org.

Executive Yuan, Taiwan (2016). New Southbound Policy, ey.gov.tw.

Hsiao, H. H. M., Kung, I. C. and Wang, H. Z. (2008). Taishang: A Different Kind of Ethnic Chinese Business in Southeast Asia. In K.-B. Chan, T.-S. Cheung and A. S. Ku (eds.), *Chinese Capitalisms: Historical Emergence and Political Implications* (pp. 133–151). London, Palgrave Macmillan.

Hsu, K. T. T. (2017). A Review of Taiwan's Old and New Go South Policy: An Economic Perspective. *Prospect Journal*, 18: 63–87, https://www.pf.org.tw/files/5976/20F5B418-F25E-469F-B347-F564B17D433B.

Hsu, K. T. T. (2020). Taiwan's Participation in the World Trade Organization — Strategy, Interests and Prospects. In Rabea Brauer and Cristita Marie Perez (eds.), *The Multilateral Trade System under Stress: Charting Asia's Path Forward* (pp. 73–105). Tokyo, Konrad-Adenauer-Stiftung Japan.

Investment Commission, MOEA, Taiwan (2021). FDI statistics of Southeast Asian Countries, https://www.moeaic.gov.tw/english/.

Ku, Y. H. and Hsu, K. (2017). The White Book for Business and Investment in Vietnam (in Chinese and Vietnamese). Hanoi, Taiwan Chamber of Commerce Vietnam.

Ma, Y.-J. (2008). Inaugural Address. May 20, 2008, https://china.usc.edu/ma-ying-jeou-%E2%80%9Cinaugural-address%E2%80%9D-may-20-2008.

OCAC, Taiwan (2018). Annual Statistics Book, https://english.ocac.gov.tw/OCAC/Eng/Pages/VDetail.aspx?nodeid=323&pid=13712942.

Office of the President, Republic of China (Taiwan) (2002). Vice President Returned from Indonesia Visit (in Chinese), Office of the President, Republic of China (Taiwan), August 17, 2002, https://www.president.gov.tw/NEWS/1160.

Pesek, W. (2019). Is Southeast Asia's Safe-Haven Halo for Real? *Asia Times*, June 16, 2019, https://asiatimes.com/2019/06/is-southeast-asias-safe-haven-halo-for-real/.

Schubert, G., Rui-hua, L. and Yu-Chen Tseng, J. (2016). Taishang Studies — A Rising or Declining Research Field? *China Perspectives*, 1: 29–36, http://journals.openedition.org/chinaperspectives/6900.

Schubert, G., Rui-hua, L. and Yu-Chen Tseng, J. (2017). Are Taiwanese Entrepreneurs a Strategic Group? Reassessing Taishang Political Agency across the Taiwan Strait. *Asian Survey*, 57(5): 856–884.

Taiwan-Asia Exchange Foundation (2019). *The Image of Taiwan and Taiwanese Businesses in Vietnam*. Taipei, Taiwan-Asia Exchange Foundation, https://www.taef.org/doc/296.

Thornton, M. (2017). Taiwan's International Space: Walking Toward China or Toward the World, https://sentinel.tw/taiwan-intl-space-china-world/.

Trade Negotiating Committee (RCEP TNC) Meeting (video conference), April 24, 2020, https://asean.org/storage/2017/11/RCEP-TNC-29-Joint-Statement_Final_ForUploading.pdf.

Tong, L. (2016). Vietnam Fish Deaths Cast Suspicion on Formosa Steel Plant. *The Diplomat*, April 30, 2016.

USTR (2020). The Economic and Trade Agreement between the Government of the United States and the Government of the People's Republic of China. January 15, 2020, https://ustr.gov/about-us/policy-offices/press-office/press-releases/2020/january/economic-and-trade-agreement-between-government-united-states-and-government-peoples-republic-china.

Vuong, Q. H. (2014). Vietnam's Political Economy in Transition (1986–2016), https://worldview.stratfor.com/article/vietnams-political-economy-transition-1986–2016.

White, L. (1999). Globalization and Taiwan. *Asian Perspective*, 23(4): 97–141.

Yeh, C.-C. (2018). *The White Book for Business and Investment in the Philippines (in Chinese)*. Manila, Taiwan Chamber of Commerce Philippines.

https://doi.org/10.1142/9789811250668_0009

Chapter 9

Marrying out of Indonesia and Global Householding: Chinese Indonesian Women from West Kalimantan across Taiwan and Transnational Chinese Community

Sachiko Yokota

University of Shiga Prefecture, Japan

Introduction

Singkawang, West Kalimantan, Indonesia is known for its high concentration of Chinese residents and is referred to as the "City of Beautiful Women" (Kota Amoy). The phrase acknowledges the prominent role that the city has come to fill for foreigners seeking a bride. Since the late 1970s, Singkawang has sent a huge number of Chinese brides to Taiwan, Hong Kong, and Malaysia. The migration phenomena initially emerged in response to exclusionary policies against Chinese living in Indonesia, especially to the 1967 Dayak Raids, through which about 70,000 Chinese became refugees. In addition to these political factors, "the division of reproductive labor", which has gained strength since the 1970s throughout Asia, also has driven Indonesian Chinese women to marry out. In this chapter, I discuss the forces driving marriage migration and the practices of "global householding" and moral economy in the Singkawang context. My research was conducted in a former refugee camp. Through elaborating three particular cases in detail, I suggest the following four features to the phenomenon of marriage migration. First, female marriage migrants come from lower socioeconomic classes. When they lose financial supporters, such as husband or father, the women choose to marry abroad in order to secure financial support. Second, a single family sends several members as brides or workers abroad. Third, sisters tend to marry out in order of seniority. Fourth, sisters who marry abroad assume the central role in maintaining the welfare of their families of orientation over a long period of time.

This chapter examines a historical change of marriage migration of West Kalimantan Chinese Indonesians and their moral economy in marriage migration. This chapter also focuses on marriage migrants, their families, and local Chinese Indonesian society.

Indonesia has been sending migrant workers and marriage migrants abroad since the end of the 1970s (Hugo, 2005: 56–67). Migration phenomena from Indonesia also progress along with "global division of reproductive labor" in East Asia. "Global division of reproductive labor" means reproductive labor concerning "reproduction of human being", "reproductive economy/sex service/fostering children/care for older person/ reproduction of human resources", and maintaining social system is being divided between advanced countries and the Third world. Then, those who are engaged in reproductive labor with the stream of the global division of reproductive labor are defined as "reproductive worker".

Due to globalization, changing lifestyle, and changing employment structure, advanced countries accordingly suffer from lack of reproductive labor. Especially in global cities,[1] along with the growing demand for high-salary specialists, the demand for low-salary, low-skilled labor who support high-salary specialists also has grown. Women who had not joined the labor market have been newly incorporated into the latter sector as well as foreign workers.

Since reproductive labor in most societies traditionally belongs to women's line of work, women foreign workers are favored. And this favor has caused the "feminized migration" phenomenon (Truong, 1996: 33).

---

[1]Global cities refer to cities that are centers of innovation and businesses, such as New York, London, Shanghai, Tokyo, Dubai, Singapore, Hong Kong, Dubai, Paris, and Beijing.

"Reproductive workers" who are engaged in domestic work from the third world can be divided into family members as a marriage migrant, and a non-relative member of a household as a caregiver or maid in advanced countries. Both "reproductive workers" contribute to maintaining family welfare, offering domestic work. Here I define "welfare" as "happy life" and "public-help, co-help, self-help to maintain happy life".

On the other hand, reproductive workers economically support their families of orientation so that they can live healthy. Thus, reproductive workers contribute to enriching both families' welfare. In this way, Michael Douglas calls the practice to enrich welfare of family/household globally as "global householding" (Douglas, 2006, 2010).

Women of reproductive labor contribute to supporting their family of orientation, local society, and their mother country economically. Aihwa Ong calls their contribution and sacrifice as "moral economy". This anthropological term means that the subsistence ethic is rooted in the economic practices and social exchanges, and also forms the standards to maximize peasants' utility (Scott, 1976). Quoting the term moral economy, Ong describes migrant workers' moral economy as "the emerging cross-race, cross-ethnic economy of female migrant workers intersects with multiple moral economies rooted in kinship, religious ethos, and ethnic communities" (Ong, 2006: 199). In their families, communities, and even homeland where people can't sustain a level of development without remittances from abroad, moral economies are the fundamental stimulus for the outflows of the young women as migrant workers in Southeast Asia (*ibid.*).

Indonesia continues to send reproductive laborers to the world, including marriage emigrants from Indonesia. The marriage emigrants whom I discuss in this paper are from West Kalimantan. Among the studies about them, Mary Somers Heidhues's work and Hsia Hsiao-chuan's work are remarkable. Somers Heidhues pointed that the Dayak Raids in 1967 became the background of marriage migration rush and described poor women's situation (Somers Heidhues, 2003). Hsia analyzed the motivation of marriage migrants from West Kalimantan to Taiwan in her book. She also criticized that Taiwanese society stigmatized cross-border marriage severely (Hsia, 2002). Though these works offer valuable information, they lack the description about migration experience and their families and have not caught up with the changes of cross-border marriage as times change.

In Indonesia, marriage migration boom in West Kalimantan has been reported as momentous, unmoral, social problem again and again (cf. Anonymous, 1995: 51–65; Bektiati and Kleden, 2001: 67–80). These reports analyzed that the background of cross-cultural boom is poverty and criticized match-making system as inhumane. Cross-border marriage boom is often described as vulgar, gossip, and less regarded as an academic issue.

This chapter examines the change of marriage migration since the late 1970s in West Kalimantan, their practices of "global householding", and their family's strategy to make up the deficit of previous research.

My report is based on data that I got through fieldwork at Singkawang City on August 2011, from January to February 2012, September 2012, March and September 2013, March 2017, and August 2018. During the interviews, I spoke Mandarin Chinese and Indonesian. Also, my assistant translated Hakka into Mandarin for me.

Cross-border Marriage in Singkawang, West Kalimantan

Singkawang is the second largest city in West Kalimantan Province, and her population amounted to 190,801 people; male 98,117, female 92,684 in 2011 (Pemerintah Kota Singkawang, 2011: 28).

The population of Singkawang consists of Chinese, Malay, and Dayak. According to 2006 statistics, Chinese account for about 40.26%, Malay 35.61%, and Dayaks 7.16% (La Ode, 2012: 18). Singkawang is a Chinese-dominant city. Dawis described her as follows.

> Chinese Indonesians in Medan, Singkawang, and Pontianak tend to practice Chinese traditions and customs to a greater degree than those from Manado. They also prefer to associate with fellow Chinese and frown upon intermarriage with the indigenous population. (Dawis, 2009: 28, 83)

As a backing of these descriptions, Singkawang also goes by the name of "Kota Seribu Kelenteng", city with thousands of Chinese temples. As this nickname describes, huge numbers of Chinese temples are interspersed throughout the city, and Taoism and Buddhism are very popular. Yearly events and ceremonial occasions among Chinese Indonesians are quite similar with the customs of South China and Taiwan.

The ancestors of Singkawang Chinese came from *Hepo, Hai-feng, Lu-feng, Feng-shun, Hui-lai*, of Guangdong Province in the 19th century to West Kalimantan to work at gold mines (Somers Heidhues, 2003: 36). Both Hakka (*Hoppo*) dialect and Indonesian are mainly spoken, and Mandarin is partly spoken. Mandarin speakers are either over 60 years old elders who had studied at Chinese schools at the beginning of 1960s or teenagers and people in their 20s who are studying at restored Chinese schools after the 2000s.[2] Among other ethnic groups, Indonesian, Malay dialects, and Dayaks are also spoken.

The economic system of Singkawang is agricultural based. The main crops are corn, cassava, and sweet potato. Rubber, coconut, and oil palm are also main cash crops in plantation (Badan Pusat Statistik Kota Singkawang, 2010: 145–146). Rice for self-consumption is not enough, so rice is imported from Java. There are no big industries in Singkawang (Figure 1).

Attributes of marriage migrant

Besides the nickname about religion, Singkawang also goes by the name "Kota Amoy": city of beauty. But now the nickname has been changed

Figure 1: Singkawang, West Kalimantan

[2] Since the New Order, all phenomena about communism had been prohibited including the use of Chinese characters and Chinese education. But in the 21st century, the restriction to maintain Chinese culture have been lifted, so that Chinese language education are revived.

Table 1: Number of new cross-border marriage spouses by country of origin, registered in Singkawang since 2005 until August 25, 2011

		County of origin of foreign spouses			
Year	**Bridegroom/bride**	**Taiwan**	**Malaysia**	**Others**	**Total**
2005	Bridegroom	4	—	—	4
	Bride	—	—	—	—
2006	Bridegroom	9	2	1	12
	Bride	—	—	—	—
2007	Bridegroom	47	—	—	47
	Bride	1	—	—	1
2008	Bridegroom	47	—	3	50
	Bride	—	—	—	—
2009	Bridegroom	76	—	1	77
	Bride	—	—	—	—
2010	Bridegroom	70	4	—	74
	Bride	1	—	—	1
August 25, 2011	Bridegroom	80	2	—	82
	Bride	—	—	—	—
Total		335	8	5	348

into "homeland of foreign brides" or "city sending brides abroad", somewhat dishonorable ones. How many people ever did get married with foreigners and emigrate from Singkawang?

Table 1 shows the numbers of cross-border marriage since 2005 until August 25, 2011 by country of origin.[3] It shows that most of the foreign spouses are women, and Taiwanese are the dominant foreign male spouses.

On the other hand, based on the statistics of the Taiwanese government on January 1, 2014, the number of spouses who live in Taiwan with Indonesian origin was estimated at 27,974; with 27,474 women, accounting for 98.21%.[4] This number shows Indonesia–Taiwan cross-border

[3]This table is based on the data collected at the Catatan Sipil Singkawang on August 26, 2011.

[4]Cf. National Immigration Agency of Republic of China (2014)〈各縣市外裔、外籍配偶人數 按性別及原屬國籍分76年1月~103年1月分〉(http://www.immigration.gov.tw/).

marriages are mainly composed of "Indonesian wife and Taiwanese husband" couples. But since this statistic does not work out numbers by origin of province in Indonesia, I cannot show the quantities by origin of province. Therefore, I am still continuing my investigation on how many spouses migrated from Singkawang.

I did research on marriage migration toward Taiwan mainly, but in my research, I found a lot of cases, which also sent family member to Hong Kong and Malaysia, so I added this information to Table 2. All of families whom I interviewed sent marriage migrants and migrant workers to foreign countries and other domestic areas.

The time period of Table 1 is quite limited, so it does not show long-term tendency. Though it shows that cross-border marriage cases were fewer between 2005 and 2006, it suddenly increased since 2007. Especially in 2011, the number reached 80 cases by August 25. I am researching now what factors influenced the number of cases. Then, by nationalities of foreign spouses, Taiwanese are the biggest group, followed by Malaysians.

Figure 2 shows the age distribution of cross-border marriage couples married in 2010.[5] Though the age of Taiwanese men varies greatly from 20s to 50, the age of Chinese Indonesian women is mainly from the later teen years to the early 20s. The average age when they get married is 35.8 years old for Taiwanese men, and 23.1 years old for Chinese Indonesian. According to an Indonesian broker, ethnicity of marriage migrant is only Chinese.

Taiwan is the main destination

In Taiwan, as the main destination for Chinese Indonesian marriage migrants, cross-border marriage phenomenon has begun at the end of the 1970s, and the earliest marriage immigrants were from West Kalimantan, Indonesia.[6] This trend has exploded from 1990s to the early of 2000s. The origin of marriage immigrants became diversified: not only from Indonesia but also from Mainland China, Thailand, Philippines, Vietnam, and Cambodia.

---

[5]This figure is based on the data collected at the Catatan Sipil Singkawang on August 26, 2011.

[6]About how the cross-border marriage started, see Hsia (2002) and Yokota (2017).

Table 2: Sending migrant of *RT* A

No	Name	Age	Family type	No. of cohabitant	No. of children	Sex and children's position on seniority	Year of migration	Age	Current place of residence	Type of migration	Academic background	Occupation	Husband's occupation
1	LNC	79		2	7	F/1st	1977	58	Guishan, Taoyuan	Brokered	2	Housewife	Abandoned by 1st husband→ Veteran
						F/2nd	1982	52	Miaoli	Introduced by sister	none	Housewife	Carpenter
						F/3rd D	1983	48		Brokered and introduced by sister	2	Running store	From farmer to Veteran
2	TSF	50	N	3	10	Sister	1982	48	Taiwan	Brokered	none	unknown	Unknown
3	YCH	66	N	2	8	F/1st D	1994	41	Jia-yi	Brokered	6	Casual employment	Iron worker
						F/2nd D	2012	43	Jakarta			Cloth print	
						F/3rd D	2012	30	Jakarta		6	Cloth print	
						M/5th SF	2012	24	Jakarta			Cloth print	
4	PCK	62	S	5	8	F/1st D	1997		Zhu-bei Hsin-chu	Brokered	9	Casual employment	Carpenter
						F/2nd D	2005		Da-du, Tai-chung	Brokered	9	Factory worker	Factory worker
						F/3rd D	2012		Malaysia		9	Waitress	

						M/1st S	2012		Zhu-bei Hsin-chu		9	Factory worker	
						M/2nd S	2012		Pontianak		9	Cock	
5	LHQ	36	S	8	6	F/1st D	1997	36	Sha-lu, Tai-chung	Brokered	9	Waitress	Factory worker
6	HXL	36	S	5	6	F/1st D		39	Hong Kong	Introduced by relative	?	Housewife	Office worker
						F/2nd D	1994	37	Taiwan	Migrant worker	13	Housewife	Office worker
						F/3rd D	1994	36	Ping-zhen, Taoyuan	Migrant worker	13	Housewife	Office worker
						F/4th D	2007	23	Taipei	Study	Bachelor	Student	Office worker
						1st S	2012	41	Jakarta		?		
7	HSK	59	N	2	5	1st D	2000	34	Malaysia	Brokered	6	Housewife	Factory worker
						F/2nd D	1999	30	Taiwan	Brokered	2	Housewife	Factory worker
						M/1st S	2012	32	Kuching, Malaysia		2	Factory worker	
8	CRK	57	S	5	6	D/1st D	2003	30	Johor, Malaysia	Brokered	9	Housewife	Factory worker
9	XYM	59	S	3	5	F/1st D	2009	35	Taiwan	Brokered	13	Housewife	?
						M/1st S	2012	35	Taiwan		14	Factory worker	
						M/3rd S	2012	26	Taoyuan City		9	Factory worker	
10	ZHT	50	N	5	4	F/2nd D of BSS	2010	18	Hua-lien	Brokered	4	Waitress	Factory worker
						F/1st D	2012	22	Miri, Malaysia		9	Waitress	
11	ZMM	18	S	7	6	M/2nd S	2012	25	Taipei		?	Factory worker	

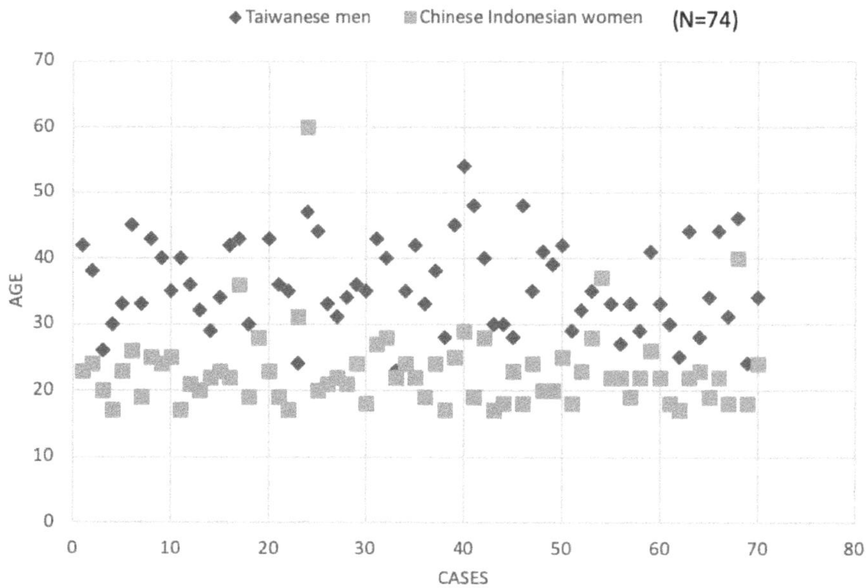

Figure 2: Age when married in 2010

In the late 1980s, Taiwanese society suffered from the shortage of labor. Taiwanese government took a measure to put foreign workers into the productive industry suffering from shortage of labor. Since the 1980s until 1990s, the demand for young local female labor rose dramatically because their academic background was getting advanced. At that time, Taiwanese business community worried that Taiwanese women would stop their career due to marriage, childbirth, child raising, and care (Asato, 2005: 7–9). They pushed Taiwanese government to import more foreign workers as reproductive labor, so that Taiwanese women could continue to work as paid workers.

In May 2020, the population of foreign worker in Taiwan was 707,308 people: male 319,829, female 387,479. Among them, 274,269 were Indonesian workers: male 67,714, female 206,555. Indonesian female worker account for about 30% of all foreign workers, and about 53% of all female foreign workers.[7] Since 2005 until May 2020, the

[7]The Minister of Labor "Table 12-6 Foreign workers in Productive Industries and Social Welfare by Nationality and Sex in May 2020" (労動部 「表12-6産業及社福移工人数—按國籍及性別分 109年5月底」).

population of foreign workers has doubled in 15 years. As mentioned earlier, marriage migration phenomenon in Taiwan reached its peak before 2004. After that, Taiwanese government controlled the expansion of marriage migration by illegalizing profit-making brokers. Due to this control, the number of cross-border marriage has hovered around 15% of total foreign immigrants every year.

Since 1987 until May 2020, the total population of Indonesian spouses is estimated at 30,614: 740 male spouses and 29,874 female spouses. However, this number may not include all Indonesian spouses because the statistics started after the advent of marriage migration phenomenon. In addition to the start of the statistics, based on my life history research, early marriage immigrants with Chinese ethnicity were covered by special laws for Overseas Chinese. There is a possibility that early marriage immigrants were not counted as foreign spouses.

How has the Taiwanese government responded toward this cross-border marriage phenomenon? Since 1980s until 1998, Taiwanese government did not take any special policy toward marriage immigrants except on immigration control, family register, and medical care. First support to marriage migrants came out of a civil volunteer group. Taiwanese sociologist Hsia Hsiao-chuan and her friends organized a Chinese learning class for marriage migrants in Mei-nong town, Kaohsiung in 1992, which also offered support for them to integrate into the Taiwanese society. NGO/NPOs and scholars appealed to Taiwanese government to acknowledge a necessity of support by showing the result of the Chinese learning class, and Taiwanese government finally started a supporting project in 1998.

The project named "Guidance Project for Foreign Spouses" (外籍新娘生活輔導実施計画)[8] continued from 1998 until 2006. The "Funds for Foreign Spouses" (外籍配偶輔導基金) was budgeted since in 2005. A total of 3 billion NT dollars were collected to set up a support system to guide marriage immigrants in the following 10 years. This fund covered marriage immigrants as well as their children, offering medical service, education for marriage immigrants, childcare service, community-based support service, and so on. The central government entrusted local governments and NGOs/NPOs to provide the services.

[8]The project was renamed the "Developmental Funds for Immigrants" in 2015, which covers not only marriage immigrants but their children. IFI Network+ (新住民培力發展資訊網) http://ifi.immigration.gov.tw/ (Accessed on December 18, 2017).

From 2006 to 2011, Taiwanese government institutionalized services for immigrants, and also extended the target from immigrants to immigrants and their children. The following project "Lighting Project for New Immigrants" (新住民火炬計畫) promoted multicultural education from 2012 to 2014. This project entrusted elementary schools to teach foreign spouses' mother tongues, to organize multicultural festivals, and so on. Elementary schools with a certain number or a certain percentage of students with marriage immigrant parent could apply for financial support from the central government.

After the "Lighting Project", "New Residents Empowerment Policy" started in 2015, which targeted children with immigrant parents. The new policy encourages these children to develop their multicultural background.

Marriage migrants and children under the "New South-Bound Policy"

As mentioned previously, the priority of integration program shifted from marriage immigrants themselves to their children. Furthermore, various support programs also started as part of the "New South-bound Policy" since around 2015–2016.

In 2015, "The Funds for Foreign Spouses" (外籍配偶輔導基金) was replaced by the "New Immigrants Development Fund" (新住民発展基金). It allocated a budget of 10 billion NT dollars to promote various projects.[9]

Since 2016, "New Immigrants and Children's Dream Program" (新住民及其子女築夢計畫) has awarded new immigrants and children grants to fulfill their wishes related to their Southeast Asian roots. They are expected to deepen Taiwanese citizens' understanding of Southeast Asian countries.[10]

---

[9]The projects include "New Immigrant Social Security Network Service Project" (新住民社會安全網絡服務計畫), "New Immigrant Family Education and Multiculturalism Promoting Program" (新住民家庭學習成長及子女托育、多元文化推廣及相關宣導計畫), "Family Service Center Program" (家庭服務中心計畫, and "New Immigrant Innovation Service, Manpower Empowerment and Activating Communal Industry Program" (新住民創新服務、人才培力及活化產業社區計畫).

[10]Similar projects such as "New Immigrant New Star Training Camp" (新住民新星培育営) have started since 2014. "New Immigrant Second Generation Training Project" (新住

The real aim of these "empowerment" projects is to develop talents with Southeast Asian roots, who "can improve Taiwan's international competitiveness and serve as a pioneer in a new market for Taiwan (See "New Immigrants New Star Cultivation Camp" (新住民新星培育営) prospects). Although the empowerment projects under "New South-Bound Policy" will take a positive attitude to children with marriage immigrants, there is also fear that Taiwanese government will sort children into valuable/invaluable citizens.

Research Data

I mainly interviewed inhabitants in *RT* A (A neighborhood unit),[11] *Kelurahan* S (S village),[12] Singkawang. Chinese and Dayaks are the main inhabitants in *Kelurahan* S. In 2011, the total population was 8,785: 4,717 male and 4,068 female, with a total of 2,149 households (Pemerintah Kota Singkawang, 2011: 44). I interviewed 46 households in *Kelurahan* S, and 11 households in *RT* A. *RT* A has a special history in *Kelurahan* S. After the Dayak Raids in 1967, four refugee camps were built in Singkawang. *RT* A was an administrative unit composed by a former refugee camp. The reason why I chose RT A as a study site is because stagnation of economic condition caused by the Dayak Raids might be a push factor of marriage migration.

Table 2 shows a condition of sending migrant from *RT* A. From the left, it shows a case number, a name and age whom I interviewed, and the details of migrated family members. About the family type, "N" means a nuclear family, and "S" means a stem family. "The children's position on seniority" means a position among siblings.

Table 2 data show: out of 18 migrants to Taiwan, 14 were women, of which 13 migrated to Taiwan because of marriage. And the rest, three men moved to Taiwan for work, one woman moved to study, seeking assistance from her sisters who migrated as brides. Migrants to Malaysia included five persons, with two women migrated for marriage, and one

民二代培育計畫) and "New Immigrant Children International Training Program" (新住民子女海外培育計畫) have started since 2016.

[11]"RT (*Rukun Tetangga*)" means a neighborhood unit, which is the smallest unit in Indonesia, consisting of 10–20 households.

[12]"Kelurahan" means a village.

man and two women moved for work. As I mentioned earlier, Taiwan is the main destination for cross-border marriage migrants, followed by Johor, Malaysia, and Hong Kong. On the other hand, Jakarta is the main destination of domestic migration, and Kuching, and Miri, Malaysia are favorable destinations for migrant workers.

The inhabitants of those destinations are similar in ethnicity with Singkawang Chinese Indonesian. Oxfeld reported that Chinese Canadian men show a preference of the same or similar ethnicity when they seek brides at their ancestor's homeland, Mei-xian, Canton (Oxfeld, 2005). Those Chinese Canadian men imagine that Mei-xian Chinese women share an ethnicity of "Chinese-ness" or "Hakka-ness" with them.

We can find similar phenomenon in cross-border marriage between Taiwanese men and Chinese Indonesian women. Taiwanese match-making brokers can introduce women from China, Thailand, Vietnam, and the Philippines, but Hakka Taiwanese men show a preference for Hakka women as foreign spouse. Based on my research, a Hakka man, aged 39 when married, went to Singkawang to seek a Hakka bride, because his mother only can speak Hakka, and she ordered him to marry a Hakka Indonesian. Like him, if the communication between his wife and mother in Hakka, and transmitting his own mother tongue to the next generation are considered, "Hakka-ness" of the bride becomes an important factor.

There are a lot of Hakka in Kuching, and to some extent Hakka also inhabit in Miri, Johor, Malaysia. It seems that migrating destination is also related with "Hakka-ness" ethnicity in Malaysia, but I am still studying this correlation.

Next, we move to the age of marriage. For women, the youngest one was 17 years old, the oldest one was 32 years old, and the average age was 20.23 years old. In February 2012, the youngest one was 20 years old, the oldest one was 58 years old, and the average age was 38.85 years old. The number of cases of migration by chronological order is one case in 1970s, three cases in 1980s, seven cases in 1990s, and five cases in 2000s.

On academic background of the marriage migrant, two cases had none, four dropped out of elementary school, two finished 6th grade, four finished 9th grade, and three finished high school, and one unknown. Although it seems that many years have passed from graduation to marriage, it is rare that children graduate according to normal school age. Girls often are 15–16 years old when they graduate from elementary school. When they get married at a young age, only several years have passed from graduation to marriage.

On their recent occupation in 2012, nine were housewives, one owned a store, two were part-time workers, two were waitresses, and one unknown. Their jobs were mainly helping farming and processing agricultural products at home.

Their places of residence in Taiwan: four in Taoyuan, four in Hsinchu, four in Miaoli, two in Tai-chung, one in Jia-yi, one in Hua-lien, and one unknown. Meanwhile, one migrated to Hong Kong, and two migrated to Malaysia. One case included both sisters migrating to Taiwan and living in two different places.

Householding for Family and Individual: Case Study from a Former Refugee Camp A Village

In this section, I will describe the motives for migration and family situation of the female marriage migrant according to my research.

Case 1: Abandoned by husband, and seeking new support in Taiwan: Early female marriage migrant

LNC, 79 years old, Hakka woman, lives with one sister in a tiny house, which sits slightly away from the main street, and is surrounded by rubber trees and pigpens. Her husband died when she was 50 years old in 1982. They got seven children, one son and six daughters. Three daughters migrated to Taiwan as marriage migrants.

Eldest daughter had stayed home after she dropped out of second grade. One day she got pregnant with a Chinese from Pontianak, but he abandoned her. Then, in 1977, 3–4 months later she gave birth to a son at 23 years old, and she decided to get married with a Taiwanese serviceman who moved from Mainland China to Taiwan. LNC said, “We didn’t have any other choice but to get married with Taiwanese”. Their son had grown up at LNC’s house until 8 years old before his mother took him to Taiwan. Eldest daughter does not have biological children with her Taiwanese husband, because her husband’s job ranking is relatively high and supported by good welfare, she could keep being a housewife.

Second daughter got married with a *Benshenren* (Taiwanese local) from Miaoli in 1982. Her husband was a carpenter. A Chinese Indonesian from Jakarta adopted the third daughter. Thereafter, she was taken by a friend to Taiwan, and got married with a poor farmer in 1983. Eldest daughter made her divorce the poor husband and introduced a serviceman to her to remarry. Now she runs a store. The third daughter visits Singkawang once a year. Her son born from her second marriage is 27 years old and is married to a flight attendant.

Both fourth daughter and fifth daughter died young. Only sixth daughter got married with a Chinese Indonesian from Singkawang with three children. Her husband takes rubber sap from rubber trees and she is a housewife. Then, LNC's son, the youngest child, married a local Chinese Indonesian with nine children. They process coffee beans, but they are very poor.

LNC's family finance depends on the remittances from her three daughters in Taiwan every month. LNC manages to raise the money to support her youngest son. In 2008, LNC built a concrete house with two bedrooms, one living room, kitchen, and bathroom thanks to the remittances from her daughters.

In the beginning of the marriage migration phenomena in Singkawang, Chinese Indonesian women who were abandoned by their husbands, divorced, or lost their husband like LNC's eldest daughter were dominant migrants to Taiwan. Documents relating to this situation are also kept in Taiwan. The following passage is taken from a report from the Taiwanese diplomatic establishment abroad to the Ministry of Foreign Affairs.

> Because veterans longed for spouses to marry from the beginning of 1970s to the beginning of 1980s, Overseas Chinese returnee from Indonesia who stayed in Taiwan introduced West Kalimantan women as brokers … brokers got carried away with business opportunity. In a rise in demand, broker one after another imported West Kalimantan women, and women were sold when the price jumped. Imported women were sold to Waishengren (Mainlander veterans). These brides included a lot of prostitutes and bogus marriage women. That caused a social unrest of public order. (Hsia, 2002:58)

Waishengren were desirable partners for marriage, because the veterans could receive pension and provide foods like rice and seasoning. Besides, the veterans were secured for housing and medical care. Life security by the government was very attractive for divorced women and widows from Singkawang area.

As Case 1 shows, after divorce or separation, Singkawang Chinese Indonesian women become financially vulnerable. The norm that woman should be supported financially by husband is very strong-rooted, besides there might not have been enough job opportunities for women to be independent financially due to the employment structure. Because of these reasons, Singkawang Chinese women had to secure life security through marriage.

In the late 1970s, when this case's eldest daughter married a Taiwanese husband, working abroad was not common. In addition, the norm and the necessity for life security drove women to marry abroad. Cross-border marriage seemed to be a "kill two birds with one stone" choice, which could fulfill moral demands and solve financial problems.

Case 2: Born as eldest daughter: Woman as long-term economic supporter

YCH's house stands near the entrance of A village. As a refugee of Dayak Raids, she moved to this village from the inland area at 21 years old. Her husband was also a refugee. They had lived in a leased land since 1960s, but in 2008 she finally bought it, and built a new house. In 2012, most of the A villagers still leased land to build houses. A new house with satellite dish receivers suggests the family is supported by remittance from the daughters.

YCH manufactures and sells confectionary. In the Singkawang area, regardless of ethnicity, people not only usually eat confectionary but also entertain a guest with homemade confectionary, which are filled in bottles on festival days. As confectionary for sale is very expensive, so women make various confectionaries at home, using gas oven. YCH is very good at manufacturing confectionary, so she does it for a living. Her husband was a barber, who went everywhere by bike to cut hair. He had already passed away.

YCH had five sons and three daughters with him. The eldest son has married three times, and now lives with his third Dayak wife and a daughter in Mempawah. His ex-wives are Chinese. After his first wife divorced him, she was demanded by her parents to remarry a Hong Kong man.

Her second son was engaged in the spinning industry, but he also died of illness. His wife lives with their two children at her home in Mempawah. The third son with mental disability is supported by YCH.

The fourth son also had died. The fifth son and the third daughter work in a spinning industry in Jakarta.

The eldest daughter is a marriage migrant to Taiwan. After she graduated from an elementary school, she helped her mother to manufacture confectionary and do housework. When she was 23 years old in 1994, she married a Taiwanese who worked in Jia-yi as a blacksmith. They have two sons and one daughter. Although the eldest daughter is a part-time worker with low salary, she saved money, and offered to pay for all the cost for her parent's house. She comes back to Singkawang every 5 years. They usually communicate through phone. She often says: "every time I see an airplane flying in the sky, it makes my heart fly to Singkawang."

YCH's house is a one-story concrete house, where the floor is covered with blue and green tiles, and is kept clean. The house consists of a terrace, a living room, one bedroom, a kitchen, a bathroom, a laundry room, which is a typical house in Singkawang. On the wall of the living room, the marriage photograph of the eldest daughter is hung to commemorate her contribution to the family.

Since the eldest daughter married, she has been offering most of the expenses for YCH, her disabled brother, and her nephew. YCH's eldest son sometimes sends money and rice; other daughters also sometimes send money. But YCH mostly depends on the eldest daughter. She said crying: "we didn't have other choice but to let her marry abroad. Because of her sacrifice, we could build a house."

First, Case 2 shows that the eldest daughter's devotion is significant. She not only supports her parents, and her disabled brother and nephew, but also offers all the cost for the land and house just by herself.

Second, this case also shows us that the unstableness of marriage links to another cross-border marriage. The ex-wife of the eldest son remarried a Hong Kong man after the divorce, which is another survival strategy.

Third, this case represents cross-ethnic marriage situation. The eldest son married the current Dayak wife in his third marriage. In Singkawang, while betrothal money for Chinese bride is about Rp. 50,000,000, betrothal money for Dayak bride is only Rp. 1,000,000. Therefore, relatively poor Chinese men often marry Dayak women, or remarriage case with Dayak women often happen.

Finally, I would like to introduce a young female case. Case 3 is different from the former two cases where moral economy works well. In Case 3, marriage migration seems to be an extension of seeking a job, and the woman fails to support her family of orientation.

Case 3: Seeking a job: A case study of migrant in the 2010s

Mr. ZHT, 50-years old Hakka, lives with his wife (36 years old), third daughter (16 years old, high school student), eldest son (13 years old, junior high school student), and two nieces (16 and 2 years old) (No. 10 of Table 2). His eldest daughter (22 years old) went to Miri, Malaysia to work, and his second daughter BSS (18 years old, main marriage migrant) married a Taiwanese when she was 17 years old.

ZHT's house is a wooden house with no air conditioner. His house has a terrace, a living room, a bedroom, a kitchen, and a bathroom, all in a straight line. At night, women sleep together in the bedroom, and men sleep together in the living room. The facility is not enough for the family members. ZHT works at construction sites, and his wife grows rice for home consumption. This means their source of income is very limited.

BSS worked as a part-time waitress after she dropped out of fourth grade. She asked a broker to introduce a foreign groom to marry. Soon after she moved to Hua-lien City, she came to know that her groom was quick to use violence. She could not endure to his violence, and ran away without bringing her passport. "He dares to hit his own mother. If he could be gentle with me, I wouldn't run away," BSS said. Fortunately, she was able to stay with her aunt in Chu-pei City, Hsin-chu County, who was working illegally. In Chu-pei, a broker introduced her to work at a vegetarian restaurant.

Her family in Singkawang asked the author to help her. I visited BSS in March 2012 in Hsin-chu. At that time, she had already changed jobs, and started to work at another vegetarian restaurant in Hsin-chu City. During the Lunar New Year vacation in 2012, her aunt was arrested for illegal stay, so BSS lost her house. She traveled from her friend's house to house until she could find live-in work. Her colleagues were both marriage migrants and illegal workers from West Kalimantan. Some of them escaped from their Taiwanese husbands, like BSS did.

When I met her in Hsin-chu, she was dressed in short pants with dyed hair, like a Taiwanese teenager. Her salary was about 28,000 NTD (Rp. 12,607,286). She worked as a cashier and cleaner at the restaurant. When a policeman came as a customer, she hid herself in the backyard in order to hide her identity. Foreign brides can work legally when they marry a Taiwanese, so she did not need to hide from the police. But she escaped without any ID, and she heard that her husband had reported to the police that she stole his goods, and she did not know where she could get help. Before everything else, she wanted to stay and work a little longer in Taiwan.

In summer 2013, BSS finally got help with the department of social welfare in Hsin-chu. With their help, she could take back her passport and divorce her husband. When she was done with the divorce process, she was still a minor and needed a guardian's guarantee, but she did not have one. After the divorce, she bought a plane ticket with her money, and came back to Singkawang. At that time, she had an older Taiwanese boyfriend, so she was planning to go to Taiwan to remarry after a while. But few months later, her boyfriend posted a photograph with a new girlfriend. She lost love, and her plan fell through.

She was trying to find a new job when I visited her in September 2013. "It's very difficult to find a good job. There are only low salary jobs. Because people are willing to work even with low salary, so employers won't raise the salary," she said. Since she dropped out of fourth grade, her job opportunity was very limited. If some weddings or funerals were held, she worked as a waitress at ceremonies. Aside from that, she did piecework at home, shelling macadamia nut with her sisters. However, with these jobs, she could not get a stable income. She lamented her unemployment: "after the Lunar Chinese New Year, job offers will increase". There were still 4 months before the Lunar Chinese New Year at that time. She started to have a pessimistic outlook on job hunting.

One day she sent me a photograph in which she smiled with a red wedding dress with an unknown man. She explained the man was from Hong Kong. Before the Lunar Chinese New Year of 2014, she gave up job hunting, instead, she asked a broker to introduce a foreigner to remarry. That man was actually from Henan Province, China.

BSS described later that she had stayed home in Henan for 1 year. In 2015, she came back to Singkawang during her pregnancy with her husband. But he left her in Singkawang, and they never met each other again. She complained "he sent me a photograph with another woman, never asked about his son." She gave birth to her first son and remarried again with a local Chinese man in 2016. Now she became a mother of two children. Nevertheless, she seemed to be ready to work abroad. "I would go abroad again after my children have grown up," she said. Although she became a mother of two children, her dream to financially support her family of orientation is yet to come true.

I would like to summarize the life cycle and job of Singkawang Chinese Indonesian women. They enter national elementary school for compulsory education, but dropping out is not rare. By earning a high school diploma or higher, people can work as white-collar workers. College graduate are elites who can work at leading banks or multinational corporations. Without a high school diploma, men would work as blue-collar workers, like as service engineer or construction worker; women often work as clerk at clothing shops or restaurants.

Even if one has not finished compulsory education, there is another option to get a high salary: to learn Mandarin Chinese. Young Chinese Indonesian proficient in Mandarin Chinese can work as translators with a good salary. Students with good grades at Chinese private schools could study in China supported by the Chinese government.

Nevertheless, the working condition of Singkawang women is tough. According to my research, most of the young Chinese Indonesian women engage in supplementary jobs. They work six days a week from 8 a.m. to 6 p.m. and the salary is about Rp. 500,000. They usually engage in these jobs for several years after graduation and become a full-time housewife. They usually take care of the children, do piecework at home, or make and sell confectionary and food.

Like Case 3 in a relatively poor family, the division of gender roles between the husband and wife is very clear. The husbands earn their living; the wives are assigned to grow rice and vegetables for home consumption instead of earning a wage. It also means that financial resources may be very limited.

Marriageable age of women makes them vulnerable, too. Early 20s are considered marriageable age, but women in their late 20s are recognized as too old to marry. To make matters worse, even job opportunities of simple work decrease for women in the late 20s. Therefore, marriage is an influential way of life security for Singkawang Chinese Indonesian women. These circumstances drive them to marry.

On the other hand, those who do not resign themselves to marriage go to Jakarta, and Sabah Province, Malaysia. In Jakarta, they engage in spinning industry which is monopolized by Singkawang Chinese, or in cell phone shops and beauty salons targeting customers from the same area. In Sabah, they generally work as waitress at Internet cafés and restaurants. At Internet cafés, they offer a kind of sexual service: chatting up customers with suggestive words. These paths of migration appeared after cross-border marriage.

BSS and her elder sister tried to support their family of orientation as a marriage migrant and a migrant worker. BSS's challenge to remarry shows how she was eager to marry abroad. Whether marrying abroad or working abroad, it is a serious problem for themselves and their family to survive.

Discussion

Based on the three cases, I would like to point out some characteristics of international migration from Singkawang. First, the migrants from the three cases are from relatively low class. Before daughters married abroad, the conditions of three families needed to be improved. If a woman marries a foreign groom, she can offer not only considerably more wealth to her family of orientation but also support them for a long time, taking an advantage of the economic disparity between Taiwan and Indonesia. Therefore, cross-border marriage is a powerful option of survival strategy for families.

Second, one family sends multiple marriage migrants abroad (Case 1 and Case 3). As the two families also sent male migrant workers abroad, it could be said that not only female migrants but also male members supported family finances. In Case 3, one person emigrated and married repeatedly. According to my research, main contributions are from the daughters.

Michael Douglas pointed that people are practice householding to satisfy family welfare globally. He calls these dynamic processes in social reproduction which both shape and maintain a household, covers the whole life cycle, and expand beyond the family as "global householding" (Douglas, 2006: 421). The practices of the three cases also show that multiple family members get married abroad or work abroad and keep sending remittance. Thus, they are also practicing "global householding".

Third, daughters marry abroad in the order of seniority. In Case 1 and Case 2, the eldest daughters married abroad first. In Case 2, when the family lost their father as the breadwinner, the eldest daughter volunteered to marry abroad to send remittance. But, in Case 3, the eldest daughter just went to Malaysia to work, while the second daughter married to foreign men again and again.

Fourth, marriage migrant to Taiwan have been sending remittance for a long time (Case 1 and Case 2). Foreign grooms pay on purchases for the family of the bride, such as house, boat, motorcycle, and cost for painting house. Besides, after marriage, marriage migrants keep sending about 15,000 NTD (Rp. 6,753,903) every month to support parents and younger siblings. In general, educational background of younger siblings is higher than the migrants' one. In addition, many years later after marriage, marriage migrants would build a house for her family of orientation. Although in Case 3 BSS has failed to send remittance during both her marriages, she is still eager to work abroad to support her family financially.

The above is practices of "global householding" which has been around for more than 30 years. Cross-border marriage is not a special option but a practical option, which Singkawang Chinese Indonesian women need to consider through their life course.

Since not only marriage migration but also labor migration of men is general, we have to argue different ways of migration by gender and male contribution toward moral economy. But, in my research, moral economy by marriage migrants played a greater role in the practice of "global householding."

Conclusion

Cross-border marriage of Chinese Indonesian women has been reported many times in local newspapers and major magazines. But few anthropological case studies exist. Besides, though globalization and global division of labor, of course, have influenced the way of migration of Overseas Chinese, those former studies have not contextualized marriage migration to the migration history of Overseas Chinese.

In order to fill in the blanks of previous studies, this chapter examined the practices of migration and cross-border marriage of Chinese Indonesian by taking into account the universality and the features by ethnicity in the globalization era. The cases show four points. First, female marriage migrants come from lower socioeconomic class. When they lose financial supporters such as husband or father, they choose to marry abroad in order to secure financial support for them and their family of orientation. Second, a single family sends several members as brides or workers abroad. Third, sisters tend to marry abroad in order of seniority. Fourth, it can be assumed that sisters who marry abroad play the central role in maintaining the welfare of their families of orientation over a long period of time.

References

Dawis, A. (2009). *The Chinese of Indonesia and Their Search for Identity: The Relationship Between Collective Memory and the Media.* New York, Cambria Press.

Douglas, M. (2006). Global Householding in Pacific Asia. *IDPR*, 28(4): 421–446.

Douglas, M. (2010). Globalizing the Household in East Asia. *The Whitehead Journal of Diplomacy and International Relations*, Winter/Spring, 11(1): 63–78.

Hugo, G. (2005). Indonesian International Domestic Workers: Contemporary Developments and Issues. In S. Huang, B.S.A. Yeoh and Noor Abdul Rahman (Eds.), *Asian Women as Transnational Domestic Workers*. Singapore, Marshall Cavendish Academic.

Ong, A. (2006). *Neoliberalism as Exception*. Durham, Duke University Press.

Oxfeld, E. (2005). Cross-Border Hypergamy? Marriage Exchanges in a Trasnational Hakka Community. In N. Constable (Ed.), *Cross-Border Marriages: Gender and Mobility in Transnational Asia*. Philadelphia, University of Pennsylvania Press.

Scott, J. C. (1976). *The Moral Economy of the Peasant: Rebellion and Subsistence in Southeast Asia*. New Haven, Yale University Press.

Somers Heidhues, M. (2003). *Golddiggers, Farmers, and Trades in the "Chinese Districts" of West Kalimantan, Indonesia*. Ithaca, New York, Cornell University.

Truong, T. (1996). Gender, International Migration and Social Reproduction: Implications for Theory, Policy, Research and Networking. *Asian and Pacific Migration Journal*, 5(1): 27–52.

Japanese

Asato, W. (2005). The Position of Foreign Workers in Care Sector: From the Case of Taiwan. *Ryukoku University Institutional Repository*, 44(5): 1–29. (安里和晃「介護労働市場の形成における外国人家事•介護労働者の位置づけ: 台湾における事例から」『龍谷大学経済学論集』44(5): 1–29.)

Yokota, S. (2017). Life History of Chinese Indonesians Who Migrated to Taiwan: Studying at "Homeland" Republic of China and Marriage Migration. In Y. Kitamura (ed.), *Chinese Indonesians on the Move within the International Relations of 20th Century Asia.* Kyoto, Kyoto University Library. (横田祥子「台湾に移住したインドネシア華人のライフヒストリー: 中華民国へ

の『帰国』進学と結婚移住」北村由美編著『20世紀アジアの国際関係とインドネシア華人の移動』京都大学図書館.)

Chinese

Hsia, H. C. (2002). Wandering to Search for a Place: The "Foreign Brides" Phenomenon Under the Globalization of Capital. Taipei, Ton San. (Hsia, H. C. 夏暁鵑 (2002).《流離尋岸——資本国際化下的「外籍新娘」現象》台北: 唐山).

National Immigration Agency of Republic of China. (2014). Foreign Residents and Foreign Spouses by Sex and Original Nationality for Countries and Cities, Jan. 1987 to Jan. 2014. (National Immigration Agency of Republic of China 中華民國内政部移民署 〈各縣市 外裔、外籍配偶人數按性別及原屬國籍分76年1月~103年1 月分〉).

The Minister of Labor Republic of China. (2020). Table 12-6 Foreign Workers in Productive Industries and Social Welfare by Nationality and Sex, May 2020. (The Minister of Labor of Republic of China中華民國勞動部〈表12-6產業及社福移 工人数—按國籍及性別分□109年5月底〉).

IFI Network+ http://ifi.immigration.gove.tw/. (IFI Network+ 新住民培力發展資訊網 http://ifi.immigration.gov.tw/) (Accessed on December 18, 2017).

Indonesian

Anonymous (1995). Dari Singkawang Mencari Cinta. *Gatra*, June 10, pp. 51–65.

Badan Pusat Statistik Kota Singkawang (2010). *Kota Singkawang Dalam Angka 2010*. Jakarta, Badan Pusat Statistik.

Bektiati, B. and Kleden, H. Y. (2001). Mimpi Jadi Cinderella di Singkawang. *Tempo*, March 25, pp. 67–80.

La Ode (2012). *Etnis Cina Indonesia Dalam Politik: Politik Etnis Cina Pontianak dan Singkawang di Era Reformasi 1998–2008*. Jakarta, Yayasan Pustaka Obor Indonesia.

Pemerintah Kota Singkawang (2011). *Database Kota Singkawang Tahun 2011*. Singkawang.

https://doi.org/10.1142/9789811250668_0010

Chapter 10

Indonesia–Taiwan Relationship Under the New Southbound Policy: A Perspective from Jakarta

Rita Pawestri Setyaningsih

Researcher, National Research and Innovation Agency (BRIN)

Introduction

Since the leadership of Tsai Ing-wen, Taiwan has adopted the New Southbound Policy (NSP). NSP targets 10 of the South East Asian countries, six South Asian countries, Australia and New Zealand. It aims to deepen economic co-operation with the partner countries to improve the scope and economic variety in the manner of not over relying on one market. Four dimensions are highlighted in this NSP, namely economics, talent exchange, resource sharing and regional co-operation. Unlike previous co-operation, the NSP not only relies on economic co-operation but also on people-to-people (P-to-P) exchanges. Within this NSP framework, Indonesia expects to receive benefits from the co-operation with Taiwan.

Although Indonesia has no formal diplomatic relations with Taiwan due to its One China Policy, their relation has been nurtured for an extended period. The relationship has expanded from economic co-operation to socio-cultural ties. Three kinds of interactions that connect Indonesia and Taiwan are (1) official interaction, (2) semi-official interaction and (3) unofficial interaction (Kabinawa, 2013). The official interaction contains official government exchanges and has the significant political implication. The semi-official interaction is done through economic activities, such as trade and investment by Indonesian and Taiwanese businesspeople. This type of interaction creates moderate political implications. The unofficial interaction is done through economic and socio-cultural interactions and has low political implications. The first and second types of interactions still include official governmental exchanges, while the last type of interaction does not. However, with the absence of diplomatic relations, the formal G-to-G interaction seems difficult to be upgraded. It becomes the reason why P-to-P connectivity can contribute more.

Based on the outline and limitations aforementioned, Indonesia and Taiwan try to upgrade their relationship, primarily through P-to-P relations. This chapter tries to answer questions: (1) How is co-operation under the NSP perceived from Indonesia's point of view? (2) Is NSP in line with Indonesian's interests? (3) How to enhance the P-to-P relationship between Indonesia and Taiwan?

Many studies on the P-to-P relations between Indonesia and Taiwan have been done (Paramitaningrum, 2013; Elias, 2013; Kabinawa, 2013; Tsay, 2018). P-to-P interaction is believed to be a suitable way to bridge Indonesia–Taiwan relations since it has less political constraint (Paramitaningrum, 2013; Kabinawa, 2013). Kabinawa (2013) discusses Taiwan–Indonesia relations in economic and socio-cultural aspects from an Indonesian perspective. She states that Indonesian people who promote the ideas play an important role in keeping certain relationship with Taiwan so that its economic and socio-cultural relations with Taiwan is well maintained despite the absence of diplomatic relations. She further categorizes three types of actors in Indonesia–Taiwan relations, namely Indonesian businessmen, Indonesian workers and Indonesian students. They are influenced by personal understanding and socially shared knowledge in conducting the P-to-P interaction with Taiwan. The P-to-P interactions between Indonesian and Taiwanese businesspeople create common economic interests; while P-to-P interactions formed by Indonesian workers and Indonesian students in Taiwan create cultural interests.

Paramitaningrum (2013) focuses on Indonesian students' role in Taiwan as actors to enhance P-to-P co-operation with Taiwan, especially in raising Indonesian soft power. Education becomes a medium to share knowledge, skills and experience with the Taiwanese. Hence, she suggests Indonesia and Taiwan to assign specific official in IETO/KDEI to support the P-to-P relation so as to foster an epistemic community for both countries. They have shared positive achievements and helped Taiwanese society understand more about Indonesia, although the Taiwanese society has not responded to them. Elias (2013) argues that Taiwan has not yet utilized the increasing number of Indonesian students in Taiwan that has the potential to improve Indonesia–Taiwan relations. The success of promotion in higher education is not complemented by better treatments when they are in Taiwan. All the previously mentioned literature above discuss the Indonesia–Taiwan relations from the Indonesian perspective before the NSP was implemented. None of them address the relation after the NSP. Tsay (2018) discusses the P-to-P relation after the NSP focusing on the Indonesian migrants from Taiwan perspectives. He also pinpoints other actors besides workers and students, namely immigrant spouses and the professionals/skilled, who also contribute to the bilateral relations. However, the relations of those actors have shown an imbalance relation between Indonesia and Taiwan. To make it less asymmetrical, he suggests the Taiwanese people improve the bilateral relationship by traveling to Indonesia and learning its language, people and country. In addition, Taiwanese students need to be encouraged and facilitated.

This chapter discusses capital and people's flows from the Indonesian perspective by using an economics schemes. The people flow aspects include the international student, transnational marriage, migrant workers involved in the Indonesian Diaspora Network (IDN) and *halal* tourism. As the first path in Indonesia–Taiwan relations, economic relations are also discussed, particularly the Taiwanese capital inflows to Indonesia. Data utilized in this chapter are mainly obtained through secondary resources and interviews. This chapter is organized into four sections; first section is the introduction. Second is the NSP implementation in Indonesia, which discusses the flagship programs in the NSP implemented in Indonesia. Third section explains the Indonesia–Taiwan relation with specific focus on: developing the substantial relation for both sides. This section discusses economic and socio-cultural co-operation between Indonesia and Taiwan, particularly the capital and people flow. In the people flow, the main focus is the IDN, including the international students, Indonesian workers, and the tourists. Finally, the fourth section is the conclusion.

Implementation of the NSP in Indonesia

The NSP aims to utilize Taiwan's cultural, educational, technological, agricultural and economic strengths and resources, to deepen its regional integration with 18 countries, including all ASEAN countries. Four main aspects have been addressed, including:

(1) Encouraging economic collaboration, focusing on supply chains, domestic market demand and infrastructure projects.
(2) Carrying out talent exchange through educational relationships, industrial talents and new immigrants.
(3) Resource sharing, including health care, culture, tourism, technology and agriculture.
(4) Strengthening regional relations, regional integration and negotiations.

Different from the previous efforts, this NSP focuses more on P-to-P relations, for Taiwan wants the relations to be more comprehensive culturally. The policy's main aims are to facilitate the connection among the people, developing ASEAN's talents through academic and job training programs at Taiwan's colleges and universities. Hence, overall Taiwan wants to cooperate with the Southbound partner countries in the area of economic relations, market, science and technology, and culture; share resources and talents. It means that there are two-way exchanges in the area mentioned above. Moreover, Taiwan would like to impel people to acquire skills needed to support the NSP.

In relation with Indonesia, the NSP has been focused on some dimensions; namely (1) education, (2) industry, and (3) new immigrants. In terms of education, the key agenda include increasing scholarship for ASEAN students depending on the need of industry in Taiwan, opening up internship programs under the industrial-academia co-operation and providing suitable jobs for graduate students. Additionally, it also encourages universities and schools to establish courses or study abroad programs, provide language courses at the elementary and secondary levels for new immigrants and encourage universities to cultivate experts in Southeast Asian languages and areastudies, and, then, train regional trade professionals. Meanwhile, the implementation of resource sharing is done through tourism.

Indonesia itself has a national vision, which during President Joko Widodo's leadership, is called *Nawacita*. *Nawa* means "nine", himself and *Cita* means aspiration. This platform was initiated by the president himself and the vice-presidential candidate, Jusuf Kalla, in their speech in the presidential election campaign in 2014. It demonstrates the national priorities to improve Indonesia as a major power that is politically sovereign, independent in the economic field, and having a personality in culture (Wedhaswary, 2014). In the implementation, the *Nawacita* is carried out within intermediate and long-term plans. Hence, the implementation of the NSP is supposed to be in line with Indonesian interests.

Through co-operation with other countries, Indonesia targets at high economic growth in terms of technological progress, improvement in education, skills as well as expertise of the workforce, and additional capital. However, Indonesia has faced a lack of capital and expertise, a rapid population growth that becomes a challenge to its economic growth. That is a large population may harm development efforts unless they have the resources and capabilities to contribute to development.

Foreign investment is vital for the Indonesia's economic development not only in the sense of increasing capital but also creating jobs, facilitating exports and transfer of technology. Capital is in great demand to build infrastructure while educating knowledgeable personnel is essential for carrying out development projects and overseeing industrial activities' implementation can make it efficient.

To accelerate economic development, Indonesia needs various policies to enhance people's economic activities to increase productivity. Increasing infrastructure development can also contribute to modernizing the economy. It is believed that, education is a significant investment to improve the quality of human resources — the refined education performance will directly influence the prosperity of the country and its people.

Indonesia needs co-operation with other countries to solve its problems and also establish mutually beneficial foreign cooperative relations. For attracting investment, it needs some determinants such as high economic growth levels, availability of human resources, a stable political situation and a supportive investment climate to attract foreign investors. In foreign co-operation, through the Ministry of Foreign Affairs, the Indonesian Government has tried to make mutually beneficial co-operation by creating economic opportunities. One of Indonesia's foreign policy pillars is economic diplomacy, where the main agenda is to develop a long-term resilient economy. Indonesia views the importance of a collaborative strategic outlook as a strategy to encourage higher world economic growth. Economic diplomacy focuses on attracting foreign investment that supports Indonesia's sustainable development and infrastructure development, including human resource development.

Indonesia–Taiwan Relations: Developing Substantial Relations

Supamijoto and Herlijanto (2016) explain the historical relation between Indonesia and Taiwan. Both of them started their relationship after the Dutch colonial era in Indonesia in the first half of the 20th century. The ROC that established a formal relationship with the Netherland in the 1940s tried to continue its formal relations with Indonesia after its independence, expecting that Indonesia might recognize Taiwan's status. However, instead of recognizing it, the Indonesian Government decided to recognize PRC by hailing the One China Policy.

During the Cold War era, Indonesia and Taiwan relations began in the 1950s. Indonesia's political situation impelled some Chinese overseas from Indonesia to study somewhere else. However, since the Indonesian Government considered those who went to PRC as communists, most Indonesian Chinese selected Taiwan as the destination to study. Due to Indonesia's political upheaval in the 1960s, Taiwan also became the destination of run-away Indonesian Chinese from Indonesia. They settled in Taiwan and became citizens of Taiwan (Riskianingrum, 2012). Furthermore, they formed the Indonesian Overseas Chinese Association (IOCA), which later became one of the Indonesian diaspora's forerunners in Taiwan.

Indonesia and Taiwan's official relations began in the early 1970s when they agreed to establish representative offices. Indonesia established the Indonesian Chamber of Commerce (KADIN) in Taipei, and Taiwan set up its Chinese Chamber of Commerce in Jakarta. Further, through the Presidential Decree number 48/1994, the KADIN was upgraded into the Indonesian Economic and Trade Office (IETO) Taipei as a non-governmental economic institution under the Ministry of Trade (KDEI, 2014). Meanwhile, the Chinese Chamber of Commerce was changed into Taipei Economic and Trade Office (TETO). The establishment of these offices has enhanced Indonesia and Taiwan's co-operation that labeled politically meaningful status to Taiwan (Kabinawa, 2013). Later, more intensive co-operation between Indonesia and Taiwan has impelled the Indonesian Government to approve the other TETO establishment in Surabaya in 2015 (Marboen, 2015).

Until today, Indonesia–Taiwan relations have progressed in the form of economic, social, and educational engagement. The economic co-operation has been carried out through trade and investment, while social co-operation has been promoted through sending Indonesian workers to

Taiwan, and educational co-operation has been facilitated through international student exchanges.

Flow of capital

One feature of the economic co-operation between Indonesia and Taiwan is the capital flow. Taiwan has been one of the significant sources of Foreign Direct Investment (FDI) in Indonesia. From 2004 to 2017, Taiwan investment in Indonesia ranked no. 13, with a total investment of US$2.4 billion and 2,500 projects, or US$265 million per annum on average. Taiwan investment reached the top in 2012 with a total amount of US$646.9 million but continuously declined until 2015 as US$108 million. Compared to the other non-ASEAN countries, Taiwan ranks the top five sources of FDI in Indonesia, just after Japan, South Korea, China and Hong Kong.

The launch of the NSP increased the investment inflow which jumped by 166% to more than US$390 million in 2017. The number of projects also increased from 150 projects in 2014 to almost 530 projects in 2017, dominated by the manufacturing sector (Plessis, 2018). Until 2019, Taiwan's investment in Indonesia ranked No. 15. It indicates that the NSP fosters a positive Taiwanese contribution to investment in Indonesia, albeit relatively not significant. Factors such as vast market opportunity, higher GDP growth and abundance of natural resources have still determined Taiwan's capital inflow into Indonesia. Besides, the Indonesian middle class's growth, boom in manufacturing, *halal* and creative industries, agriculture products, technology, green energy, tourism, steel and education in Indonesia seem to attract Taiwan investors in Indonesia (Plessis, 2018).

However, in terms of geographical distribution, most of the investments have concentrated on Java Island. Although the Indonesian Government has developed other areas than Java, few investment amounts are located in Indonesia's eastern part. In line with the Indonesian Government policy that develops infrastructure in those areas, Taiwan investment has gradually spread to the eastern parts of Indonesia, such as in South Sulawesi and North Maluku. Taiwan investors have also shown interest in infrastructure construction, such as in building up a water reservoir. Today, building infrastructure has become Indonesia's priority nowadays. The Government has encouraged foreign investors to focus on this sector by offering better infrastructure and services (Sundaryani and Wirayani, 2016). However, President Tsai's promise to boost its investment in Indonesia's infrastructure, in fact has not yet come to fruition.

From 2007 to 2016, the service sector became the primary Taiwan's investment in Indonesia, particularly the finance and insurance (42.06%), followed by the manufacturing sector, mainly the rubber product (12.91%) and plastic products (10.33%). All the products were exported to foreign countries. In terms of characteristics, the Taiwan investment in Indonesia is different from those in other ASEAN countries, which mainly are electronic components and semiconductors. These indicate that Taiwan has still preferred to invest in Indonesia's natural resources-related sector besides the financial sector. In terms of trade, Taiwan ranked No. 14 trade partner of Indonesia. The trade volume rose by 15% in 2017 to US$8 billion; therefore, Indonesia enjoyed surplus after Indonesia-Taiwan's trade deficit for four years (Christianto, 2018). In 2018, both Indonesia and Taiwan signed an MoU on comprehensive economic co-operation to enhance bilateral co-operation.

Through NSP, Taiwan intends to invest in other sectors, such as agriculture, fishery, infrastructure, logistics, marine transportation and shipbuilding, electronic equipment industry, information technology and tourism sectors. These preferences are also in line with Indonesian interest. Especially in the tourism sector, the Indonesian Government also intends to create 10 "New Bali" as tourism destinations (Badan Koordinasi Penanaman Modal, 2017). Special Economic Zone will be established in these locations. In Morotai Island (North Maluku), Taiwan is eager to build infrastructure. To attract more foreign investors, the Indonesian Government established a one-stop service mechanism and an electronic automation platform for investment in licensing and non-licensing services.

Flow of people

The NSP places people as the center of co-operation to make it more comprehensive culturally. The P-to-P relations have been done through educational exchanges, sending of migrant workers, transnational marriage and tourism. The relations have involved key actors, namely the IDN Taiwan that consists of international students, migrant workers, transnational married spouses and tourists.

Indonesian Diaspora Network (IDN)

The IDN Taiwan was established in 2013, just a year after the Indonesian Diaspora Network Global was set up. The IDN Taiwan that covers

Indonesians living in Asia and the Pacific, bridges relations between communities to promote cultural understanding and co-operation between Indonesia and Taiwan, improve business, and facilitate economic co-operation.

Regardless of the definition[1] of the Indonesian diaspora which has not yet been clear, the Indonesian Government intends to increase their contribution to Indonesian economic development. In Taiwan, the IDN Taiwan includes all Indonesian citizens and non-Indonesian citizens residing in Taiwan (including migrant workers, students, transnational marriage spouses), Indonesian descent (ex-Indonesian citizen, the second generation of Indonesian-Taiwanese marriage) and Taiwanese citizen linked to Indonesia.

Despite the Indonesian diaspora's immense economic potential, there are no exact data on the number of the Indonesian diasporas abroad. The Indonesian Ministry of Foreign Affairs estimates the number as 6 million people (Rositasari *et al.*, 2019). Meanwhile, the Indonesian diasporas in Taiwan is estimated to reach 1% of the Taiwan population (Effendy, 2016). In this chapter, the diaspora refers to Indonesia–Taiwan marriage spouses. In 2018, the number of spouses with Indonesian nationals reached 29,451 people that represented 19% of the Southeast Asian transnational marriage in Taiwan. It makes the Indonesians the second largest of the transnational marriage in Taiwan (Tsay, 2018). They mostly reside in Taiwan and have a second generation.

Taiwan has paid more attention to the second generation of the Indonesian diasporas. There are approximately 20,000 of the second-generation diasporas from Indonesian married to Taiwanese. Under the NSP, Taiwan has encouraged the second generation to learn their mother language and culture. It also provides them with subsidy to visit their motherland to better learn about their heritage.

Most of the second generation is more fluent in Mandarin than their mother language because of the teaching system since an early stage.

[1]Indonesian Diaspora Network (IDN) Global was established at the 1st Congress of Indonesian Diaspora in Los Angeles. The establishment was generated by the Indonesian Government's intention to pay more attention to Indonesians living abroad to serve their potential contributions to national development. Generally, diaspora terms used to be defined as those who migrate to another place of origin and create a new community (Braziel, 2008). However, the founder of the IDN Global, Dino Patti Djalal, defines it in a broader definition, as an Indonesian citizen who lives in foreign countries, foreign citizens but having Indonesian descendent, and individuals with Indonesian linkage.

Moreover, the Indonesian and the other Southeast Asian languages were put as the subordinate language in Taiwan. With the NSP, Taiwan realizes the importance of learning Southeast Asian languages for the second generation. Even, they can study the languages at elementary school since the languages become required courses for mother tongue. They are also broadcasted through television programs. Consequently, Taiwanese society have been more familiar with the Southeast Asian languages and social dynamics.

Although there are no data on the number of the second-generation diasporas who have taken these programs, at least by encouraging them to learn their mother language and culture, they are expected to understand their roots and reconnect with their identity. Visiting their motherland will enable them to learn their heritage, which is an excellent way to maintain the bonds between them and Indonesian people as an emotional need. Hence, it will create a more robust infinity and network with their ancestral motherland.

The Indonesian Government is hoping for a more significant role from the Indonesian diasporas by emulating the world's Chinese diaspora's experiences. They constitute as Indonesian assets, either as a source of remittance or investment, which contribute to many areas of national development. Understanding the cultural identity and root can play a role in closer Indonesia and Taiwan relations. It is undeniable that their bilingual abilities will become essential factors in pursuing bilateral collaboration. Moreover, they can also act as agent of change that may influence specific foreign policy.

Up to the present, Indonesian diasporas in Taiwan have played essential roles, including developing Indonesian image, transferring knowledge and facilitating the P-to-P relations between Indonesia and Taiwan (Effendy, 2016). They can unite all Indonesians with different backgrounds residing in Taiwan and impel them to contribute to Indonesian economic development. Unfortunately, there has been a lack of government structural support (Effendy, 2016).

Mok Ai Fang is an example of a successful Indonesian married to Taiwanese, who has become a famous artist in Taiwan. She, who originally comes from Pontianak–Kalimantan, has starred in many movies to promote Taiwan to the world (Nanda, 2016). She has also become a bridge to introduce Indonesia to Taiwanese society. By having a better understanding of Indonesian culture, it is hoped that Taiwanese will understand better the way of life of Indonesian people so that Taiwanese can live together with Indonesians in harmony. As a result, more Taiwanese are getting more familiar with Indonesian culture, including its gastro economy, society and cultures.

Given the so-called "people-centered" nature, the NSP hopes to help the second generation connect with their ancestral countries. By improving Indonesian language skills, it will provide them future career opportunities that are related to Indonesia. Hence, their participation will be significant in enhancing or at least maintaining the existing Indonesia–Taiwan ties.

International students

Collaboration in the field of education between Taiwan and Indonesia has been going on for a long period. This collaboration resulted from bilateral ties with some universities in Indonesia. Since 2000, more than 256 MoUs has been signed between universities in Indonesia and Taiwan (Mubah, 2019). However, since the launch of the NSP, this collaboration has been more intensified.

There are several NSP agendas in the field of education, namely increasing scholarships for ASEAN students depending on the needs of industry in Taiwan, opening an internship program under industrial-academic' co-operation and providing jobs suitable for students who have graduated. Moreover, the NSP also encourages universities and schools to establish courses or study abroad programs, provides language courses at primary and secondary levels for new immigrants and encourages universities to cultivate experts in the language of Southeast Asia or area studies and educate professionals in the field of regional trade.

Taiwan has encouraged Indonesian students to study in degree and non-degree programs in Taiwan. They study there at their own expense and scholarships from Taiwan and Indonesia. According to Taiwan's Ministry of Education, between 2008 and 2016, Indonesian students in Taiwan increased from only 534 to 1,923 people, as shown by the Figure 1. It means that the average Indonesian student in Taiwan increased by 174 people each year. Indonesian student was the third largest population after Malaysia and Vietnam. However, from 2016 to 2018, there has been a significant increase to almost doubled yearly, from 1,923 to 5,686, while in 2019, the number reached 6,460 (Ministry of Education ROC (Taiwan), 2020a). The increasing number of Indonesian students since 2018 makes Indonesian students as the second-largest group after Vietnam.

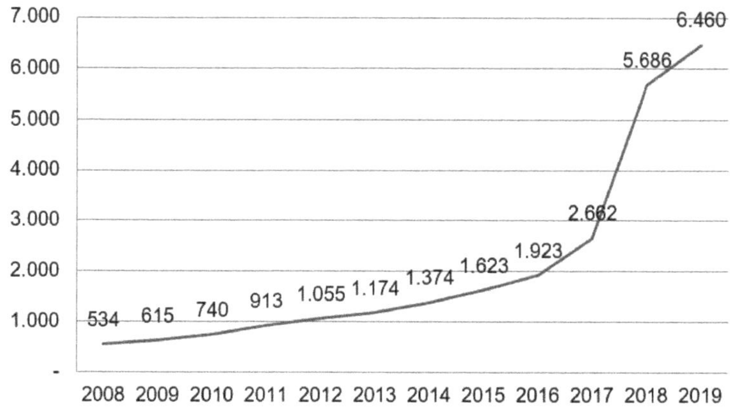

Figure 1: Number of Indonesian Students in Universities, Colleges and Junior Colleges in Taiwan, 2019–2020 (persons)
Source: Ministry of Education ROC (Taiwan), (2020a).

Generally, Indonesian students studying in Taiwan are interested in the fields such as Business Administration and Engineering. It is related to Taiwan's position as a business center globally and as a leader in technology. However, since 2016, more Indonesian students have been interested in studying other fields, such as architecture and construction, language and literature as well as arts. Since 2017, several universities in Taiwan have also opened new programs in hospitality, tourism and personal services, information and communication technology, beside medical and health.

For some Indonesian students, the current employment conditions in Indonesia have encouraged them to pursue higher education. According to the Central Bureau of Statistics, in 2019, there were 6.82 million unemployed persons, which were dominated by students from vocational school (8.63%), diploma (6.9%), senior high school (6.8%) and bachelor's degree (6.2%). Some factors caused this situation: (1) unmatched skills with the employment opportunity; (2) higher salary and higher status expectations; and (3) a limited number of employment opportunities (Newswire, 2019). Instead of getting a low-level job, they preferred to pursue higher education.

Meanwhile, with similar amount of tuition fees to those universities in Indonesia, Indonesian students prefer to study abroad. Taiwan becomes an attractive destination for studying for various reasons: (1) Taiwan's prospects become a vital entity, (2) the availability of the international environment, (3) the availability of right research equipment and professors, (4) the similarity of the education system with the US and Europe (Kabinawa, 2013), (5) competitive tuition fees compared to that in other countries and (6) in terms of quality, Taiwan provides international standardized universities, and (7) availability of scholarships and educational funding assistance from universities (Fikri, 2017). Finally, more environmental-friendly conditions for the Muslims may be a new attraction for prospective Muslim students from Indonesia.

In the NSP, Taiwan offers jobs that are suitable with their fields of study. The employment opportunity might be another incentive for Indonesian students since this becomes an opportunity to gain work experience once they return to their homeland. Working experiences in foreign companies in Taiwan can be used to establish interactions with other foreign workers so they can feel the competitive climate. Such experiences will be beneficial when they have to face competitors (Mubah, 2019).

There are unique characteristics of the Indonesian students in Taiwan. Since 2005 they are no longer dominated by Chinese Indonesians (Supamijoto, 2014). They come from various backgrounds, ethnicity and professions (Elias, 2013). Besides, some are having single status, while some are married and came to Taiwan with their family members. There are increasing numbers of Master and PhD degree students. For this reason, encouraging more entry of undergraduate students to study in Taiwan is strongly recommended (Mubah, 2019). So far, Taiwan has attracted international students, primarily for Masters and PhDs, to overcome the problem of meeting the shortage of student quotas at several universities in Taiwan. Therefore, Taiwan need to provide subsidies to several universities as financial support to international students. This kind of subsidy constitutes one form of scholarship schemes offered by Taiwan to the Southbound partner countries, including Indonesia.

Education is an investment in human resources. Increasing the level of public education will be beneficial to national & individual prospering. Investment in education will also increase individual productivity and income. Through education improvement, human resources will support for more efficient management, use more sophisticated technology, expand public knowledge and cultivate specialists in various fields of knowledge. Hence, the Indonesian Government welcomes the education program of the NSP because Indonesia has faced a fundamental problem: the low quality of human resources, making it insufficient to compete globally (Mubah, 2019). The learning process toward higher education becomes Indonesian Government's crucial agenda for the next five years. Therefore, the Indonesian Government has encouraged Indonesian students to improve the quality of their education in many ways. Besides providing scholarships, the Indonesian Government has also signed MoU with universities abroad to work on academic co-operation.

Since the NSP was launched, the number of recipients of Taiwan scholarships from Indonesia has also increased, both for attending Chinese language training, tiered education and research/fellowship. These scholarships generally target professionals, government officials, NGOs or other candidates from institutions with strategic positions in Indonesia, hoping that their existence can improve Taiwan's relations with Indonesia. However, Paramitaningrum (2014) found that professionals and students are currently not capable enough to support state actors to carry out such interactions because of a number limitations. If this program is successful, it still takes some years to be productive (Huang, 2018). Different experiences were given to Japan and the US, where the graduates later held important positions as policymakers in Indonesia. During Suharto's leadership, most government officials were Berkley graduates, while during the leadership of Susilo Bambang Yudhoyono, many essential officials were Japanese graduates. The selection of these scholarships' target recipients may become Taiwan's soft power in enhancing co-operation with Indonesia in the future.

The establishment of the Taiwan Education Center (TEC) in Indonesia is appreciated as an information and promotion center of the Taiwan education system. At least three TECs in Indonesia are on Java Island, that is in Jakarta, East Java and Yogyakarta. The establishment of this TEC shows the seriousness of Taiwan in attracting Indonesian international students. Besides, TEC is a forum that connects prospective Indonesian students who will study in Taiwan. The increasing number of Indonesian students in Taiwan currently shows that Taiwan has successfully promoted its education system in Indonesia. At the same time, it shows that academic exchange is a crucial instrument in bilateral relations with Indonesia (Mubah, 2019).

However, there has been an imbalance in educational relations between Indonesia and Taiwan. Few Taiwanese students are studying in Indonesia, only few scientists are researching Indonesia. This situation is likely due to the lack of promotion from the Indonesian side to Taiwanese students. It also happened in field of area study, where Vietnamese studies and Thailand studies were more desirable than Indonesian studies. The

Directory of the Indonesian Ministry of Research and Technology and Higher Education in 2018 did not record Taiwanese researchers applying for research permits. It seems that most of them have researched in Indonesia using their network.

In 2018 Indonesia and Taiwan signed another MoU to improve academic co-operation, especially in vocational training. The signing of this MoU was a continuation of the previous MOU, signed in 2011 on co-operation with higher education and Taiwan's commitment to NSP through the Industry Academy Collaboration (IAC) program. With the MoU, it is hoped that there will be an increase in the number of trainings for students and teachers, vocational student exchanges and scholarships (Taiwan Today Indonesia, 2018).

The IAC was part of the NSP flagship that provides talent development programs established by MOE. The Indonesian students have to follow it for 2-year, known as the 2+i program. This program contains 1.5 years of professional knowledge courses or about 30–40% of the program, and one to one and a half years off-campus internship at institutions in the same professional field to obtain a bachelor's degree. Scholarships are given to students for the first year, as well as plane tickets to Taiwan and living expenses (Ministry of Education ROC (Taiwan), 2020b). At the same time, students pay the rest of any expenses from the salary they receive during internship.

Meanwhile, the types of courses are tailor-made based on the needs of the Indonesian industry. By joining Program 2+i, Indonesian students can learn professional knowledge in specific fields, learn Chinese and have life experiences in a new environment. Life experience, understanding Taiwanese culture are other essential factors beneficial to student's future career.

A total of 88 Indonesian students attended the first wave of this program. Because of the massive promotion, up to 2019, 1,000 Indonesian students took part in the program. They were distributed into eight universities and colleges. At the beginning of the program, a problem arose because of Taiwan's media coverage of Indonesian students being treated as forced labor at a factory in Taiwan. It was reported that they were forced to work for 40 hours per week (Marboen, 2019). After an investigation and evaluation, the program was officially suspended (BP2MI, 2019).

The Indonesian Government has actively promoted higher education and technology through vocational education to improve workers' future qualifications. Departments such as agriculture, medicine, engineering and information technology are encouraged to prepare for Indonesia's future development. Through the Ministry of Education and Culture's strategic plan of 2015–2019, the Indonesian Government aimed to train secondary school graduates to market-relevant jobs. Although the idea of the IAC is excellent, the implementation has caused various problems. A third party (agent) in Indonesia and Taiwan probably has used this IAC program to exploit the students. Such action can damage the image of Taiwan's education system. So far, the pros and cons of internships are whether it is for education or as a mere exploitation of international students (Satoshi, 2008). Companies pay less for student with trainee status because they believe internship is an opportunity for students to learn and gain experience. However, learning opportunities should be emphasized without ignoring their rights. Finally, Indonesia and Taiwan agreed to conduct a joint-evaluation and monitoring of the student recruitment process, the implementation of the program while being implemented in Taiwan and then to the end of the program after the student returns to Indonesia.

Indonesian workers

Indonesian worker is the other actor that has played a significant role in maintaining Indonesia and Taiwan relations. Since 1992 Indonesia has sent its workers to Taiwan after Taiwan authority allowed foreign workers to involve in specific job of particular sectors, such as construction and social welfare sectors. The excess man power supply from Indonesia has met the demand for human resources in Taiwan. Indonesian workers as new players with fewer numbers than Vietnamese and Thai workers has turned out to take the lion share in Taiwan's labor market, particularly after 2004. According to the CLA (Ministry of Labor ROC (Taiwan), 2020), among the 718,056 foreign workers in Taiwan in 2019, 36.5% (276,411) were Indonesian people. While 456,601 (63.5%) of foreign workers work in productive industry, about 261,457 (36.5%) of them work in the social welfare sector, in which Indonesians took the most significant share, accounting for 77.12%, followed by Filipinos (11.8%) and Vietnamese (10.9%). The number of Indonesian labors in 2019 was six times larger than that in 2005. The increasing demand for Indonesian workers has been in line with the need for elderly caregivers for Taiwan's aging population.

Some Indonesian workers consider Taiwan as the most attractive destination for workplace, just after Malaysia. Previously, Saudi Arabia was in the second place, followed by Hong Kong. However, the Indonesian Government under Joko Widodo's leadership stopped the delegation after implementing the "zero maid policy" in 2015. As a result, Taiwan replaced it as the second place. Though working conditions in Taiwan were challenging, factors such as better wages and working time as well as a little freedom allowed have made them satisfied with their job as elderly caregivers. Moreover, Taiwan's location, which is not too far away from Indonesia, and its people's friendliness have strongly attracted them to work in Taiwan (Setyaningsih, 2011). Meanwhile, factors such as faster process and procedure of placement in Taiwan (Kabinawa, 2013) and following the footsteps of relatives or friends who have migrated earlier (Setyaningsih, 2011) have also influenced their decision to work in Taiwan.

In the beginning, sending workers abroad was Indonesia's strategy to cope with their labor surplus and seek employment. However, later it became one of the significant sources of national income contributing to economic growth. They are considered as "heroes of foreign exchange" or "*Pahlawan devisa*". Every year, they transfer a considerable amount of remittances to Indonesia. For example, in 2018, the total amount of remittance accounted for US$10.8 billion (CNN Indonesia, 2019b) in which Indonesian workers in Taiwan reached 12%, the third largest just after Saudi Arabia (37%) and Malaysia (31%) (Figure 2). Thus, the Indonesian Government is expected to give better protection to those workers. The launch of Law No. 18/2017 is designated to better secure migrant workers. The government has also tried to send more skilled and more professional workers abroad to reduce the number of low-educated workers (CNN Indonesia, 2019a).

Basically, even before the NSP, co-operation between Indonesia and Taiwan in this field have worked quite well. The demand for Indonesian labors seems to be continuously high[2] since Taiwanese employers would prefer[3] to hire Indonesian labors compared to other foreign workers. They

---

[2]Due to the high demand from the Taiwan side, sometimes agencies force workers to go Taiwan even though they have not met standard training before departure (Setyaningsih, 2011).

[3]Although taking care of the elderly constitutes hard work and may create a burden (Novak, 2006), Indonesian workers are acknowledged to be more patient and suitable to take care of older people. Even, according to CLA, the Indonesian workers' work performance in Taiwan is relatively better than those from other countries (Setyaningsih, 2011),

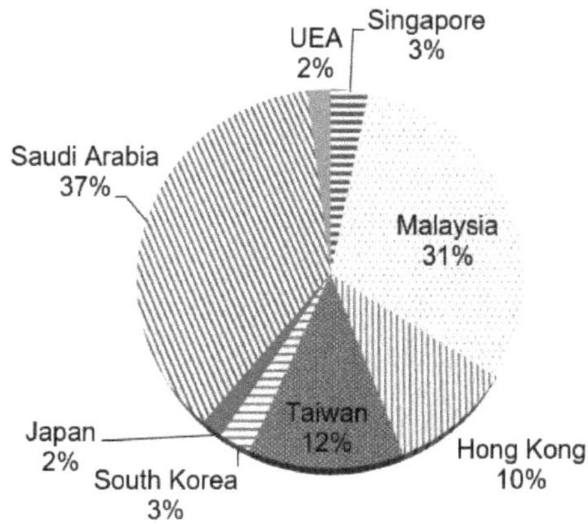

Figure 2: Remittances of Indonesian workers by host countries in 2018 (%)
Source: Bank of Indonesia (2019).

consider the Indonesian female workers to be more patient and thus suitable to take care of elderly people. The preference of Taiwanese people toward Indonesian workers and the increasing demand for elderly caregivers have also relaxed Taiwan policies on foreign workers. For example, the working permit of migrant workers that used to be only limited to 2 years with possible extension up to two years could be extended up to three times so the total could be up to 9 years, was extended again to 12 years in 2009 and finally up to 15 years in 2016 (Setyaningsih, 2016). In addition, the amendment of the Employment Service Act allows direct hiring of Indonesian workers. They no longer need to go abroad to be rehired by the employer. This preference shows that Indonesian workers have a comparative advantage compared to foreign workers from other Asian countries. In 2015, Indonesian workers' minimum wage increased, especially for the re-entry worker (Hardum, 2015).

Through the NSP, Taiwan wants to create a multi-culture environment by allowing foreigners, including workers, to develop their own culture. Further, this way has facilitated cultural exchanges between Indonesia and Taiwan. Pina, an Indonesian worker is a good example. She develops crafts made of clay with funding support from Taiwan. Clay, which is very popular in Taiwan, is created into a traditional Indonesian puppet. Pina who had lived in Taiwan for 10 years, got this

---

though Lan (2006) argue that this may be the agency's own preference by stereotyping the Indonesian workers.

skill from her Taiwanese friend. Even now she could earn some money from this business. Furthermore, she transferred her skill of making craft to some Indonesian people in Taiwan, and in her village. She also distributes her work to Taiwanese people for free as gifts. Gradually, her craft was widely recognized and sought after by the Taiwanese. Starting from there, more and more Taiwanese wanted to know more about Indonesia. She often takes Taiwanese tourists to Indonesia because they want to know other areas besides Bali. Besides introducing Indonesian culture to Taiwanese, Pina often introduces respectable Taiwanese behavior to Indonesian people, such as managing the waste, managing time, being disciplined and hard work.

In August 2019, the Indonesian migrant workers from all over Taiwan took part in a parade that starting from the Taipei Main Station to the National Taiwan Museum, enliven the 4th Indonesia Independence Day Art and Culture Festival in Taiwan. They sang the Indonesian national anthem along the way while waving the Indonesian flag. The festival that was themed *Sensasi Kebebasan* was a form of cultural exchanges promoted by the National Taiwan Museum. The theme was the expression of workers' wish for freedom. Such cultural exchange attracted numerous onlookers, and it gave the opportunity for Taiwanese people to understand the Indonesian history and culture; hence, it created a harmonious cultural development of Taiwan (Ministry of Culture, 2019).

There are still many examples of anonymous outstanding Indonesian workers. At best, Pina has proved that foreign workers can act not only as a hero of foreign exchange but also as an agent of enabling cultural exchange between Indonesia and Taiwan. In addition, improving skills through involvement in empowering social groups in Taiwan allows them to empower themselves and their community. Hence, allowing workers to develop their skills during the days off is essential. Their acquired skills will economically benefit to their individual or family once they return to Indonesia. In fact, there were many migrant workers who do not want to return to Indonesia (Saputri, 2020).

Additionally, the cultural exchange program promoted by the NSP enable new opportunity for the society to understand each other. It also greatly impacts workers' life and welfare. From Pina's experience, it shows that money flow from host to home country is not the only aspect that signifies their contribution to the Indonesia's economic development. Ironic as it may seem, but they might a hero of cultural exchange.

Tourists

Tourism is another way to enhance P-to-P connectivity. The NSP includes the development of Muslim-friendly tourism, also known as the *halal* tourism industry, as one of the platforms of resource sharing. This development aims to attract more Muslim tourists from Muslim-majority Southbound countries into Taiwan. The declining number of tourists from Mainland China into Taiwan has generated this development initiatives. Two aspects that become the focus of Taiwan Government are issuing *halal* certificates[4] for restaurants and accommodation, including Muslim-friendly guidebook. Moreover, Taiwan has also created more Muslim-friendly environments.

Although Taiwan's Muslim community is only 1% of its total population, Taiwan sees great potential from this Muslim-friendly tourism programs. There are several reasons for Taiwan to work on developing this industry. According to the Pew Research Forum on Religion and Public Life, in 2015, there were 1.8 billion Muslim populations in the world, which represented 24.1% of the world's population. The number will increase to 2.2 billion people by 2030 or represent 26.4% of the projected population of 8.3 billion (Pew Research Center, 2011). Whereas according to the Thomson Reuters Global Islamic Report Economy, in 2017 the most significant products of consumption among Muslims were food, tourism, cloth, pharmacy, media/recreation and cosmetics, that accounted for US$2 trillion or equaled to 11.9% of the total consumption of the People's Republic of China's population in those six sectors, that accounted for US$1.8 billion or equaled to 11.3% of the world's population consumption (Djakfar, 2017).

Taiwan has seen the increasing number of foreign Muslims in Taiwan and the growing number of Muslim population in the world as an economic potential that needs to be responded to. Furthermore, the increasing

---

[4]Five categories of authentication are given, namely: Muslim Restaurant (MR), Muslim-Friendly Restaurant (MFR), Muslim-Friendly Tourism (MFT), Halal Kitchen (HK) and Muslim-Friendly Tour Guide (MFTG) (Tsay, 2018). MR refers to the Muslim owner restaurant, while the MFR refers to that belongs to the non-Muslim owner. MFT refers to any accommodation that received *halal* certification, whereas the HK provides *halal* catering service for tourist hotel industry, hotel industry, and sightseeing and amusement industry. The last one is MFTG, a certificate for a tour guide, as she or he is a significant other that will guide the tourists during traveling in Taiwan (Setyaningsih, 2019).

trend of Muslim tourists visiting Taiwan has created a new driving force for Taiwan's tourism industry.

Though Taiwan's *halal* tourism industry has targeted Muslim tourists since 2009, the authority has just formally developed it in 2016 by including the subject in the NSP platform. This is why from 2009 to 2016, the development of this industry has been so slow (Setyaningsih, 2019). Before it was stipulated in the NSP, some restaurants were *halal*-certified, but in a limited quantity. After the launch of the NSP, more and more restaurants are *halal*-certified with a more even distribution in the whole country. According to the China Muslim Association (CMA), until 2018, more than 200 restaurants and accommodations have received *halal* certification from the authority. Besides issuing *halal* certificates for restaurant and accommodation, the authorities have also created a more Muslim-friendly environment. By establishing more Muslim prayers room in public areas, Taiwan expects to facilitate Muslim tourists, both foreign and domestics, to enjoy traveling without leaving worship.

Taiwan's dedicated effort in developing this industry must be appreciated, as could be seen from the Global Muslim Travel Index's increased performance. The International Mastercard announced the 2019 Global Muslim Travel Index that among the non-OIC destinations, Taiwan, for the first time, ranked no. 3 as the top destination of Muslim travelers, just after Singapore and Thailand (Huang, 2019). Taiwan's achievement as a top destination increased from previously ranked 10 in 2015 to rank 5 in 2018 and rank 3 in 2019. This progress shows that Taiwan is indeed serious about developing this industry.

Indonesia, whose Muslim population reached 80%, becomes one of the targeted countries for this *halal* tourism market, besides Malaysia, Middle East and Africa. In 2017, the number of Indonesian Muslim tourists who visited Taiwan reached 189,000 people, an increase by 46% compared to that in 2016 (Ambari, 2018). Since the flow of Muslim tourists into Taiwan is rather low compared to that of the non-Muslim one, Taiwan needs to promote more. One of the efforts is by making the visa application procedure easier[5] for Southeast Asian citizens.

---

[5] Indonesians and from some other countries who hold permanent residence permits issued by Taiwan Government (except for the working visas), or are the holders of a visa or valid residence permits from one of these countries that is valid or that expired within 10 years of the date of expected arrival in Taiwan, and those who have no record of violating

Globalization, where advanced information and technology have a strong influence, makes the spread of information faster. The visitor often expresses their experiences on social media and shares the stories with public. A good and satisfying experience from tourists will also create a profound influence and confidence in the Taiwan tourism industry. With the increasing number of *halal*-certified restaurants, it is easier for Muslim tourists to find *halal* food. For Muslims, this *halal* certificate is essential because it is a proof and guarantee that the food they consume is approved by Islamic Law. *Halal* food is not only beneficial for Muslims but also for non-Muslims.

In particular, some of these restaurant entrepreneurs are Indonesian people. However, compared to other Muslim restaurants such as Indian, Pakistani, Indonesian restaurants are relatively of small number. Therefore, there is potential to develop this *halal* restaurant in Taiwan. The opportunity for Indonesian diaspora to take part in the *halal* tourism industry as a guide is too quite significant to expand relations and exchange information. Taiwanese hospitality, coupled with the natural beauty of Taiwan, creates good impression as well as a stable and permanent emotional connection for tourists. Of course, all of these will bring a good impact on the increasingly widespread dissemination of information about Taiwan itself. This information is crucial because even though Taiwan has co-operated with Indonesia, not all Indonesian people know Taiwan well.

Unfortunately, there has been no survey in a broad scope of Taiwan's image from the Indonesian perspective. A small-scale little survey that I conducted[6] shows that when someone hears something about "Taiwan", they think about Meteor Garden (7), China (7), street culinary (Shihlin, Bubble tea/pineapple pie/spring roll (8), (5), IT/Lenovo (3), scholarship (1), traveling sites (101, CKS)/eva air (3), spare part producer (3), not part of China (3), Indonesian workers (4), gambling (1), slum/old (1), super agricultural product (1). These various answers indicate that some of the Indonesian understanding of Taiwan is still limited and needs

---

Taiwan's Law, can apply for an online visa on the website of the Immigration Department of the Taiwan Ministry of Interior (Ambari, 2018).

[6]This survey used WhatsApp to ask some Indonesian people. I asked them about "what comes into your mind when first you hear about Taiwan." The answers at least could show their perceptions about Taiwan. In answering, one respondent might give more than one answer. Hence, the total number of answers did not indicate the total number of respondents.

improvement. Those who have visited Taiwan might give the right answer, but others who have never visited might rely on media information. The result also shows that culture, including movie and culinary, seems to work better in introducing Taiwan to Indonesian. Taiwanese movie, namely Meteor Garden, was popular in Indonesia in the 1990s. Meanwhile, Taiwanese cuisines have also been popular in recent years through franchise business.

For Indonesia, Taiwan's *halal* tourism industry's development should benefit Indonesia more than a market for Taiwan. It can also create a new market for Indonesian *halal* products. Indonesia has various kinds of *halal*-certified products that can be exported to Taiwan to fulfill the demand for *halal* products of Moslem tourists and Indonesian Muslims residing in Taiwan. It includes products of foods, beverages, cosmetics, pharmaceuticals and fashion. Moreover, Taiwan's *halal* tourism can also create more significant opportunities for Indonesian businesspeople who want to invest in such sectors, including restaurants, accommodation or travel agencies. Setyaningsih (2019) found that the number of Indonesian *halal* restaurants in Taiwan is relatively fewer than that of other countries. For the individual, it also provides employment opportunities to provide services as a Muslim-friendly guide.

Indonesian students' involvement in making Apps on smart phone about Taiwan *halal* should also be considered vital in providing service to Muslim tourists in Taiwan. In the beginning, the Apps creation was aimed to assist Muslims in Taiwan to get information on the nearest *halal*/Muslim-friendly restaurant, prayer room, the Muslim community or mosque. Yet, it finally won a competition organized by the Ministry of Education and now it is a startup. Hence, the Taiwan's *halal* tourism industry's development has also offered job creativity for Indonesian students in Taiwan.

As the environment has become more friendly to Muslims, Muslim students or Muslim workers can do their daily activities more comfortably. The greater Taiwanese's understanding toward Muslims is, the better is the environment for Moslems. Hence, performing five times a day worship that used to be a challenge for Muslims can now be carried out with more conveniently.

Conclusion

This chapter has shown how various types of NSP implements run and brought different outcomes. The actors, that is the international students,

Indonesian diaspora and their second generation, workers and tourists have played their roles respectively in fostering P-to-P relations. They have played roles not only to economic development but also to cultural development. However, it is undeniable that unsymmetrical relations have still existed, particularly in the education field.

Some part of the co-operation is in line with *Nawacita* that targets at technology transfer, improvement in education and skills, as well as human resources for Indonesian development. The NSP provides more opportunities for Indonesian students to achieve higher education and obtain other skills that benefits to Indonesian economic development. If the knowledge accumulation exists while studying in Taiwan and Indonesian students could transfer their knowledge once they return, Indonesia would very likely get a brain gain from Taiwan. However, the NSP could only generate little capital supply through the investment.

Unfortunately, within the P-to-P relations, there has not been a structured institution that can bridge communication between Indonesians and Taiwanese. The existing communicating media are in the form of communities that consist of memberships from one party, or not-institutionalized forums that are temporary in nature. As a result, P-to-P relations have not run optimally. Hence, establishing an institutionalized institution that really bridges the P-to-P relation with clear structures in it, is necessary to be considered.

References

Ambari, L. W. (2018, October). *Taiwan Offers Halal Tourism to Indonesians*, AntaraNews.com, https://en.antaranews.com/news/119137/taiwan-offers-*halal*-tourism-to-indonesians.

Badan Koordinasi Penanaman Modal (2017). *All You Need to Know about the 10 New Bali Project in Indonesia*, Badan Koordinasi Penanaman Modal, https://www.investindonesia.go.id/en/article-investment/detail/all-you-need-to-know-about-the-10-new-bali-project-in-indonesia.

Bank Indonesia. (2019). Remitansi Tenaga Kerja Indonesia (TKI) Menurut Negara Penempatan, https://www.bi.go.id/seki/tabel/TABEL5_31.pdf.

BP2MI (2019, September). *MOE Taiwan Resmi Hentikan Program Kuliah — Magang IAC di Taiwan*, Badan Perlindungan Pekerja Migran Indonesia, https://bp2mi.go.id/berita-detail/moe-taiwan-resmi-hentikan-program-kuliah-magang-iac-di-taiwan.

Braziel, J. E. (2008). *Diaspora: An Introduction.* Oxford, Longman Publishing.

CNN Indonesia. (2019a). BNP2TKI Diubah Jadi Badan Perlindungan Pekerja Migran, https://www.cnnindonesia.com/nasional/20191104162132-20-445495/bnp2tki-diubah-jadi-badan-perlindungan-pekerja-migran.

CNN Indonesia. (2019b). Tahun Lalu, Pengiriman Uang TKI Capai US$10,8 Miliar, https://www.cnnindonesia.com/ekonomi/20190211102744-78-368033/tahun-lalu-pengiriman-uang-tki-capai-us-108-miliar.

Djakfar, M. (2017). *Pariwisata Halal Perspektif Multidimensi: Peta Jalan Menuju Pengembangan Akademik dan Industri Halal di Indonesia.* Jakarta, UIN-Maliki Press.

Effendy, T. D. (2016). The Roles of Diaspora Community in Indonesia–Taiwan Relations. *International Journal of International Relations, Media and Mass Communication Studies*, 2(4), 25–36.

Elias, R. A. (2013). Invisible Agent in Taiwan–Indonesia Cooperation. A paper presented at the TASEEAS Conference in May 31, 2013, http://fgumail.fgu.edu.tw/~cseas2013/1-2-2.pdf.

Fikri, C. (2017). Ribuan Siswa Indonesia Lanjutkan Pendidikan di Taiwan, *BeritaSatu*, https://www.beritasatu.com/nasional/447282/nasional/447282-ribuan-siswa-indonesia-lanjutkan-pendidikan-di-taiwan.

Hardum, S. E. (2015). Gaji TKI di Taiwan Naik Jadi Rp 7 Jutaan, *BeritaSatu*, https://www.beritasatu.com/ekonomi/302568-gaji-tki-di-taiwan-naik-jadi-rp-7-jutaan.

Huang, K.-B. (2018). Taiwan's New Southbound Policy: Background, Objectives, Framework and Limits. *Revista UNISCI / UNISCI Journal*, 46: 47–68.

Huang, T.-T. (2019). Taiwan Ranked 3rd Most Attractive Country on Global Muslim Travel Index 2019, *taiwannews*, https://www.taiwannews.com.tw/en/news/3681395.

Irianto, A. (2011). Pendidikan Sebagai Investasi dalam Pembangunan Suatu Bangsa. KENCANA.

Kabinawa, L. N. (2013). Economic and Socio-Cultural Relations between Indonesia and Taiwan: An Indonesian Perspective, 1990–2012. *Journal of ASEAN Studies*, 1(2): 140–163.

KDEI (2014). Sejarah KDEI Taipei, http://www.kdei-taipei.org/index.php/berita/item/1701-Sejarah-KDEI-Taipei.

Lan, P.-C. (2006). *Global Cinderellas: Migrant Domestics and Newly Rich Employers in Taiwan*, Durham and London, Duke University Press.

Marboen, A. P. (ed) (2015). TETO Akan Buka Kantor Perwakilan di Surabaya, *AntaraNews.com*,https://www.antaranews.com/berita/527780/teto-akan-buka-kantor-perwakilan-di-surabaya.

Marboen, A. P. (ed) (2019). Kementerian Luar Negeri Tindaklanjuti Laporan Mahasiswa Indonesia Kerja Paksa di Taiwan, antaranews.com, https://www.antaranews.com/berita/783207/kementerian-luar-negeri-tindaklanjuti-laporan-mahasiswa-indonesia-kerja-paksa-di-taiwan.

Ministry of Culture (2019). 2019 Indonesian Independence Day's Art and Culture Festival in Taiwan, https://www.moc.gov.tw/en/information_260_101920.html.

Ministry of Education ROC (Taiwan) (2020a). *Gender Statistic*, Ministry of Education ROC, https://english.moe.gov.tw/cp-87-14508-95005-1.html.

Ministry of Education ROC (Taiwan) (2020b). *The New Southbound Talent Development Program*, Ministry of Education ROC (Taiwan), https://www.edunsbp.moe.gov.tw/intro_en.html.

Ministry of Labor ROC (Taiwan) (2020). Statistics of Foreign Workers, Ministry of Labor ROC, http://statdb.mol.gov.tw/html/mon/i0120020620e.htm.

Mubah, A. S. (2019). Menyambut Kerja Sama Pendidikan dengan Taiwan, *detikNews*, https://news.detik.com/kolom/d-4773822/menyambut-kerja-sama-pendidikan-dengan-taiwan.

Nanda, G. N. (ed). (2016). Membanggakan, Wanita Pontianak Ini Jadi Artis Terkenal Di Taiwan, tribunpontianak.co.id, http://pontianak.tribunnews.com/2016/07/03/membanggakan-wanita-pontianak-ini-jadi-artis-terkenal-di-taiwan.

Newswire (2019). Perbandingan Tingkat Pengangguran Terbuka, Zaman Siapa Lebih Baik? Business.com, https://ekonomi.bisnis.com/read/20190811/12/1135052/perbandingan-tingkat-pengangguran-terbuka-zaman-siapa-lebih-baik#:~:text=Badan%20Pusat%20Statistik%20(BPS)%20mencatat,berjumlah%26%2C82%20juta%20orang.

Paramitaningrum (2013). Enhancing People-to-People Cooperation between ASEAN and East Asia Countries through Counterparts: The Case of Indonesian Students in Taiwan. *Journal of ASEAN Studies*, 1(2): 164–175.

Paramitaningrum (2014). Human Interactions between Indonesia and Taiwan: Characteristics and Implications for Bilateral relations. A presentation presented in Binus, Jakarta in December 2014.

Pew Research Center (2011). *Pew Research Center. The Future of the Global Muslim Population*, Pew Research Center, https://www.pewforum.org/2011/01/27/the-future-of-the-global-muslim-population/.

Plessis, C. D. (2018). *Progress and Prospect Taiwan's New Southbound Policy.* Taipei: Office of Trade Negotiations, Executive Yuan, Bureau of Foreign Trade, Ministry of Economic Affairs.

Riskianingrum, D. (2012). *Chinese Overseas Who Returned to Taiwan 1950s–1960s*. Report for the Research Grant for Foreign Scholars in Chinese Studies, Center for Chinese Studies.

Rositasari, B. *et al*. (2019). *Mendefinisikan Diaspora Indonesia.* Jakarta, Pusat Penelitian Sumber Daya Regional, LIPI.

Saputri, D. S. (2020). 141.423 Pekerja Migran akan Kembali ke Indonesia, Republika.co.id., https://republika.co.id/berita/qbfgig396/141423-pekerja-migran-akan-kembali-ke-indonesia.

Satoshi, K. (2008). Japan's Internship Training Program for Foreign Workers: Education or Exploitation? *The Asia-Pacific Journal*, 6(7): 1–7.

Setyaningsih, R. P. (2011). Job Satisfaction of Indonesian Workers in Taiwan. Thesis for the International Master's Program in Asia Pacific Studies (IMAS). Taipei, College of Social Science, National Chengchi University (NCCU) (unpublished).

Setyaningsih, R. P. (2016). Tenaga Kerja Indonesia Dalam Konteks Masyarakat Taiwan yang Menua. *Jurnal Kajian Wilayah*, 7(2): 113–127.

Setyaningsih, R. P. (2019). Taiwan Halal Tourism Industry: Policy and Practice. Research report for the POSCO Asia Forum, POSCO TJ Park Foundation, Korea (unpublished).

Strong, M. (2017, August). Taiwan Wants Indonesian Students To Double Within 3 Years. Retrieved from taiwannews.com.tw: https://www.taiwannews.com.tw/en/news/3240171.

Sundaryani, F. S. and Wirayani, P. (2016). Taiwan Promises Increased Investment in Indonesia, *The Jakarta Post*, https://www.thejakartapost.com/news/2016/12/01/taiwan-promises-increased-investment-in-indonesia.html.

Supamijoto, P. (2014). *Human Interactions between Indonesia and Taiwan: Characteristics and Implications for Bilateral Relations* (Roundtable Discussion Indonesia–Taiwan Relations, Indonesian Ministry of Foreign Affairs, Jakarta, December 30, 2014. Jakarta, Indonesia), https://www.researchgate.net/publication/280111080_Roundtable_Discussion_Indonesia_-_Taiwan_Relations_Indonesian_Ministry_of_Foreign_Affairs_Jakarta_30_December_2014.

Supamijoto, P. and Herlijanto, J. (2016). Economic Diplomacy, Soft Power, and Taiwan's Relations with Indonesia. *Contemporary Chinese Political Economy and Strategic Relations: An International Journal*, 2: 1173–1194.

Taiwan Today Indonesia. (2018). Taiwan-Indonesia Tandatangani MOU di Bidang Pendidikan Tinggi dan Kejuruan, Taiwan Today Indonesia, https://id.taiwantoday.tw/news.php?unit=465&post=145214.

Tsay, C.-l. (2018, October). Characteristics of Indonesian Migration to Taiwan and Implications for Enhancing Bilateral Relations. A presentation on The 2nd International Conference on Social Sciences and Humanities (ICSSH), Jakarta, Indonesia.

Wedhaswary, I. D. (2014). Nawa Cita, 9 Agenda Prioritas Jokowi-JK, Kompas.com, https://nasional.kompas.com/read/2014/05/21/0754454/.Nawa.Cita.9.Agenda.Prioritas.Jokowi-JK.

https://doi.org/10.1142/9789811250668_0011

Chapter 11

Taiwan's NGOs and Southeast Asia

Kevin Chen

Founder, One-Forty, Taiwan

Current Status of Migrant Workers in Taiwan and the Background of One-Forty

The history of foreign migrant workers in Taiwan can be traced back to the 1980s. At that time, Taiwan saw an increase in national income, yet the labor-intensive industries that underpin the Taiwan economy still required a vast pool of low-wage labor. In 1987, Taiwan's manufacturing industry experienced a massive shortage of labor and businesses urged the government to legalize the introduction of foreign migrant workers. In response, the Taiwanese government formally introduced migrant workers on a project basis in 1990. The Employment Service Act was passed in 1992, stipulating in detail the industries and conditions for hiring migrant workers, officially opening the door to legal migrant workers.

Meanwhile, Taiwan has been facing an ongoing trend of aging and declining birthrates, with the elderly population increasing rapidly. How to cope with the aging population and the long-term care manpower needs of people with mobility and functional disabilities is becoming an important and urgent issue that necessitates attention from the Taiwanese people. However, there is a shortage of Taiwanese caregivers willing to be on the frontline of long-term care. To address the imbalance the supply and demand of long-term caregivers in Taiwan, the government decided to open up her doors to migrant caregivers to solve the long-term care needs of a large number of families.

As of yearend 2019, the total number of migrant workers in Taiwan registered at 718,058, mainly from four Southeast Asian countries: Indonesia, Vietnam, the Philippines and Thailand. Among them, Indonesians accounted for 276,411, the largest, followed by 224,713 Vietnamese, 157,487 Filipinos and 59,445 Thais.

The main line of work migrant workers are engaged in Taiwan can be divided into two general categories. The first category is "social welfare and migrant workers", which includes domestic helpers, home-based caregivers and institutional caregivers. They are shouldering the long-term care of families by filling in the inadequate supply of Taiwanese caregivers. At the end of 2019, social welfare and migrant workers totaled 261,457 people or 36.4% of the total number of migrant workers. The second category is "industry migrant workers", who are engaged in construction, manufacturing and offshore ocean fishing. They are involved in many of Taiwan's major transportation infrastructure projects, such as the Taiwan high-speed rail, highways and Taipei metro. At the end of 2019, the total number of industry migrant workers was 456,601, accounting for 63.6% of the total number of migrant workers.

Since the Taiwanese government officially opened her doors to migrant workers in 1992, the number of migrant workers from Southeast Asia has been rising rapidly every year, indicating that Taiwan is increasingly dependent on Southeast Asian migrant workers to support industrial and social welfare needs. In 2016, the Taiwanese government launched the New Southbound Policy to actively expand its links with ASEAN, India, Australia, New Zealand and other economies, establishing economic, trade, educational and cultural exchange policies to attract Southeast Asian students to study in Taiwan, as well as drawing in people for medical checkups, tourism and investment. With people at the heart, it also aims to assist Taiwanese businessmen in the ASEAN and Indo-Pacific regions to facilitate bilateral talent flow and build sustainable new partnerships.

Under the New Southbound Policy, migrant workers from Southeast Asia are receiving greater attention in Taiwan, which has led to changes in the political, economic and cultural landscape of Taiwan's society. In addition to various government agencies, e.g. the Ministry of Labor and local government labor bureaus, rolling out various forms of Southeast Asian migrant worker programs, colleges and universities are also actively promoting students' understanding of Southeast Asian culture. Many large enterprises have started to pay attention to migrant worker's needs in Taiwan by releasing products and services catered to them. Moreover, a variety of non-profit organizations that focus on Southeast Asian migrant workers have been set up, including organizations that promote their rights and offer legal assistance. Emergency placement centers are established to assist migrant workers experiencing emergency difficulties.

Generally speaking, there are two different types of attitude toward migrant workers. The lack of real-life interactions with migrant workers has made it difficult for some people to understand the life stories and transnational experience behind them, not to mention the generally negative portrayal of migrant workers on the news. As a result, some have developed prejudice and stereotypes about migrant workers, believing they have a higher crime rate and indirectly cause social disorder in Taiwan. Another part of the population is gradually understanding the importance of migrant workers in Taiwan, and cherishes the multiculturalism brought by their different national backgrounds. Aside from expanding their own international perspective, they are genuinely grateful to the migrant worker community for supporting the development of Taiwan over the years. But while these people want to learn more about migrant workers, they have to proactively seek ways to interact with them due to the language and cultural barriers and unfamiliarity with each other.

One-Forty, a non-profit organization, was established in 2015 against this backdrop. With the vision of serving as the first window into the general public's understanding of migrant workers, One-Forty offers an array of ways for the people of Taiwan to interact with them. By allowing the entire Taiwanese society to gain a better understanding of the transnational journey and stories behind the migrant workers, it is hoped that the prejudice and stereotype can be broken to shape a more diverse and inclusive Taiwan. At the same time, One-Forty also comes in from the perspective of migrant workers, understanding they have high learning needs. Thus, the largest migrant learning community in Taiwan is now up and running to make their Taiwan experience a memorable one.

The Founding Story of One-Forty

At the end of 2014, a group of young college graduates headed out to Taipei Main Station concourse every Sunday to conduct in-depth interviews with migrant workers. Hearing from first-hand accounts, they were listening to the real voices of the migrant workers. What motivated them to leave their home country to work abroad? Why did they choose to work in Taiwan? Working and living in Taiwan, what kind of needs or difficulties do they have? And what sort of goals or dreams do they have when they return home?

After compiling interviews from over 100 migrant workers, the team found that most of them choose to work abroad owing to family financial difficulties. The future goal of many is to save up enough money during their years working in Taiwan and then open and run a small business, let it be a grocery store, clothing shop, beauty salon or a restaurant, after they return home; some hope to find a stable job with a steady income after going back. There is one thing in common: they want a steady income for their families so they do not have to work abroad again. Unfortunately, most migrant workers in Taiwan are working in low-level labor-intensive jobs, which makes it difficult for them to accumulate knowledge and skills that will help them start their own small businesses or find employment in the future. There is also a shortage of friendly learning channels outside of work, resulting in a vicious cycle where many people return home unemployed again, or they fail to run a business and spend all their savings, ending up leaving their families again to work abroad.

On the other hand, One-Forty observed that there's pervasive stereotype and prejudice against these "foreigners" in the general public and the media. Taiwanese people keep migrant workers at arm's length due to different nationalities, languages, religions and cultural habits. Media coverage of migrant workers often shine them in a negative light, reporting crimes committed by them and implying they are the indirect source of social disorder. In the face of the increasing number of migrant workers in Taiwan, the general public deliberately avoid contact and interaction with migrant workers because they do not understand and are unfamiliar with them, and the gap between the two populations persists.

Officially established in July 2015, One-Forty is a non-profit organization composed of a group of young people with diverse professional backgrounds — corporate management, education, social work, design, art and so on. One-Forty's mission is "Make every migrant's journey worthy and inspiring" with the hope that every migrant worker's journey in Taiwan can become an important experience in their lives. One day when they return home, they will remember this journey as a life-changing memory. For this reason, One-Forty focuses on the educational nurturing of migrant workers from Southeast Asia, allowing them to learn practical knowledge and skills while working in Taiwan. Hopefully they will be able to return home financially independent, breaking the vicious cycle of poverty to create a better life for themselves, their families, their hometowns and even for their next generations. One-Forty is also committed to making Taiwan a truly diverse and friendly society. By organizing regular cultural exchange activities every month, Taiwanese are given the opportunity to interact and communicate with migrant workers from Southeast Asia, so they can empathize and learn the stories and values in each other.

Over the past 5 years, One-Forty has launched three major initiatives: One-Forty School, Open Sunday and Migrant Life Channel.

One-Forty School is a learning community specially tailored to the needs of Southeast Asian migrant workers, with the goal of charting an alternative path in life through educational nurturing. Located in Taipei, One-Forty School welcomes migrants on Sundays to attend classes. To date, more than 1,000 Indonesian migrant workers have completed six months of learning courses, including Chinese learning, finance, entrepreneurship, computer learning and more. There are also other professional courses like photography, hair styling, art creation and makeup.

The Chinese classes offered at One-Forty School have become an important part of migrant workers who have just arrived and are adjusting to a new life in Taiwan. One-Forty designs materials and group games based on the work-life scenarios of migrant workers, such as taking the bus, going to the market to buy groceries or visiting the doctor in the hospital. The course is divided into basic, intermediate and advanced classes, and migrant workers are placed in appropriate classes according to their level. After completing the course, they will take an official Chinese certification exam to obtain a certificate. In the future, they will be able to leverage their Chinese skills to increase their competitiveness in employment after returning to Indonesia.

Aside from language learning, One-Forty School specializes in helping migrants foster practical skills for future employment and starting their own businesses upon returning to their hometowns. In finance classes, they learn how to manage their income, set up savings plans for themselves and work with family members to discuss how to use the money to achieve their goals. The entrepreneurship classes are aimed at migrant workers who plan to open a business when they return home. They are instructed in basic business concepts, including business plans, cost and profit management, marketing and promotion methods, e-commerce and operation, to increase their success rate of running a business.

So far, about 300 One-Forty graduates have returned home to Indonesia after completing their work term in Taiwan. The One-Forty team conducts field surveys in Indonesia every year, visiting homes of returning migrants to learn more about their entrepreneurship and employment experiences. There are already a number of success stories. For example, Adi, a student in the entrepreneurship course, has opened a ranch in his hometown and is now raising 150 goats, and he plans to expand the scale to 600 goats in the future. Another student Warti returned to Indramayu in West Java to open a clothing store, where she has six employees and nine sewing machines. The store has significantly improved her life as well as her family's. Besides buying a new house for her family, she is giving her two children better education and learning resources. Yani and Yusni, students in the Chinese course, received their Chinese language certificate. After returning to Karawang in West Java, Indonesia, they were offered the opportunity to work as Chinese translators and administrative assistants in a Taiwanese business in Indonesia, earning a monthly salary thrice the local average.

One-Forty School is more than a place for migrant workers to learn knowledge and enrich themselves in Taiwan, and also a supportive community where they can meet friends from the same country and feel a closer sense of belonging. When migrant workers first arrive in Taiwan from a foreign country, they are able to quickly establish connections with other fellow migrants, share living information, ways of adjusting to work and goals after returning home. Many say that One-Forty School is like their second home in Taiwan.

One-Forty's second initiative is Open Sunday, which aspires to establish a friendly cultural exchange between Taiwanese and Southeast Asian migrant workers. By striking real-life conversations between the two sides during the activities, migrant workers have the opportunity to learn more about Taiwan's culture while Taiwanese locals can catch a glimpse into the migrant workers' stories and lives by directly interacting with them. Open Sunday is held regularly every month on Sundays. More than 100 events have been held so far, with an average of 40 plus people attending each event. Over the years, more than 5,000 Taiwanese people have been introduced to the migrant community. These events encompass a variety of themes, such as migrant holiday get-together mini-tour, Southeast Asian kitchen parties, social design workshops and many more.

In Taipei alone, there are many migrant weekend congregations, such as the "Indonesian street" near Taipei Main Station, where there are money transfer shops, beauty salons, chain supermarkets, specialty restaurants and electronics stores that are specially targeted to Indonesian migrant workers. In another part of Taipei, a community of Filipino migrant workers is centered around St. Christopher's Church, the only church in Taipei that offers Sunday Masses in Tagalog. The surrounding neighborhood has gradually developed into a Filipino business district, which has become the biggest Filipino migrant worker congregation in Northern Taiwan for nearly two decades. Over the past 5 years, One-Forty has been organizing migrant weekend get-together mini-trips with migrant workers acting as tour guides to Taiwanese people to experience a migrant worker's weekend off. During the tour, these migrants break away from their roles as low-level laborer on the weekdays, as they become storytellers to narrate their experiences in a foreign country and share their Southeast Asian culture to the people of Taiwan who rarely have the opportunity to come in contact with them. The one-day tour also gives people an idea of what a weekend off is like for migrant workers — going to the bank to transfer their paycheck home, sending a package to their family at a courier, or enjoying a home-style buffet at an authentic Southeast Asian restaurant. These day-to-day activities may seem routine, but they actually overturn a common misconception in Taiwan about migrant workers' days off. Many people believe that they go out and make bad friends when they are off work, so many employers do not allow them to go out on weekends.

An employer who participated in the tour said, "I used to be afraid to let my caregiver have a day off, because I heard many neighbors saying that they would learn bad things and make bad friends who would egg them on to run away. And I was very nervous about it. After this Indonesian get-together mini-trip, I came to realize that weekends for migrant workers are just like weekends for us. They meet with friends who they haven't seen in a while and enjoy a hometown meal. They are no different from us." As for the migrant workers, these rare opportunities to be a guide give them a chance to see themselves in a new light. "The opportunity to share my stories made me see myself again, and not just as a laborer, but a person with many precious life experiences," said Halim, an Indonesian migrant worker. "The journey from Indonesia to Taiwan is making me think about what my culture can bring to Taiwanese. I hope they can learn and see a different side of Indonesian culture from me."

Open Sunday, more like a kitchen party, is another popular event. Southeast Asian cuisine has long been integrated into the daily life in Taiwan, as people fill up Vietnamese and Thai restaurants everywhere. Many people's first impression with Southeast Asia starts with food. Therefore, the point of these kitchen parties is to use these Southeast Asian flavors familiar to Taiwanese people as a cultural medium, through which they can learn about the food culture behind the fascinating and delicious food, before diving deeper into the cultural values behind their daily diet. In each Open Sunday event, One-Forty asks three migrant workers to put on their chef hats and bring Taiwanese people together to make Southeast Asian dishes, such as *klepon*, an Indonesian dessert where palm sugar is wrapped in glutinous rice and sprinkled with grated coconut, a popular Indonesian childhood snack that brings back memories or *es buah*, an Indonesian iced fruit cocktail dessert with dragon fruit juice as the base, giving the whole bowl a pink glow.

In the process of preparing and cooking with the migrant workers, the Taiwanese people begin to understand the authentic spices and seasonings as well as the different cooking methods in the Southeast Asian region. Comparing with Taiwanese cooking, they would often share the cooking methods between the two cultures. Once the cooking is done, people start to enjoy the food, as migrant workers share their hometown's cultural customs. For example, when celebrating important occasions such as birthdays and marriages in Indonesia, people like to enjoy *nasi tumpeng* (turmeric rice cone), which is quite different from the birthday cakes commonly used for birthday celebrations in Taiwan.

Another activity in Open Sunday is called the Social Design Workshop. This activity is designed for people who are already familiar with the issue of migrant workers, where they get to explore the structural issues and dilemmas faced by migrant workers in Taiwan in greater depth and see how they can act to make a difference. The migrant journey map developed by One-Forty is used during the event. It clearly distinguishes a migrant's cross-country journey — preparing to leave their home country, their first arrival in Taiwan, their life of working and living in Taiwan, preparing to return to their home country and their life after returning home. This allows event participants to use empathy and role-playing to imagine the difficulties they may encounter and their needs in different stages of the journey if they were to become a migrant worker from Southeast Asia. Participants are also divided into breakout groups during the event, and they would actually go to stations or parks on the weekends to interview migrants and get real first-hand feedback.

Once the participants have collected enough feedback, they use the migrant journey map to classify various difficulties for different stages of the journey, and compile the issues into themes, such as cultural adaptation, legal rights, institutional improvement and home country family relations. Then, participants would begin to brainstorm how to come up with solutions for improvements from the perspectives of various stakeholders, such as the government, businesses, NGOs, employers and the general public. The participants have actually come up with many practical solutions. For example, ideas for improving the Muslim prayer room at Taipei Main Station allow better user-friendly experience and flow of movement consistent with the needs of most Muslims. Another example is how to provide migrant workers who have just arrived in Taiwan to effectively obtain practical living information. Participants hope to set up an online portal to record short videos of migrant workers who have lived in Taiwan for many years to share practical information on living in Taiwan, such as various modes of transportation, recommendations on tourist attractions and restaurants, and migrant communities. This platform gives migrant workers a place to quickly access important information to help them adjust to a new environment when they first arrive in Taiwan.

The last of One-Forty's three initiatives is Migrant Life Channel. We believe that "every story deserves to be heard", so our team collects a large number of migrant stories and presents them in creative ways through texts, videos, artistic creation and more. The project came into being because we found migrant workers did not have a channel to voice their stories in Taiwan's past social context. Most people perceive migrant workers as mere labor, with few opportunities or channels to see their real-life stories outside of work. The public gets most of their information from the media, and the second-hand information often shine them in a negative light, causing a general stereotype of migrant workers. Through the Migrant Life Channel project, One-Forty's team continues to write personal stories about migrant workers. So far, 80 interviews have been published, documenting their life in Taiwan, their living situation after returning home and their observation of Taiwan's society. Besides being published on One-Forty's blog site, these articles are presented as columns via the collaboration with eight well-known Taiwanese online media outlets, where they are featured monthly for more people to read.

The One-Forty team aspires to spread migrant stories beyond certain filter bubbles and reach people of all walks of life. In addition to regular monthly web articles, the team also invites migrant workers to appear on radio and TV shows or record their own podcast. Via these different media channels, Taiwanese people get a chance to see the many faces of migrant workers. For instance, One-Forty once invited Indonesian caregiver Umy, who is also a novelist, to share her stories on the radio. Before working in Taiwan, where she has worked for 5 years as a caregiver, she worked in Singapore and Hong Kong for 7 years. In her spare time, she has written over 50 short stories and poems, and they can be seen in newspapers, magazines and anthologies. She once won first prize in Taipei's Poetry & Essay Writing Contest, a literature award for migrants. Meanwhile, Umy is also serving as the vice-president of GEMAS, the Indonesian reading culture promotion society, and has been actively assisting returning migrant workers to set up charity libraries in their hometowns. Her first novel *Genderang Cinta Nia* (Nia's Love Drum), is the culmination of Umy's creative writings after more than 10 years of working in Singapore, Hong Kong and Taiwan. Aside from using her own life experience in the story, she is representing a voice for other fellow migrant workers.

In One-Forty's podcast, Indonesian migrant worker Maya was invited to share her story. In 2017, Maya founded the Universal Volunteer charity community. Every month, migrant workers are invited to pick up trash in the mountains or take part in a beach cleanup. Having accumulated more than 50 such events, Universal Volunteer, originally targeted at Indonesian migrant workers, is now attracting Taiwanese and white-collar expats from various countries. "I hope to raise more awareness of the migrant worker community through this kind of charitable action, so that migrant workers can do more meaningful things to the society on their days off," said Maya. "Taiwan is our second home after leaving our home country for so many years. I would like to say thank you to Taiwan through action and express my love for Taiwan. Moreover, I also hope that through the power of this community, more Taiwanese people will be able to change their negative perceptions of migrant workers and see the more realistic and diverse faces that we are."

Expanding Impact through Social Innovation

One-Forty set a vision called Redesign NPO in the early days of its establishment, hoping to transform the established public perception of NGOs by leveraging social innovative thinking to design each action to drive social impact on a larger scale. We believe that NGOs offer more than care to the less privileged and the weak, they shouldn't provide a work environment that sucks the enthusiasm out of employees, and they are much more than boring publicity and event planning. Instead, we expect our operations to be professional, innovative and flexible, as we constantly think, observe and listen to design experiences and mechanisms that best meet the needs of users. We brainstorm ideas for engaging ways of fundraising and advocacy, and make adjustments quickly. We establish a one-of-a-kind organizational culture to attract the most qualified partners to join our warm and cohesive team. At the end of the day, we want to let every moment of contact and interaction with One-Forty to exceed public expectations and leave a lasting impression.

To achieve Redesign NPO, one must first start with a new way of assembling a team. Service-based NPOs are usually composed of members with professional backgrounds in social work, whereas One-Forty has recruited professional designers, photographers, artists and experts in business or sociology since day one. The average age of our team is 26 years old, and we also recruit 50 cross-disciplinary professional volunteers, who work pro bono, every year. We introduce design thinking to re-understand the pain points of Southeast Asian migrant workers in Taiwan from a people-oriented perspective, and use observation, interviews, focus groups and role-playing to gain insights into their unmet needs. Through brainstorming, international case studies and consulting with cross-disciplinary experts, we have come up with a number of prototypes. By directly inviting migrant workers to participate in the experimental pilots, the rapid experimental trial-and-errors receive first-hand feedback for adjustments and fine-tuning to finally produce a feasible project plan with scaling potential and innovative elements.

The enrollment each semester at the One-Forty School has always been very high, indicating that there's a high level of unmet learning needs among the migrant workers. Since 2017, One-Forty has received a large number of inquiries from migrant workers about additional courses. They were asking whether classes can be open in other counties or cities outside of Taipei. We soon observed that at that time, One-Forty School only offered classes in Taipei, the capital city, but migrant workers were located all over Taiwan, thus it failed to meet the huge demand for migrant workers elsewhere. In 2017, One-Forty began to think about how to use social innovation to grow the impact of the project by 10-fold, and we decided to introduce digital learning and set up a One-Forty School online platform. Educational videos are recorded in migrant workers' mother tongue and put on the online platform, where they can access and learn at any time and any place, completely free of charge.

Over the past 3 years, over 280 educational videos have been uploaded to the platform, with 46,500 Indonesian migrant workers throughout Taiwan registered for long-term online learning. One-Forty's audiovisual production team is responsible for planning, script writing, shooting and editing of the educational short videos. From situations where the workers have just arrived in Taiwan to learning basic Chinese language skills, these videos cover topics as variegated as body parts, care-giving methods, basic safety guidelines for factory workers, as well as experienced migrant workers who are invited to share their work experience. At the same time, the videos also address real-life scenarios for migrant worker's days off, such as going to a doctor's appointment, taking a bus, making purchases and more. Digital learning has reshaped how people learn and it has solved the problem of irregular days off for migrant caregivers, who can use their spare time to quickly absorb practical sentences in the videos and use them in real life, greatly reducing the language barrier upon their first arrival in Taiwan. In addition, the videos are complemented by lively and interesting animations to meet the needs of young migrant workers who are more audio-visual learners. They can also share the videos on their own social platforms. Peer recommendations and digital sharing are helping subscribers to grow exponentially, with each video averaging 10,000 views.

In 2019, One-Forty School once again proposed an innovative solution to provide learning package delivery services for migrant workers who are in their first year in Taiwan and live in a remote area. A customized learning package, containing Chinese learning textbooks, workbooks, a guide to Taiwanese life and culture and a letter to the employer, is sent to migrant workers' homes throughout Taiwan for free. The learning package program was officially open for application in June 2019, and it immediately received more than 2,800 active sign-ups. When registering, the migrant worker must clearly state their time of arrival in Taiwan, frequency of days off, where they live and motivation for learning. To date, 1,000 learning packages have been successfully sent out to kick start their one-year remote learning journey.

Once the migrant worker receives the learning package, they will be immediately added to an online learning community to start their learning progress. Each week, there are scheduled learning topics, assignments, quizzes and exams, and live audio-visual interactions. Any difficulties or questions encountered can be answered by teachers or other migrant workers in the group. This learning package program not only assists migrant workers who are adjusting to their new life in Taiwan, but it also helps them form a good relationship with their employer family. Working as a home caregiver, language barriers can often cause misunderstandings and conflicts with the employer family, whiles risks can run high when they cannot understand the needs of the elderly they are supposed to take care of. After the migrant workers receive their learning package, we encourage them to learn together with their employers and care recipients. Many of the activities designed in the textbook are expected to be completed together by migrant workers and employers. Employers can teach migrant workers Chinese writing and pronunciation to create a better communication relationship, allowing the whole family to live more harmoniously. In the coming years, One-Forty will continue to send out 1,000–1,500 study packages to new migrant workers every year. When the migrant workers have gained the language and life skills, we hope they can give the package to other migrants in their community to pass on the learning opportunity.

On top of Open Sunday and Migrant Life Channel, in view of enabling more people in Taiwan to understand the situation and stories of migrant workers and changing the stereotypes and prejudices about migrant workers, One-Forty wants to create large-scale social change through social innovation. In 2017, *600,000 JOURNEYS*, One-Forty's first large-scale non-profit exhibition, was held. Using art as a medium to reinterpret the migrant stories through collaborations with multiple artists, it attracted 27,000 visitors in two weeks. This exhibition, in collaboration with Filipino artist couple Alfredo and Isabel Aquilizan, featured installation artworks, using more than 1,000 slippers worn by Filipino migrant workers to form a pair of colorful wings, symbolizing the heart's longing for their home and the desire to fly freely. Another exhibit drew "Ballikbayan box" as its inspiration. Ballikbayan boxes are parcel boxes used by overseas Filipino migrant workers to send home to their families.

The objects in the box become the medium for migrant workers to convey their emotions to their families afar, letting Taiwanese people see and feel their homesickness.

In 2019, One-Forty held its second large-scale exhibition — *Turning Point: Taiwan* — a photo exhibition that attracted 10,000 visitors in one week. This exhibition focuses on the journey of migrant workers, taking Taiwanese to see Southeast Asian migrant workers' hometowns, their work and life when they first arrived in Taiwan, as well as their lives after returning home. Featuring 300 photographic works, combined with new VR experiences, the exhibition allowed the public to glimpse into what life is like in migrant workers' hometowns. In addition, there was a special exhibition area called "Voice of Migrant". One-Forty collected 200 photographs taken by migrant workers all over Taiwan and let them tell the story behind the photo. Through the exhibition, their voices could be heard, where they observe Taiwan's society, express their homesickness and their relationships with their employers.

In the exhibition, Joan Pabona, a migrant worker in Hong Kong turned professional street photographer, was invited to stage her first overseas solo exhibition in Taiwan. Since 2015, Joan has been shooting on the streets of Hong Kong. Her favorite spots are Hong Kong's popular attractions like the bustling Tsim Sha Tsui and Causeway Bay. However, her works are hardly reminiscent of the glamorous and flamboyant Hong Kong. Under her lens, Hong Kong is lonely, quiet and desolate. In 2018, Joan won the National Geographic Wheelock Hong Kong Photo Contest. In the same year, she debuted her first solo exhibition *Empathy in a Click* in Hong Kong. Joan Pabona succeeded in letting the people of Taiwan see another side of migrant workers, empowered with confidence and in courageous pursuit of their goals in life.

One-Forty aspires to truly bring the issue of migrant workers from Southeast Asia to a wider public community. Through the collaborative storytelling with artists, designers and photographers, we recognized that this issue is a complex and institutional one, involving a mix of labor rights, government regulations and policies, agency systems and human resources supply chains, ethnic co-prosperity and social prejudice. If a social issue is to be promoted to the general public, they key lies in how to present it in a way that people find interesting and worth exploring. At One-Forty, we believe we are a bridge connecting this issue to the general public by transforming the issue through innovative and cross-disciplinary perspectives. We are presenting the journeys and stories of migrant workers and connecting the dots to reach various communities, creating long-term social impact. In 2015, One-Forty was honored with the Taiwan Design Best 100 award by *Shopping Design*, a well-known design magazine in Taiwan. The reason for the award: One-Forty is a representative in the Social Design arena, as it takes advantage of the power of design to communicate social issues and bring about changes in public awareness. In 2017, the non-profit art exhibition organized by One-Forty won the La Vie Taiwan Creativity Award, another well-known design award in Taiwan, as an exemplary model of non-profit exhibitions.

This concept of cross-disciplinary connection goes beyond collaborations with the design and art worlds, but the way One-Forty operates also sees co-operation with the corporate sector. In 2018, One-Forty launched a partnership with the world-renowned National Palace Museum in Taiwan to help boost the number of visitors from Southeast Asia. One-Forty shot a "brand image" video featuring well-known Indonesian migrant workers on a day trip at the Museum. In the video, many visitor-friendly facilities are showcased, including the Southeast-Asian language audio tour guide and prayer rooms, and it successfully reached 150,000 Indonesian migrant workers through social media. Later in 2019, One-Forty partnered with Taipei 101, the tallest building in Taiwan and one of the most iconic landmarks for Southeast Asian migrant workers working in Taiwan. One-Forty collaborated with Taipei 101 on the "Bring a book from Southeast Asia" charity project, where migrant workers who are coming to Taiwan from Southeast Asia to work can bring a book in their native tongue with them and donate it once they are in Taiwan. Through this project, books in their native language can be sent to other migrant workers in Taiwan, so that their homesickness can be somewhat allayed by reading in their native language even though they are on a foreign land.

In 2019, One-Forty co-operated with Taiwan Fu Hsing, a well-established manufacturing company in Taiwan, to launch a series of customized physical and online training courses for 300 Filipino workers at their plants. The contents cover Chinese language, work adjustment, personal savings and financial management, team communication and co-operation to effectively improve the performance of Filipino migrant workers on the job, while reducing the communication barriers and frictions between foreign and Taiwanese colleagues. This project has attracted the attention of many companies in Taiwan which employ a large number of migrant workers, prompting them to think about how to treat their foreign colleagues in a CSR-oriented manner to create a more friendly work environment and better performance. Also in 2019, One-Forty co-operated with Far EasTone Telecommunications (FET), one of Taiwan's largest telecom providers, to provide e-care services to tens of thousands of migrant workers using the FET network. One-Forty produced a series of life adjustment educational videos, which are sent to the migrant workers through mobile messaging service. Migrant workers using FET will receive such videos on a regular basis, teaching them how to adapt to work and life in Taiwan, such as going to the doctor and shopping.

One-Forty's vision for the future is to allow every returning Southeast Asian migrant worker to bring back fond memories of Taiwan. This is true citizen diplomacy in action. Over the past few years, migrant workers whom One-Forty has assisted have one by one returned to their hometowns and they are living their lives in meaningful ways. One worker published a novel after returning to Indonesia, writing about her experience of her journey in Taiwan. Some brought back the altruistic spirit they learned from One-Forty to their hometowns and established volunteer groups to start cleaning roads and rivers to form non-profit entities centered around communities, evoking a sense of cohesion in the neighborhood. Others formed a band after moving back and wrote songs about Taiwan, allowing more Indonesians to learn Taiwanese culture through music. In the meantime, One-Forty also plans to launch a returning migrant community project in Indonesia to organize community activities in Jakarta, West Java, Central Java, East Java and Sumatra, for returning migrants to meet regularly to talk about how to re-adjust to their families, how to run a small business, how to improve their job competitiveness and find good job opportunities, as well as giving advice to prospective workers who are about to leave for Taiwan. One-Forty hopes that one day Taiwan can truly become an important layover stop for all migrant workers to realize their lifelong dreams and improve their lives. We genuinely hope that their time in Taiwan is worthwhile, and their experiences can inspire their imagination for the future before they return home to shine.

Future Trends and Positioning of the New Form of Transnational Labor Migration

Looking into the future, globalization and regionalization of economic development will bring about greater flux of capital, goods, information and human resources. In the process of regional economic and free market integration, migrant-importing countries are experiencing demographic changes and labor shortages due to long-term declines in fertility rates, dwindling population growth and increasing aging population. Meanwhile, migrant-exporting countries are giving their people job opportunities. In addition to helping migrant workers realize personal interests and earn a higher income, labor migration is also accelerating the transnational economic, social and political interconnections and is changing the cultural landscapes of various countries.

Therefore, how to see labor migration in a new light is an issue of urgent importance for both migrant-exporting and migrant-importing countries. Based on the new perspectives driven by One-Forty's accumulated experience, we believe that migrant workers are taking on three roles: Labor, Talent and Ambassador.

For migrant-exporting countries, migrant workers are considered labor export, where transnational workers earn a large amount of foreign currency to send back home, and they earn a higher income to improve their family's quality of life. If we look at migrant workers from the perspective of "talent", they can take advantage of the valuable knowledge and skills acquired during their time working overseas, so that they are professionally upgraded when they return to their home country to engage in jobs with higher knowledge demands and economic value. In a way, they present a pool of potential talents in their country. If we look at migrant workers as "ambassadors", every migrant worker abroad represents the culture of their home country. This creates the opportunity for the other country to understand their culture and in turn deepens the bilateral cultural exchange.

For migrant-importing countries, migrant workers can be seen as "labor" that help fill the labor gap in their own country, including caregivers in an aging society and grassroots labor in traditional industrial factories. These migrant workers are important and indispensable for the sustainable operation of society. If we look at migrant workers from the "talent" viewpoint, the local languages and cultures that they learn in the migrant-importing country can give them broader perspectives and experiences that arm them to be highly sought-after talents. For instance, Taiwanese companies are now actively branching out to Southeast Asia and they need local talents on the ground. Returning migrants who have the Taiwan experience and are proficient in Chinese are the best talents to help Taiwanese businesses make inroads in Southeast Asia. Migrant workers can be viewed as "ambassadors", as they may very well become citizen ambassadors of the migrant-importing country. When they have lived in the migrant-importing country for many years, and if they are treated well during this transnational journey and given valuable knowledge and skills, they will leave the country with a good impression and only good things will come out of this positive relations. Some tens of thousands of migrant workers in Taiwan return to Southeast Asia every year. If everyone leaves with a fond impression of Taiwan, it will greatly enhance Taiwan's international image in Southeast Asia, which is solid citizen diplomacy in the long run.

For every country and city in the world, people are learning how to live with people of different languages, races and cultures, seeing each other's values, being able to have more empathy, so that we are guided by core values that lead the way to a more globalized future. This is the value that migrant workers can bring. And it is something we must start to value from now on.

Part 3

Socio-Cultural Connections

https://doi.org/10.1142/9789811250668_0012

Chapter 12

The Socio-Cultural Connections: The Chinese Indonesian Popular Magazines on Taiwan and China in 1945–1955

Yerry Wirawan

Lecturer, Sanata Dharma University, Indonesia

Introduction

After World War II, Indonesia was in the middle of a divided world. The foundation of the People's Republic of China (PRC) and the relocation of the Nationalist government to Taiwan represented the beginning of the Cold War in Asia. This conflict affected the Chinese Indonesia society as one of the significant Chinese diasporas in Southeast Asia. Clashes between the PRC and the Republic of China's (ROC) supporters occurred in Indonesian big cities. The Indonesian government carefully took a non-aligned side in this issue, in order to gain support from both political powers for the benefit of its independence struggle in the diplomatic arena.

During this period of social and political tension, Peranakan Chinese magazines emerged and reached a wide readership.[1] The most

[1]During the Japanese occupation, Indonesian Peranakan publications that supported China in her fight against Japan were banned. The only publication allowed was *Kung Yung Pao* (1942–1945).

prominent were: *Star Weekly* (1946–1963), *Java Critic* (1948–1950) and *Pantjawarna* (1948–1963).[2] All of them were published in Jakarta, showing the leading role of this city for the Indonesian intellectual life after the war.[3]

With the revival of the press, some Indonesian writers undertook to discuss the concept of modernity. The main issue was how Indonesia should be modernized and how to place the local tradition in that context. However, we hardly find Sino-Indonesian writers involved in the discussion in Indonesian cultural magazines (such as *Mimbar Indonesia, Siasat* and *Indonesia*) despite their historical role in Indonesian cultural life.[4] The exclusion of Chinese from the intellectual debate may be explained by the long period of colonial segregation system that had placed them as outsiders in Indonesian colonial society.[5]

The Chinese Indonesian publications during the decolonization period has remained understudied.[6] From the 1950s to the 1960s and even later, scholars were more interested in political divisions within the Chinese Indonesian community than socio-cultural issues. These studies often overlook Chinese Indonesian magazines in which the Chinese writers expressed their fascination for modernity and progress as perceived in other Asian countries.[7]

---

[2] In later years, there are slightly changes in the title's writing such as *Starweekly* to *Star Weekly* or *Pantjawarna* to *Pantja Warna*. For consistency, I adopt *Star Weekly* and *Pantjawarna* as their first version.

[3] Jakarta was also the birthplace for the publication of prominent Indonesian cultural magazines such as *Mimbar Indonesia* (1947–1966), *Siasat* (1947–1961) and *Indonesia* (1949–1965; this magazine slightly changed its name over time but maintained the title *Indonesia*).

[4] For the role of *Mimbar Indonesia* in the Indonesian cultural debate in this era, see Bogaerts (2012).

[5] However, *Sin Po* had promoted the modernization of Sino-Indonesian in Netherlands Indie since its early edition 1910–1912. See Song Ge (2018). We thank Claudine Salmon for this reference.

[6] On nationality status of the Chinese, see Suryadinata (1984); on the Chinese organization, see Heidhues (1964); see also Blussé (1991) and Twang (1998).

[7] We noted few works on the Chinese Indonesian press in post-colonial Indonesia (Soejatmiko 1946; Dea Letrina Cesaria 2018).

Here, I intend to investigate a sample of socio-cultural articles — emanating from three leading Chinese Indonesian magazines *Star Weekly*, *Java Critic* and *Pantjawarna*. I compare how those magazines presented newness and modernity from Taiwan, Hong Kong and China. I also look at the conception of modernity of the writers and their reflection on Indonesia. I argue that these magazines had played an important role in delivering the image of Asian modernity to Indonesian readers.

Political Situation of the Chinese during the Decolonization Era

In September 1945, the Dutch returned to Indonesia to establish NICA (Netherlands Indies Civil Administration, the office of which was in Jakarta). They were faced with the outbreak of the Indonesian independence war in Jakarta and forced the Republic Indonesia to find a safer place in Yogyakarta.[8] During this revolutionary war, the Chinese were often the target of violent attacks by Indonesian militias. The Chinese were often perceived as aliens by the Indonesian majority due to their difference in religion, physical appearance and economic status. In Tangerang, the most notable atrocities occurred, hundreds of Chinese were massacred. Heidhues (2017) who compiled reports from the Chinese organizations has this to say:

> In May 1946, Dutch forces attacked and occupied the town of Tangerang, and Republican army forces withdrew from the town and its surrounding region. Irregular troops (*laskar*) remained behind in rural areas, encouraging violence against Chinese villagers, burning their houses, murdering some, forcibly circumcising men and sometimes raping women. An estimated Chinese population of 25,000, over 1000 were dead, over 200 missing, and 15,300 refugees, overwhelmingly Chinese, fled to the city of Jakarta". (Heidhues, 2017)

[8]Meanwhile, the Indonesian republic moved its capital to Yogyakarta where it was hosted by Sultan Hamengkubuwono IX until 1949. For the anti-Chinese violence during the revolution, see Heidhues (2012).

This very fact compelled the Chinese community to realize their social and political powerlessness in Indonesia. It also revealed how fatal the shortcoming of Indonesian nationhood for the minority groups at that time.

In the meantime, there was a rise of nationalistic feelings where the Chinese encountered national identity issues that reflected in the citizenship status. During the colonial period, the Chinese were Dutch subjects. Expecting support from the Chinese community, the Indonesian government adopted a passive citizenship policy toward the Chinese in Indonesia in 1946. This means that every Chinese person would automatically be an Indonesian citizen by law, unless he refutes the status. However, this regulation covered the republic areas in which Chinese communities were relatively small and had little influence on the Chinese community (Suryadinata, 1984: 116).

Meanwhile, the China government established diplomatic relations with the Dutch government by opening one of its consulates in Jakarta. This diplomatic tie was an attempt by the Dutch government to prevent the China Government from recognizing the newly proclaimed Indonesian government residing in Yogyakarta. However, Dutch troops overran most of West and East Java, while the Republic controlled most of Central Java and Sumatra (Heidhues, 2012: 388). Aiming to gain full coverage of the area, the China government insisted on establishing relations with the Indonesian government in order to protect the Chinese population in the Republican side.

The Dutch widely reported the Chinese victims. However, we need to be careful when we look at this report as Mary Sommers Heidhues indicates "Dutch efforts to record Chinese losses also unquestionably had the purpose of blackening the reputation of the Republic and winning Chinese sympathy. At least one communication of the government information service deliberately attempted to use photographs of Chinese atrocity victims to turn China and the local Chinese community against Yogyakarta" (Heidhues, 2012: 396). After the 1949 Round Table Conference agreement, this regulation was later amended so that Chinese people have to choose their citizenship status before the court.

Political instability was the main concerns of the Chinese in Indonesia throughout the early years of independence. While anti-Chinese violence occurred in countries and cities, the Chinese Indonesian press played an important role in discussing the issues of the Chinese at that time. Moreover, they kept attracting Indonesian readers with interesting articles and beautiful photos from foreign countries.

Chinese Magazines in Post-Colonial Indonesia

The major Chinese magazines in this era were part of a well-established Chinese media who had a considerable circulation and networks since the colonial era. For example, *Sin Po*, established in 1910 and pro-China, issued the bi-monthly magazine *Pantjawarna*.[9] Its rival, *Keng Po*, which was a well-established journal since 1923 and known as a Dutch sympathizer, published its magazine *Star Weekly*. An exceptional case was *Java Critic*, which had no link with the major daily from the pre-war era and was instead edited by Kwee Kek Beng, a senior Chinese journalist at that time.

Star Weekly

The first issue of this weekly magazine was published on 6 January 1946.[10] Being part of the well-known *Keng Po* daily, *Star Weekly* rapidly gained popularity among Indonesian readers.[11] But *Star Weekly* appeared less attractive than other Chinese magazines at that time. It did not have a cover page or nice illustrations. On the contrary, *Star Weekly* placed national news in its front-page story and lengthy political information more than other Chinese magazines. Starting in 1951, Auwjong Peng Koen was named the chief editor.

Auwjong Peng Koen was a well-established journalist during post-colonial Indonesia. He was born on 20 July 1920 in West Sumatra. Auwjong Peng Koen went to a Christian *Hollands Chinese School* in his hometown. After finishing MULO (Dutch middle school) in Padang, he continued his study at a Chinese teacher school (*Hollands Chinese Kweek School*) in Jakarta (Steenbrink, 2015: 210; Suryadinata, 2015: 209–210).[12] Auwjong Peng-koen worked as a teacher in 1940–1944 before

[9] *Sin Po* was the first newspaper in the colonial era that published the Indonesian national anthem in November 1928. They had a wide range of Indonesian readers, especially among the nationalists, as it supported the Indonesian independence movement. See also Lie (2018) and Tirto, 7 November 2018, https://tirto.id/sejarah-sin-po-koran-tionghoa-yang-menyuarakanindonesia-merdeka-c8Vq.

[10] During the pre-war era, this magazine was entitled *Star Magazine* (Cesaria, 2018: 109).

[11] Previously, *Keng Po* had published *Star Magazines* in the early 1940s.

[12] Later on, Auwjong Pengkoen changed his name to Petrus Kanisius Ojong.

joining journalism. During the Indonesian revolution war, he studied law in Jakarta (1946–1951). He headed *Star Weekly* soon after he finished his law study until this magazine was banned by the Sukarno government in 1960.

As a devout Catholic, Auwjong Peng Koen was a member of the Catholic Political Party. He also signed "Piagam Asimilasi" (Assimilationist Charter) in 1960. It means Auwjong Peng Koen supported the Chinese to abandon their Chineseness to adopt a full Indonesian identity. This political stand placed him in opposition to the leftwing group in Baperki. In 1964, he led a daily newspaper, *Kompas*, which became the largest daily in Indonesia after the fall of Sukarno in 1965. Auwjong Peng Koen passed away in 1980.

Java Critic

Java Critic was a monthly periodical. Its first issue appeared on October 10, 1948 in Bandung. In an article in 1949, a writer named "WB" wrote that *Java Critic* was inspired by a well-known English-speaking periodical published in Shanghai, *The China Critic Weekly*[13] and by a Chinese Western educated writer, Lin Yutang (1895–1976).[14] By referring to *the*

[13] *The China Critic Weekly*, an English newsletter focusing on the social and political issue published in May 1928 in Shanghai, proclaimed as the first Chinese edited press in the English language at that time. This periodical was published in the period when Shanghai was growing rapidly as an urban center with its cosmopolitan profile and openness. This city was also the center of publishing, attracting writers of various styles. Meanwhile, the political conflict between the Nationalist and the Communist spread out in the countryside. *The China Critics* was "a unique forum for authors to present a 'Chinese perspective' to a foreign world that generally did not, or did not care to, read the ebullient Chinese press. It also acted as an important conduit of Western ideas for urban Chinese students and other readers who were proficient in English." *The China Critic* was a forum for the discussion of social, cultural, scientific and educational ideas and trends (Sima, 2012).

[14] *Java Critic* no. 6, 1948, 1949, p. 18. A prominent writer in *The China Critic Weekly*, Lin Yutang was a Chinese translator and philosopher. In the English-speaking world, he was well-known for his role in promoting Chinese culture to the West. Lin Yutang is a fine example of a modern Chinese man in a crisis identity in the 1920s. In his belief: "to be brought up as a Christian was synonymous with being progressive, Western-minded and in sympathy with the New Learning. It meant, on the whole, acceptance of the West, with particular admiration for the Western microscope and Western surgery." However, he was not familiar with his own Chinese culture, tradition and philosophy. He believes that Christianity is responsible for this loss. In 1959, Lin Yutang declared his return to

China Critic and Lin Yutang, it demonstrates the modernity conception of *Java Critic* is a confluence of Asian and Western values. This principle was then strongly presented in the articles of this magazine.

Java Critic was founded by Kwee Kek Beng (1900–1975), who was a prominent Chinese writer. He went to *Hollandsch Chinesche school* (HCS), a prestigious Dutch primary school at that time. After attending secondary school at *Kweekschool* (Dutch teacher training school), he worked as a teacher in Bogor in 1922. Soon, Kwee realized that being a teacher was not his passion. In the same year, he started his career as a journalist in the biggest Chinese newspaper, *Sin Po*. Unlike Lin Yutang, who was a devout Christian, Kwee Kek Beng was a secular nationalist. He was also well-known for his staunchly anti-Japanese stance. During the Japanese occupation, *Sin Po* was closed down. Kwee Kek Beng and his family moved to Bandung.[15]

Concerning his political preference, Kwee Kek Beng was known for his pro-Mao Zedong stance (Lee, 2013). But if we look at his publications in *Java Critic* in 1948–1950, one may have a different image. In the first issue, Kwee Kek Beng wrote his standpoint in the editorial:

> Lebi Jaoeh ini madjalah berdiri di loear semoea party sebab pemimpinnja tida ngekor dibelakang party ini atawa itoe; meski begitoe "Java Critic" boekan bendera zonder tiang, sebab sembojannja ada "impartial, not neutral".

Christianity that surprised a lot of people. Lin Yutang gave a lecture at the English Language at Peking University. In 1926, he moved to Xiamen university for a year and in 1927 lived in Shanghai as a creative writer. In 1936, Lin Yutang migrated to America for 30 years. In 1966, he returned to live in a beautiful villa on Yanming mountain, Taiwan. Lin Yutang passed away in Hong Kong and his remains buried in Taipei in 1976 (Liu, 2011: 159).

[15] While Lin Yu Tang was fluent in the English language, Kwee Kek Beng wrote several books on China mostly in the Dutch language. Traveling to Singapore and Malaya in 1929, Kwee Kek Beng was amazed by the pro-China Chinese community. In 1933, he visited China and was impressed by the relics of China civilization. During this visit, Kwee Kek Beng was awarded a medal by the Red Cross of China for his role in fundraising for the poor. Returning to Indonesia, he became a Chinese chauvinist. He wished Chinese *Peranakan* in Indonesia should be re-sinicized through Chinese language training. Kwee Kek Beng also suggested Chinese history, geography and Chinese culture should be introduced in the Chinese school (Kwee 1948 a,b; Lee, 2013).

> [Furthermore, this periodical stands beyond all the parties because the editor in chief does not follow any party. However, "Java Critic" is not a flag without a pole. It has a motto: "impartial, not neutral"].[16]

Java Critic, April 1949

Pantjawarna

In 1948, one of the biggest Chinese Indonesian newspapers, *Sin Po* published a richly illustrated monthly magazine *Pantjawarna* in Jakarta. This newborn magazine appeared more attractive than other Chinese publications at the time. It had beautiful photographs on its cover page and within its articles. This was an entertaining magazine for Indonesian readers

[16] *Java Critic*, Th. 1 No. 1, October 10, 1948.

where they could read synopsis of new films or have the latest photo of their favorite movie stars. *Pantjawarna* also provided articles on literature, art, history, philosophy and science.

Pantjawarna was led by Nio Joe Lan who was a senior Chinese writer and journalist (Suryadinata, 2015: 184–185). Nio Joe Lan was born in 1904 in Jakarta. He went to *HCS met bijbel,* and *Koningen Wihelmina School*, a prestigious Dutch school. Unlike Auwjong Peng-Koen, Nio Joe Lan was more interested in Chinese culture. He purposely learned Mandarin from a private course. Nio Joe Lan started his career in journalism when he started to work for *Keng Po* in 1928. In 1935, he moved to *Sin Po* until 1942. During the Japanese occupation, Nio Joe Lan was interned in a camp. After Pacific war, he soon rejoined *Sin Po* by leading the *Pantjawarna* editorial board.

The Chinese World as Perceived by the Three Magazines

Comparing the news in these magazines, we immediately realize that China and Hong Kong were dominantly reported. Meanwhile Taiwan was modestly presented, a fact that may be simply caused by a lack of correspondents and networks. This part will focus on observing the articles of Taiwan, Hong Kong and China that these places represented three completely different features of the Chinese world in the post war era. For the readers, Taiwan was seen as the representation of the nationalist Chinese and Hong Kong was a perfect sample of Westernized Chinese city. On the other hand, China remained as the ancestral home for the Chinese diaspora. The readers attempted to understand the rapid changes of the Chinese world through the articles of these three magazines.

Taiwan, a little-known modernity

The Chinese Indonesian magazines shared little information on Taiwan during this period. Through my reading, I could only find two magazines that provided socio-cultural articles of Taiwan during this time: *Star Weekly* and *Java Critic*.[17] On September 12, 1948, an article written by

[17] In fact, *Star Weekly* occasionally mentions Taiwan in their political news that is beyond our discussion here.

Mrs. Huang Giok Huey, was published in *Star Weekly* (Huang, 1948). This one-page article might be the translation of an unspecified source.

Mrs. Huang Giok Huey's article sketched a general economic situation by providing a list of export goods from Taiwan, the prices of which were more expensive than in China. In her report, Mrs. Huang Giok Huey highlighted the advantage of Taiwan with a population of 6 million people who experienced modern industry and hardworker. Mrs. Huang Giok Huey expressed her admiration of the nationalistic spirit of the people who had suffered 50 years of colonization of Japan. She also pointed out the language issue between the mainland Chinese who spoke Mandarin and the local Chinese people who spoke Taiwanese.

Another brief article, maybe also a translation, was published in *Java Critic* in 1948 by a writer using the initials "KHG" (KHG, 1948). Its author also shared a positive image of Taiwan in which the writer was especially impressed by their high level of education system. This article reported there were 1,241,234 students in elementary school, 40,148 students in high school and 11,637 students in university. The library fascinated the writer where it had 200,000 book collections. The writer then went further by comparing the medical doctors between Taiwan (1 medical doctor for 2,300 people) and Indonesia (1 medical doctor for 35,000 people). We learn from this article that the Indonesian education system far lagged behind Taiwan at that time. The Indonesian first national university was opened only in 1949 in Yogyakarta.

Looking at the length of both articles, they seem not direct reportage from Taiwan. It is more plausible that the writers translated it from other sources to give a quick image of Taiwan for the readers. Despite the lack of extensive information, the readers could learn the superiority of Taiwan over Indonesia. The people in Taiwan had a strong workforce, a good education system and a modern industry. They were also more advanced in the education system than Indonesia. It was unfortunate that the Chinese Indonesian writers at that time were unable to go further than that limited information on the socio-cultural side of Taiwan.

Hong Kong, a beautiful modern trading city

Hong Kong was always remembered as a beautiful trading port. Its natural beauty captivated everyone when they visited the city. During the post-Pacific War, Hong Kong became more central as a connection hub to the developing cities in East Asia. Travelers have to transit at its port before going further north to Japan or entering mainland China. Staying there for a couple of days allowed the travelers to observe the city.

The beauty of Hong Kong was also enjoyed by writers from Indonesia, though they understood this city was under political tension.[18] A travel report written by Oei Son Hok was published in *Star Weekly* 1948 (Oei, 1948). The writer started his article by describing the details of his trip to Hong Kong. It took a 7-day journey by ship from Jakarta before he arrived at the port of Hong Kong. Oei Son Hok portrayed Hong Kong's busy urban life. There were only three options to travel in Hong Kong such as buses, trams or taxis that allowed tourists to explore the city until near midnight. In his observation, he found Hong Kong enjoyed the typical modern city life. The people stayed in the same building but on different floors without knowing their neighbors.

Oei Son Hok appreciated Hong Kong's nightlife, but he seemed not impressed with the streets. Compared to Java, where the homeless people started to exist on the street only during the Japanese occupation, Oei Son Hok noticed homeless people in Hong Kong at night. But he had a more entertaining nightlife in that city than in his hometown in Jakarta. For him, the area inhabited by Europeans was cleaner and well maintained than the China area. That was his preference for the hotel where he chose an English hotel rather than a Chinese hotel. Oei Son Hok also provided detailed information on how to visit Kowloon or to Canton that was helpful for anyone in Indonesia who wished to visit China via Hong Kong. Portraying Hong Kong in the day and at night, we can perceive the writer's definition of a modern city that is characterized by transportation, entertainment facilities and cleanliness.

[18]A two-page article was published in *Star Weekly*, January 25, 1948, discussing an incident that just erupted in Kowloon. On January 5, 1948, the incident started when the British government attempted to expel Chinese refugees. A riot then occurred a week later causing injuries. This news rapidly spread and incited student protests in Shanghai. They burned down the British consulate. This news was published two weeks later in *Star Weekly*. In general, the article gave a favorable voice for the Hong Kong government. It reminded the readers of the Chinese people in Taiwan and Singapore who prefer to stay away from the Chinese government. Additional photo news of the student protest in Shanghai was published a week later. More details on the incident and its background, see Jones (2011).

Two other travel reports on Hong Kong were written by Goei Tek Tjiang in the two editions of *Pantjawarna* in 1950 and 1958 (Goei, 1950; 1958). The first report in 1950 portrayed Hong Kong in a way almost similar to Oei Son Hok's article, saying that this city was a busy but well-maintained and prosperous city. It was the center of trading, government offices and houses. The most prominent edifice was the ten floor-building of the Hong Kong and Shanghai Corporation (HSBC). The most interesting part of this lies in its comparison to Jakarta. For example, Goei Tek Tjiang observed that the commercial center in Hong Kong was as busy as the one in his hometown. He also found that the restaurants and coffee shops were open until midnight. But during the summer, Hong Kong was hotter than Jakarta.

Portraying social life, Goei Tek Tjiang, provided a different picture of Hong Kong than Oei Son Hok's report. He noticed the problem of housing due to the influx of political exiles from China. Unlike the homeless refugees in other cities, the political exiles in Hong Kong were the riches and elites who stayed in the hotels, villas and expensive flats. He observed that Hong Kong was more secure than in Java. Oei Son Hok missed to report the political life, whereas Goei Tek Tjiang realized the political tension in Hong Kong when he saw barbed wire and many worker union meetings in the city. Goei Tek Tjiang also admired the beauty of Hong Kong, especially during the night where the city lights look beautiful from Hong Kong's port. Despite the political crisis, he found the nightlife kept entertaining Hong Kong people during those days.

The second travel report in 1958 was on his journey from Japan to Indonesia when Goei Tek Tjiang made a stopover in Hong Kong for four days. Since it was not his first visit, he could observe the changes. For Goei Tek Tjiang, the most striking transformation was the increased amount of new high buildings and houses in the city as compared to 8 years ago. He understood that the government constructed new buildings to provide housing for 12,000 new residents in Hong Kong at that time. Due to the short visit, Goei Tek Tjiang did not explore the city like Oei Son Hok did in 1948. There is no detailed information on social or cultural life. However, he did observe the market where, unlike 8 years ago, the prices were cheap. He concluded that Hong Kong had become a paradise for shoppers.

Hong Kong was not only impressive for Chinese reporters but also for a journalist like Hassan Taa'lab. His piece was published in *Pantjawarna* in 1959 (Taa'lab, 1959). Reading his article, we learn that Hassan Taa'lab did not visit Hong Kong, his piece was probably based on written sources. Hassan Taa'lab was particularly fascinated by the construction of a new runway for Kai Tak airport in 1957–1960. This was a mega project involving 2,000 workers. The government started the project by flattening two hills to secure the air traffic. The project also implied land reclamation for a runway over the sea. A bypass road was specially created to ease the traffic to the site. The government projected to build a six-floor new terminal to welcome more visitors.[19] This construction demonstrated an advanced technology that placed Kai Tak airport as the biggest and most modern airport in Asia, defeating Tokyo. This was wonderful news for Indonesian readers because it means there would be more options to reach Hong Kong from Jakarta.

Hong Kong in *Pantjawarna* 15 July 1958

---

[19]Kai Tak airport was opened as Hong Kong's main airport in 1925 and was closed in 1998.

Mainland China reconstructs

Compared to Taiwan and Hong Kong, China was devoted more space within the magazines. The readers could easily find news and photos from there almost in every issue.[20] We also notice that that news was based often on a direct reportage, which means that the journalists from Indonesia used to travel to China. One of that news was published in *Java Critic* in 1948.[21] Its author, named TS Hsieh, reported his three-day visit to Nanking. TS Hsieh was invited on a maiden trip by KLM (*Koninklijke Luchtvaart Maatschappij*, Dutch Royal Aviation Company) that just opened a flight from Jakarta to Shanghai. During this trip, TS Hsieh profited from his free time to travel to Nanking and he found that the city was more attractive than Shanghai.

Traveling to Nanking was intended by TS Hsieh to clarify the negative image of China in Indonesia. Contrary to the news, TS Hsieh found that the daily life in the city had few shortcomings, though China had suffered the civil war. In his opinion, Nanking is a modern city in the broad sense where the high buildings and streets had been rapidly restored from Japanese bombings. But he observed that there were fewer cars in Nanking than in Jakarta and the living cost was high.

While the train approached Nanking station, TS Hsieh also felt moved, that he believed would happen to every Chinese who is visiting China's capital for the first time. He was pleased to find the China nationalist flags on the government buildings. But when he visited the Dutch embassy, TS Hsien would have liked to find the Indonesian embassy and its flag instead.[22] This thought reflects the typical character of Chinese Indonesians who have dual identity: being Chinese and Indonesian at the same time. The writer then provided some practical information for other Indonesian readers, i.e. information on transport cost from Batavia to Nanking, facilities on plane and hotel accommodation in Nanking.

In their quest of modernity, the Chinese Indonesian magazines provided strong support to women's issues. They frequently published articles and photos of prominent women in their respected fields. Moreover, an exceptional article was published in *Star Weekly* of May 16, 1948.

[20]Most of the articles on China were certainly political news that I have to omit because it is beyond our discussion here.

[21]*Java Critic*, No. 3, December 10, 1948, pp. 14–17.

[22]*Ibid.*

It consists a list of prestigious women in China history which is a summary of "Chinese Women, Yesterday and Today", authored by Florence Ayscough (1878–1942, a Canadian sinologist) (Anonymous, 1948).[23] At that time, women's issues commonly referred to Western tradition, but this article provided reference to China. In so doing, *Star Weekly* incorporated Chinese history into the modernity issue.

During the 1950s, we also noticed the increasing number of articles on cultural relations between Indonesia and China. This was an interesting development in relation of both countries since, as Taomo Zhou (2019) concludes, Beijing attempted to steer away from the Chinese diasporic politics. Interestingly, the news was written by and about non-Chinese artists. For example, in 1954 there was a report of the first Indonesian cultural mission prepared by the government in response to an invitation from China (Anonymous, 1954). This mission consisted of 60 persons who were mostly students. They were divided into two groups who traveled to China for a month, one group for dance performances and another for painting exhibitions. A second article by Pramoedya Ananta Toer was published in *Pantjawarna* in 1957. After having traveled during a month in China in 1956, Pramoedya was favorably impressed by China because of her ability to blend modernity and Chinese tradition (Toer, 1957).[24] The visits of Indonesian artists to China had significantly changed the image of that country and brought China as a sample of Asian modernity in the cultural field.[25]

Concluding Remarks

The first decade of post-colonial Indonesia was a harsh time for the Chinese. It was the independence era, but the Chinese were still marginalized in social, cultural and political life and, even worse than in the colonial time, being attacked by anti-Chinese militias. However, the Chinese were able to publish their magazines and provided the image of modernity in Asia. They reported the progress of Taiwan, Hong Kong and China and inspiring stories from those places. In so doing, these magazines introduced the modern lifestyle in the Asian big cities for Indonesian readers.

[23] Anonymous (1948). This book was actually first published in 1937.

[24] Pramoedya second visit to China was 1958 and the third one in 1960.

[25] For a detailed analysis of Pramoedya's visits in China, see Liu (1996).

To collect first-hand information, journalists visited Hong Kong and Nanking in China. Their travels were supported by good transportation networks and facilities to those places that demonstrated preparedness of the Asian cities to be important hubs in the Eastern world. However, we understand the choice to visit those places must be related with the socio-cultural connection of the Chinese diasporas in Indonesia. Interestingly, despite their fascination with modernity, these journalists always had Indonesia in mind by comparing those places with their hometown.

Observing these magazines, Taiwan was disproportionately represented than Hong Kong and China. This discrepancy might be due to the limited access and network of journalists to reach Taiwan. However, the news was relatively neutral that helped these magazines to provide a balancing image on Taiwan and maintain their wide audience when the political conflict started to divide the Chinese Indonesian community at that time.

One might find the writers did not provide deep analysis except sharing impressions of their travels or fascination of newness from Taiwan, Hong Kong and China. But reading closely, they offer another perspective. In the effort of highlighting the Asian style of modernity, the writers expressed their admiration of Western management systems and technology in the city (Hong Kong) or education (Taiwan). However, they respected tradition and originality (Nanking) and the importance of China history (in the topic of women issues). Therefore, we may conclude here the definition of modernity from *Star Weekly*, *Pantjawarna* and *Java Critic* was a simple combination of modernity and tradition. There are no theoretical conceptions of modernity or cultural polemic in these magazines that may disappoint the Indonesian intellectuals. But these magazines had brought factual references of Asian modernity to the general public in Indonesia on what modernity life is.

References

Anonymous (1948). Wanita Tionghoa Termashoer (The Famous Chinese Women), *Starweekly*, May 16:5–6.

Anonymous (1954). Missi Kesenian dan Persahabatan ke RRT (The Cultural and Friendship Mission to PRC). *Pantjawarna*, August, 2.

Blussé, L. (1991). The Role of Indonesian Chinese in Shaping Modern Indonesian Life: A Conference in Retrospect. *Indonesia*, 1–11.

Bogaerts, E. (2012). "Whither Indonesian Culture?" Rethinking "Culture" in Indonesia in a Time of Decolonization. In Jennifer Lindsay and Maya H. T.

Liem (eds.), *Heirs to World Culture: Being Indonesian, 1950–1965* (pp. 223–253). Leiden, KITLV Press.

Dea Letriana Cesaria. (2018). "Kontribusi Majalah Star Weekly, Liberal, dan Pantjawarna Pada Perkembangan Sastra Melayu Tionghoa tahun 1950-an". *Prosiding Seminar Sejarah Sastra "Memutakhirkan Kajian dan Penulisan Sejarah Sastra",* Departemen Ilmu Susastra, FIB UI, 105–120.

Goei, T. T. (1950). Melihat-lihat ke Hong Kong (Traveling to Hong Kong). *Pantjawarna*, 14–15, 32.

Goei, T. T. (1958). Melawat ke Negeri Matahari Terbit (Visiting Japan). *Pantjawarna,* 4–7, 48–49.

Heidhues, M. S. (1964). *Peranakan Chinese Politics in Indonesia. Theses.* Ithaca, Cornell University.

Heidhues, M. S. (2012). Anti-Chinese Violence in Java during the Indonesian Revolution, 1945–49. *Journal of Genocide Research*, 14(3–4): 381–401.

Heidhues, M. S. (2017). Violent, Political, and Administrative Repression of the Chinese Minority in Indonesia, 1945–1998. *Wacana*, 18(1): 94–105.

Huang, G. H. (1948). Taiwan di Masa ini (Taiwan on the Contemporary Days), *Starweekly*, September 12, 141.

Jones, G. (2011). The Kowloon City District and the Clearance of the Kowloon Walled City: Personal Recollections. *Journal of the Royal Asiatic Society, Hong Kong Branch*, 51: 266.

KHG (1948). Serba Serbi Tentang Formosa (Miscellaneous on Taiwan). *Java Critic*, November 10:12–13.

Kwee, K. B. (1948a). *Doea Poeloe Lima Tahon Sebagai Wartawan (1922–1947)* (Twenty-five years as a Journalist). Batavia, Kuo.

Kwee, K. B. (1948b). Pengantar Kata (Introduction). *Java Critic.* Java Critic, Th. 1 No. 1, October 10.

Lee, K. C. (2013). *Golden Dragon and Purple Phoenix: The Chinese and Their Multi-ethnic Descendants in Southeast Asia* (pp. 176–177). Singapore, World Scientific Publishing Co.

Lie, R. (2018). "Sejarah Sin Po, Koran Tionghoa yang menyuarakan Indonesia Merdeka" [The History of Sin Po, a Chinese newspaper voicing Indonesia's Independence], Tirto, November 7, https://tirto.id/sejarah-sin-po-korantionghoa-yang-menyuarakan-indonesia-merdeka-c8Vq.

Liu, H. (1996). Pramoedya Ananta Toer and China: The Transformation of a Cultural Intellectual. *Indonesia, Pramoedya Ananta Toer and His Work,* 61: 119–143.

Liu, R. Y. (2011). Lin Yutang, Astride the Culture of East and West. In Carol Lee Hamrin and Stacey Bieler (eds.), *Salt and Light, Vol. 3, More Lives of Faith that Shaped Modern China, Studies in Chinese Christianity* (pp. 158–175). Eugene, Pickwick Books.

Nio, J. L. (1962). *Sastra Indonesia Tionghoa* (The Chinese Indonesia Literature). Jakarta, Gunung Agung.

Oei, S. H. (1948). Menindjau di Hongkong dan Kowloon (Inspecting Hong Kong and Kowloon). *Star Weekly*, February 15:11–12.

Taa'lab, H. (1959). Kai Tak Lapangan Terbang diatas Lautan (Kai Tak, an Airport over the Sea). *Pantjawarna*, September 16, 36–37.

Toer, P. A. (1957). RRT Bagi Saja (PRC for Me). *Pantjawarna*, May 1, 12–13.

Twang, P. Y. (1998). *The Chinese Business Elite in Indonesia and the Transition to Independence 1940–1950*. Kuala Lumpur, Oxford, Singapore, New York, Oxford University Press.

Sima, W. (2012). Re-introducing *The China Critic. Chinese Heritage Quarterly*, 30/31, June–September.

Song, G. (2018). Indes Néerlandaises et Culture Chinoise Deux Traductions Malaises du *Roman des Trois Royaumes* (1910–1913), https://journals.openedition.org/archipel/1074#tocto1n2

Soejatmiko, B. (1982) Etnis Tionghoa di Awal Kemerdekaan Indonesia, Sorotan Bok Tok Pers Melayu-Tionghoa (The Ethnic Chinese in the Early Independence Indonesia, the Highlight of Bok Tok on the Chinese-Malay Press, December 1945–September 1946). Surabaya, Liberty.

Suryadinata, L. (1984). *Dilema Minoritas Tionghoa* (The Dilemma of the Indonesian Chinese minority). Jakarta, Grafitipers.

Suryadinata, L. (2015). *Prominent Indonesian Chinese: Biographical Sketches* (4th edn.). Singapore, ISEAS.

Steenbrink, K. (2015). *Catholics in Independent Indonesia: 1945–2010*. Brill, Leiden.

WB (1949). Doenia Soerat Kabar di Indonesia Sehabis Perang (Indonesian Newspaper After the War). *Java Critic*, 6:17–19.

Zhou, T. (2019). *Migration in the Time of Revolution: China, Indonesia and the Cold War*. Cornell: Cornell University Press.

https://doi.org/10.1142/9789811250668_0013

Chapter 13

Wayang Potehi: Cultural Connection between Taiwan and Indonesia

Kaori Fushiki

Professor, Taisho University, Japan

Brief Introduction on *Wayang Potehi* in Indonesia

Indonesian *wayang potehi* is mostly performed in *klenteng* (Chinese temples). And it is also performed at shopping malls and cultural events held in various places during *Imlek* (Chinese New Year) and other occasions. In addition, as its presence in television news programs has increased in recent years, *wayang potehi* performances have also begun to increase in areas that had not seen it in a long time or areas that it have not been performed.[1]

However, with details to be described later, the unique characteristic of *wayang potehi* is the use of the Indonesian language. *Wayang* in various parts of Indonesia uses their local languages, such as Javanese, Balinese, etc., with Kawi, old Javanese, which is the language of poetry, whereas *wayang potehi* uses Indonesian "national" language, Bahasa Indonesia, as the main language of its performance except for Hokkien 福建語 in a very little poetry part of the first appearance of each character in the performance

[1]As for the change of social context, see Fushiki (2019b).

which is called *su liam pek*[2] 四聯白 or *suluk*. It is only *wayang potehi* that uses the national language for its performance mainly.

To say about its performance style, the *wayang*, *wayang potehi* can be considered as retaining the old style of *potehi/budaixi* 布袋戲.[3] The figure of the puppets, the *hi-tai* 戲台 (stage) that imitated temple buildings, and the performance style that the *dalang* (puppeteers) are sitting while they are performing are quite similar with old *potehi* styles and look, keeping well its Chinese-ness. However, if we look at the actual performance, it certainly has features that can only be said as Indonesian *wayang*.

From such appearance of *wayang potehi*, it may be thought what Indonesia-ness of wayang *potehi* is compared to the practice of *potehi* in other countries described later. In fact, *wayang potehi* has suddenly attracted attention in the field of ethnomusicology in recent years, and there are quite a few PRC and Taiwanese students doing fieldwork on this subject. At that time, after all, Chinese-ness or Sino-ness in *wayang potehi* is often referred to consciously or unconsciously. Even though the successors do not mention technical terms in Hokkien or Mandarin, it happens that technical terms of *wayang potehi* are replaced with Hokkien or Mandarin in academic presentations. For example, the music of *wayang potehi* basically inherits the form of *pak koan/bei guan* 北管, but the successors themselves did not know the name of music genre. They did not have the opportunity to learn music theory properly, but because their practice was an imitation of their predecessors and passed down orally, they have only given a general outline. In the past, they added gamelan and Western music instruments in the accompanying music, and in recent years, they have taken in some Chinese musical instruments and songs that they like on YouTube. Certainly, people who know *potehi* in China and Taiwan will recognize the things that have changed from *pak koan*, but since the successors themselves do not mention them, the usage of the Hokkien or Mandarin technical term to describe the actual performance/phenomenon is the act of unconsciously searching for Sino-ness. And if we try to derive Indonesia-ness from a comparison of how it differs from practice in China and Taiwan, that Indonesia-ness may only be the view of the researchers, but later the Sino-ness and Indonesia-ness are materialized,

---

[2] This is not misspelled, but Indonesian spelling.

[3] In the following, when I mention "historical Chinese" one and Taiwanese one, I am going to write it as *potehi*. Because before the Minguo era, the theater form was just called as *potehi* in Nanyang.

and there is a possibility that they will become the cause of local conflict. It is not such Sino-ness or Taiwan-ness that I would like to clarify in this chapter.

The main point of this chapter is to clarify how the current successors of *wayang potehi* interact with Taiwan between the longing for the clear roots lost in the traditional process and the recent practice. What kind of new practice did they get from this? Therefore, this chapter begins by looking at the history of how *wayang potehi* settled in Indonesian society. How did *wayang potehi* come to Indonesia and settle down? And after that, what was the conflict/repression on it? In addition, how did *wayang potehi* meet with Taiwanese *potehi*, especially *wai jiang budaixi* 外江布袋戲 in the removal of the ban of the Chinese culture in Indonesia and the research and practice that became popular with it? In the process, what did Indonesian successors seek by meeting Taiwan, which is close to its roots? And in the process, they get a new idea and take it home, return to Indonesia and start a new practice. I would like to clarify what it is.

Prior Research and Papers

There are some important prior studies on *wayang potehi* in the field of ethnomusicology. Victoria M. Clara van Groenendael's paper, "*Po-té-hi*: The Chinese Glove Puppet Theatre in East Java", is probably the earliest paper introducing *wayang potehi* in Indonesia and describes its practice in 1980s based on her field research in the late 1980s. The article is an off-shoot of her research of *jaranan*[4] in East Java at the time. The article is very informative, although some details are inaccurate, unfortunately.[5]

Margaret Kartomi researched the history of varieties of entertainments including *wayang potehi* that were sponsored by Indonesian-Chinese *tauke* (patrons) during celebrations such as Chinese New Year (春節), *Capgohmeh* (十五暝), *Rebutan* (*Pudu*, 普度), and Indonesian-Chinese

---

[4]*Jaranan* is a horse dance in East Java and Central Java, and the East Javanese one is famous for the dancers going to trance while they are dancing.

[5]For example, when she describes about the prior performance, the most important ritual part of *wayang potehi* that is performed prior to the main story, she describes a character as a "clownish actor" as the "locally known … god of the theatre" (van Groenendael, 1993:30). This would have been neither a theater god nor a clown but the "masked prime minister", Tek Jin Kiat, performing the ritual called *ke kwan/pai siu* as part of the *wayang potehi* (Purwoseputro, 2014: 103).

music such as the accompaniment of *wayang cokek*,[6] *tandhak* (dancing), *wayang* (theater) from the colonial era to 1990s with Western influences from Portuguese and Dutch and the changes of economic situations. Through the colonial era, Indonesian-Chinese or peranakan *tauke* provided some syncretic forms of music, and later, one of the music forms was used in *wayang potehi*. In the past, there was an era that *wayang potehi* was accompanied by *gambang kromong*. According to her, *gambang kromong* was a form of mixture of Chinese bowed string instruments (called *hyan* and *sukong*) and side-blown flute (*suling*) with Sundanese xylophone (*gambang*) and a set of Sundanese drums (*kendang*), and it changed its style in the 1870s to include Sundanese instruments such as suspended gongs and gong-chimes (Kartomi, 2000: 291–292). Today, *gambang kromong* is not popular, though the names of the musical instruments are still used from this ensemble.

Tsai Tsung-te (蔡宗德) also researched about the succession of *wayang potehi* and its music based on interviews with puppeteer Thio Tiong Gie 張忠義 in Semarang and Sukar Mudjiono in Surabaya (Tsai, 2015). In his paper, he described a little bit about the differences of the Indonesian *wayang potehi* and Taiwanese *potehi* and clarified their accompanying music. In other papers, there is no information about the musical pieces directly, though his paper clarified four musical genres that is used in *wayang potehi*: traditional *budaixi bayin* music (传统布袋戏八音音乐), Chinese folk songs, Chinese popular songs and Indonesian folk songs (*ibid.*: 87). And importantly, he did not translate any related technical terms that was told by puppeteers to Mandarin or Hokkien. Although some technical terms were already translated into Mandarin in some references, it can confuse researchers and successors of *wayang potehi*, and the translation also can change their technical terms in the practice forever.

Stenberg has several publications about a detailed history of *wayang potehi* from its origins in the East Indies to the present and those publications are very informative and important. Interestingly, in his most recent publication (Stenberg 2019), he mentions the *wayang potehi* performance is considered an Indonesian art by many, including some Indonesian politicians, former presidents Abdurrahman Wahid (Gus Dur) and Megawati

[6] *Wayang cokek* is "performances which were of Chinese origin and in which female singer-dancers danced with male customers." To accompany *wayang cokek*, a syncretic musical form called *gambang* (later known as *gambang kromong*) was used (Kartomi, 2000: 281).

Sukarnoputri, the current president Joko Widodo and former mayor of Jakarta Basuki Tjahaja Purnama (Ahok). In the publication, he also surveys the new performance models of *wayang potehi*.

History: Migration from China

Before writing about its brief history, it would be better to explain the name *wayang potehi*. In East Java, the current center of *wayang potehi*'s succession, it was originally called as *wayang titik*. *Wayang potehi* was the designation in other areas, Central Java and West Java. However, the same name, *wayang titik*, in Central Java means *wayang kulit Cina-Java* (*wayang cinwa/wacinwa*) that is a kind of *wayang kulit Jawa* using Chinese stories. Because the name causes confusion, I decided to follow Ardian Purwoseputro, author of *Wayang Potehi in Java* (Purwoseputro, 2014) and a counterpart of collaborative research, to use the name *wayang potehi* for the glove puppet theater. Therefore, I also use the term of *wayang potehi* for the glove puppet theater in this chapter.

Potehi was brought to Java by immigrants from Fujian, China, in the middle of the 18th century. According to the oldest record, there was a group of *potehi* in Semarang and the group came to Batavia in 1772 for their performance. There is also a record that when Tay Kak Sie 大覚寺 in Semarang was established, there was a big ritual, and at the time, *potehi* was performed for two months (Stenberg, 2015a: 396). From then on, *potehi* was actively performed in Semarang, and Semarang became an important area that could also be called the center of *potehi*.

Thus, *potehi* began to be performed in various places in Java afterward. In the 19th century there are many records that it was performed in various places in Java. And at the end of the 19th century, mixing had already begun, as seen in the story of *potehi* being written in *Aksara Java* (Javanese character) (Figure 1).[7]

In the first half of the 20th century, there were also performances recorded in various parts of Java, Sumatra, such as Padang, Medan and Solok. The first half of the 20th century was the golden age of *potehi* in Indonesia (Stenberg, 2015b: 46). *Gambang kromong*, a mixture of Javanese (Sundanese) gamelan and Chinese pentatonic scale, became

[7]Toni Harsono's collection. This book does not have a title or any information on the publication. However, the handwriting indicates the year 1888.

Figure 1: A copy of handwriting book in Javanese character back in 1888

Source: March 19, 2018, photo taken by author.

popular (around the late 1930s was the golden age of *gambang kromong*), and some of the instruments and music of *gambang kromong* also diverted to *potehi*.[8] The influence can still be seen in musical instruments used in accompaniment of *potehi* and their names.

[8] Instead of using slendro scale, an Indonesian pentatonic scale, Chinese pentatonic was introduced in the Javanese (Sundanese) gamelan. And *gambang kromong* also used some Chinese musical instruments especially for the strings, furthermore, even Western musical instruments, such as guitars, were also added to the ensemble.

After the Japanese occupation period, in the latter part of the 20th century, the popularity of *potehi* began to decline gradually. In the 1950s, Chinese films became popular, and its songs were also adopted to *potehi* (Stenberg, 2015b: 51). However, it was the incident of September 30, 1965 that became a decisive factor for the decline of *potehi*. After this coup, the Indonesian Communist Party was repressed, and the Chinese descendants were also repressed because of the suspicion of being connected with the Communist Party of the People's Republic of China. Therefore, *potehi* that was thought as one of Chinese matters was also repressed.

The repression against *potehi* was done in the form of restriction of occasion and place of performance, and advanced application of performance permission including contents to be performed needed to be filed. *Potehi*'s *Hi-pen* 戲棚 and *Hi-tai* were hidden inside temple buildings especially in urban areas, such as Hong Tek Hian 鳳德軒 of Surabaya,

Figure 2: *Hi-tai* of wayang potehi inside a temple building, at Hong Tek Hian 鳳德軒, Surabaya

Source: March 8, 2014, photo taken by author.

Figure 3: *Hi-tai* and *Hi-peng* in front of temple buildings at Hong san kiong 鳳山宮, Gudo

Source: March 6, 2014, photo taken by author.

so-called Klenteng Dukuh or Kampong Dukuh, and it was covered with walls so as not be seen by nearby citizens (Figures 2 and 3).[9]

It is said that interactions with others have been broken except interactions with a few Javanese children living near the temple. Prior to the

[9]Mudjiono, Sukar (Alias: Jhon"R"). Personal communication, March 8, 2014.

performance, people needed to apply to *Kantor Sosial Politik* (the Social and Political Bureau) in the provincial government, and it was needed to write detailed information such as where and what kind of occasion, who was the client, who was the *dalang*. Moreover, it was necessary to write the title and the outline as to what the story to be performed was. And even if the performance was about a story of the Tang Dynasty era, if it was a scene including politics or a conflict involving war or weapons, the content was not permitted, and the scene using weapons had to be deleted. At the same time, as *dalang*s were against these applications and brought in politics and governance-related matters in their performances or inserting scenes of fighting with weapons, they were arrested and jailed. For example, Ki Susomo, who was the keyperson of the largest "*potehi* family" in Java, was jailed eight times in his life under these circumstances.[10]

At the same time, as a means of protecting their lives, the Chinese themselves also gave up keeping materials of *potehi*, and actively changed its form. Because documents written in Chinese characters could not be read by Indonesians, they raised suspicions about the contents, which raised concern that it could lead to red scare and related riot. As a result, all of them were alphabetized by Soewandi spelling and then incinerated by themselves. They also abolished the belief and practices of the theater god that was worshiped in the backstage.

In addition, until the early 1990s when the political power of Suharto began to decline from the 1980s, there were situations where people who had succeeded or were related to *potehi* forbade their succession to their children. The second generation of *dalang totok* who succeeded *potehi* and continued its performance thought that it only faced political, social and economic difficulties, so they prohibited their children, the third generation, to learn *potehi*. Many children turned to doing business and *potehi*'s tradition was ceased once and for all.[11]

Owing to this situation, *potehi* was nearly abolished in the 1990s.[12] Mainly the Javanese successors continued their performances on small requests from temples. There was no money to charter a car when going out to the other temples, and the *potehi* group had to hitchhike at the roadside, according to people who know that time.[13] The main performing

[10] Susomo. Personal communication, March 6, 2014.

[11] Harsono, Toni. Personal communication, September 3, 2016.

[12] Purwanto and Widodo. Personal communication, September 3, 2016.

[13] Purwanto. Personal communication, September 3, 2016.

Figure 4: The oldest puppet that Harsono's grandfather brought from Quanzhow

Source: March 7, 2014, photo taken by author.

place was no longer limited to East Java and a part of Central Java, but still *potehi* had declined so much as the logistics was more difficult.

That situation changed in 2001. Abdurrahman Wahid (Gus Dur) who was born in the Jombang prefecture where the center of succession of the present *potehi* is, became president and removed the ban of Chinese culture officially. Gus Dur was from the village just next to Gudo, one of the bases of *potehi* in Jombang prefecture, and was the leader of Islam who co-existed with the Chinese in the community. When the restoration of Chinese culture began, among the third generation of *dalang totok*, a person forbidden to carry the torch became a patron of *potehi*, Toni Harsono (Tok Hok Lai 卓

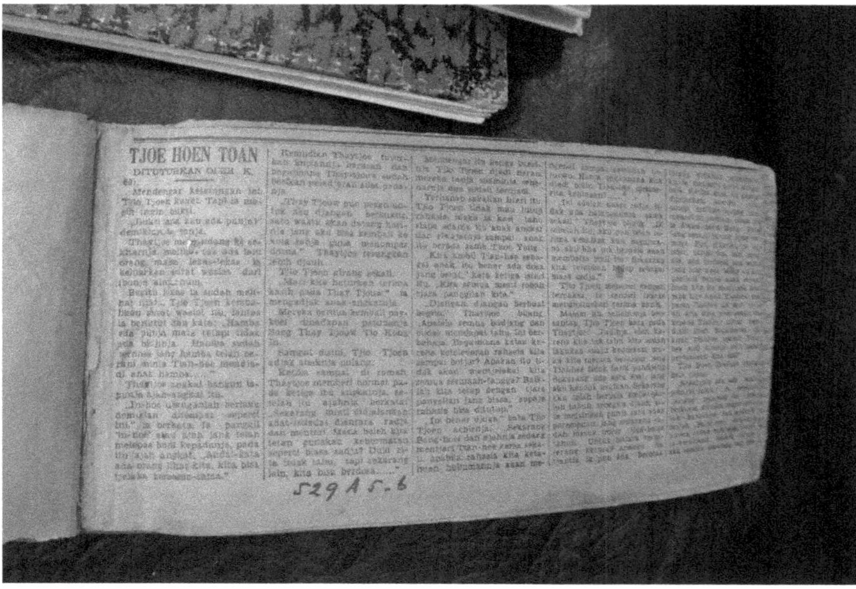
TJOE HOEN TOAN

Figure 5: Old newspaper clips

Source: March 7, 2014, photo taken by author.

福来).[14] Beginning with contributing a car for the transportation of *potehi*'s group, his support eventually reached a wider range, such as support for puppets and *Hi-tai* production and collection of materials. He collected puppets left by the *dalang totok* who passed away one after another (Figure 4), memorandum for performances, rips of story books and newspaper novels circulating in rental book stores that could also be called antiques (Figure 5), and shared them with members of *wayang potehi*'s group.

Among these reconstructions, a message from Ardian, the author of the book of *wayang potehi in Java* and a relative of Toni, was directed to me, and finally *wayang potehi* encountered Taiwanese *potehi*.

Wayang Potehi Met Taiwanese *Potehi*: International Collaborative Research Project "Potehi: Glove Puppet Theater in Southeast Asia and Taiwan"

To be honest, before I started planning a project and starting networking, there was already some connection with *wayang potehi* and Taiwan.

[14]In his biography, this prohibition is not mentioned (Kuardhani, 2011).

In 2010, Olivia Xiao Feifei 蕭翡斐, who was an Indonesian-Chinese lecturer in the Chinese studies of Petra Christian University in Surabaya, wrote a paper on the history of *wayang potehi* at Hong Tek Hian in the Taiwanese academic journal of folklore studies 民俗曲藝 (Xiao, 2010). That paper was related to her master's thesis, and her advisor was Professor Tsai 蔡欣欣 of the Chinese studies of National Chengchi University. Naturally, as the existence of her paper and thesis suggests, the information of the *wayang potehi* in Indonesia was already known in Taiwan at the moment. And a professor of the Graduate Institute of Ethnomusicology, Tainan National University of the Arts, Professor Tsai 蔡宗德 regularly visited Java with many of his students, and during that time, he was interacting with people related to *wayang potehi*.[15] It has been mainly known in the academic world, especially in the fields of Chinese studies and ethnomusicology.

However, it can be said that the people directly involved in *wayang potehi* performance had never had the chance to see Taiwanese *potehi*. In Indonesia, where the development of information infrastructure related to internet had not progressed much, it was not easy to get any foreign information on the internet at the beginning of the 2010s. In such circumstances, the research of *wayang potehi* and the publication of its result as a book was done by the relative of *wayang potehi*'s patron Toni, Ardian who lived in urban areas at the time. In the process of writing, he envisioned "*wayang potehi* Indonesia go international" and started to contact foreign researchers.

At that time, while I was doing field research in Singapore, I posted some photo series of Singapore's *potehi* called as *zhangzhongxi* 掌中戲 while exposing a part of the research records/results on social media, sharing them with related persons and researchers. Ardian found it and contacted me. The first contact was on February 16, 2013. Initially, he meant to plan "a Japan tour of *wayang potehi Indonesia*". However, there was not enough funds or subsidy to do it in Japan, nor any support to incarnate it. As for the invitation performance of overseas artists in Japan, the scale of the subsidy has been reduced year by year, and it is currently difficult to obtain subsidies in most cases. Therefore, at that time I agreed to his plan, but since then I have gathered information on *wayang potehi* in Indonesia.

[15] His most recent paper about *wayang potehi* have been published in Chinese, in 2015 (Tsai, 2015).

Figure 6: Malaysian *zhangzhongxi* 掌中戲 by Beng Gek Hong 鳴玉鳳 in Penang. The first paper about the Malaysian potehi was written in 1981 by Tan (Tan 1981)

Source: March 4, 2014, photo taken by author.

Figure 7: Banxianxi 扮仙戲 (Ritual play) in Singaporean *zhangzhongxi by* Xin Yi Sheng Zhang zhong ban 新藝聲掌中班 in Singapore

Source: March 10, 2014, photo taken by author.

However, the information in front of me was so different from Singapore's *potehi* at the time. Also, it was different from Taiwanese *potehi*, which is rich in materials and resources for research. In addition, *potehi* in Singapore and Malaysia are also different from those in Taiwan, so I did not know what I had to refer to know details about *wayang potehi*. All of them can be called *potehi*, and all glove puppet, but are they the same? To clarify that question by one person was too wide of an area and academic field, and I had absolutely no idea what to do.

However, in the fall of that year, the call for the grant for collaborative research project came out. At this time, the countries covered by the collaborative research in the grant were five countries: Indonesia, Malaysia, Thailand, the Philippines and Japan. However, as it allows the organization of collaborative research including researchers from other countries, I immediately planned an international collaborative research on *potehi*. Professor Tan Sooi Beng, an ethnomusicologist from Malaysia, was also in the midst of investigating and inheriting *potehi* in Penang (Figure 6). But the Malaysian *potehi* that she showed me was different from that of Singapore (Figure 7). It looked quite similar, but different. Therefore, it was necessary to put Singapore in international collaborative research, as well as Taiwan as an important base of *potehi*.

The project based on this grant began in 2014. The aim was to conduct field survey in each country and mutual cultural exchange based on creativity, and the first symposium and exchange were held in Tokyo (Figure 8).[16] The reason why it was held in Tokyo was due to political considerations still necessary in Malaysia and Indonesia and we could not organize it in Taiwan and Singapore with that grant. Moreover, the Indonesian group also aimed to "go international". In that context, I chose Japan that is politically neutral as the place of exchange. At that time, Dr. Robin Ruizendaal and Taiyuan Puppet Theater Company went to Tokyo with the subsidy of the Republic of China's Ministry of Culture. This was the first opportunity when *wayang potehi* met Taiwanese *potehi*.

During their stay for about a week, members of Fu He An, *wayang potehi* group, got conscious about the differences, such as differences in the performance styles and the story performed, differences in the manipulation

---

[16]Those related events were held from September 17–23, 2014. And the symposium was held on September 19 at Taisho University, Tokyo.

Figure 8: The first demonstration of Indonesian *wayang potehi* and Taiwanese *potehi* in an International collaborative research project, Tokyo

Source: At the Nippon Foundation building, September 17, 2014, photo taken by author.

of puppets, differences in languages, and learned new things and way of making the head of the puppets (Figure 9).[17]

The following year, with the support of the Ministry of Culture, Taipei Culture Bureau and The Taipei National University of the Arts, an international symposium and festival of *potehi* in Taipei was held to publish the results of the collaborative research.[18] In this festival, we were able to see some kinds of *potehi* in Taiwan, and a group doing performances at a temple daily in Malaysia was also invited to perform. Therefore, their differences were more clearly recognized. And this opportunity became important for the successors of *wayang potehi* in Indonesia.

[17]This grant was in the API (Asian Public Intellectuals) fellowship program, named as API collaborative grant 2014, supported by Nippon Foundation.

[18]These related events were held from December 12–16, 2015, in Taipei and Beitou. And the symposium was held on December 16. The result of this project was published as Fushiki & Ruizendaal eds. 2015.

Figure 9: The delightful author of *Wayang Potehi in Java*, Ardian Purwoseputro, when he found the same character in Indonesian *wayang potehi* and Taiwanese *potehi*. Left is the Taiwanese, right is the Indonesian

Source: September 17, 2014, photo taken by author.

Toni, who is a patron and accompanying the group as an assistant for the puppeteers, wanted to search the "*asli* (original/authentic) *potehi*" in Taiwan, especially the original style and meaning of *su liam pek* of *potehi* that was already lost. Toni's grandfather was *dalang totok* who came from Quanzhou to Indonesia, and his father was also *dalang*. However, he was forbidden to inherit *potehi* from his father in the era of repression and because he progressed to the world of business, he had no chance to learn *wayang potehi*. Toni was unable to learn Hokkien language that was his grandfather and father's mother tongue in the era when all Chinese-related things were forbidden, and also could not learn Mandarin. Because of this reason, he cannot read nor write Chinese characters. To make matters worse, when the times changed and *potehi* came to light again, his father had already died, and he could not learn anything from his father at all. He noticed that there were lots of knowledge he had lost because he did not learn from his father and he hoped to "get it back" in Taiwan. And, as a

Figure 10: Indonesian group visited Master Chen to seek "the original" *su liam pek*

Source: December 14, 2015, photo taken by author.

part of it, he wanted to find out the meaning about a part of *su liam pek*[19] in Taiwan.

A part of that meaning was easily found by the Malaysian group. Members of Malaysian group were able to recognize that some of *su liam pek* in Indonesian *wayang potehi* was the same even though the sounds of Indonesian *dalang*'s pronunciation was strongly affected by Bahasa Indonesia. One of the members could speak Bahasa Malaysia, which is quite similar to Bahasa Indonesia, so he could talk with Javanese members directly.[20]

However, for most of the meaning of *su liam pek/suluk* which was still not found, members of the group of *wayang potehi* in Indonesia co-operated with the Taiwanese classical *potehi* group and asked directly to several masters including Master Chen Xi Huang 陳錫煌 (Figure 10). Finding out the meaning was extremely difficult. For those Indonesian members who could not understand Hokkien (Taiwanese) nor Mandarin and Taiwanese masters, many people were present as interpreters. *Wayang potehi*'s *dalang* read alphabetized *su liam pek*. Interpreters explained that this *su liam pek* was "the word is for this kind of specific character...". However, it was impossible to find anything in the Taiwanese *su liam pek*. That work continued for two days, but only a small amount of the meaning was found, and in most cases, it was only found that *su liam pek* seems not to

[19]Toni Harsono. Personal communication, December 15, 2015.

[20]This interaction was done on December 13, 2015.

be shared between Taiwan and Indonesia. It goes without saying that Toni seeking the original, lost meaning was very disappointed.[21]

But on the other hand, there was something new for the Indonesian members. It was the figure of the theater god that they lost in the past and its practice of belief. In the process of mutual exchange, the identity of one of puppet heads whose origin and characters were unknown among the people of *wayang potehi* in Indonesia was revealed. It was a head of *Tian Du Yuan Shuai* 田都元帥. Belief of the theater god had been abandoned during repression and no one remembered about it, therefore, the figure of the theater god was also forgotten. However, during the festival in Taiwan, they saw the figure of the theater god at the museum, and by accidently visiting a temple dedicated to *Tian Du Yuan Shuai* while walking around the city, they learnt about the figure of the god and brought it back to Indonesia.

Currently, they do a practice of the belief of the theater god in their own way. After failing several times, they finally made a puppet of the theater god. Because they recorded and memorized the figure of the *Tian Du Yuan Shuai* in the style of 嘉礼戲（Marionette), their figure of the theater god came to look like it, although construction of the puppet is still in glove puppets (Figure 11). However, it does not mean changing their *wayang potehi* performance, as they do not prepare the altar for the god in *au-tai* (backstage) area, and they also do not make any offerings to the god at the beginning.[22] Despite this, when members of *wayang potehi* participate in the temple's *kirab* (procession of the gods), etc., they bring it and hung on their drum set.[23] There is even a *dalang* who always carries the head that failed to make a proper puppet, and when he does his performances as *dalang*, he puts it in backstage area like a guardian.[24]

---

[21] Toni Harsono. Personal communication, December 15, 2015. A part of this process was reported in Fushiki (2019a).

[22] A few years later, they started to pray the theater god at their base in Gudo, and in February 2020, they started a new ritual for the theater god before they start their *wayang potehi* performance and putting the theater god statue in a box at *au-tai*. The situation related to the theater god is drastically and rapidly changing now.

[23] It happened for the first time on the *kirab* of a *klenteng* in Malang, October 21, 2018. And there were also some people who wanted to pray for the theater god (Widodo. Personal communication, March 3, 2019.)

[24] It happened on September 10, 2018 at Hong San Kiong, Gudo. The *dalang* for the day was the son of Ki Susomo, Sonny Frans Asmara.

Figure 11: The recently made altar for the theater god. The right end is the first theater god Fu He An made. The center above one was brought from Taiwan and gifted by someone to the group of Fu He An

Source: March 2, 2020, photo taken by author.

The desire to revive their lost tradition gave birth new practices within them during the exchanges with Taiwan (Figure 12).[25]

Recognition of Indonesia-ness and *Wayang-ness*

Since the exchange in Taipei, the yearning for Taiwan has expanded among the successors of *wayang potehi*. Especially young members who were unable to go to Taiwan want to study in Taiwan. Generally, they are eager to incorporate various Chinese elements. For example, in terms of

[25] Even the statue for the belief of the theater god also is accepted in Indonesia nowadays. There was someone who went to Taiwan and brought back the statue of *Tian Du Yuan Shuai* and gave it to the reader of the *wayang potehi* group Fu He An, Toni Harsono. Since then, he does the practice of the belief of the theater god in his house. The statue has been brought to Hong San Kiong Gudo for a *kirab* in September 2019.

Figure 12: A new ritual praying to the theater god to start *wayang potehi* performance in Kong Ling Bio, Temanggung

Source: February 29, 2020, photo taken by Lydia Sia Lie Bing.

music, when Toni buys and gives them Chinese musical instruments, they learn music by themselves through YouTube, etc., and bring it into *wayang potehi* performances. As a result, the small backstage can be filled with many musical instruments, and often there is not enough space for all the members. These aggressive young people began to say that they wanted to go to Taiwan to learn the art of delicate and skilled manipulation technique of puppets.[26]

[26] Sonny Frans Asmara. Personal communication, September 10, 2018.

Also, although they are often Muslims or Christians on their identity cards, *Kejawen*'s practice, which is folk belief of Java and also syncretism of various religions, is always familiar with them. They are forgiving and aggressive to receive other religious factors in their practice as well, accepting the gods brought back from Taiwan without hesitation.

On the other hand, however, the exchange with Taiwan has also made them realize that their *wayang potehi* is no longer unique. Initially, when Indonesia applies for *wayang* as an intangible cultural heritage of UNESCO,[27] the successors have strongly insisted that their practice is "*wayang* of Indonesia" as a strategy to survive *wayang potehi*. Even when a research team in Indonesia such as SENAWANGI[28] visited to the *wayang potehi* group, they emphasized how much *wayang potehi* has Indonesia-ness and has been loved in Indonesian society. Even though no matter how puppets and performances look like Chinese, they insisted that everything is from Indonesia, both the successors, the puppets and the performance themselves.

Indeed, many of successors of the descendants of *dalang totok* have already insisted that they are *Orang Indonesia* (Indonesian) rather than *Orang Tionghoa* (Chinese/overseas Chinese), and even there are some descendants who do not want to use their Chinese name in the newest generation. And many of successors are also Javanese. After the era when the production of puppets and *Hi-tai* could not be borrowed by the craft-workers of PRC or Taiwan, home-made production is possible and there are many Javanese craftsmen. In fact, if politically subtle problems occur, Chinese-ness will be pointed out easily, and it is easy to exclude it as *Tionghoa* (Chinese). They, therefore, strongly insist its Indonesia-ness. It can also be said that the memory of repression and decline in the past strongly emphasizes Indonesia-ness.

And that claim cannot be said to be wrong. Even if we look at its performance style, they who already recognized the different form from the Taiwanese *potehi* are cherishing their style and trying to make the difference clearer. Basically, *wayang potehi* is a narrative as well as other *wayang kulit* in Indonesia. It places more emphasis on telling the story than manipulating the puppets. Therefore, sometimes by leaving the manipulation of puppets to the assistant, *dalang* may even

[27] Indonesian Wayang puppet theater inscribed on the Representative List of the Intangible Cultural Heritage of Humanity in 2008 by UNESCO.

[28] SENA WANGI (*Sekretariat Nasional Pewayangan Indonesia*) is the Indonesian national secretariat of *wayang* and puppetry art organizations.

Table 1: Comparison of the structure of performance with *wayang kulit* and *wayang kulit Bali*

	Potehi	**Wayang Purwa Jawa**	**Wayang Purwa Bali**
Sitting piece	—	O Songs	O Petugak
Overture	O Lautai	O	O Pemungkah
[Ritualistic part]	O Pai siu	O Gunungan/Kayonan	O Kayonan
Part 1	O Suluk	O Suluk	O Petang kilan
	O [Main]	O [Main]	O [Main]
Intermission	O Liau lo	O Goro-goro	O Delem Sangut
Part 2	O [Enemy/bad]	O [Enemy/bad]	O [Enemy/bad]
	—	O kembang perang	—
	—	O [Real purpose]	—
	O Battele or insidents	O Final Battle	O Battle
Ending	O Liau lo	O Penokawan	O Delem Sangut
	O Pai siu	O Gunungan/Kayonan	O Kayonan

Note: Until recent years, the structure of Indonesian *wayang potehi* was not divided in two scenes in main part/scene (the story part), and there was no clear intermission in their performance. They had a structure following to the story of the day, though nowadays the young *dalang*s make their performances like in the chart, and clearly recognize the character of *Liau lo* as a comedian and interpreter, and its role is the same with *goro-goro* in *wayang kulit Java*.[29]

concentrate on talking and singing, playing melodic musical instruments himself. When songs in Hokkien, Mandarin and other Chinese dialects are needed, and if *dalang* does not understand the language well, *panjak* (musician) in the backstage sings on behalf of *dalang*. However, basically the storytelling and singing a song are recognized as most important acts for *dalang*.

Also, the theatrical performance has been standardized as good as Indonesian *wayang* (Table 1). There is no literal "scenario" consisting of directions and lines in *wayang potehi*, and the actions of the puppets and lines in the performance are ad libs other than being conveyed as oral tradition as a pattern. This is the same with other *potehi*, but due to that

[29]Sonny Frans Asmara told it in a program on CNN Indonesia, *Rumah Torelansi Gudo* (broadcasted on October 19, 2019, https://www.youtube.com/watch?v=-n0gfMQ3fzU).

ad lib, it is also possible it is similar with Indonesian *wayang*. Following points are examples.

The follower *Liau Lo/Ya Olo*[30] exists as an important character in the performance and plays a *Punokawan* (comical followers of *Wayang Kulit Jawa*) role. He is usually following the master, complementing the words of the master, explaining the background and behavior of the story, the behavior of the master and complaining about his master behind his back. There is also a scene especially for him in the middle of the story, and it is a scene of entertainment for the audience.[31] In addition, sometimes *Liau Lo* receives some money from the audience directly to accept their special requests to insert announcements, welcome greetings, etc., in a performance and enjoy dialogue with the audience. Moreover, it also appears at the end of every performance and tells that "it is so sad to say that the performance will end soon. If you want to see what happens next, please come on...."[32]

The structure of the performance is almost fixed (Table 2), starting from *Lau-tai* (鬧台, percussion music) part, continue to *pai siu*[33] (拜寿) and *ke kwan*[34] (加冠), before the start of the story. The story itself is also well-constructed as first half, comedy, to latter half, strife and battle.[35] And soon after the short end scene of *Liau Lo/Kepala Gede* a very short part

[30]There are some figures of the puppet for *Liau Lo/Ya Olo*. The one is usually known as *Kepala gede* (*Tua Tau Pio*) which is the big head puppet. The other is *Ya Olo* which has dark chocolate color skin.

[31]During this, *dalang*s usually make some comedies by ad lib and sometimes directly communicate with audiences who are in front of the stage.

[32]In the case of *wayang kulit Java* and *wayang kulit Bali*, at the end of every performance, *Punokawan* and *Sangut* (one of comical followers of Balinese *wayang kulit)* appear and say some moral messages and instructive comments.

[33]*Pai siu* usually called as *Fu Lu Shou* (福禄寿) because it consists the performance of *Fu Lu Shou* and *Tong Cu* (a little red child). And in case of *wayang potehi*, the puppet of *Tong Cu* was made in normal size of glove puppets. Because of the reason, this part should be thought as *Sam Sian* (三仙), though it looks like four deities playing (see Arif 2019, Kuardhani 2018, Mustuti 2013, van Groenendael 1993). The reason why they make *Tong Cu* in normal size is "it is too small to manipulate if we make it as a baby doll" (Widodo. Personal communication, September 3, 2019).

[34]*Pai siu* and *ke kwan* are constructing the part of Banxianxi 扮仙戲 (Ritual play/sacred play to celebrate the peoples, communities, and temples).

[35]As for the story parts, sometimes they can be different from this construction especially at the very beginning of the story or the very end of the story. And the stories usually continue for more than 2 weeks.

Table 2: The structure of *wayang potehi*

0-[purify]		Burning Kim-chua (金紙)	Just only first moment of long term performance
1-overture		Lau-tai (鬧台)	Overture [drum only]
2-[扮仙]	2-1	Pai Siu (拜寿): Hok Lok Siu [H] (福禄寿) + Tong Cu [H] (童子) Su liam pek /Suluk	Appearance of Hok Lok Siu and Tong Cu
	2-2	Pai Siu (拜寿): Hok Lok Siu (H) (福禄寿) + Tong Cu [H] (童子) [Blessing of the deities]	Hokkien version
	2-3	Pai Siu (拜寿): Hok Lok Siu (H) (福禄寿) + Tong Cu [H] (童子) [Blessing of the deities]	Bahasa Indonesia version
	2-4	Ke Kwan [加官]	Blessing from dancing Tek Jin Kiat [Masked dance, nowadays, it is rare to put a mask on the puppet of Tek Jin Kiat] bring and showing Kim long/Sbda (The scroll of "Hap Ke Peng An (合家平安)") *Kim long will keep hanging on Hi-tai while whole performance
3-Part1		First part of the day (mostly main and good characters scene, in a court, etc.)	Depends on the story development, sometimes bad character comes first part. (A scene of main character of the day)
Intermission		Liau lo/Ya Olo	A servant of the enemy or bad character come out singing, talking jokes [comedy]
4-Part2		2nd part of the day (mostly enemies side or bad characters Scene, at the end, some incidents happens or go battle)	Usually the end goes to battle at the end of a performance But in case of very first scenes of the story. it goes to Incidents such as murder/ manslaughter instead of battle
5-ending	5-1	Liau lo/Ya Olo	Announce of the end of performance attractions (lottery etc.)
	5-2	Pai Sia Di [團圓] (man and wife living in harmony)	Wishing prosperity and happiness end with the sentence "Pai sia shin min/bin" "Pai sia hon thian"

Note: Nowadays, *pai siu* in Hokkien (2-2) and in Bahasa Indonesia (2-3) are mixed and become just only one scene in mixed language. It happened because of the death of a dalang who could speak Hokkien fluently and today all *dalang*s cannot speak Hokkien anymore.

pai sia di[36] is continued. This structure is used for almost all performances and stories.

In addition, for the people who are familiar with *wayang kulit*, it is very common that some characters speak their lines in unfamiliar language in their performance, because *Kawi*, language for a poetry, is usually not familiar with the audience. Because of this reason, even some characters in *wayang potehi* speak Hokkien as *su liam pek*, the audience do not mind it.

Thus, even the figures of the puppets are different, the told story is different, the accompanying music is different, the basic form of the performance has been assimilated with *wayang*. The successors of *wayang potehi* are clearly aware of these *wayang*-ness of *wayang potehi* and they perform it as a kind of *wayang*. Some of the *panjak*s were also involved in the performance of Javanese *wayang kulit* for a long time, and their *panjak*s feel equally accompanying *wayang kulit* with Gamelan Jawa and accompanying *wayang potehi* with other musical instruments.[37] While *wayang potehi* has a lost original figure and yearning for Taiwan, it has been established as *wayang* in Indonesia.

Conclusion

In this chapter, following the history of *wayang potehi* in Indonesian society, we have been looking at how *wayang potehi* was influenced from Taiwan after exchanging with Taiwanese *potehi* through international collaborative research and exchange projects.

It was in the middle of the 18th century when the group of *potehi* arrived in Indonesia. Along with the immigrants who came from Fujian, the group of *potehi* also arrived in Indonesia and expanded its area of activity to Sumatra, including West Java, while settling at Semarang as the center of its activities. After the heyday in the first half of the 20th century, the occupation of the Japanese, and the revolutionary war and steadily declining, it has been exposed to repression after 1965. Eventually it

---

[36] Very short play of a set of male and female puppets. The male one is called as *Cong Keng Ki*, and the female one is called as *Kat Bing He*. In this part, the puppets only come out from the back and bow, and dalang says "*Pai Sha Sin Bin*" or "*Pai Sha Hong Tian.*" Selecting which words to use to end the performance depends on its situation.

[37] Selamet Lamalan. Personal communication, September 5, 2018.

almost died in the 1990s. In the past, however, there has not been any information or evidence about the relationship between each group of *potehi* in Indonesia and Taiwan.

With the revival of the Chinese culture from 2001 in Indonesia, thanks to the appearance of patrons, *wayang potehi* that once declined was also revived. With the effort of relatives and researchers, the group of *wayang potehi* who aimed for "go international" met Taiwanese *potehi* in an international collaborative research. While paying attention to the fine technique such as the manipulation technique of the classical *potehi* that was not in their own *wayang potehi*, the way to add a sound effect, they were most interested in *su liam pek*. They asked for the meaning and original/authentic form and accent that they lost in the history of repression of *wayang potehi*. Among the *wayang potehi* successors, there was a yearning for Taiwan, as a homeland of *potehi,* where there must be an original/authentic form, and generations forbidden to inherit the performance from parents wanted to regain the lost tradition in Taiwan. However, that was a failure. They could not find *su liam pek* in Taiwanese classics. The experience in Taiwan, including the fact that it was decisive that not being able to regain original figure in this way, made *wayang potehi* successors strongly recognized that their *wayang potehi* was unique to Indonesia.

As *wayeng potehi*'s survival strategy, Indonesia-ness of *wayang potehi* has been actively claimed so far, and exchanges with Taiwan have made the successors to get conscious about the uniqueness strongly. Reconsideration spanned various points; the point that seems to be the most important is that they recognized *wayang potehi* as an art of storytelling. On the one hand, while witnessing the splendor of Taiwan's puppets manipulation method, there is a yearning for it mainly among young people. On the other hand, while styles that talk stories little by little every day, as the puppets do not move much, *dalang* tells a story and sings a song uniquely. They recognize objectively that it is their greatest feature. And with such a recognition, they try to pass their unique *wayang potehi* that have been a great influence of *wayang kulit* to the next generation. They are also aggressive to incorporate new things, while introducing a part of the belief of the theater god from the exchange with Taiwan, however, they do not want to change their performance style and their theatrical style.

As generations go on, the usage of Hokkien is declining, and more parts are spoken in Indonesian. Although I did not describe in detail in this chapter, until the second generation of *dalang totok*, they also performed *potehi* in Hokkien. However, through experience of repression, its style has been lost mostly. Nowadays, even the Hokkien version of *pai siu* and *ke kwan* parts are also being changed. It will not change the fact that *su liam pek* does not allow the change of wording, even it becomes meaningless words or sounds like Hokkien. However, *wayang potehi* deeply engraved with Indonesia-ness and *wayang*-ness has gained the identity of a kind of *wayang* in Indonesia, while the addition of the atmosphere of Chinese on its music, etc., as it evolves in Indonesian society.

References

Arif, A. R. (2019). Reaktualisasi Wayang Potehi Gudo Tahun 2001–2016: Studi Tentang Hibridasi Budaya Tionghoa Indonesia di Kecamatan Gudo Kabupaten Jombang. *Avatara, e-Journal Pendidikan Sejarah* 7.2, https://jurnalmahasiswa.unesa.ac.id/index.php/avatara/article/download/29027/26576.

Fushiki, K. (2019a). Oto to Natta Kotoba: Indonesia, Wayang Potehi no Shutujoshi (Words Became Sounds: Poetry of *Wayang Potehi* in Indonesia). In Ikuya Tokoro and Kaori Kawai (eds.), *Mono no Jinruigaku 2: Nin'gen to Hi-nin'gen no Dainamikusu* (Anthropology of Things 2: Dynamics of Human and Inhuman), (pp. 209–215). Kyoto: Kyoto University Press.

Fushiki, K. (2019b). Embracing New Performance Spaces to Survive: The Changing Social Context of Indonesian *Wayang Potehi*. *The Journal of the Oriental Society of Australia*, 51: 70–83.

Fushiki, K. and Ruizendaal, R. eds. (2015). *Potehi: Glove Puppet Theatre in Southeast Asia and Taiwan*. Taiyuan, Taipei.

Kartomi, M. (2000). Indonesian-Chinese Oppression and the Musical Outcomes in Netherlands East Indies. In Ronald Radano and Phillip V. Bohlman (eds.), *Music and the Racial Imagination* (pp. 271–317). Chicago, University of Chicago Press.

Kuardhani, H. (2011). *Toni Harsono Maecenas Potehi dari Gudo*. Yogyakarta: Isaac Book.

Kuardhani, H. (2018). Potehi Puppet (布袋戲) in Java. *Dance and Theatre Review, Jurnal Tari, Teater, dan Wayang*, 1(1): 18.

Mastuti, D. W. R. (2013). Wayang Potehi di Gudo. *Proceedings, Festival Wayang Indonesia*, July 6, 2013.

Purwoseputro, A. (2014). *Wayang Potehi of Java*. Jakarta, Afterhours Books.

Stenberg, J. (2015a). Wayang Potehi: Glove Puppets in the Expression of Sino-Indonesian Identity. *Journal of Southeast Asian Studies*, 46(3): 391–416.

Stenberg, J. (2015b). Wayang Potehi: Hokkien Origins, Indonesian Context. In *Potehi: Glove Puppet Theatre in Southeast Asia and Taiwan*. Taipei: Taiyuan.

Stenberg, J. (2019). Glove, String, and Shadow: Sino-Indonesian Forms of Wayang. In *Minority Stages: Sino-Indonesian Performance and Public Display* (pp. 50–75). Honolulu, University of Hawai'i Press.

Tan, S.-B. (1981). The Glove Puppet Theater (*po te hi*) in Malaysia. *Asian Music*, 13(1): 53–72.

Tsai, Tsung-Te (2015). 印度尼西亚华人布袋戏的历史，演出形态与音 Transculture and Identity: Historical and Social Environment of Chinese Indonesian Wayang Potehi. 中央音乐学院学报 *Journal of the Central Conservatory of Music*, 139: 69–108.

van Groenendael, V. M. C. (1993). *Po-té-hi*: The Chinese Glove Puppet Theatre in East Java. In Bernard Arps (Ed.), *Performance in Java and Bali: Studies of Theatre, Narrative, Music and Dance* (pp. 11–33). London, School of Oriental and African Studies.

Xiao, Fei-Fei (2010). 「印尼泗水的「鳳德軒」廟宇布袋戲團發展史」 History of Affiliation with the Fengdexuan Temple Puppet Theatre Troupe in Surabaya, Indonesia 『民俗曲藝』. *Journal of Chinese Ritual, Theatre and Folklore*, 170: 233–281.

Interviews

Ardian Purwoseputro (Poo Thian An). March 6–8, 2014, September 2, 2016.

Purwanto. September 3, 2016.

Purwanto and Widodo. September 3, 2016.

Selamet Lamalan. September 5, 2018.

Sonny Frans Asmara. September 10, 2018.

Sukar Mudjino (alias: Jhon "R"). March 8, 2014.

Susomo (Cak Di), March 6–7, 2014.

Toni Harsono (Tok Hok Lay). March 6–7, 2014, December 15, 2015, September 3, 2016.

Widodo. September 3, 2019.

https://doi.org/10.1142/9789811250668_0014

Chapter 14

Screen Connections between Malaysia, Taiwan, Hong Kong and China*

Thomas Barker

Research Affiliate, Faculty of Arts and Social Sciences,
University of Nottingham, Malaysia

This chapter contributes to the understanding of Chinese transnationalism by focusing on the screen industry connections between Malaysia and production centers in Hong Kong, Taiwan and China. Transnational screen industries connections are formed through creative labor migration, the flow of capital and investment across borders, co-production partnerships and out-sourcing, as well as the establishment and acquisition of screen industries companies and businesses. Alongside a conceptual perspective drawn from Chinese transnationalism, this study engages with scholarly work in East Asian pop culture, Chinese cinemas and studies of creative labor migration within the context of a growing and regionally assertive China (Percival, 2007). It contributes to a growing body of work that seeks to understand how a "rising China" is reshaping Chinese language screen industries through the circulation of cultural products, capital, imagery and people.

*Screen Connections between Malaysia, Taiwan, Hong Kong, and China, THOMAS ALEXANDER CHARLES BARKER, Issues & Studies, Vol. 54, No. 01, 1840002 (2018)., Copyright @ 2018 Issues and Studies and World Scientific Publishing Co. Pte. Ltd. https://www.worldscientific.com/doi/10.1142/S1013251118400027.

As the screen industries of China, Hong Kong and Taiwan have become more intertwined and interdependent, it is useful to posit Malaysia as a new vantage point from which to consider transnational connections. Malaysia is geographically distant from East Asia and provides a counterpoint to the work that has been done on the Chinese diaspora in North America (Lu, 1997). Driving these connections are Chinese Malaysians who utilize their linguistic and cultural resources to become participants as mobile creative labor and co-production partners. In examining the evolving China–Malaysia relationship, this chapter describes new patterns of migration and interaction between Mainland China and Malaysia that form part of the "new Chinese mobility landscape" (Chan and Koh, 2017).

In particular, this chapter focuses on two vectors of this relationship linking the screen industries of Malaysia and China. The first set of relationships is forged as Chinese Malaysians travel to China either temporarily or permanently to work on film and television projects. These moves are supplanting the more established destinations of Hong Kong, Taiwan, Singapore or the United States as Malaysians see China as a viable destination to develop and forge a media career. The second vector consists of the outbound productions coming to Malaysia to use locations, facilities and engage co-production partners. These provide opportunities for local co-production businesses in Malaysia to build relationships with China and its screen industries. Together they develop connections between Malaysia and China that speak of a growing relationship between the two countries.

Defining "China" for the purposes of this chapter is fraught not only with historical, territorial and administrative complexities but also the processes of Chinese transnationalism and globalization have made societies and economies much more integrated and interdependent. This recalls the debate around the concept of "greater China" and how the People's Republic of China (PRC), the Republic of China (Taiwan) and the territories of Macau and Hong Kong are situated in discourse (Harding, 1993). Although Hong Kong returned to PRC rule in 1997 thereby enlarging the administrative territory of the PRC, Hong Kong retains quite a distinctive identity, culture, as well as some administrative autonomy under the "one country, two systems" concept (Lu, 1997: 2). China in this chapter refers primarily to Mainland China as a territory and people, without wanting to reify China as meaning the Chinese Communist Party or Chinese state, while being cognizant of the diversity and complexities within the PRC itself.

Malaysia has come under increased interest recently due to the flow of capital and investment linked to China's ambitious Belt and Road Initiative (BRI, formerly One Belt One Road). Located strategically along the Strait of Malacca, Malaysia has been the focus of Chinese investment in ports, rail, and been willing to take over assets linked to the multi-billion-dollar 1MDB Development Fund scandal (Lopez, 2017). Accompanying this has also been soft power initiatives including the establishment of two Confucius Institutes in Malaysia, the opening of Xiamen University Malaysia Campus in 2016, and increasingly outreach efforts in culture and media (Barker, 2017; Su, 2010). This speaks of both a new recognition of Malaysia's importance to the Southeast Asian region and to China's ambitions but also to the growing power and wealth of China in the region.

This chapter is based on ongoing research into the screen industry connections between China and Malaysia. Alongside an evolving database of productions and projects that see the participation of Chinese and Malaysians parties, I have interviewed a number of Malaysians who have worked in China or with Chinese companies or on Chinese projects. Some of these interviews have been conducted in person in Malaysia, in China or via Skype. Those interviews are interested in learning about the experiences of working in China, motivations and impressions of China's media industries, and thoughts about the relationship between Malaysia and China. They represent an important new dimension in the study of transnational media production, the growth in Chinese media, and how East Asian pop culture is being re-conceptualized in the era of a rising China.

Chinese Transnationalism and the Rise of China

Since the 1980s, the growth and integration of economic activity in the Asia-Pacific region can in part be attributed to what Aihwa Ong and Donald Nonini dubbed "Chinese transnationalism" (Ong and Nonini, 1997). They sought to account for increased flows of people, capital and ideas in the Asia-Pacific region and the particular role and importance of the region's ethnic Chinese populations. Through the vector of Chinese communities, businesses and *guanxi* networks, new flows of capital and investment have been activated. Since 1978 and into the 1980s, this has centered on Mainland China with the development of the Guangdong industrial area attracting significant investment from Taiwan, Hong Kong and Singapore. At the same time, Chinese transnationalism yields new Chinese identities linked to diaspora experiences and a reshaping of social and institutional arrangements across the Asian region (*ibid.*).

Considerable attention has been placed on the Chinese diaspora who are a "transnational community" (Ang, 2004: 179) in the creation of transnational networks and connections. In further defining Chinese transnationalism, Sun and Sinclair (2015) propose the three dimensions of movement and circulation; connectedness, flows, linkages and networks; and a distancing from traditional culture. While Mainland China remains the "center of culture" (Lu, 1997: 12), the realities of diaspora, media making and ongoing hybridization means that Chinese identity and definitions of Chineseness are multiple both within China itself and globally (Ang, 2004: 193). For Sun and Sinclair, diasporic lines of communication provide "a material and cultural geography of belonging" (2015). Here media, such as Chinese language film and television, provide imaginations and representations of identity and culture as well as opportunities for business, collaboration and cultural production.

Chinese transnationalism and the media networks associated with it challenge national models of media production and media markets. In particular, Yue and Khoo (2014) have proposed using "Sinophone" to conceptually capture the diverse range of Sinitic language cinemas and diversity of representations of Chineseness in Chinese language cinema. Chinese cinemas are therefore theorized as both transnational and plural at the same time (Berry and Pang, 2008), thereby challenging the national cinema models and assumed cultural center of Mainland China (Ang, 2004: 184). This has been reflected in the scholarly and popular interest in film production in Taiwan and Hong Kong, and in the Chinese diaspora, especially in the United States (Lim, 2006; Lu, 1997).

Within media economies and markets of the East Asian region more broadly, until recently China has not been seen as a significant production center. As media theorists sought to decenter globalization away from the West (Curran and Park, 2000), production and circulation of pop culture in East Asia provoked the conceptualization of an East Asian pop culture (Chua, 2004) in which countries such as Japan took an important lead role (Iwabuchi, 2002). Chua's conceptualization of "East Asia" is characterized by an unevenness of role of which the most notable was the position of Mainland China which was a large consumer but insignificant producer of cultural content. It was taken that China with its authoritarian political structures, widespread state-ownership and strict censorship, would not be able to produce pop culture as cool or appealing as that produced by market-based capitalist economies such as Japan or South Korea. China-made content would therefore not appeal to audiences outside its borders. Rather, audiences in China were seen to be hungry for cooler and more trendy material from elsewhere — especially music and drama from South Korea and Japan.

Although China has remained somewhat peripheral to studies of Chinese cinemas and East Asian pop culture until very recently, its integration into regional media industries and the importance of the Mainland market is beginning to reshape the contours and definitions of Chinese cinemas. By the 1990s, global media companies, many in advertising, were moving into China to take advantage of the emerging consumer economy and new opportunities for market development. China's ascension to the World Trade Organization (WTO) in 2001 followed by the Beijing Olympics in 2008 further opened China's media and its markets to foreign players and market forces (Kokas, 2017; Lee, 2003; Shirk, 2011). More media partnerships were developed to help modernize and internationalize China's media including Hong Kong's Television Broadcasts Limited (TVB) who partnered with China Media Capital (CMC) and Shanghai Media Group (SMG) in China to establish TVBC in 2012 (Sun and Sinclair, 2015).

Mainland China is altering this narrative as its domestic production increases and as it carves a significant presence in global media industries through private enterprise and state led initiatives such as "media going global" (Sun and Sinclair, 2015). Marketization and the establishment of privately owned production companies, such as Bona Film Group, Huayi Brothers and Wanda, have marked the emergence of commercially driven production and a corresponding growth in the exhibition sector. Through capital accumulation, Mainland Chinese companies are now making significant and strategic acquisitions of media assets in Hong Kong, Singapore and the United States. When Wanda purchased AMC Cinemas in 2012 and Legendary Pictures in 2016 in the United States, many observers began to take note of China (Rainey, 2016). Signs of China's global ambitions are evident in films made and set overseas including the jingoistic action films *Wolf Warrior 2* (Wu Jing, 2017) and *Operation Red Sea* (Dante Lam, 2018) both set in Africa, and comedies such as *Lost in Thailand* (Zheng Xu, 2012) and *Detective Chinatown 2* (Sicheng Chen, 2018). These films are also beginning to be screened commercially overseas — for example, *Operation Red Sea* was released in AMC Cinemas in the United States.

One phenomenon linked to the growing importance of the Chinese media market is the emergence of co-productions that often aim for distribution in China to circumvent the import quotas on foreign films and thereby enjoy a wide release (Kokas, 2017). The most prominent example of this was the Hollywood–China co-production *The Great Wall* (Zhang Yimou, 2015) which starred Matt Damon, Pedro Pascal, Willem Dafoe, Hong Kong megastar Andy Lau, and Chinese actress Jing Tian. With a budget of US$150 million, making it the most expensive film to be shot in China, it saw American and Chinese crews working alongside each other. *The Great Wall* was envisaged as a Chinese blockbuster that could be big in both China and the United States although on its release, it failed to get much traction in either market. Nevertheless, it speaks of the growing sophistication of the Chinese film industry and the importance of its market to the global film industry.

What is occurring then is a rapid reshaping and reorientation of East Asian pop culture, and indeed parts of global pop culture, toward China. Definitions and understandings of Chinese cinemas will invariably accommodate these changes, not just to include greater Mainland product, but also to account for the variety of content from within China itself. It is important to note that media production happens all over China and complicating any simple definition of a Chinese cinema (Zhang, 2008). Nor is China just a captive market of one billion people but is a complex site for negotiation in terms of co-productions which are increasingly competitive as Chinese companies and producers become more assertive and globally savvy. China is thus drawing in foreign participants just as much as it is now looking outward for new markets for its products, acquisitions, and to exert its cultural influence or soft power.

Malaysia in Chinese Media Transnationalism

If China has only recently became a country of interest to studies of Chinese cinemas and East Asian pop culture, Malaysia is even less visible. It has rarely figured in studies of Chinese cinemas and is neither seen as a significant source or consumer of pop culture. It is overshadowed by the more prominent nodes of Chinese language production in Taiwan or Hong Kong and does not command the interest and excitement of a rising

China. Nevertheless, Malaysia is home to Southeast Asia's largest ethnic Chinese population of 6.52 million people, more than the total population of multi-ethnic Singapore (5.89 million) but less than the population of Hong Kong (7.19 million).[1] If it is not a function of population, then other factors contribute to Malaysia's role and prominence in Chinese media transnationalism. Indeed, Chinese Malaysians have a long history of engagement and participation in Chinese media circuits through "*mahua*" or "South Seas" (Nanyang) literature (Bernards, 2017; Raju, 2008) and film companies such as the Shaw Brothers and Cathay-Keris organizations (Muthalib, 2013).

With China closed off after 1949, Mandarin-speaking Malaysians seeking to connect with greater China have seen Taiwan as their natural destination to pursue education related to the media or to pursue a career in the creative industries. Connections to Taiwan developed in the context of Cold War geopolitical alignment away from Communist China, led first by the British and later by the independent Malaysian government. As a result, Malaysian indie filmmaker Tan Chui Mui notes that:

> The Chinese community in Malaysia is closer to Taiwan than to China. Cultural exchanges between China and Malaysia began as late as 1990s. Many Malaysians who were educated in the Chinese language, especially those in their 40s or 50s now, studied in Taiwan. So, there's quite a strong connection with Taiwan. (quoted in Segay, 2007)

Of the Malaysians that moved to Taiwan, the most notable case is filmmaker Tsai Ming-Liang who studied in Taiwan in the early 1980s and has remained there as a prominent artist and filmmaker. Other recent creative migrants to Taiwan include actors Lawrence Ong and Daphne Low, and director Ho Wi-Ding (although he later moved to China).

Other prominent cultural connections to Taiwan are evident in the music industry as many Chinese Malaysian singers since the 1980s have emigrated to Taiwan to take advantage of its larger audience base, music industry infrastructure, and distribution and marketing networks. One of the first notable musical émigrés to Taiwan was Malaysian singer Eric Moo whose career took off after he relocated in the late 1980s. Many other singers have followed including Lee Sinje (Angelica Lee), Fish

---

[1]See The World Factbook 2017, https://www.cia.gov/library/publications/the-world-factbook/index.html.

Leong and Michael Wong. Many of these artists have been reimported back into Malaysia via their Taiwanese labels or concert promoters. They too are part of the transnational circulation of Chinese pop culture and performers, circulating between Taiwan, Singapore, Malaysia and increasingly China.

Hong Kong also offered similar opportunities to Malaysians in the 1980s with the development of broadcaster TVB and a buoyant film industry. Michelle Yeoh, born in Ipoh, moved to Hong Kong in the mid-1980s to pursue a modelling career, before becoming an actress starring in titles such as *Police Story 3: Supercop* (Stanley Tong, 1992) alongside Jackie Chan. In the years since, she has become an international superstar acting in *Crouching Tiger Hidden Dragon* (Ang Lee, 2000) and *Crazy Rich Asians* (Jon M. Chu, 2018). Similarly, Willie Chan (born Chan Chi-Keung) migrated to Hong Kong in 1970 where he met Jackie Chan and became his agent and promoter, especially to support Jackie Chan when he moved to the United States in the 1990s. Willie Chan was also the agent for many other Hong Kong stars of the 1980s and 1990s including Maggie Cheung, Tony Leung Ka Fai, Simon Yam and Edison Chen.

In Malaysia at least, Chinese language filmmaking has only become notable in the years since 2000 (Raju, 2008). Although there are Chinese language television stations, opportunities are limited, and many Chinese diverted into other careers or went overseas. After 2000, a new generation of indie filmmakers have remained in Malaysia to produce work in Chinese whilst retaining a cosmopolitan outlook (Khoo, 2007). Notable names include James Lee, Tan Chui Mui, Liew Sengtat, Ho Yuhang and Teck Tan. Teck Tan's *Spinning Gasing* (2000) for example features Malay, English and Cantonese dialogue. Many found exposure at international film festivals and tapped into the growing interest in digital and indie production from Southeast Asia at the time. They have also sought work overseas as well with Tan Chui Mui, for example, spending a number of years in China working alongside Chinese luminary Jia Zhangke making advertisements and contributing to the omnibus documentary *Yulu* (2011).

In the last 10 years, Chinese language filmmaking in Malaysia has undergone a revival, both commercially and critically. Box-office success of titles like *Nasi Lemak 2.0* (Namewee, 2011) and *The Journey* (Chiu Keng Guan, 2014) have shown the commercial potential of Chinese language films, alongside the critical success of films like *Shuttle Life* (Tan Seng Kiat, 2017) which won awards at the 20th Shanghai International Film Festival. Many of these films take advantage of the Chinese New Year screening slot to maximize their audience such as the comedy *Think*

Big Big (Chiu Keng Guan, 2017). Director Chiu Keng Guan has become a significant mainstream director since graduating from the Beijing Film Academy and returning to Malaysia. Likewise, Ho Yuhang recently directed the Malaysia–Hong Kong–China produced triad-revenge film *Mrs K* (2016) with Hong Kong actors Simon Yam, Kara Wai and Taiwanese singer Wu Bai. Currently about 10 Chinese feature films are released annually, mostly in Cantonese or Mandarin.

As members of an ethnic minority in Malaysia, Chinese filmmakers are presented with limited opportunities in Malaysia's already small market. Malaysia's film market is divided ethnically and linguistically into four "racial" groups — English, Malay, Indian (Tamil) and Chinese (primarily Mandarin and Cantonese).[2] Aspiring Chinese filmmakers are thus left with a series of choices: remain in the limited Chinese language market; go mainstream into the commercial Malay market; or seek opportunity overseas. Many Chinese Malaysians have been willing to move overseas for opportunities. Whereas Taiwan was often the most obvious choice, China has become a new option for Malaysian filmmakers. As a Malaysian actress now in Beijing says "Trust me, when I was young I never thought I would end up in China. I always wanted to go to US." Commenting on her own options for work, one Malaysian freelance producer notes:

> I was thinking, should I stay in China because everybody tells you it's more prospective to work in China and [there are] opportunities there ... it's like an eye-opener etc. [...] money's there and [the] Malaysian film industry was really [small].

Just as China's market is at a moment of expansion and internationalization, Chinese Malaysian filmmakers are looking for greater opportunities. There is a moment of confluence between the two countries which is prompting many Malaysians to see China as a viable destination.

Moving to Mainland China

Concurrent with observations about Chinese transnationalism, scholars of migration are tracing the new migration patterns of the Chinese in

[2]Malaysia's first Hokkien film *You Mean the World to Me* (Saw Teong Hin) was released in 2017. Shot in Penang, the film stars a number of Malaysian and Singapore actors with cinematography by Christopher Doyle.

Southeast Asia. Yuk Wah Chan and Sin Yee Koh (2017) describe a "new Chinese mobility landscape" in which new flows and directions of migration are being activated both to and from the Mainland and from within the diaspora. Through migration, both temporary and permanent, and transnational collaboration new "transnational social fields" are created (Willis, Yeoh and Fakhri, 2004: 3). Over the past 20 years, as Thunø suggests, "Chinese migration experiences [...] are shaped in new ways by global capitalism, globalization, and the rising economic significance of China" (2007: 2). Routes back to the Mainland are being opened again as China liberalizes and has even recently proposed a special category of residency visa for "Overseas Chinese" who want to return to China (Luo and Li, 2018).

Historically, as the work of Wang Gungwu suggests (Wang, 2000), much of the migratory patterns were outward from China, creating the diaspora populations across the world. With the PRC inaccessible for decades during the twentieth century, overseas Chinese populations developed distinctive regional identities that diverged from those on the Mainland. This saw the "development of new (global and hybrid) Chinese identities" (Chan and Koh, 2017) of which Chinese Malaysians represent a very broad category. Chinese Malaysians are shaped by their experience as a minority population in Malaysia: politically marginalized but with high socio-economic status (Freedman, 2000). As a former British colony, English has also been widely adopted as a language in the education system and broadly in the media, thus entrenching broad fluency in English across much of Malaysia's educated and urban populations.

Malaysian independence in 1957 wedded many Chinese Malaysians to the new nation, but they retained transnational linkages and ties to Chinese cultural traditions and practices. This differed from the experience of ethnic Chinese in Indonesia who were forced to assimilate to the majority national culture accompanied by a ban on Chinese languages in 1966, and in Singapore where the state insisted much more tightly on English language in education and official discourse. In Malaysia, Chinese language education was able to continue providing a pathway for students in Malaysia to learn in Mandarin and graduate with a Unified Education Certificate (UEC). Due to state education policies however, Malaysians earning a UEC are unable to enroll in the state university system. As most UEC graduates are Mandarin-speaking Chinese, many of them pursued further study overseas. In more recent years, this maintenance of linguistic and cultural links has given Chinese Malaysians a lead in recent "resinicization" efforts as Southeast Asian Chinese populations seek to reconnect with China and take advantage of China's growth (Wang, 2000: 84–85).

Communal and linguistic linkages are not the only reasons provoking Chinese Malaysians to seek opportunities outside Malaysia. As discussed in the previous section, the small size of the Chinese language market in Malaysia is a factor, but there are larger trends seen in the migration desires and patterns of Chinese Malaysians that also shape the pathways of migration for film workers. Nationalist policies and rhetoric in Malaysia lead by the ruling UMNO party have positioned ethnic Chinese as tenuous citizens through such labels as "pendatang" (visitor/outsider) and via pro-*bumiputera* (Malay) economic and social policies implemented since 1971.[3] These conditions have created uncertainty in the minds of many Chinese Malaysians and a feeling of what Sin Yee Koh calls "unbelonging" (Koh, 2014). As a result, trends of outward migration from Malaysia by members of the minority Indian and Chinese communities have been noted especially via the phenomena of "brain drain" as highly skilled and educated Malaysians seek permanent emigration elsewhere (Hugo, 2011: 148). Traditionally, migrants have focused on destination countries such as Singapore and Australia, rather than China (Hugo, 2011).

Throughout China's post-independence era until its opening up and marketization from 1978 onward, Chinese Malaysians were unable to migrate to China for business or work. As noted in the previous section, if they wanted to work in a Chinese milieu, they sought opportunities in Hong Kong, Singapore, or Taiwan. By the 2000s, China was also beginning to liberalize its media industries with the privatization of state-owned media companies, the creation of a domestic commercial film industry, and the proliferation of digital and online platforms such as Youku and Tudou (Kokas, 2017). China has only recently become a viable destination for Malaysian creative labor seeking work in China's media sector.

Much of the concern with creative labor migration has been framed within the creative cities discourse initiated by Richard Florida (2003). Providing a playbook for urban administrators, Florida argues that for cities to remain competitive in the globalized knowledge economy, cities need to attract young, creatives through incentives such as high-speed

---

[3] This chapter was written before the defeat of the UMNO-led ruling Barisan Nasional coalition in the May 2018 General Election. The point still stands, however.

internet, liberal social policies and art districts. Such superficial prescriptions have been rightly critiqued (Peck, 2005), with others placing emphasis on how established "media cities" (e.g. Shanghai, Los Angeles, Tokyo and London) are able to attract migrants due to the existence of global media companies, job opportunities and peripheral services (Krätke, 2003). Push and pull factors drive Chinese Malaysians to move to China, but the attractiveness of China as a destination is in part due to the advantageous position they have in the networks of Chinese transnationalism.

As media production expands in China, many migrants have sought work in its media centers. Primarily this is to the urban centers of Shanghai and Beijing which remain important media cities hosting global companies as well as domestic production houses, but new production centers are emerging around the Hengdian World Studios and in Qingdao where Wanda have recently built studios. Hengdian World Studios is estimated to account for 70% of domestic film and television production in China due to its permanent and largescale sets and locations and has attracted many internal migrants (Johnson, 2013). Centers of media production are also emerging at the provincial level — usually in the capital cities — as provincial media businesses seek to modernize their infrastructure and product and compete nationally. With Beijing and Shanghai rapidly becoming global cities, they simultaneously become sites for "transnational community" (Ang, 2004: 190).

Creative labor migration to Mainland China has been led primarily by Taiwanese and Hong Kong above-the-line talent including cinematographers, directors, producers, art directors and actors. Writing from Hong Kong, Szeto and Chen (2012) have described this phenomenon as "mainlandization" noting that the skimming off of above-the-line talent from Hong Kong has left below-the-line crews out of work, but also opened space for a new kind of Hong Kong filmmaking to emerge that is much more local in its orientation and Cantonese in its dialect. Mainlandization also sees the Mainland market and political interests infiltrating into film content, with the increased use of Mandarin and deference to Mainland sensitivities and political concerns. This has also resulted in the blurring of what is a "Chinese film" as a production may involve Mainland money and locations, Hong Kong above-the-line talent, and feature actors from Taiwan, Hong Kong and China.

Malaysians are also drawn into these circulations of production with many Chinese Malaysians moving to China becoming new actors in the networks of Chinese transnationalism. Some respondents reported moving to China for only a few months whereas others have settled permanently there, marrying PRC citizens, and establishing families. This variety of migratory patterns reflect an "open-ended rather than finite process" (Ip *et al.*, 2006: 3) as China may not be the final or permanent migration destination. Instead, China becomes a new node in the creative labor networks alongside Taiwan, Hong Kong, Singapore, as well as Japan, South Korea, and extending as far as Indonesia and the United States. No doubt there are more workers from Taiwan and Hong Kong working in China due to the geographical proximity and the earlier integration of their markets and the first mover advantage.[4] Moreover, both countries had much more high-profile film and media industries through into the 2000s and can offer greater expertise. However, Malaysians are beginning to find a niche for themselves in China's media industries due in part to their mobility, transnational vision, linguistic abilities and exposure to international media business practices.

How Mainland China now appears in circuits of creative labor migration is evident in the trajectory of Malaysian director Ho Wi-Ding who after graduation from NYU Tisch School settled in Taiwan where he directed his first feature *Pinoy Sunday* (2009) for which he won the Best New Director award at the Golden Horse Awards. From his base in Taipei, he worked on two telemovie projects on the Mainland (*My Elder Brother in Taiwan*, 2010; *The Biggest Toad in the Puddle*, 2014) which he described in one interview as "stepping into the Wild West. [...] It was a tough situation to work in, but it was good training" (Koay, 2014). More recently he completed a feature in Singapore *Our Sister Mambo* (2015) for Cathay — their first production in 15 years. Then in 2017 he released *Beautiful Accident* (2017) made in China for Huayi Brothers and Taihe Film Investment and as of January 2018 is working on a Taiwan–France co-production called *Cities of Last Things*. Now based in Beijing, Ho displays a transnational sensibility in which Mainland China has become a central node in his filmmaking network and thereby creating new circuits and connections within Chinese cinemas.

A similar trajectory is seen in the career of Malaysian singer-actor-director Namewee who now circulates between Taiwan, China, Singapore

[4]The exact numbers of migrants are not known. It is outside the scope of this research project to know exactly how many Malaysians are working in China presently. Some informants mentioned a "Malaysians in China" WeChat group with a few hundred members.

and Malaysia. Originally from Johor and developing a media career in online video and hip-hop music, Namewee moved into feature film as an actor and sometime director. After his sixth feature film *Banglasia* (2013) was banned in Malaysia, Namewee largely abandoned feature filmmaking to concentrate on his music career. He moved to Taiwan where he is able to work more freely — but returns to Malaysia for tours and recording — including filming for his music video *Oh My God* (2016) which led to him being arrested due to scenes in the video showing him dancing in a mosque and *Like a Dog* (2017) ostensibly to celebrate the Year of the Dog but also a satire on Malaysian politics. Earlier in 2017, Namewee collaborated with American-Chinese singer Wang Leehom to release *Stranger in the North* which describes the life of migrant workers in Beijing.

Namewee's producer Fred Chong also now works cross-border looked beyond Malaysia to develop a new trans-Asia music and entertainment business called WebTVAsia (http://webtvasia.com). WebTVAsia was established in 2013 and promotes Asian pop music and video content to audiences in China, Korea, Japan, Hong Kong, Taiwan, Thailand, Malaysia, Indonesia and Singapore via its 600 channels aggregated on YouTube. At the same time, WebTVAsia is able to cross-promote between different national markets developing a trans-Asian brand and market presence. WebTVAsia is headquartered in Kuala Lumpur but have an office in Beijing (Prodigee Media) with plans to produce feature films in China including a remake of the Thai film *Teacher's Diary* (Nithiwat Tharathorn, 2014). We see here the ways in which Malaysian media companies and individuals are moving into trans-Asian circuits of production, promotion and consumption that includes China.

China now becomes a logical destination for Malaysians seeking their next big project or wanting to step up in their career. Malaysia's market remains limited in terms of the budgets available to directors and the ambitions of local television producers. One Malaysian cinematographer — Stephen Chua — who worked on a number of Namewee's films is the DOP for a 50-episode Chinese TV series called *God of Lost Fantasy* (Hu Chuxi and Chen Weixiang, 2018) shot partly at the Hengdian World Studios and locations in Tongzhou grasslands, Yellow River Hoodoo National Geopark and Yuanmou forests. This kind of large-scale project is rarely produced domestically in Malaysia and gives Chua not only larger sets, budgets and scale to work with but represents a means to network further in China's media industry.

Linguistic ability is important for China's rapidly globalizing media industries as it seeks to host more co-productions, invite foreign talent and negotiate for distribution deals overseas. While English is the language of international business, to work in China in the media requires Mandarin. Many Western workers therefore struggle in this environment or require translators or other linguistic assistance. In other instances, bi-lingual employees are preferred including American Born Chinese (ABC), Singaporeans, or Chinese Malaysians. Co-productions which involve delicate negotiations and relationships between different parties may look to Malaysians as neutral arbiters between the English-speaking and Mandarin-speaking sides. As one Beijing based Malaysian actress notes:

> That's why I have more chances to get in English or bi-lingual project or co-production project in the film industry. Because I'm still Chinese but just that I was born in Malaysia.

In other instances, Malaysians speaking Mandarin, Cantonese and English are able to operate on multi-cultural productions. Another Beijing based Malaysian producer notes that

> I grew up speaking Mandarin, Cantonese, and a bit of English, but mostly I grew up with a bunch of friends and relatives who are Chinese educated that's why I am very familiar, and I see myself very close to these Mainland Chinese or Taiwanese Chinese culture as well.

Cantonese helps in relationships with Hong Kong filmmakers also working on the Mainland. On the production side, Chinese Malaysians tend to be polyglots who have gone through the Chinese education system attaining fluency in Mandarin but also fluency in English.

Within the rapidly globalizing Chinese media, Malaysians become intermediaries in between Mainland partners and foreigners. One interviewee worked for a Japanese company in Shanghai producing co-productions in part because of his command of English, Mandarin and Japanese after graduating from a Japanese university. This pattern of being cultural intermediaries extends to Willie Chan, Jackie Chan's long-time agent, who became an important middleman for Jackie Chan as he noted in this 1998 interview:

> Jackie has no education. Since he was seven he was at Beijing Opera School. As he goes on in his career, he will need me more and more. It cannot be less. I spent two years at the East-West Center in Hawaii in 1966 getting my master's degree in marketing, the best years of my life.

> And handling a movie star is like marketing. It's a product — that may not sound nice, but the principles are the same. He needs someone to handle his finances, and he needs me for the American market because I know English very well. (quoted in McHugh, (1998))

Another Malaysian producer worked on the French-China production *Le Portrait interdit* (*The Lady in the Portrait*, Charles de Meaux, 2017) mediating between the French team and the Chinese team. Although somewhat difficult to negotiate, her experience speaks of her role in-between the two sides:

> So when I'm with the Chinese, they felt that I'm a foreigner because I'm not a real Chinese to them, but when I'm with the French, the Chinese would think that "Hello, you are Chinese. How could you side [with] the French?" So, I'm like "Okay, who do you want me to be?"

Despite these difficulties, Malaysians come to occupy an important and needed function within the Chinese media industries. But like many Hong Kong and Taiwanese creative migrants, Malaysians are also occupying important roles in China's media productions.

Taking on these roles allows Chinese Malaysians to participate in the internationalization of China's media industries which can be a point of pride. Chinese Malaysians help connect China into networks of production, capital flow, skills transfer and product distribution both in the region and globally. The actress based in Beijing sees her role partly as a cultural ambassador for China, helping the world to see and understand China better:

> So, I think that… I'm a Chinese I should try out in China … at the end of the day you still want to promote this culture outside. Because I'm more strong [sic] in Chinese culture then you need to bring this Chinese culture outside China. This is the exchange. There is a value there.

What we are seeing then is a growing integration of China into cultural and media circuits of Chinese transnationalism. Chinese Malaysians become a vector for China's integration as they seek opportunities and take operational roles in the Chinese media market. This represents one way in which new relationships are being forged between China and Southeast Asia through the region's local Chinese population.

China's Film Industry in Malaysia

At the same time, as more Malaysians have been moving to China to seek work in the entertainment industries, Chinese productions have been looking outwards for locations, facilities, talent and co-production partners. In other cases, Mainland actors, talents and other filmmakers are featuring in Malaysian productions. The Malaysian horror film *Haunted Hotel* (Ryon Lee, 2017), for example, featured a young Mainland Chinese couple who are chased by a ghost in Genting Highlands while on holiday. The film features Thai Chinese actress Aom (Li Haina) and Mainland actor Leon Li Chuan. *Haunted Hotel* was later released in cinemas in China, completing its transnational journey in both production and exhibition. These screen industries linkages carry new interactions and create new networks of transnationalism between Chinese populations in China and Southeast Asia.

Scholars have previously noted how the United States, Australia and Canada have figured in the new networks of Chinese outbound investment and productions, with specific services catering to facilitating co-productions emerging in different locations (Walsh, 2012; Yue, 2014). In Canada for example, Leung (2016) notes how Canadian-Chinese become co-production partners for Chinese film projects providing location and production support. Malaysia has hosted foreign film shoots and crews using its locations for various types of films. Some of the most famous films shot in Malaysia include *Anna and the King* (Andy Tennant, 1999) starring Chow Yun-Fat and Jodie Foster, *Entrapment* (Jon Amiel, 1999) starring Sean Connery, and *Police Story 3: Supercop* (Stanley Tong, 1992) with Jackie Chan and Michelle Yeoh. Since 2000 though, there has been an increase in the number of productions originating from China and/or Hong Kong. Romantic drama *Summer Holiday* (Jingle Ma, 2000) filmed on location in Redang Island initiated the flow of new Chinese productions into Malaysia. *Summer Holiday* earned 21,336,647 Hong Kong dollars (US$2.7 million) at the Hong Kong box office making it the second highest grossing Hong Kong film for that year. In the years since 2000, over 20 Chinese productions have come to Malaysia.

What needs to be noted here is that identifying a "Chinese" project or production is increasingly difficult as more productions become transnational in their design, production, content and distribution. With the return of Hong Kong to China in 1997, Hong Kong's status is somewhat ambiguous — retaining some of its identity and autonomy through the use of Cantonese for example, but in reality, rapidly integrating with Mainland

China. Hong Kong still hosts many established film companies such as Golden Harvest, Media Asia and Emperor Pictures but these are now either collaborating increasingly with Mainland companies or being bought over. Hong Kong film mainstay Golden Harvest for example was bought over by Mainland company Orange Sky in 2007. A similar integration between Hong Kong and China occurs in productions as a result of "mainlandization" as discussed earlier.

To aid China's growing collaborations with foreign partners and in overseas locations, a number of co-production agreements have been signed with other countries and there are film exchanges, festivals and government-to-government forums to promote China overseas. While no co-production agreement has been signed between China and Malaysia, in 2017 the Beijing-based ASEAN–China Centre (ACC) hosted the China ASEAN Film Festival in Kuala Lumpur, hosting officials from China, filmmakers from across ASEAN, and screening a number of Chinese films including *Wolf Warrior 2*.[5] China presented itself as a logical partner to Southeast Asian filmmakers in the hope for more cultural exchanges and filmmaking collaborations. Choosing Kuala Lumpur as the venue also spoke of the receptiveness to China in Malaysia and the existing screen industries and business relationships between the two countries. Although these operated at the official level, China–Malaysia projects have been proceeding through private initiative and based on company-to-company partnerships.

To service these productions, a small number of local companies provide co-production services, the most prolific assisting Chinese language production is Asia Tropical Films (ATF) based in Petaling Jaya. ATF was formed in 2008 by CEO Adrian Teh, alongside Production Controller Allyan Too, and Senior Executive Producer Matt Lai,[6] both of whom had associations with film and television production in China and Hong Kong. ATF markets itself as a production company "providing one-stop professional film production services" with "vast joint venture experiences with filmmakers from around the region." ATF have provided assistance or co-produced a number of Chinese productions including *The Viral Factor*, *Conspirators* (Oxide Pang Chun, 2013), *Death Trip* (Li Tian and Chen Liu, 2014), and *Operation Mekong*. ATF themselves produced a local version of the hit Chinese film *Goodbye Mr Loser* (Adrian Teh, 2017) based

[5] See http://www.asean-china-center.org/english/2017-12/01/c_136830299.htm.

[6] See http://www.atfilms.com.my/index.php/about/key-person.

on the 2015 original by directors Yan Fei and Peng Damo. ATF further strengthened their ties to China by opening an office in Beijing in 2017.

In assisting Chinese productions incorporate international locations and talent, Chinese Malaysian companies are playing the role of bridge or conduit. Adrian Teh's profile on the ATF website states: "Work with us, together we introduce Malaysia production to the world!"[7] This sentiment is echoed by a former producer at ATF and now marketing manager at Pinewood Iskandar Malaysia Studios (PIMS) who says that:

> I tried to build the bridge, the communication bridge between Malaysia and China and let them know that they can always find Chinese-speaking crew in Malaysia and they also work with China production before.

At PIMS in the southern state of Johor, there has been a similar reorientation toward projects from China as the studios try and pick up the increased interest from outbound Chinese productions. PIMS most recently provided sets for the airplane crash movie *Lost in the Pacific* (Vincent Zhou, 2016), a US–China co-production starring Brandon Routh and Zhang Yuqi.

As Chinese Malaysians position themselves as a bridge to China, they contribute to Chinese transnationalism alongside other members of the Chinese diaspora in Southeast Asia. Researcher Setijadi (2016) has found similar patterns in the case of Chinese Indonesian businessman who play a crucial function as "trade and cultural intermediaries" with China, or what she calls a "beautiful bridge". Chinese Malaysians are already facilitating the internationalization of China's media industries and becoming active participants in developing overseas linkages and networks. By playing this intermediary role and linking China to the other parts the world, Chinese Malaysians become nodal agents in furthering Chinese transnationalism.

Malaysia is attractive for Chinese filmmakers for its variety of locations that include natural and manmade landscapes, and also importantly its multi-lingual speaking population which makes working relationships easier to manage. This has been partly the motivation of Hong Kong director Dante Lam who shot *The Viral Factor* (2012) and *Operation Mekong* (2015) in Malaysia. Working with a Hong Kong crew, and actors

---

[7] See http://www.atfilms.com.my/index.php/about/key-person.

from Hong Kong, Taiwan, China and Malaysia, Lam says for *The Viral Factor* "everything fell into place when we decided that the movie would be mainly set in Malaysia" (Seto, 2012). Funding for the film came through Emperor Motion Pictures (Hong Kong), and the two Mainland companies Beijing Universe Starlight Culture Media and Huayi Brothers. Lam returned to Malaysia to shoot *Operation Mekong* (2015) for Bona Group.

Likewise, China's capital investment in media and entertainment is expanding into Southeast Asia. In February 2018, the Bona Group opened their first overseas cinema in Malaysia at the casino complex in Genting Highlands. At the opening with Bona Group boss Yu Dong, attendees watched *Operation Red Sea* (Dante Lam, 2018), the latest action film funded by Bona. China's biggest special effects company BaseFX head-quartered in Beijing, expanded to Malaysia opening an office in Kuala Lumpur (Frater, 2018). This complements their established offices in Xiamen and Wuxi and takes advantage of Malaysia as a low-cost location that can mediate between China and the West. With the acquisition of Malaysian-based regional streaming service iflix in 2020 by Tencent, other Mainland Chinese companies will expand to Malaysia or acquire local media operators as they seek to consolidate their market presence in Southeast Asia and use them as avenues of distribution and exhibition over the coming decade.

As Mainland China commands greater interest and leverage in these media relationships, Mandarin increasingly becomes the required working language. As in Hong Kong where Cantonese films have become a form of resistance and alternative to Mainland China (Szeto and Chen, 2012), there will be ongoing challenges and interpretations of Chinese culture and Chineseness. Nevertheless, Malaysia will remain attractive for Mainland filmmakers looking for locations to shoot in, just as Malaysia will remain receptive to Chinese productions because they contribute to the local film industry. These productions accompany a range of other "soft power" or cultural initiatives that seek to promote China in the region and to bolster its image and regional presence (Su, 2010).[8]

---

[8]For example, China recently promoted the "Information Silk Road" through news and broadcast media in Thailand. See http://www.asean-china-center.org/english/2018-02/02/c_136953748.htm.

Conclusion: China Dream Factory

As China becomes a more assertive player in Chinese transnationalism, it also draws Malaysia and Chinese Malaysians into its economic and cultural orbit. Chinese Malaysians become important partners and participants in the growth of China's screen industries. This is due to the large Chinese population in Malaysia, including many Mandarin speakers, the continued linguistic and cultural attachments to Chinese culture, the small domestic Chinese media market, and the precarious political position of the Chinese in Malaysia. We will therefore see more Chinese Malaysians consider China as a destination to pursue their ambitions as cultural producers, resulting in deeper integration between the two countries.

For Malaysian companies and individuals, this means a much clearer role in a reshaped East Asian pop culture in which China now plays a much larger role. It sees China emerging as a powerful source of capital and content that is reshaping the film and media industries across the region as it has already in Hong Kong and Taiwan and drawing in others attracted by the possibilities of co-productions and access to China's massive market. What is obvious is that our understanding of Chinese transnationalism is changing with China becoming a much more active and powerful participant.

As Nyíri and Tan (2017: 22) note however, China's "rise" is by no means just a top-down, coordinated process and involves much negotiation and diversity "on the ground." This means that the rise and power of China in East Asian pop culture will not homogenize the region, making it the same as China. One of the clearest manifestations of this is in the relative political openness and opportunity for critique and opposition in each country. In recent years for example, a number of Taiwanese and Hong Kong artists have been forced to publicly apologize to China following their support of independence movements.[9] At the same time, filmmakers and others seeking greater cultural freedom and space for expression may look to countries like Taiwan where different norms and traditions exist. Tsai Ming-Liang for example works with controversial material in his films and has found Taiwan conducive to his work — a situation unlikely in either Malaysia or China. Similarly, talented Mainland filmmakers who face censure at home, look abroad to explore possibilities for their filmmaking (Marchetti, 2006).

---

[9]Examples include Taiwanese pop singer Chou Tzu-yu and Hong Kong actor Wong He.

It is important to note that not all Chinese Malaysians are aligned to China, use Mandarin, or see China as a benign and benevolent actor. China has attempted to use the overseas Chinese community as a community of influence overseas and to cultivate and suggest that their ultimate allegiance is to China, rather than their adopted home. Many Chinese Malaysians are dedicated citizens of Malaysia and have established roots in the country, building lives and families, and do not recognize or feel attachment to the PRC which itself has undergone significant political change since the ancestors of many Chinese Malaysians migrated. The ongoing attachments, identifications and relationships with China will remain complicated.

By examining screen industries connections, we are reminded that the product also carries cultural meaning and significance. The choice of language, themes, narrative resolutions and so on can all be significant for different audiences. While film is often treated as a commodity for capital accumulation, it also draws attention to representations, imagery and ideas in ways that other products do not. Scholars in Chinese cinemas have developed these themes much more strongly as the transnational nature of Chinese cinemas itself gives rise to diversity and different possibilities of representation. The politics of representation will increasingly become more contentious and complicated.

As screen industries relationships develop between Malaysian and China there is a reshaping of our understanding and parameters of Chinese transnationalism. Not only does it mark the rise of China as an active participant in developing new networks and relationships but highlights the new roles that Chinese Malaysians are playing. Their presence helps globalize the Chinese screen industries and thereby develop a more international outlook. It also marks a realignment toward Mainland China from Taiwan and Hong Kong for Chinese Malaysians and therefore part of a larger reshaping of the transnational Chinese language media economy and market.

References

Ang, I. (2004). Beyond Transnational Nationalism: Questioning the Borders of the Chinese Diaspora in the Global City. In B. S. A. Yeoh and K. Willis (eds.), *State/Nation/Transnation: Perspectives on Transnationalism in the Asia-Pacific* (pp. 179–196). London, Routledge.

Barker, T. (2017). The Real Source of China's Soft Power. *The Diplomat*, November 18, https://thediplomat.com/2017/11/the-real-source-of-chinas-soft-power/.

Bernards, B. (2017). *Writing the South Seas: Imagining the Nanyang in Chinese and Southeast Asian postcolonial literature*. Seattle, University of Washington Press.

Berry, C. and Pang, L. (2008). Introduction, Or, What's in an "S"? *Journal of Chinese Cinemas*, 2(1): 3–8.

Chan, Y. W. and Koh, S. Y. (2017). Introduction: New Chinese migrations. In Y. W. Chan and S. Y. Koh (eds.), *New Chinese Migrations: Mobility, Home, and Inspirations* (pp. 1–18). Abingdon, Routledge.

Chua, B. H. (2004). Conceptualizing an East Asian Popular Culture. *Inter-Asia Cultural Studies*, 5(2): 200–221.

Curran, J. and Park, M.-J. (eds.) (2000). *De-Westernizing Media Studies: Communication and Society*. London, Routledge.

Florida, R. (2003). *The Rise of the Creative Class: And How It's Transforming Work, Leisure, Community and Everyday Life*. New York, Basic Books.

Frater, P. (2018). FilMart: China's BaseFX expands to Malaysia. *Variety*, March 18, http://www.variety.com/2018/digital/asia/filmart-china-basefx-expands-malaysia-1202728678/.

Freedman, A. L. (2000). *Political Participation and Ethnic Minorities Chinese Overseas in Malaysia, Indonesia, and the United States*. New York, Routledge.

Harding, H. (1993). The Concept of "Greater China": Themes, Variations and Reservations. *The China Quarterly*, 136: 660–686.

Hugo, G. (2011). Malaysian Migration to Australia. *Malaysian Journal of Economic Studies*, 48(2): 147–174.

Ip, D. F.-K., Hibbins, R. and Chui, W. H. (2006). *Experiences of Transnational Chinese Migrants in the Asia-Pacific*. New York, Nova Science.

Iwabuchi, K. (2002). *Recentering Globalization: Popular Culture and Japanese Transnationalism*. Durham, Duke University Press.

Johnson, I. (2013). Studio City. *The New Yorker*, April 22, https://www.newyorker.com/magazine/2013/04/22/studio-city.

Khoo, G. C. (2007). Just-Do-It-(Yourself): Independent Filmmaking in Malaysia. *Inter-Asia Cultural Studies*, 8(2), 227–247.

Koay, A. (2014). Filmmaker Ho Wi Ding Has Best Job in the World. *The Star Online*, November 6, http://www.thestar.com.my/lifestyle/entertainment/movies/news/2014/11/06/filmmaker-ho-wi-ding-has-best-job-in-the-world/.

Koh, S. Y. (2014). Diasporic "Unbelonging" to Malaysia and Singapore: Second-Generation Malaysian–Chinese Migrants in Singapore. In Y. W. Chan, D. Haines and J. H. X. Lee (eds.), *The Age of Asian Migration: Continuity,*

Diversity, and Susceptibility (pp. 358–372). Newcastle upon Tyne, Cambridge Scholars.

Kokas, A. (2017). *Hollywood Made in China*. Oakland, University of California Press.

Krätke, S. (2003). Global Media Cities in a World-Wide Urban Network. *European Planning Studies*, 11(6): 605–628.

Lee, C. C. (2003). The Global and the National of Chinese Media: Discourses, Market, Technology, and ideology. In C. C. Lee (ed.), *Chinese Media, Global Contexts* (pp. 1–31). London, Routledge Curzon.

Leung, H. H.-S. (2016). Hollywood North, Asiawood West: Vancouver as a Transpacific Film Location. In D. Black, O. Khoo and K. Iwabuchi (eds.), *Contemporary Culture and Media in Asia* (pp. 31–48). London, Rowman & Littlefield.

Lim, S. H. (2006). A New Beginning: Possible Directions in Chinese Cinemas Studies. *Journal of Chinese Cinemas*, 1(1): 3–8.

Lopez, L. (2017). Malaysia's 1MDB Settles Debt Owed to Abu Dhabi with China Backing. *The Straits Times* (Singapore), December 27, http://www.straitstimes.com/asia/se-asia/malaysias-1mdb-to-settle-debt-owed-to-abu-dhabi-with-china-backing.

Lu, S. H. (1997). Transnational Chinese cinemas. In S. H.-P. Lu (Ed.), *Transnational Chinese Cinemas: Identity, Nationhood, Gender* (pp. 1–34). Honolulu, University of Hawai'i Press.

Luo, W. and Li, L. (2018). New Rules for Visas to Help Chinese "Return Home." *China Daily*, January 23, http://www.chinadaily.com.cn/a/201801/23/WS5a668664a3106e7dcc135dfb.html.

Marchetti, G. (2006). *From Tian'anmen to Times Square: Transnational China and the Chinese diaspora on global screens, 1989–1997*. Philadelphia, Temple University Press.

McHugh, F. (1998). Willie Chan. *South China Morning Post*, May 10, http://www.scmp.com/article/240239/willie-chan.

Muthalib, H. (2013). *Malaysian Cinema in a Bottle: A Century (and a Bit More) of Wayang*. Petaling Jaya, Merpati Jingga.

Nyíri, P. and Tan, D. (2017). China's "Rise" in Southeast Asia from a Bottom-Up Perspective. In P. Nyíri and D. Tan (eds.), *Chinese Encounters in Southeast Asia: How People, Money, and Ideas from China are Changing a Region* (pp. 3–22). Washington, University of Washington Press.

Ong, A. and Nonini, D. (1997). Chinese Transnationalism as an Alternative Modernity. In A. Ong and D. Nonini (eds.), *Ungrounded Empires: The Cultural Politics of Modern Chinese Transnationalism* (pp. 3–36). New York, Routledge.

Peck, G. (2005). Struggling with the Creative Class. *International Journal of Urban and Regional Research*, 29(4): 740–770.

Percival, B. (2007). *The Dragon Looks South: China and Southeast Asia in the New Century*. Westport, Praeger Security International.

Rainey, J. (2016). Wanda's Legendary Buy is Just the Beginning of China's Investment in Hollywood. *Variety*, January 13, http://variety.com/2016/film/asia/wanda-legendary-buy-china-1201678463/.

Raju, Z. H. (2008). Filmic Imaginations of the Malaysian Chinese: "Mahua Cinema" as a Transnational Chinese Cinema. *Journal of Chinese Cinemas*, 2(1): 67–79.

Segay, J. (2007). Discussion with Director Tan Chui Mui on her experience at Résidence du Festival of Cinéfondation. *Culture 360*, http://culture360.asef.org/film/discussion-with-director-tan-chui-mui-on-her-experience-at-residence-du-festival-of-cinefondation/.

Setijadi, C. (2016). "A Beautiful Bridge": Chinese Indonesian Associations, Social Capital and Strategic Identification in a New Era of China Indonesia Relations. *Journal of Contemporary China*, 25(102): 822–825.

Seto, K. Y. (2012). Chasing the Action. *The Star Online*, January 20, https://www.thestar.com.my/lifestyle/entertainment/movies/news/2012/01/20/chasing-the-action/.

Shirk, S. L. (2011). Changing Media, Changing China. In S. L Shirk (ed.), *Changing Media, Changing China* (pp. 1–37). New York, Oxford University Press.

Su, W. (2010). New Strategies of China's Film Industry as Soft Power. *Global Media and Communication*, 6(3): 317–322.

Sun, W. and Sinclair, J. (2015). Rethinking Chinese Diasporic Media. In W. Sun and J. Sinclair (eds.), *Media and Communication in the Chinese Diaspora: Rethinking Transnationalism* (pp. 1–14). London, Routledge.

Szeto, M. M. and Chen, Y. (2012). Mainlandization or Sinophone Translocality? Challenges for Hong Kong SAR New Wave Cinema. *Journal of Chinese Cinemas*, 6(2): 115–134.

Thunø, M. (2007). Introduction. Beyond "Chinatown": Contemporary Chinese Migration. In M. Thunø (ed.), *Beyond Chinatown: New Chinese Migration and the Global Expansion of China* (pp. 1–34). Copenhagen, NIAS Press.

Walsh, M. (2012). At the Edge of Asia: The Prospects for Australia–China Film Co-Production. *Studies in Australasian Cinema*, 6(3): 301–316.

Wang, G. (2000). *The Chinese Overseas: From Earthbound China to the Quest for Autonomy*. Cambridge, Harvard University Press.

Willis, K., Yeoh, B. S. A. and Fakhri, S. M. A. K. (2004). Introduction: Transnationalism as a Challenge to the Nation. In B. S. A. Yeoh and K. Willis (eds.), *State/Nation/Transnation: Perspectives on Transnationalism in the Asia-Pacific* (pp. 1–15). London, Routledge.

Yue, A. (2014). Contemporary Sinophone Cinema: Australia-China Co-Productions. In A. Yue and O. Khoo (eds.), *Sinophone Cinemas* (pp. 185–202). Basingstoke, Palgrave MacMillan.

Yue, A. and Khoo, O. (2014). Framing Sinophone Cinemas. In A. Yue and O. Khoo (eds.), *Sinophone Cinemas* (pp. 3–12). Basingstoke, Palgrave MacMillan.

Zhang, Y. J. (2008). *Cinema, Space, and Polylocality in a Globalizing China*. Honolulu, University of Hawai'i Press.

https://doi.org/10.1142/9789811250668_bmatter

Index

Lightning Source UK Ltd.
Milton Keynes UK
UKHW020654040123
414807UK00002B/27

9 789811 250651